D0926695

Presented to

_____

On _____

By _____

A YEAR IN THE NOW!

a dynamic devotional
dedicated to the daily discovery of destiny

Bishop Jim Earl Swilley

All Scripture quotations, unless otherwise indicated, are taken from the New King James Version. Copyright 1979, 1980, 1982, 1992 by Thomas Nelson, Inc. Used by permission. All rights reserved.

Scripture quotations marked (AMP) are taken from THE AMPLIFIED BIBLE, Old Testament copyright © 1965, 1987 by the Zondervan Corporation. The Amplified New Testament copyright © 1958, 1987 by The Lockman Foundation. Used by permission.

Scripture quotations marked (The Living Bible) are taken from The Living Bible, copyright © 1971. Used by permission of Tyndale House Publishers, Wheaton, IL 60189, USA. All rights reserved.

Scripture quotations marked (The Message) are taken from The Message, copyright © by Eugene H. Peterson, 1993, 1994, 1995, used by permission of NavPress Publishing Group.

Scripture quotations marked (New English Bible) are taken from The New English Bible, copyright © The Delegates of the Oxford University Press and The Syndics of the Cambridge University Press 1961, 1970.

Scripture quotations marked (NIV) are taken from the Holy Bible, NEW INTERNATIONAL VERSION®. Copyright © 1973, 1978, 1984 International Bible Society. All rights reserved throughout the world. Used by permission of International Bible Society.

Scripture quotations marked (NLT) are taken from the Holy Bible, New Living Translation, copyright © 1996. Used by permission of Tyndale House Publishers, Inc., Wheaton, IL 60189, USA. All rights reserved.

Take note that the name satan and related names are not capitalized, as we do not recognize him as either supreme nor revered, to the point of violating grammatical rules.

A Year In The Now!
a dynamic devotional dedicated to the daily discovery of destiny
ISBN 0-9716838-1-6

Copyright © 2002 by Jim Earl Swilley

First Printing: November 2002 / Second Printing: February 2003
Printer: United Book Press, Inc., Baltimore, MD
Cover designer: Chris Haler
Technical/Production Editors: René Babcock, Jane Conyers, Robyn Darby

Published by Church In The Now Publishing
1873 Iris Drive, SE
Conyers, GA 30013

Printed in the United States of America. All rights reserved under International Copyright Law. Contents and/or cover may not be reproduced in whole or in part in any form without the express written consent of the Publisher.

TABLE OF CONTENTS

INTRODUCTION

Presenting people with the prospect of living their lives "in the now" is the major theme of my ministry, but practicing it personally has become the leading quest of my life. Through the long, arduous process of navigating my personal journey toward discovering the authentic Christ, I have become convinced that He can be found ONLY in the eternal "now," where true seekers of His Kingdom can experience Him in a way that is relevant to their everyday existence.

My message in microcosm is this: Those who seek the Kingdom must make a constant effort to embrace the now when they recognize it, and then commit to the continual conforming of their lives to it. In so doing, they are able to avoid the distractions produced by living in the past or in the future, and can begin to comprehend a real Christ for their current real world.

But herein lay a conflict. The concept of conceiving a life in the now consumes me, but it confounds me, as well. I find that I am both intrigued and intimidated by the idea of it, finding it fascinating and frightening at the same time. I am intrigued with the notion that life could be lived with absolutely no regrets over the past and no fear of the future - but intimidated by the reality that leading a life like that would require one to take enormous personal responsibility and ownership of their own destiny.

Simply put, if you live in the now, you don't get to blame anybody but yourself for what's wrong with you, and you forfeit the luxury of using guilt over past mistakes as an excuse for incompetence, inadequacy, and feelings of inferiority.

My theology – and this is the part that fascinates me - is one that demands my acceptance of the authority made accessible in the now, through the completed work of Christ on the cross. Jesus was telling the truth when He declared, "It is finished!" However, there is a requirement imposed by the realization that comes with that revelation, and that is the part that is somewhat frightening.

In other words, once you know who you are in Christ, and that satan has been completely put out of commission by Him, you are taken to an even higher level of personal responsibility for the quality of your life. By simply refusing to give him place by resisting him, the enemy is **altogether taken out** of the equation of your life circumstances.

When I was a boy, I regularly watched (and loved) the Flip Wilson TV show, particularly enjoying the comedy sketches in which he played the character known as "Rev. Leroy, Pastor of the *Church of What's Happenin' Now!*" The talented comedian's outrageous impersonation of the flamboyant preacher with attitude was very funny to me and, for some unknown reason, I found the name of his fictitious church exceptionally appealing.

People laugh when I tell them this, but on some level, I really believe that my affection for that character created in me a subliminal desire to pastor a church with "now" in its name, even though I had no idea at that young age that I would ever actually pastor a church. I'm not saying that I think I received a call to the fivefold ministry from a late 60's weekly primetime television network comedy/variety show – my calling is a holy thing, and it was mine from the foundation of the world. But God does use the foolish things of the world to confound the wise and, in my case, the *Church of What's Happenin' Now* helped to shape a certain mindset in me, concerning the relationship of the church to its contemporary culture, which manifested itself in my life many years later.

When I first changed the name of our ministry (Word of Faith Christian Center) to Church In The Now, I did not realize what I was getting myself into. I thought, at the time, that the name just sounded cutting-edge and modern, and that it described our non-traditional and unconventional approach to communicating the gospel to the world.

I even admitted to the "Rev. Leroy" connection from childhood, in keeping with my penchant for referring frequently to secular media as a point of reference for our decidedly non-religious congregation, and for not taking myself too seriously. But something very profound started happening deep within me with that name change, because name changes can be prophetically meaningful (Abram/Abraham, Sarai/Sarah, Jacob/Israel, Simon/Cephas-Peter, Saul/Paul, etc.), and they speak to the development of destiny and the promotion of purpose. Pastoring a church with "now" in the name became less of a novel and amusing idea – a clever method of marketing our ministry's message - and began to dramatically alter my life!

Since then, the message of now has completely affected my lifestyle, my theology, my eschatology, my world-view, and my self-concept. But the more I have realized that living in the now is the only way to experience the Christ of the now, I have been made painfully aware of how difficult it can be to do so. Hurtful memories, unhealthy relationships, unfinished emotional business, religious tradition, strongholds, unforgiveness, and familiar spirits can make it seemingly impossible to ever totally escape the clutches of living in the past. Also, anxiety, worry that history might repeat itself, fear of the unknown, lack of vision, and emotional stress can cause an unbalanced preoccupation with the future. In the natural world, it is just plain hard to live in the now!

This realization initiated a search for a practical and efficient way to harness such an abstract idea, and to make it work in reality where people actually live. That search led me to the Lord's Prayer – the Blueprint of Christ's vision for His Kingdom – and particularly the line that reads "Give us this day our daily bread."

The bottom line is this – you have to live in the now to really know God, but you can only do it one day at a time! Otherwise, you will inevitably become overwhelmed by the enormity of trying to live a "now life" in a "yesterday/tomorrow world," and will resort to old patterns of thinking from your familiar comfort zones.

This devotional is designed to deliver a useable format for bringing your life in Christ into the now on a daily basis. No interesting stories or anecdotes – just real affirmations that can and will help you get your life on the right track in realistic increments.

I have written this book from the paradigm of a Pastor, but also, hopefully, with the viewpoint of a visionary. The vision for my life is that I will experience the living presence and appearing of the genuine Jesus Christ in every day of my life on earth, so that I can express His reality to my world – His will being done on earth as it is in heaven. I want to help you realize that vision for your own life, too, if you so desire.

Included here are most of my favorite elements of communication – the inspired, written Word of God, the power of positive confession, the number seven (I usually preach/teach from 7-point outlines), a sense of humor, and creative and interesting ways of ordering and arranging words, particularly with the use of alliteration. For some reason, I am quite fond of (maybe slightly obsessive about) grouping words together that start with the same letter. I hope that my excessive use of it will amuse, rather than annoy, you!

My suggestion is that you read each day's affirmations **aloud**, before you start your regular routine. You might not "get it" at first, but if you will be diligent in your daily discipline to do it, I believe that something very significant will start to work in your spirit, changing you from the inside, out. The Word of God does not return to Him void or empty – it always accomplishes something good.

Adopt the two-word title for each day's affirmations as the theme for that day, as you live all 365 of them throughout your "year in the now." When you do that, notice how many times that theme is either confirmed or challenged in a 24-hour period. You will find it interesting and inspirational (and sometimes irritating).

I believe that you CAN and WILL learn to live in the now, and that you can inspire others who are tired of living in the past or future to do the same. You can change your world by changing your mind – one day at a time! My sincere prayer is that this book will help you to do it!

       Bishop Jim Earl Swilley
       Church In The Now
       Now Ministries

THE PURPOSE OF THE BOOK:

To provide the authentic Kingdom-seeker with a practical primer that progressively presents the "now-ness" of God through personal, prophetic prayers.

THE PREMISE OF THE BOOK:

1. Jesus is the King (1 Timothy 1:17).

2. The King can only be comprehended within the context of His Kingdom (Revelation 12:10).

3. The Kingdom must come (Matthew 6:10), but it can only come in through the heart of the believer (Luke 17:21).

4. The believer must seek the Kingdom first (Matthew 6:33), but because it is not visibly obvious (Luke 17:20), it must be pursued violently (Matthew 11:12).

5. The violent pursuit of the Kingdom can only be accomplished by a determined effort to live life "in the now" (Matthew 6:34).

6. Living in the now is a constant and consuming challenge and, therefore, can only be attempted one day at a time (Matthew 6:11).

7. One day at a time is how destiny is discovered (2 Peter 1:19).

THE PATTERN OF THE BOOK:

1. 365-day devotional

2. 2-word title conveying an easily remembered theme for each day

3. 1 (or more) foundational Scripture(s) for each day's theme

4. 7 scriptural confessions/positive affirmations to confirm each foundational Scripture

5. 1 concise prayer to confirm each day's confessions/affirmations

6. 12 monthly faith overviews

7. 1 year in the now!

⋄J⋄A⋄N⋄U⋄A⋄R⋄Y⋄

The month that sets the tone for the entire year —

New beginnings . . . a fresh start . . . putting the past behind you . . .

A time for discovering destiny through the door of dreams —

. . . for voicing vision

. . . for prophesying possibilities

. . . for sowing seeds for success.

Write down your goals for the new year, but write them in pencil.

Speak your faith:

. . . declare the end from the beginning

. . . call those things that are not as though they are

. . . prophesy to the wind —

but in all of your endeavors of faith,

always leave room for God to do

exceeding, abundantly above all that you can ask or think.

*"For I know the thoughts and plans that I have for you, says the Lord,
thoughts and plans for welfare and peace and not for evil,
to give you hope in your final outcome." (Jeremiah 29:11 – AMP)*

January 1
NEW BEGINNINGS!

"Then He who sat on the throne said, 'Behold, I make all things new.'" (Revelation 21:5)

1. Today I will live in the now! I will live in the now because He who sits on the throne declares that He makes all things new for me! I will behold His power in my life as I allow the renewal process to take place without any fear of the unknown. I can begin again! I am a pioneer! I am not afraid to explore new territory!

2. Today I will accept new beginnings in every area of my personal world, even if they challenge all of my comfort zones. I will embrace the now, with no unnecessary allegiance to the past. My only obligation is *to the now*. My only interest is *in the now*. My total focus is *on the now*.

3. Today I will share the concept of new beginnings with others as I allow them the grace to start over. I will not bind others with the words "you always . . ." or "you never . . .;" I will give them the gift of new beginnings, and I will reap in my own life what I sow into theirs. I will live in the now and love in the now. I will give someone who has disappointed me another chance.

4. Today I will see the chaos and disorder around me as a necessary means to a new beginning. I will not be moved by what I see. What would normally appear to me as a negative circumstance or situation will be seen by me today simply as the natural messiness of the birth process.

5. Today I will not be afraid to embrace the essential experience of death in my life — to die on one level, so that I can be resurrected to the next one. "Most assuredly, I say to you, unless a grain of wheat falls into the ground and dies, it remains alone; but if it dies, it produces much grain" (John 12:24). I will celebrate the mercy killing of all that needs to die in me.

6. Today I will rethink an old problem. Because of the possibility of new beginnings, I will be proactive and innovative in my approach to that which has been all too familiar. The prospect of beginning again will resurrect hope in me.

7. Today I will open a new chapter in the book of my life. I will learn something that I did not know before (or didn't know that I knew); I will think a new thought . . . speak a new word . . . sing a new song . . . pray a new prayer. I make the choice today to live in a world full of new beginnings as darkness is replaced by dawn, and winter is replaced by spring. Today is a new beginning for me, and today I will live in the now!

Father, help me to believe for new beginnings today. In Jesus' name, amen.

January 2
"I AM!"

"And God said to Moses, 'I AM WHO I AM.' And He said, 'Thus you shall say to the children of Israel, 'I AM has sent me to you.'" *(Exodus 3:14)*

1. Today I will live in the now! I will live in the now because the same God who revealed Himself to Moses as "I AM" is revealing Himself to me in the same way. He is speaking to me in the now because I live by every word that proceeds from His mouth. I am standing on holy ground today.

2. Today I will recognize that He is not the "I WAS." Even though He has always been there for me in the past, He is speaking to me in the now. I can only hear His voice in the present – "God is our refuge and strength, a very PRESENT help in trouble" (Psalm 46:1). I will not listen to the voices of regret, bitterness, and painful memories. I will not live in a haunted house. My God is the "I AM!"

3. Today I will recognize that He is not the "I WILL BE." Even though I trust Him with my tomorrow, I will take no thought for it, for His Kingdom only exists in the now (Matthew 6:33, 34). I will not listen to the voices of fear, worry, and anxiety. I will not ask for more than my daily bread. My God is the "I AM!"

4. Today I will let that abide in me which I heard from the beginning (1 John 2:24). I will listen for my eternal voice and live my eternal life. I will not be manipulated or limited by time, but I will locate the eternity that He has planted in my heart, and let it rule my day. One day with me will be as a thousand years, and a thousand years as one day. Time is irrelevant to the real me today, and yet I will get every necessary thing done on time!

5. Today I will walk in wholeness by integrating all the parts of my life: past, present and future. Like God, I also "am who I am." I will accept and make peace with my whole life – who I was, and who I will be — for they are both a part of who I am. I will be complete in Him. I will be perfect (mature) and entire, lacking nothing.

6. Today I will be myself. I will walk in the truth of who I really am. I will not have the need to impress anyone, or to try to gain anyone's approval. I am accepted in the Beloved. I will simply manifest my own uniqueness with no apology. Today, I will let God be God, and He will let me be me.

7. Today my revelation of God as the "I AM" will give others around me the courage to live in the now. The atmosphere of peace and liberty that my faith will create will encourage them to be who they are. Today I will be a burning bush for them, with God speaking through me, and today I will live in the now!

Father, reveal Yourself to me as the "I AM" in a new way today. In Jesus' name, amen.

January 3
NO REGRETS!

"Brethren, I do not count myself to have apprehended; but one thing I do, forgetting those things which are behind . . ." (Philippians 3:13)

1. Today I will live in the now! I will live in the now because I can, and will, move past my temptation to be bound to the past by regret. I make the conscious effort to forget those things that are behind me, knowing that the past is the one thing that I cannot change.

2. Today I will accept the forgiveness of God as a real thing, and will believe that He is true to His Word concerning the absolution of my sins. I will walk in the reality of the fact that I am the righteousness of God in Christ. I will glory in the cross, celebrating the power of Christ's blood which is alive through the Eternal Spirit.

3. Today I will honor God by refusing to feel guilty or oppressed over past mistakes. I will accept no accusation but, instead, will demonstrate the triumph of grace. I will believe that His mercies are new every morning and I will think, talk and act like I believe it.

4. Today I will take responsibility for my actions toward others. I will claim ownership to my mistakes. I will admit that I was wrong if I was, indeed, in the wrong. If possible, I will take appropriate action to rectify any and all situations where I have acted dishonorably, or have caused hurt or pain.

5. Today, after I have made the effort to right any of the wrongs I may have committed, I will move on. I will learn from my mistakes, but I will not dwell on them. Whether or not my attempt to fix the damage that I may have caused is received, I will know that I have made the effort, and *that* will be sufficient. I will accept the forgiveness of others, and will forgive myself.

6. Today I will believe that all things are working together for my good because I love God and am called according to His purpose. I will not regret wasted time, knowing that He redeems my time and restores to me the years that the pests ate away from my life. I will understand the miracle of the eleventh-hour-wage.

7. Today I will believe that I am exactly where I need to be on my path. I will be thankful in everything, believing that He perfects that which concerns me. I will rejoice that my coat of many colors is woven with many different threads – threads of victory, defeat, joy, sorrow, triumph, failure, accomplishments and mistakes – and the finished product is a beautiful garment of praise. I will be able to say that I wouldn't change a thing in my biography, and really mean it. Today I will have no regrets, and today I will live in the now!

Father, help me to live this day with no regrets. In Jesus' name, amen.

January 4
ONLY BELIEVE!

"As soon as Jesus heard the word that was spoken, He said to the ruler of the synagogue, 'Do not be afraid; ONLY believe.'" (Mark 5:36)

1. Today I will live in the now! I will live in the now because I hear the voice of Jesus speak to my inner man the words that He spoke to Jairus, and I will obey those words. I will not be afraid today, but I will **ONLY believe**. God has not given me a spirit of fear, and my faith in the now will be enough to put me over, no matter what happens.

2. Today I will not be devastated by any bad news, or negative report that I may hear. I will not overreact, because my heart is established and I walk in the illogical peace that passes understanding. I will believe the report of the Lord. I will overcome all obstacles to my faith by His word spoken to my heart.

3. Today I will prevail over my emotions, and will conduct myself according to what I believe rather than by what I feel. I will resist the temptation to be anxious or fretful. I will not waste my time worrying, because the Lord, my Shepherd, will make me to lie down in green pastures, and lead me beside still waters. He will restore my soul.

4. Today I will be calm and steady in my mind. The circumstances around me will not distract me. I will focus on what God is doing in the now, and in the now I will find my confidence. I will rise to the occasion today. I will accomplish my goals for today. I will win!

5. Today my words will reflect that I **ONLY believe**. I know that I cannot believe and doubt at the same time, any more than I can travel north and south simultaneously. My words will be words of faith, victory and success today. My tongue, like the rudder on a ship, will guide me through dangerous waters into safety all day long. I will have what I say.

6. Today I will avoid negative people and their influence as much as possible. I will not believe the words of those who do not **ONLY believe**. I will attract faith-filled and positive individuals who will inspire me to continue to believe, and will confirm the truth on which I stand. Our speech together will be seasoned with salt.

7. Today I will understand what the word ONLY means in a whole new way. Because I declare the end from the beginning, I call this day a good day even before I live it. I will not dilute my pure faith with compromise. I will be radical in my ability to believe, and things will change in my life for the better because of it. Today I am fearless! Today I will **ONLY believe**, and today I will live in the now!

Father, help me to ONLY believe today. In Jesus' name, amen.

January 5
NEW CREATION!

"Therefore if any person is [ingrafted] in Christ (the Messiah) he is a new creation (a new creature altogether); the old [previous moral and spiritual condition] has passed away. Behold, the fresh and new has come!" (2 Corinthians 5:17 - AMP)

1. Today I will live in the now! I will live in the now because I am in Christ, and in Him I am continually renewed to new creation status. In my life, old things have passed away; they have died and have been buried. Today I will make the effort to rethink my own self-perceived identity by seeing myself as God sees me.

2. Today I will abandon stale and unproductive patterns of conduct. I will begin to forsake what is obsolete and atrophied in the way that I think, speak and act. I will seek the new. I will welcome what is fresh and vibrant with the enthusiasm of a happily excited child.

3. Today I will not shy away from those who challenge me or even disagree with me. I will gladly engage in vigorous conversation with others who stimulate me spiritually and intellectually, and will be open to new ideas. I will not defend myself from those who would expose my predictable comfort zones and defense mechanisms, but will, in fact, thank God for their purpose in my life.

4. Today I will know no person according to the flesh, but, rather, will allow them the freedom to also be recognized as a new creation in their own right. I will see the butterfly instead of the caterpillar. I will help to locate and celebrate what is new in them.

5. Today I will walk in a deeper revelation of what it means to be "in Christ," and will thoroughly meditate on the prospect of it. The Scriptures will come alive in me as I am tutored by the Holy Spirit all through the day. My heart and mind will be open to significant words, phrases, ideas and paradigms that will further unveil the real Christ, and will awaken in me a new dimension of enlightenment concerning Him.

6. Today my concept of the new creation phenomenon will bring a greater sense of wellness and wholeness to my soul. Healing, therapy and refreshing will be available to me as I realize more and more that my sins *really* are forgiven, and my past *really* is behind me. The concept of the new creation is my **reality**.

7. Today it will be easy for me to receive miracles. I understand that the same power that translated me out of darkness into the Kingdom of light can do anything else that I need for it to do. My faith as a member of the new creation species will be strong today, and today I will live in the now!

Father, help me to live today like the new creature that I am. In Jesus' name, amen.

January 6
THINK "NOW!"

"Therefore do not worry about tomorrow, for tomorrow will worry about its own things. Sufficient for the day is its own trouble." (Matthew 6:34)

1. Today I will live in the now! I will live in the now because I know that I can seek first the Kingdom of God only by refusing to take thought for tomorrow. The Kingdom does not exist in the future, because there is no future or past in the eternal "now." Because the King is eternal, the "I AM" reigns in my life *now* as Lord *now*!

2. Today I will make the effort to keep my thoughts, my focus, and my attention on what is happening in the immediate. I will be aware of my surroundings. I will live in the moment, for this is the day the Lord has made. I will live this day like it is the only one I have to live.

3. Today I will not be distracted by an obsession with the **past**. Today is a day to clean house . . . to erase tapes . . . to delete files . . . to break ties with that which is negative and contrary to a now mentality. I will remember what needs to be remembered . . . my testimony of God's goodness to me . . . pleasant memories . . . the lessons learned from past mistakes . . . traditions that do not make the Word ineffective – but my memory will not bind or hold me. I forget what needs to be forgotten.

4. Today I will not be preoccupied with the **future**. I will make necessary plans. I will speak prophetic words. I will call those things which are not as though they were. I will study. I will prepare. I will look forward to good things coming up. But I will not worry, fret, toil or spin. Because I also consider the lilies of the field, I can relax without anxiety, knowing that the Father knows that I have need of all these things.

5. Today the Kingdom will not only come in my heart, it will also come in my mind. My mind will not be my enemy today but, rather, His will shall be done in my mind, on earth as it is in heaven. My effort to think "now" will open new doors in my thought-life. I will discover new possibilities . . . new potential . . . new wisdom.

6. Today I will **speak** differently because I will **think** differently. I will surprise the people in my life, and will even surprise myself, by my new way of reacting to the world around me. I will prevail over tormenting, familiar spirits by simply doing the unfamiliar.

7. Today I will hear God's voice and will discern what He is saying. The heavens will declare His glory to me today. His Word will be a lamp unto my feet (for what is happening in my immediate circumstances), and a light unto my path (for what is happening with my purpose and destiny). He is speaking right now, and I am hearing Him right now. I will think "Kingdom" today, and today I will live in the now!

   Father, help me to think eternally — to think "now" today. In Jesus' name, amen.

January 7
WAKE UP!

"And do this, knowing the time, that NOW it is high time to awake out of sleep . . . . "
(Romans 13:11)

"Therefore He says: Awake, you who sleep, arise from the dead,
and Christ will give you light." (Ephesians 5:14)

1. Today I will live in the now! I will live in the now because my spiritual eyes are wide open, and I am aware of all that God is doing for me . . . in me . . . through me . . . today. I will not sleepwalk through this day. I am alive! I am awake! I am aware! My spiritual senses are heightened! I am sensitive to God's presence in me and all around me! And, because I have been awakened, I have also been enlightened – Christ has given me light! I will walk in the *light* today.

2. Today I will recognize the positive. I will appreciate the beauty in the world. I will locate the noble in others. I will be thankful. I will be grateful. I will be aware of the benefits with which I am daily loaded. I will believe that all things are at work together today for my good.

3. Today I will notice the needs of people around me. I will be moved with compassion for others. I will make the effort to be less self-centered than usual. I will prefer my brother/sister. I will be aware that it's not all about me today, and will find joy in caring about someone else. The selflessness will be a relief to me. I will find pleasure in listening – really listening. I will look at people. I will make eye contact. I will make spirit-contact. I will make a difference.

4. Today I will not complain about my surroundings or my routine, but will see, instead, how blessed I really am. I will notice the details of my life today, and will enjoy them. I will embrace and celebrate my normal life. I will even find excitement in the usual as I stay "awake."

5. Today I will look at things from God's perspective. I will empathize with God, and try to discern His perspective on things. I will sit with Him in heavenly places.

6. Today I will rightly divide the Word, and my state of awareness will produce new revelation in me. I will awake to the necessity of spiritual warfare when needed, and will fight the good fight of faith. I will not wrestle with flesh and blood. I am spiritual first and, therefore, will live spiritually today. I will awaken to spiritual reality and will not be bound to the limits of the natural realm.

7. Today my spirit is awake. My soul is awake. My mind is awake. My creativity is awake. My perception and discernment are awake. My wisdom and understanding are awake. My body is awake. My senses are awake. Because I am awake, I will see things that I never saw before, and today I will live in the now!

Father, help me to wake up today. In Jesus' name, amen.

January 8
FAITH IS!

"NOW faith is the substance of things hoped for, the evidence of things not seen."
(Hebrews 11:1)

1. Today I will live in the now! I will live in the now because I understand the now-ness of the God-kind of faith. My faith has a voice that speaks in the present tense, and today it will produce results for me because of the power of these three words: NOW FAITH IS!

2. Today I will live my life according to what I believe. The faith-realm, rather than the sense-realm, is my reality today. Because of that reality, I will not be moved by what I see, hear, touch, smell or taste, but will, instead, move through this day guided by the sixth sense, which is (my) supernatural faith.

3. Today I will create the world in which I want to live by my faith-filled words. I will do this because I am in the God-class, and because God created His worlds by the words of His mouth. And, as God maintains His worlds by His words, I will maintain the quality of my world through the creativity and authority of my words. My words will have power because they will be filled with His Word, and His Word will not return to Him (or to me) void.

4. Today the pressure applied to my circumstances by my faith will change them for the better. I will re-shape the seen world by changing things in the unseen world. I will look to the unseen things because they are eternal, and will prevail over the seen things because they are temporal (2 Corinthians 4:18). My faith celebrates the triumph of what is eternally real.

5. Today I will have the substance of the things that I hope for. Although hope is in the future, the substantive material of my faith will pull what is out there in tomorrow into my eternal "now." I will believe I receive when I pray, because faith says, "I have it now." The future is now because of the substance of my faith.

6. Today I will have the evidence of things not seen. I will need no other confirmation than the evidence of my God-kind of faith. My faith is enough to overcome the natural world today, so that the material becomes immaterial to me – matter will not matter – faith is what is real!

7. Today I will live by faith because I am justified, and the just shall live by faith. My kind do not live by bread alone . . . or by the air that we breathe . . . or by the life in our physical bodies . . . we live by faith, period. Because faith IS (not WAS), I will believe and not doubt; I will walk by faith and not by sight. Today the power of faith will enable me to live the champion's life, and today I will live in the now!

Father, today I will walk in "now" faith, by Your word. In Jesus' name, amen.

REJOICE TODAY!

"This is the day the Lord has made; we will rejoice and be glad in it." (Psalm 118:24)

1. Today I will live in the now! I will live in the now because I understand and appreciate the energizing power of rejoicing in the now. Today I joyfully celebrate the present, and all of the possibilities that it presents. I exercise my will — I WILL rejoice, and I WILL be glad in this day! Today I choose to wear the garment of praise instead of the spirit of heaviness. I choose happiness! I choose joy!

2. Today I will resist the temptation to whine, complain, murmur, grumble, mourn, lament, moan and groan, be depressed, feel sorry for myself, feel down and out, feel dejected, feel discontented, feel oppressed, be sad, or even be in a bad mood. Instead, my merry heart will do me good like a medicine . . . I will glory in my infirmities (for when I am weak, then I am strong) . . . I will count it all joy when I fall into various trials . . . I will leap for joy at persecution . . . the joy of the Lord will be my strength!

3. Today I will laugh, finding the humor in my current situations. I will recognize what is funny, and I will not hesitate to enjoy it. I will not waste today by living in regret, but with joy I will draw water out of the wells of salvation. I will even find the proper way to appreciate the absurd and the ridiculous. I will let God use the foolish things of the world to confound the wise around me.

4. Today I will enter the Kingdom by becoming like a little child . . . laughing . . . playing . . . having fun . . . not taking life too seriously. I will make the effort to enjoy my day. I will smile at people. I will be a pleasure to be with. People will enjoy my company today because my joy will be both attractive and infectious. I will be a blessing to others.

5. Today, for the joy that is set before me, I will endure my cross. I will know the reality of the resurrection and, therefore, will see no situation as hopeless. Life will always triumph over death. I will celebrate my life. The same Spirit that raised Jesus from the dead will live big in me today!

6. Today I will be optimistic. I will see the glass half-full. I will think positively. I will think on those things that are true, honest, just, pure, lovely, and of a good report. I will walk in the Mind of Christ. I will be proactive in dealing with the people around me, and with all of their issues. My joyful mind will cause me to think like a winner!

7. Today I will be thankful to God, and grateful for my life. I will make melody in my heart to the Lord in an attitude of praise and worship. I will be renewed by the refreshing laughter of Christ in my spirit. This is my day that the Lord has made — I will rejoice and be glad in it and, today I will live in the now!

Father, help me to remember to rejoice today. In Jesus' name, amen.

January 10
KEEP MOVING!

"For in Him we . . . move . . . ." *(Acts 17:28)*

1. Today I will live in the now! I will live in the now because I am moving . . . I am mobile . . . I am not stuck in the past. In Him I live, and MOVE, and have my being. My life is a river, not a stagnant pool. My life is a road . . . a path . . . a highway – not a parking lot. I understand why the windshield in my car is much bigger than the rearview mirror . . . it is much more important for me to see where I am going, than for me to see where I have been!

2. Today I will keep pace with God. I will move with the cloud. I will not lag behind Him, nor will I run out ahead of Him. I will run WITH the vision for my life. I understand the importance of timing – His timing. He makes all things beautiful in His time. I am in sync with Him, moving in tandem to His direction for my destiny.

3. Today my steps are ordered by the Lord. I will move by His leading. I will not dismiss His "miracles in the now" (no matter how seemingly insignificant they may presently be) as mere coincidence or chance. I do not experience flukes. I am not "lucky." Rather, I progress daily as I move up in God, going from glory to glory, being conformed to His image. I am led by the Spirit of God, and I am a son of God.

4. Today I will accept the fact that movement inevitably brings change. I will appreciate the seasons of my life. I will release from unrealistic expectations those who cannot - or will not - change with me. I will be responsible for my own movement, and will allow others in my life to move at their own pace, without my judgment.

5. Today I will relish the excitement of not knowing every detail of my journey ("By faith Abraham . . . went out, not knowing where he was going" - Hebrews 11:8), but will simply rejoice in the fact that I am in motion. I will welcome the adventure, trusting the Good Shepherd to lead the way. I will go with the flow without question or hesitation ("The wind blows where it wishes . . ." - John 3:8), knowing that I am a visionary, not a vagabond. My movement has meaning. My path has purpose.

6. Today I will discern the necessity of baby steps. If my progress is incremental, I will not despise the day of small things, but will be encouraged that some movement is better than no movement at all. He who began a good work in me will complete it as the A and the Z, the author and the finisher of my faith.

7. Today my youth will be renewed because I keep moving . . . growing . . . learning . . . changing. Movement keeps me vital and involved with the work of God in the now. My finger is on the pulse of Christ's living body. No matter how tempted I may be to stay where I am, today I will keep moving, and today I will live in the now!

Father, help me to keep moving today. In Jesus' name, amen.

January 11
FRESH WORD!

*". . . man shall not live by bread alone; but man lives by every word
that proceeds from the mouth of the Lord." (Deuteronomy 8:3 - KJV)*

1. Today I will live in the now! I will live in the now because I do not "refuse Him who SPEAKS" but, rather, I accept the rhema word of the Lord as my manna. I appreciate and believe what He *has said,* but I live by what He *is saying* to me in the now!

2. Today I will resist religious restraints that regulate and reduce God to a managed and monitored system. Instead, I welcome the free-flowing, life-giving, ever-fresh word now proceeding from His mouth that cannot be controlled or supervised. He can say what He will, and I will receive it, even if it seems strange to my finite mind.

3. Today my spiritual eyes and ears will be open to the word of the Lord in every place. I will be sensitive to listen for the unusual and unprecedented. I will extract truth as I violently pursue His Kingdom, and will draw out revelation from the heart of God, through the mouth of God, by my strong desire to live in the now. I will recognize the pearl of great price when I find it.

4. Today I will open myself up to a fresh word through the door of meditation. I will wait on the Lord. I will keep my mind stayed on Him. My tongue will be the pen of a ready writer. My delight will be in the law of the Lord, and on His law I will meditate day and night. This book of the law shall not depart from my mouth, but I will meditate on it that I might *do* it.

5. Today I will esteem His word higher than my necessary food. His Word is forever settled in heaven as far as I am concerned, and the entrance of it gives me light. It is sweeter to me than honey in the honeycomb. It is to be desired more than much fine gold. It is a lamp to my feet and a light to my path. My house is built on the rock of it, and I rejoice over it as one having found great spoil.

6. Today I will embrace the anointed word – the word that destroys the yoke of bondage in my life. I will not be surprised at the presence of the anointing in places where I would not normally think to look for it. If the Spirit leads me to Arabia to find the word, then I will gladly go, even though conventional wisdom says that I should go to Jerusalem to find it (Galatians 1:16, 17).

7. Today I will live life to the fullest, satisfied in the inner man. I will have an edge, an advantage, because I hear and receive the fresh word that proceeds from His mouth. It will not be lost on me. I have revelation knowledge and do not deceive myself, because I am a doer of the Word. Today I will enjoy prosperity and success because of my life in His word, and today I will live in the now!

Father, help me to find a fresh word today. In Jesus' name, amen.

January 12
NEW THING!

"Do not remember the former things, Nor consider the things of old. Behold, I will do a NEW THING, NOW it shall spring forth; Shall you not know it? I will even make a road in the wilderness and rivers in the desert." (Isaiah 43: 18, 19)

1. Today I will live in the now! I will live in the now because the new thing that God is doing is causing (forcing) me to update my thinking. I am making the effort to stop considering the things of old, so that I can recognize the new thing when it springs forth. The question is, "Shall you not know it?" — and the answer is, "Yes, I will!"

2. Today I will stop complaining about the wilderness, and start looking for the road out of it. The way out is the way into the Promised Land, and if He promised that the new thing would be a road (way) in my wilderness, then I am ready to travel on that new road, no matter the condition of it. The road will give me direction.

3. Today I will stop worrying about surviving in the desert, and will search for the river that comes from the "new thing." I will not be afraid of the river, even if it is deep, and has white water rapids and treacherous falls in it. The river represents life, and I am ready to have it, and to have it more abundantly. Even if I have to move through my fears to navigate the new river, I know that it will lead me to my destiny.

4. Today I will allow the Holy Spirit to do His unique work of making all things new. He is the source of life Who causes miracles in the now. His is the only way, and I will spontaneously obey His instructions, excitedly expecting the outcome. He only brings good, life, peace, health and blessing – He is perfect in all His ways.

5. Today I will have a new outlook and attitude in preparation for the new thing that God is doing. The "springing forth" of it will not startle me, because I am flexible and aware of the work of the Spirit. I am in a state of anticipation. I am ready!

6. Today I will not fret over the chaos that the new thing may cause in my world. I will not be oppressed by the words and wishes of those who cannot accept the new or the now. If the new thing from God disrupts my life as I know it, then so be it! He is my Lord. He doesn't have to clear it with me, even though He has offered to do so. My life belongs to Him. He can do with it as He pleases, even though He has given me the control over my life. I have freely given the control back over to Him!

7. Today I will recognize the role that people play in bringing about God's new thing for me. I will be open to meeting new people who will bring new things to my life, and will rethink the people who are already affecting me. All of it will work together for my good. The Lord will perfect that which concerns me. Today I am looking for the new thing to spring forth, and today I will live in the now!

Father, help me to recognize the new thing that You are doing. In Jesus' name, amen.

January 13
LISTEN TODAY!

"Again He designates a certain day, saying in David, 'Today,' after such a long time, as it has been said: 'Today, if you will hear His voice, do not harden your hearts.'" (Hebrews 4:7)

1. Today I will live in the now! I will live in the now because I am listening for the God-word, the now-word, the rhema word to my heart *today*. My spiritual ears are open and attentive to hear His voice and, when I hear it, I will not harden my heart against it. Faith will come to me today by hearing, and hearing by the word of God.

2. Today I will understand the miracle of the confirmation in the mouth of two or three witnesses. I am in harmony with the universe, and am particularly aware that the heavens are declaring the glory of God to me. I will listen to nature. I will pay attention to the voice of children, for a little child may lead me today. I will notice the truth in what people may say to me (or what God may say through them) that even they may not be aware of.

3. Today, even though I am perceptive to spiritual things, I will not be oblivious to the voice of God should He decide to speak to me through a secular medium (the earth is the Lord's). I will notice the lyrics to songs, lines from poems, excerpts from famous speeches, etc. God can use anything as His mouthpiece - television, radio, the Internet, art – so I will embrace all forms of communication. If He is saying it, I will be listening for it.

4. Today I will not dismiss a new idea simply because it is new. I will consider what I hear, and will not resist the unfamiliar. Because my ears are open, and my heart is full of God's Word, my mind is sharp, keen, and focused on what is important. I am intelligent because Jesus is made unto me wisdom.

5. Today I will not be afraid to be impressionable. I will maintain a spark of youthfulness because I refuse to be set in my ways. Because I can hear, I can change! I am clay, and I welcome the voice (work) of the potter.

6. Today I will not rule out the possibility of an Angelic visitation or announcement. I will remember to *entertain strangers* (Hebrews 13:2), in case an angel should choose to take on such a form. By the same token, I will recognize any demonic or dark voice that tries to speak to me today, and will overcome it by my resistance.

7. Today I will listen to God when He is talkative, and will obey His instructions. I will also be patient when He is silent, and will trust that He will speak when it is necessary to do so. Either way, His presence today will be my delight, and today I will live in the now!

Father, open my ears and help me to listen today. In Jesus' name, amen.

January 14
NEW SONG!

"Oh, sing to the Lord a NEW SONG! Sing to the Lord, all the earth." (Psalm 96:1)

1. Today I will live in the now! I will live in the now because there is a new song in my mouth today – a song of victory in the now – a song of praise written on my heart by the Divine Psalmist, the Holy Spirit. He has given me the melody and the key. He has given me the tempo and the rhythm. He has given me the lyrics and the phrasing. He will inhabit my praise today.

2. Today I will sing a new song of **redemption**. I will celebrate my salvation, and sing of my passage from death unto life. I will sing the resurrection, and all of its eternal benefits. I will not take for granted my blood-bought right to the rhapsody of the redeemed, never hesitating to perform it for all to hear - in this realm, and in the next.

3. Today I will sing a new song of **war**. My song will help me fight the good fight of faith. I will sing myself to the front lines of the Lord's army, and there I will declare the end from the beginning. I will sing of triumph before the battle is over, prevailing over my enemies by confounding and confusing them. Praise the Lord, for His mercy endures forever! Mine is the song of a conquering warrior/hero.

4. Today I will sing a new song of **agreement**. "Again I tell you, if two of you on earth agree (harmonize together, make a symphony together) about whatever [anything and everything] they may ask, it will come to pass and be done for them by My Father in heaven" (Matthew 18:19 - AMP). My song, sung with others in agreement with me and around me, will cause us to be one and, therefore, nothing that we imagine to do will be impossible to us!

5. Today I will sing a new song of **love** to the One who knows me the best, and still loves me the most. I will sing a mature song of affection, intimacy, passion, and divine romance in the hidden chamber of love – the secret place of the Most High. I will sing with intense conviction and expressed desire. God will hear it and be blessed today. I will be a lover after His own heart.

6. Today I will sing a new song of **thanksgiving**. I will sing the beauty of the world around me. My song will acknowledge that God has done all things well. I will sing the glory of His creation. I will clap my hands along with the trees of the field. I will not sing a mourner's lament or a funeral dirge today, but my song will be one of gladness, born out of my joy in the Holy Ghost!

7. Today I can get through anything that comes my way, because God has given me a new song. I will not miss the opportunity to sing it today, and today I will live in the now!

Father, help me to sing a new song today. In Jesus' name, amen.

January 15
NO PROBLEM!

"And we know that all things work together for good to those who love God, to those who are the called according to His purpose." (Romans 8:28)

1. Today I will live in the now! I will live in the now because I know that there is more to what is happening in my life right now than meets the eye. I also know that my problems are actually opportunities for God to show off *for me* and *through me* and, therefore, I am excited about what is about to happen *around me* and *in me*! I feel like I have a front row seat, and it is just a few moments until Show Time!

2. Today I will not worry about the situations concerning me right now, because worrying will not change them. Instead, I will convert the mental energy that I would need to really worry into effectual, fervent prayer. I am careful for nothing, but in everything, by prayer and supplication, I thankfully make my requests known to God.

3. Today I will realize that I am not alone in this. God is for me! Who can be against me? He'll never leave or forsake me. He will be with me always, even to the end of the world. And though I walk through the valley of the shadow of death, I will fear no evil, for He is with me. His rod and staff comfort me. The fourth man in my fiery furnace will cause me to come out without even the smell of smoke on my clothes!

4. Today I will be proactive, instead of reactive, to my problems. Because I have been given dominion and authority, I can do something about my situation. I am not helpless. God will show me what I can do today that will make a difference, and after I have done all that I can, I will stand in faith for God to do the rest.

5. Today God is sending someone to help me. Someone has the answer that I am looking for. Someone has the solution to the problem. Someone has a key to unlock the mysterious part of the situation. Someone is bringing me the word of the Lord.

6. Today I will have a good attitude. My strong spirit will prevent me from being overwhelmed by my problems. The same God, who delivered me from the bear and the lion, will also deliver me from the present giant that I am facing! In all these things I am more that a conqueror!

7. Today I will rest in the faithfulness of God. He has *never* failed me, and He *never* will. I am not worried, anxious, fearful or depressed. My situation could totally change for the better today. I will keep things in perspective. I will not be negative. I will not burden others with the details. I will not exaggerate and magnify my problems – *I will magnify the Lord!* Today, God and I are bigger than my problems, and today I will live in the now!

Father, help me to see my problems today as opportunities. In Jesus' name, amen.

January 16
TRADITION FREE!

"Thus you have made the commandment of God of no effect by your tradition."
(Matthew 15:6)

". . . The phrase 'one last shaking' means a thorough housecleaning, getting rid of all the historical and religious junk so that the unshakable essentials stand clear and uncluttered." (Hebrews 12:27 – The Message)

1. Today I will live in the now! I will live in the now because I have declared my independence from meaningless forms, routines and traditions in my life that are contrary to my present reality, and that make the Word of God ineffective for me. I am moving past archaic and passé ways of thinking about God or life or myself. The limiting, antiquated ideas and philosophies that I have accumulated over the years are being exposed for the irrelevant relics that they are. I am free to think a new way!

2. Today I will not believe something just because someone told me to believe it. I will have the confidence to think for myself, and the courage to expose a lie that I have accepted when I recognize that it is, indeed, a lie. I will be able to maintain my love and respect for someone important to me, without feeling obligated to believe everything they say.

3. Today I will consider the Word of God as the final authority on every subject.

4. Today I will honor the Lordship of Jesus as the highest priority in my life.

5. Today I will cooperate with the work of the Holy Spirit in my inner man.

6. Today I will reject, resist and renounce all forms of the man-made religion that exalts itself against God's true Kingdom. I will pull down strongholds in my mind that were imparted to me from the religious system that are contrary to the knowledge of God. Religion is the enemy, and I will have no part of it and its silly fables, false doctrines, and pointless works of the flesh.

7. Today I will enjoy the good traditions from my family, my childhood, my country, my heritage. I will benefit from sage advice – the wisdom of the ages – and from lessons learned by life experience. I will restore the old landmarks, and will be a link to the next generation by passing down what is noble and worth keeping. But I will also know how to discern the difference between healthy, foundational traditions, and the ones that are holding me in the past. In that context, today I will be tradition-free, and today I will live in the now!

Father, help me to break free of all unnecessary tradition today. In Jesus' name, amen.

January 17
ACT NOW!

"Go to the ant, you sluggard! Consider her ways and be wise, which, having no captain, overseer or ruler, provides her supplies in summer, and gathers her food in the harvest." (Proverbs 6:6, 7)

1. Today I will live in the now! I will live in the now because I am a doer of the Word, someone who takes action. I will seize the day, live in the moment, perceive the power of the present – and at the same time take charge of my life by preparing for my future. What I do today will make a difference in the world around me.

2. Today I am making plans . . . planting seeds for a desired harvest . . . watching and praying; but I am doing it all without taking thought for tomorrow. I make wise preparation, all the while considering the lilies of the field! This is impossible to do in the natural, but with God all things are possible. I am blessed to be balanced in Him.

3. Today I am a co-laborer with God. I am His fellow-worker. I can decree a thing so that it can be established, but I can also cast my care upon Him. He will not do everything for me, and I do not have to do everything for myself. God and I are in perfect harmony with one another.

4. Today I will recognize opportunity when it knocks. Jesus is made unto me wisdom. I have the knowledge of witty inventions. I have the Mind of Christ. I know when to move and when to act. I also know when to be still and wait. I walk in the Spirit.

5. Today I will not walk in stress or under undue pressure. The government is on His shoulders. I have the energy and the will to pursue success, but I also have the grace to let go. Through faith and patience I inherit the promises.

6. Today I have a keen sense of timing. I will not run ahead of God, nor lag behind Him. I will move with the cloud. I will not act prematurely, nor will I procrastinate. I am in sync with God, moving in tandem to his perfect leadership.

7. Today I make good and right decisions. I am not afraid to trust my instincts. I will patiently wait for the "blade" and the "ear," but when the "full corn in the ear" is ripe, I will not hesitate to thrust in the sickle and reap! I will discern my moment of visitation. I will not miss my window of opportunity. I can do something powerful and important today, and today I will live in the now!

Father, show me today how to "act now." In Jesus' name, amen.

January 18
LET GO!

"And whenever you stand praying, if you have anything against anyone, forgive him and let it drop (leave it, LET IT GO) in order that your Father Who is in heaven may also forgive you your [own] failings and shortcomings and let them drop." (Mark 11:25 – AMP)

1. Today I will live in the now! I will live in the now because I am not held in the past by unresolved issues and unfinished business. I am too busy to be bitter. I have more important things to do with my time than to waste it by holding onto things that I cannot change in the natural. I will forgive, not just because I have been commanded to do so, but, because it is for my own benefit. Forgiveness moves me into the now.

2. Today I will let go of unrealistic expectations that I have in and for other people. Jesus is enough for me. His grace is sufficient. I can depend on Him. His faithfulness allows me to give a break to someone who has disappointed me. His power helps me to keep people in perspective.

3. Today I will let go of my regrets. That was then. This is now. I will learn from my mistakes, take responsibility for my actions, and do what I can to make my life what it should be. If I can change something that I don't like, I will. If I can't, I'll shut up about it!

4. Today I will let go of my pettiness. I will choose greatness by taking the high road with others. I will do the right thing, whether anyone else does or not. I will be mature and noble and wise. I will stop blaming everybody else for what I don't like about the world. I will not complain about what I permit.

5. Today I will let go of my anger. I will retire from nursing my high-maintenance grudges, and stop allowing myself to be exhausted and burned out from my hatred and prejudices. I will be a peacemaker, even with myself.

6. Today I will let go of my negativity. God is good. Life is good (or at least better than I usually realize or admit). The world is a beautiful place to live. So I let it all go . . . bad attitude, self-pity, pain and sadness . . . and I will not take comfort in the familiarity of these things any longer.

7. Today I will let yesterday go. I can't go back there; I have to keep moving, so I will make the journey easier by lightening my load. I will not hold on to the past, but will move with the rhythm and flow of life. Today I say "good-bye and good riddance" to what I should release, and today I will live in the now!

Father, help me to let go today. In Jesus' name, amen.

January 19
GET UP!

"For a righteous man may fall seven times and rise again . . . ." **(Proverbs 24:16)**

1. Today I will live in the now! I will live in the now because I have it in me to get back up again when I fall down. I am not just a survivor; I am more than a conqueror through Him who loves me! Because of the reality of the resurrection, I have the grace to **get up**, the power to prevail, and the will to win, even if I fall frequently.

2. Today I will **get up** out of my shackles of shame. An embarrassment is not the end. He has made me the head and not the tail, above only, and not beneath. I am the righteousness of God in Christ. I will arise and shine for my light has come, and the glory of the Lord has risen upon me!

3. Today I will **get up** out of my sewer of self-pity. A mistake is not mortal. If God is for me, who can be against me? He prepares a table for me in the presence of my enemies. No weapon formed against me can prosper, and every tongue that rises against me will be shown to be in the wrong!

4. Today I will **get up** out of my dungeon of discouragement. A defeat is not devastating. Forgetting those things which are behind, I press on to the prize. The same Spirit that raised Jesus from the dead lives in me. The joy of the Lord is my strength!

5. Today I will **get up** out of my morass of mediocrity. A failure is not forever. I can run and not be weary; I can walk and not faint. Greater is He Who is in me, than he who is in the world. I can do all things through Christ Who strengthens me!

6. Today I will **get up** out of my gulf of guilt. A fall is not fatal. Where sin abounds, grace does much more abound. He has not dealt with me after my sins, nor rewarded me according to my iniquity. He is faithful and just to forgive me of my sins, and to cleanse me from all unrighteousness!

7. Today I will **get up**, even if I fall seven times (the number representing infinity), because Jesus is praying for me. I will never give up, because He never gives up on me. And every time I get back up, I become stronger than I was before I fell. Today I am restored, renewed, revived, refreshed and resurrected by His power, and today I will live in the now!

Father, help me to get back up today. In Jesus' name, amen.

January 20
NO CONDEMNATION!

"There is therefore NOW no condemnation to those who are in Christ Jesus, who do not walk according to the flesh, but according to the Spirit." (Romans 8:1)

1. Today I will live in the now! I will live in the now because no condemnation exists for me in the NOW. He who knew no sin became sin for me, that I might become His righteousness – and I am the righteousness of God in Christ now. I am forgiven now. I am holy now. I am justified now. I am clean now.

2. Today mercy is working on my behalf, to withhold from me what I really deserve. I will make myself comfortable at the mercy seat, because Jesus has enabled me to do so. I am accepted in the beloved, and today I will act and feel like I am accepted.

3. Today grace is working on my behalf, to pour out on me what I really don't deserve. I will make myself at home at the throne of grace, because Jesus has invited me to do so. My transgressions have been removed from me as far as the east is from the west, and today I will think and speak like I am forgiven.

4. Today the blood of Jesus is working on my behalf, to wash away all of my guilt and shame. He was wounded for my transgressions, and bruised for my iniquities. His cleansing blood is alive now through the Eternal Spirit.

5. Today the word of God is working on my behalf. It is written in the logos word that my sins have been thrown into the sea, and have been cast behind His back. It is spoken in the rhema word that He is saving me to the uttermost, as He lives to make intercession for me.

6. Today the Holy Spirit is working on my behalf as He leads me into all truth. I will walk in the Spirit today, and not in the flesh. As He reveals Himself to me as the Spirit of Adoption, I will be secure in the family of God, boldly crying, "Abba, Father!"

7. Today I will enter into rest, knowing that I do not have to be motivated by fear. My heart does not condemn me and, therefore, I have confidence before God. I will glory in the cross, believe the resurrection with my heart, and confess His Lordship with my mouth. I am saved! I have eternal life! I am a new creature in Christ! I have passed from death unto life! Today I will know that God is good, and today I will live in the now!

Father, help me to walk in the Spirit today. In Jesus' name, amen.

January 21
RELATIONSHIPS NOW!

"Consequently, from now on we estimate and regard no one from a [purely] human point of view [in terms of natural standards of value] . . . ." (2 Corinthians 5:16 – AMP)

1. Today I will live in the now! I will live in the now because of the covenant relationships in my life and the way that they reveal Jesus to me. The people in my life – family, loved ones, acquaintances, business partners, neighbors, friends (both close and distant), and enemies alike – are all working out a higher purpose in me and, therefore, I will thank God for them all!

2. Today I will succeed because I walk in love, and love never fails (1 Corinthians 13:8). The God-kind of love is shed abroad in my heart by the Holy Ghost, and that love will enable me to exist in a supernatural dimension of harmony, forgiveness and grace toward everyone with whom I come into contact.

3. Today I will enjoy the comfort of friendship. Knowing that "a friend loves at all times . . ." (Proverbs 17:17), I will believe and accept that I am loved. I deserve friends because I have shown myself friendly (18:24), and today my life will be improved because of them, as iron sharpens iron (27:17).

4. Today I will embrace the benefits of commitment. I will not be hesitant to make a required withdrawal from the lives of those into whom I have made an investment. I will give of myself freely, fully understanding the demands imposed upon me by my relationships, ignoring the risks. I will ask for help when I need it.

5. Today I will speak the truth in love. ("Faithful are the wounds of a friend, but the kisses of an enemy are deceitful." - Proverbs 27:6) Life is in the power of the tongue, so I will not avoid confrontation when necessary, nor fear possible rejection, because there is no fear in love.

6. Today I will be unselfish with my time and attention. I will let those who play significant roles in my life know how important they are to me by my words and by my actions. I will be touchable.

7. Today I will work toward improving my relationship with God, with others, and with myself. My life will be enriched by relating to people. Today I will make a connection, and today I will live in the now!

Father, help me to value my relationships today. In Jesus' name, amen.

January 22
GOOD MORNING!

". . . the Lord's mercies . . . are new every morning. Great is your faithfulness."
(Lamentations 3:22, 23)

1. Today I will live in the now! I will live in the now because God's mercy endures forever - one morning at a time. The freshness of the dawn and early hours of the day are a reminder to me of how current and new God is in His merciful dealings with me.

2. Today I will praise the Name of the Lord from the rising of the sun, to the going down of the same. I will start off my day with a love song for the One Who woke me up this morning, and I will sing it to Him in my heart until I lay down to sleep this evening. I am blessed and thankful for all of God's benefits. Today I know that He is smiling on me as I sing of His greatness!

3. Today I will not be overcome by sorrow, because weeping may endure for the night, but joy comes in the morning. No matter how dark things have been, this morning I can see the light at the end of the tunnel. I will be optimistic in my thinking, and the faith in my heart will produce great expectations in my inner man.

4. Today I will go where the day takes me, without fear or dread. I declare the end from the beginning by saying that this is the day the Lord has made, so I will regard it as an open door to my future. No matter what it may bring, or what I may be up against, my faith will win the day.

5. Today, as the Daystar arises in my heart, my vision will increase like the sunlight at dawn. This day will usher in a whole new season of increase for me. I say "good morning" to my new attitude, as I welcome all the possibilities that are on the way.

6. Today I let yesterday go, and use what I have in my hand right now to maximize the day's potential. A new opportunity for me lies around every corner, and I will not let one go unnoticed by being distracted by water under the bridge.

7. Today the Bright and Morning Star shines on me - and through me. It's a new day, and everything is different in my world than it was before. I demonstrate that His mercies are new this morning by my determination to live the liberated life today, and today I will live in the now!

Good morning, Lord! Help me to see Your new mercies today. In Jesus' name, amen.

January 23
START NOW!

"Making the very most of the time [buying up each opportunity], because the days are evil." (Ephesians 5:16 – AMP)

1. Today I will live in the now! I will live in the now because I have realized how important my time is, and how necessary it is for me to stop wasting it. I can do something to advance the Kingdom of God *now*! I can do something to make the world a better place in which to live *now*! I can do something to help somebody I love *now*! I can do something to improve my life *now*!

2. Today is a day full of opportunity and promise. I don't have to be victimized by the swift passage of time, because I have the ability to redeem it. The eternal "I Am" lives in me and, therefore, time is on my side. It is never too late for a miracle!

3. Today I will stop delaying my destiny. I will be a proactive producer rather than a prosaic procrastinator. I will not be lazy. I will stop making excuses for myself. I will not put off until tomorrow what I should go ahead and do today.

4. Today I will move toward the fulfillment of the prophecies over my life. I will find ways to start making my dreams come true, and I will enjoy the journey every bit as much as I do the destination. To accomplish this, I will start making the necessary changes in my thinking immediately.

5. Today I will not allow an unfounded fear of failure prevent me from getting started. So what if I fall? Stepping *out of the boat* is more important to me now than trying to stay *out of the water*. In fact, I would rather be a wet "water-walker" than a dry "boat-dweller!"

6. Today I will trust that God will stop me before I take a wrong step, because I have prayed over my path. My faith will distance me from the pack – those who are too careful or too afraid - and I will ride with God on the high places of the earth.

7. Today I will be brave enough to take the initiative in pursuing my best destiny. I have experienced enough to know that I don't have to be afraid anymore. I am ready to get started today, and today I will live in the now!

"Jesus said, 'No procrastination. No backward looks.
You can't put God's Kingdom off till tomorrow. Seize the day.'" (Luke 9:62 - The Message)

Father, give me the courage to get started on my journey today. In Jesus' name, amen.

January 24
BIG PICTURE!

"While we do not look at the things which are seen, but at the things which are not seen. For the things which are seen are temporary, but the things which are not seen are eternal." (2 Corinthians 4:18)

1. Today I will live in the now! I will live in the now because I have made the decision to see my current circumstances in the light of the spiritual realm. I will see my life as a whole - something entire and complete. Although I am making the effort to live in the moment, I always know that there is more to my life than what is happening right now. Now is certainly important, but it is not all that there is to my life.

2. Today I will be able to regard my present circumstances as important pieces to the puzzle of my life, and I will cooperate with the Holy Spirit in assembling those pieces until the picture is complete. Seeing things come together to manifest God's purpose for my life is an enjoyable adventure, even when the process is precarious.

3. Today I don't have to understand exactly *how* the plan works for me, because I know that it *always* works out for me! In the big picture, all things are working together for my good, and that is all that really matters to me. I trust in the Lord with all my heart by not leaning unto my own understanding.

4. Today I will not allow negative, limiting voices from my past to create a defeatist mentality in me, because my spiritual eyes are on the *big picture*. I am able to maintain a "can do" attitude in all things, regardless of what I may be facing today.

5. Today, even though the big picture is painted in broad strokes, I will not be unaware of how important minute details are to the finished product. I will pay attention to the still, small voice of God in my inner man, and I will obey all of His instructions, not despising the day of small things (Zechariah 4:10). His every wish is my command.

6. Today I look at those things that are eternal, because eternity is now. I do not have to look to the past. I don't even have to look to the future. The big picture is *now*, and I walk in the revelation of it in the spirit, instead of in the intellect.

7. Today I am unmoved by natural scenarios. I am a visionary and, therefore, can see what most people can't. Because of this ability, I am strong, steady, patient, and focused as I work out my own salvation. Today I will enjoy seeing my personal path unfold as the big picture of my life manifests the glory of God. I will not underestimate the importance of today, and today I will live in the now!

Father, help me to begin to see the big picture today. In Jesus' name, amen.

January 25
KINGDOM, COME!

"Your Kingdom come. Your will be done on earth as it is in heaven." (Matthew 6:10)

*"Therefore, since we ARE RECEIVING a Kingdom which cannot be shaken,
let us have grace . . . ." (Hebrews 12:28)*

1. Today I will live in the now! I will live in the now because I am a part of His Kingdom, and His Kingdom is coming now! The King is reigning in my life now. His government is increasing now. The kingdoms of this world are becoming the Kingdoms of our God, and of His Christ, now.

2. Today I am not encumbered with the pointless rules and regulations of religion, because the Kingdom of God is not meat or drink, but it is righteousness, peace, and joy in the Holy Ghost. I will interpret my day by these three things, and will make seeking them my first priority.

3. Today is a day to demonstrate righteousness. He Who knew no sin became sin for me that I might become the righteousness of God in Christ, and it is from this righteousness consciousness that my self-esteem and confidence flow today. By this I am able to show that He has made me the head and not the tail.

4. Today is a day to walk in peace - not as the world gives - but as Jesus Himself shares His supernatural peace with me. I let not my heart be troubled because I have the peace that passes understanding. I will not be agitated, frustrated or anxious today because of my Kingdom right to walk in Kingdom peace.

5. Today is a day to celebrate joy in the Holy Ghost. I will not be sad or depressed today because His joy is in me and, therefore, my joy is full! The Kingdom joy working in me will be my strength and will give me the winner's edge.

6. Today I will seek the Kingdom *first* in every situation. Before I have a chance to think about it in the natural . . . before I analyze it, or react emotionally . . . I will look for the Kingdom before I do anything else about anything at all. He is reigning in and through me today, and every name that is named must bow to His Name!

7. Today I live a life that shows the world that I am a royal subject of the ultimate Kingdom and, therefore, I cannot fail, or lose, or be defeated. Jesus the King shall reign forever and ever, and He is my Lord . . . my personal friend . . . my elder brother. Today I say, "Long live the King!" and today I will live in the now!

Your Kingdom come, Your will be done on earth as it is in heaven – today. Amen.

January 26
DREAM BIG!

"Now to Him who . . . is able to [carry out His purpose and] do superabundantly, far over and above all that we [dare] ask or think [infinitely beyond our highest prayers, desires, thoughts, hopes, or dreams] to Him be glory . . . ." (Ephesians 3:20 – AMP)

1. Today I will live in the now! I will live in the now because I am a visionary, a dreamer, a believer and a doer of the Word. I am not afraid to put God to the test by believing for the extraordinary and the impossible. He is able, and He has enabled me by giving me the ability to dream.

2. Today I will avoid, if possible, the company of shallow and small-minded people who do not practice the power of dreaming. I will seek the fellowship of those who dare to see beyond the finite world, and, if there are none to be found, I will be content to dream alone.

3. Today I will think creatively. I will walk fearlessly on the high places without the security of a safety net – daring to dream dramatic, even dangerous dreams. I will challenge the status quo, rejecting my own self-imposed limitations. My dreams will enlarge me.

4. Today I will prophesy possibilities, voice my vision, and declare my dreams to those around me. I will not indiscriminately "cast my pearls before swine" and set myself up to be disillusioned by the influence of negative people. But neither will I hesitate to talk up my dreams when the right time or opportunity presents itself.

5. Today I will be open to inspiration . . . new ideas . . . revelation . . . enlightenment. I will not reject a radical idea if I believe that it will honor God and help to reveal His Kingdom. My big dreams create a child-like faith in my heart that causes me to truly believe that anything is possible.

6. Today I will maintain the ability to think realistically, because the fruit of the Spirit is self-control. My dreams will not prevent me from being grounded and practical. I will continue to expect the impossible, but will also be flexible in my vision, with a teachable spirit, and the patience needed to balance my faith.

7. Today I will continue to be focused and productive in the real world, but I will be ever aware that there is an unseen world of the spirit that is even more real than the natural one. Today I will work toward making my dreams come true, and today I will live in the now!

Father, help me to dream big and think out of the box today. In Jesus' name, amen.

January 27
TRY AGAIN!

"So let's not allow ourselves to get fatigued doing good. At the right time we will harvest a good crop if we don't give up, or quit. Right NOW, therefore, every time we get the chance, let us work for the benefit of all, starting with the people closest to us in the community of faith." (Galatians 6: 9 – The Message)

1. Today I will live in the now! I will live in the now because I'm not a quitter. My determination is greater than my discouragement, and my resolve is stronger than my resignation! The same Spirit that raised Jesus from the dead dwells in me, and He will not allow me to stay down, either.

2. Today I will face my failures and overcome any embarrassment connected to them. I will not allow myself to be intimidated by past mistakes, because Jesus bore my shame by hanging naked on the cross, and He gives me the courage to try to succeed.

3. Today I will not be cynical. I will not be afraid to be positive and optimistic, but will have the energy and good humor to pull myself back up again. I will not take myself too seriously, and I will humbly keep going until I break through.

4. Today I will be realistic enough to realize when I am at an impasse, but the realization will only serve to inspire me to think of a new way to accomplish my task. The indomitable spirit in me will cause me to keep searching until I find the Kingdom key needed to unlock the door to destiny. I will never say "never."

5. Today I will be innovative. As Moses did, I will use what is in my hand to fulfill God's plan for my life, and will prevail everytime. I have the substance of faith, the Mind of Christ, and the will to win - I will overcome . . . I will be victorious . . . I will win!

6. Today my determination will be an inspiration to someone. This is how I will salt the earth and light the world today – I will cause someone else to try again.

7. Today I will begin to see the first fruits of the bumper crop harvest that I am going to reap because I have refused to give up. This is my season of increase and I intend to enjoy every minute of it. Today I will try again, and today I will live in the now!

Father, don't let me give up - help me to try again today. In Jesus' name, amen.

January 28
BE YOURSELF!

"You're blessed when you're content with just who you are – no more, no less. That's the moment you find yourselves proud owners of everything that can't be bought." (Matthew 5:5 – The Message)

"For we are God's masterpiece. He has created us anew in Christ Jesus, so that we can do the good things He planned for us long ago." (Ephesians 2:10 – NLT)

1. Today I will live in the now! I will live in the now because I know that God loves me just like I am, and has given me the permission to be myself. Because I am accepted in the Beloved, I can put away the childish things that I used to do to try to gain the approval of others, and can relax in my own skin.

2. Today I will officially retire from my need to please everyone, knowing that the effort that it requires is an exercise in futility. It can't be done, and it shouldn't be done. From now on, my number one priority will be to "have this testimony that I please God." God accepts me in the now, so I can accept myself in the now.

3. Today I will enter into rest concerning how people feel about me. I will not be fretful, touchy, or easily offended. I will reject the spirit of rejection, and will not allow my ego to be unnecessarily fragile. Today my attitude will make it virtually impossible for me to get my feelings hurt.

4. Today I will love myself, and not feel guilty about it. I will maintain humility, be a servant to others, and take up my cross – but if Jesus wants me to love my neighbor as I love myself, then I must learn to first love myself. I will be good to myself and treat myself well today.

5. Today I relinquish the need to emulate others, or to compete with them. I am unique. There is only one of me. God did not make a mistake in my creation. I don't have to be jealous, envious, intimidated or untrue to myself. The truth makes me free.

6. Today Jesus is my cornerstone. He alone is my rock – my pattern – my ideal – my hero. I am being conformed to His image, without sacrificing my originality.

7. Today I am prepared to introduce the world to the real me. I will celebrate the fact that I am the workmanship of God today, and today I will live in the now!

Father, help me to be myself today. In Jesus' name, amen.

January 29
RECEIVE NOW!

"Therefore I say to you, whatever things you ask for WHEN YOU PRAY, believe that you receive them, and you will have them." *(Mark 11:24)*

1. Today I will live in the now! I will live in the now because I am receiving from God even as I pray. I am a receiver because I am a believer, and I believe now because faith is now. I trust in God with all my heart, do not lean to my own understanding, and He is directing my path for this day.

2. Today I am in a position to receive from God because Jesus has made me worthy to receive. God gives to me, not because I deserve it or have earned it. My receiving is not based on *my goodness,* but on *His grace* – not on *my performance*, but on *His performance on the cross*!

3. Today people will be able to receive from me, because I receive from God. He is my source, and I am His channel for giving. I am in the flow of supernatural reception, so I freely give because I freely receive. The cycle of sowing and reaping is working for me today.

4. Today I am excited about the power of prayer! Life is in the power of my tongue and, as I communicate with the Creator, I open myself up to unlimited possibilities and resources from Him. Out of the abundance of my heart, my mouth speaks, and my faith-filled words move mountains.

5. Today I know that all of the promises of God are yes and amen, so I repent my mind away from any thought that is contrary to His generosity. I am connected to God and His provisions by my conversations with Him, and my mind is renewed to the fact that anything is possible today!

6. Today my reception of the things of God will take me to a new level of responsibility. I will embrace the real world that lies beyond the limits of my personal comfort zone, and ignore my tendencies to always do the safe and easy thing. I will receive today, even if I have to go out on a limb to do it!

7. Today I will give God the glory and praise that He deserves. No miracle, regardless of how seemingly small, will go unnoticed by me. I am praying today, I am receiving today, and today I will live in the now!

    Father, help me to believe that I receive when I pray today. In Jesus' name, amen.

January 30
GET REAL!

"It's who you are and the way you live that count before God. Your worship must engage your spirit in the pursuit of truth. That's the kind of people the Father is out looking for: those who are simply and honestly themselves before Him in their worship. God is sheer being itself – Spirit. Those who worship Him must do it out of their very being, their spirits, their true selves, in adoration." (John 4:23, 24 – The Message)

1. Today I will live in the now! I will live in the now because I have been set free from the required pretense and phoniness of man-made religion. I know the truth, and the truth that I know makes me free! God has been looking for someone like me to worship Him in spirit and in truth, and my worship is actual and authentic.

2. Today I will be real and genuine in my relationships. I will be a servant today, without a hidden agenda. I will be a giver without a disguised motive. I will really love without any ultimatum. The God-kind of love will enable me to be transparent and pure toward everyone I encounter today.

3. Today I will not be afraid to part with illusions – to speak the truth in love – to be confrontational. There is no fear in love, but perfect love casts out fear, so I will search for honesty in everything and in every situation.

4. Today I will stop blaming and pointing the finger. I will get real about my life, and my responsibility to its integrity. I will not live a lie, and I will take ownership of the fruit of my actions. I can be honest today because God is good, and His mercy endures forever.

5. Today I will not allow pride to prevent me from admitting when I'm wrong.

6. Today I will not live in denial of negative things that need to be examined. I will not ignore the things in my life that need correcting, no matter how small, so that "acorns" cannot become "oak trees." I will call those things that are not as though they are, instead of calling those things that are as though they are not.

7. Today I will be in touch with reality, while maintaining my supernatural faith. I will make every effort to tell and live the whole truth today, and today I will live in the now!

Father, help me to get real in every area of my life today. In Jesus' name, amen.

January 31
STOP WORRYING!

"Do not fret or have any anxiety about anything, but in every circumstance and in everything, by prayer and petition (definite requests), with thanksgiving, continue to make your wants known to God." (Philippians 4:6 – AMP)

1. Today I will live in the now! I will live in the now because I am not bound to the future by unrealistic and unfounded fears. I have peace in the now . . . security and safety in the now . . . nothing to fear or dread in the future, because the image of confidence and strength is being built on the inside of me as I meditate God's Word.

2. Today I hear my Father's voice say, "Be still and know that I am God!" as He makes me lie down in green pastures, and leads me beside still waters. I keep my mind stayed on Him, and He keeps me in perfect peace as He perfects that which concerns me.

3. Today I have power and love and a sound mind, instead of the spirit of fear. I will not let my heart be troubled, but will let the peace of God rule in my heart. I cast all of my care on Him because He cares for me.

4. Today I will not accept a bad report. My heart is established, so that I am not afraid of evil tidings. I will think on those things that are true, honest, just, pure, lovely, of a good report – whatever is virtuous and worthy of praise. As much as is possible, I will surround myself with positive influences. I will walk in the Mind of Christ.

5. Today I will not worry about my family. My children are taught of the Lord, and great is their peace and undisturbed composure. I will not let the thing that I fear the most come upon me concerning my children, but will only see them with my eye of faith. My seed will be mighty on the earth!

6. Tonight I will sleep soundly, because He gives His beloved sleep, and in quietness and confidence will be my strength. No plague will come near my dwelling because the angel of the Lord encamps around me.

7. Today I am calm, undisturbed, relaxed, and serene. I know that worrying will not change things, or add anything good to my life, so I will have no part of it. Today I know that everything is going to be all right, and today I will live in the now!

Father, by Your Word I will not worry today. In Jesus' name, amen.

✦F✦E✦B✦R✦U✦A✦R✦Y✦

A month to remember that faith is the evidence of things not seen.

The bleakness of winter . . . the barrenness of the trees . . . the bone-chilling temperatures . . .

only serve to remind us of the inevitability of inconstancy and the certainty of change.

The trees will bud again . . .

. . . the birds will sing again

. . . the sky will be blue again.

A whole living creation still exists under the frozen earth, even though it is invisible.

Build a fire, wear a sweater, shovel the snow . . . but remember that you'll be warm again.

Don't be moved by what you see . . .

Don't be moved by what you feel . . .

We walk by faith and not by sight . . .

We look at the unseen things that are eternal . . .

To everything there is a season . . .

Change is coming soon . . . go put on a T-shirt and a pair of shorts!

The fundamental fact of existence is that this trust in God, this faith,
is the firm foundation under everything that makes life worth living.
It's our handle on what we can't see . . . ." (Hebrews 11:1 – The Message)

February 1
LIGHTEN UP!

"Therefore . . . let us lay aside every weight, and the sin which so easily ensnares us, and let us run with endurance the race that is set before us." (Hebrews 12:1)

1. I will live in the now! I will live in the now because I am consciously and intentionally laying aside any unnecessary baggage in my spiritual or mental life that would weigh me down, or hold me in the past. I will do what I can today to lighten my load so that I can run my individual race in the now.

2. Today I will unload my personal grudges and hidden agendas, and live honestly and simply among my peers. I will be responsible for how my race is run by doing the right thing, whether anyone else does the right thing or not. I will mind my own business, lay aside my judgmental tendencies, and work out my own salvation with fear and trembling.

3. Today I will strip off my cultural pretenses and religious facades. I am accepted in the Beloved, so I can remove all masks, knowing that I don't have to prove anything to anybody. I will liberate myself from the pressures of being a people-pleaser, and will keep my eyes on Jesus for the duration of the race. Pleasing Him is my one goal.

4. Today I will release my hold on past disappointments and regrets. I will cast off the old, familiar cloak of self-pity, and will discipline myself to run freely, wearing only the garment of praise. He will make my feet like the feet of a deer on the tops of the mountains.

5. Today I will discard my unrealistic expectations of people, along with any unreasonable demands that I may make on them. I will live and let live, freely passing on to others the grace and mercy that has been lavished on me. My only desire will be for God's will to be done in their lives.

6. Today I will throw aside the encumbrances of self-defeating and negative thought patterns. By the hidden weapons that are mighty through God, I will pull down any stronghold that exalts itself against the knowledge of Him today. My renewed mind will enable me to run and not be weary – to walk and not faint.

7. Today I will resist the spirit of heaviness, knowing that His yoke is easy, and His burden is light. I will pace myself with patience, and I will run to win! I will not put off entering the race any longer . . . this is my time to excel, so I will rise to the occasion! Today I will run like a champion, and today I will live in the now!

Father, help me to lighten up today. In Jesus' name, amen.

February 2
HOLD ON!

"Fight the good fight of faith, lay hold on eternal life . . . ." **(1 Timothy 6:12)**

1. Today I will live in the now! I will live in the now because I have the will and the tenacity to grasp my eternal life and to prevail over life's circumstances. When others give up, I will take the road less traveled, and demonstrate that I am of a different spirit. I *can* go the distance!

2. Today I will **hold on to the promises of God**, for they are all "yes" and "amen." By these exceeding great and precious promises, I have been made a partaker of the divine nature . . . a believer who knows that God is not a man that He should lie.

3. Today I will **hold on to my vision and my dreams**. No matter what my present circumstances may be - even if they are completely contrary to the consummation of my dreams – I will see the invisible! I will not perish today, because I have a vision.

4. Today I will **hold on to the prophecies spoken over my life**. Even if the word of the Lord tests and torments me as it did Joseph (Psalm 105:17-19), I will come forth as pure gold, not despising prophecies (I Thessalonians 5:20). They will edify, exhort, and comfort me, while I anticipate their fulfillment.

5. Today I will **hold on to the covenant relationships that have been given me**. I will not take the people in my life for granted, nor will I lightly esteem their importance to, and influence on, me. I am aware that the Kingdom is revealed through relationship, and all that it entails.

6. Today I will **hold on to faith**. The just shall live by faith, and without it, it is impossible to please God. I will hold on to the evidence of things not seen, and firmly and persistently grasp the substance of things hoped for.

7. Today I will **hold on to my sense of destiny and purpose**. I will not forget why I am here. I will not allow myself to believe for one second that my life is meaningless or unimportant. I will *hold on to my identity in God*. I will be unmovable, unshakable, and undefeated. Today I will not give up or let go, and today I will live in the now!

Father, help me to hold on today. In Jesus' name, amen.

February 3
ENJOY TODAY!

"Give your entire attention to what God is doing right NOW, and don't get worked up about what may or may not happen tomorrow. God will help you deal with whatever hard things come up when the time comes." (Matthew 6:34 – The Message)

1. Today I will live in the now! I will live in the now because I am focused on this 24-hour period, and on how I can make it the best that it can be. I will seize the day and live it to the fullest. I will enjoy my *life* because I can enjoy my *day*.

2. Today I will enjoy my work. I will not simply endure it, but will be thankful for the opportunity that it affords me. I will take pride in the work of my hands, finding a sense of fulfillment in the contribution that I make to the world. I will act on these words: "Servants, obey in everything those who are your earthly masters, not only when their eyes are on you, as pleasers of men, but in simplicity of purpose [with all your heart] because of your reverence for the Lord and as a sincere expression of your devotion to Him" (Colossians 3:22 – AMP).

3. Today I will enjoy my family and friends, just as they are. I will love them unconditionally, and thank God for whom they are, without feeling the need to try to change them.

4. Today I will enjoy my leisure time. I will be good to myself, enjoy some well-deserved fun, and will not feel guilty about just relaxing and taking some time off.

5. Today I will enjoy nature. "The heavens declare the glory of God . . ." (Psalm 19:1), so I will pay attention to God's beautiful creation and to what it speaks to me. I will breathe some fresh air, listen to a bird sing, and maybe even watch a sunset.

6. Today I will enjoy my environment. I will appreciate my home, my city, my country, etc. I will take care of what God has entrusted to me.

7. Today I will enjoy the presence of God. I will spend some quality time simply worshipping and communing with Him today, with no request or petition. I was created for His pleasure; so today I will be a pleasure for Him to be with. I will rest well tonight, because of how well I have enjoyed today, and today I will live in the now!

Father, help me to enjoy my day today. In Jesus' name, amen.

February 4
WORK HARD!

"Whatever your hand finds to do, do it with your might . . . ." (Ecclesiastes 9:10)

1. Today I will live in the now! I will live in the now because I am a "doer." I can get things done today. I can accomplish necessary things – important things — even great things — with my life. I am strong, able, equipped, focused, and goal-oriented. I can do all things through Christ who strengthens me!

2. Today I will make the effort to find the pleasure in my work. I will show my positive attitude toward today's tasks by doing them all in the name of Jesus. "And whatever you do in word or deed, do all in the name of the Lord Jesus, giving thanks to God the Father through Him" (Colossians 3:17).

3. Today I will give 100% of myself, but my work will not consume my life. I will not live under undue stress or pressure, nor will I allow myself to become overwhelmed or burned out. I will maintain a healthy balance in my daily routine by not allowing my diligence to become dysfunctional.

4. Today I will not let pride, or any other negative stronghold in my mind, prevent me from asking for help from others when I need it. I will make the effort to be a team player today, and will unselfishly celebrate the rewards of collaboration.

5. Today I will take advantage of the assistance offered to me from "the Helper, the Holy Spirit" who stands by me, and works with and through me. With His help, I will run and not be weary – I will walk and not faint.

6. Today I will inspire those around me to be motivated – to be thankful – to take pride in their own work. My words and actions will be a source of energy for those who interact with me. Whatever the challenge today, as a proactive participant, I will not be a part of the problem, but a supporter of the solution!

7. Today Jesus is made unto me wisdom. I have His mind, His strength, and His faith. I am not lazy, disoriented or confused. I know what I am here to do, understand my job description, and have the incentive to "make it happen." Today will be a good day for me to get things done, and today I will live in the now!

Father, help me to work hard today, while remaining in Your rest. In Jesus' name, amen.

February 5
GIVE LIBERALLY!

"The liberal person shall be enriched, and he who waters shall himself be watered."
(Proverbs 11:25 - AMP)

1. Today I will live in the now! I will live in the now because my life is improved and enlarged by the power of giving. My liberal lifestyle produces a flow of affluence that is a blessing to mankind, and enables me to salt the earth and light up the world around me.

2. Today I will sow bountifully into my world, increasing my sphere of influence by my reputation of benevolence and charity. I will be thrifty with my expressed opinions, frugal with my agendas, and stingy with my judgmental ideas. I will withhold what needs to be withheld, and give what needs to be given.

3. Today I will contribute generously. I will give of myself. I will give my undivided attention to those with whom I speak. I will be unselfish with my time, and will consider the needs of others. I will esteem them highly. I will be respectful and understanding. I will love unconditionally.

4. Today I will remember that the tithe is holy, and belongs to the Lord.

5. Today I will look for those whose giving to me has been activated by my own cheerful giving, and will allow them to return to me good measure, pressed down, shaken together, and running over. I will walk in the reality of the 100-fold return, overcoming the persecution that comes with it.

6. Today I will rise above a poverty mentality, knowing that I prosper as my soul prospers. I will not be cheap, stingy, miserly, or small-minded. I walk in a real vision of abundance. The blessing of the Lord makes me rich, and He adds no sorrow with it.

7. Today the Lord gives me the power to get wealth that He may establish His covenant with me. I will make a withdrawal from the investments that I have made into others, and from the treasures that I have laid up in heaven. People will notice my prosperity, and will be inspired by it. I will live like a well-watered garden today, and today I will live in the now!

Father, help me to give liberally today. In Jesus' name, amen.

February 6
BE FREE!

"Look at the birds, free and unfettered, not tied down to a job description, careless in the care of God. And you count far more to him than birds." (Matthew 6:26 – The Message)

1. Today I will live in the now! I will live in the now because I am free! He/she whom the Son makes free is free indeed . . . I know the truth, and the truth that I know sets me free . . . where the Spirit of the Lord is (*where the Spirit is Lord*), there is liberty!

2. Today I will live free from small-mindedness and limited vision. I will not feel obligated to think on a lower level just because the people around me are inclined to do so. I can love them unconditionally, and still move toward my higher purpose and larger destiny. Today I can see the big picture of my life!

3. Today I will live free from religious tradition. I will gladly discard whatever still exists in my belief system that is archaic, passé, or irrelevant, in an effort to repent my way into the NOW Kingdom where God lives. My liberated mind will prevent tradition from making the Word in my life ineffective.

4. Today I will free myself from the captivity of living in the past, and from the weight of my own emotional baggage, by practicing the power to forgive. I will allow myself to breathe today's fresh air, no longer having to struggle with memories that suffocate my soul and attempt to create a claustrophobic atmosphere for my spirit to contend with.

5. Today I will live free from fear and worry. I will consider the lilies of the field and will observe the freedom with which the birds of the air demonstrate a faith, and a trust, and a confidence that reveal the Kingdom. I am free to let faith come to me by hearing, and hearing by the Word of God.

6. Today I will live free from doubt and unbelief. I am emancipated to receive the evidence of things not seen, and to allow my God-like faith to give substance to those things for which I hope.

7. Today I am free to let God be God, and to allow myself to be His unique workmanship. He is the only true God, and He has set me free to be the only true me! I will celebrate my freedom today, and today I will live in the now!

Father, help me to walk in real freedom today. In Jesus' name, amen.

February 7
NO FEAR!

"For God has not given us a spirit of fear,
but of power and of love and of a sound mind." (2 Timothy 1:7)

1. Today I will live in the now! I will live in the now because I am free from the paralysis of fear . . . in Him I live and MOVE and have my being. In Christ I am a mover and a shaker . . . a Kingdom "risk-taker!"

2. Today I will not be afraid to explore the vastness of the real world that lies beyond the limits of my comfort zone. I will ignore my tendency to always do the safe and easy thing, and will accept the challenges of living the faith-life. I will violently take the Kingdom by force in my own realm of influence today.

3. Today I will look beyond my own insecurities, and see all of the possibilities around me that are worth striving for. I will not allow the fear of failure or rejection to prevent me from moving toward the fulfillment of my purpose, because I know that I will be all right, even if I fall or fail!

4. Today I will not be afraid to voice my vision. I will write it upon the tablet of my heart, so that I can read it and run with it. I am not intimidated by the potential of it, which I see moving, and growing, and evolving into something much bigger than what it is right now.

5. Today I am not afraid to do what I need to do to be productive. Productivity is a choice – my choice. My productivity will be magnetic today; it will draw success into my life and cause me to increase and multiply my own resources.

6. Today I am not afraid to be myself . . . to be real . . . to express my needs to those who can appropriately fill them. With Jesus as the Lord of my mind, I will not be afraid to think for myself – to be original and true to my own unique call and purpose.

7. Today I will live a carefree lifestyle, far removed from fear. I will not live the safe life – the sheltered life – the small life – but I will joyously break forth into a new world of freedom from intimidation and cowardice. God will approve of me today as I please Him with my faith and as I do exploits for His Kingdom! Today I am simply not afraid, and today I will live in the now!

Father, help me to live the fear-free life for Your glory today. In Jesus' name, amen.

February 8
BE SOMEBODY!

"In a word, what I'm saying is, Grow up. You're Kingdom subjects. Now live like it. Live out your God-created identity. Live generously and graciously toward others, the way God lives toward you." (Matthew 5:48 – The Message)

1. Today I will live in the now! I will live in the now because I am fearfully and wonderfully made – I am His workmanship – I am the righteousness of God in Christ – I am the head and not the tail, above only, and not beneath – I am bought with a price – I *am* somebody!

2. Today I will refuse to believe anything about myself that is contrary to what God believes about me. I will not regard any word spoken about me that does not confirm what God says about me. I will agree with God and His will for my life, even if it seems illogical and impractical to do so.

3. Today I will carry myself in a way that demonstrates my godly self-confidence. I will speak well of myself without bragging or being offensive to others. I will show that I believe in myself, without thinking more highly of myself than I ought to think. I will love my neighbor as I love myself today.

4. Today I will not waste my time on unimportant and trivial things – the "beggarly elements of the world." I will forsake the temptation to give in to silly pettiness, and will pursue great ideas and noble thoughts. I will conduct my affairs with a flair for grandeur and loftiness, without becoming pretentious and out of touch with reality.

5. Today I will feel neither superior nor inferior to anyone else.

6. Today I will remember that I am who God says that I am – I have what God says that I have – and I can do what God says that I can do!

7. Today I will walk like a winner, and lose my loser mentality. I am a champion - a king - an overcomer. I have favor, creativity, confidence, the Mind of Christ, prosperity, success, supernatural ability, and uncommon favor. Anything can happen today, and my expectation of faith will attract the positive to my life. If God is for me, who can be against me?! No matter what others have said to me or about me – no matter what I have said about myself – today is a new day of self-realization for me. Today *I am somebody*, and today I will live in the now!

Father, help me to remember today that You have enabled me to be somebody!
In Jesus' name, amen.

February 9
HE IS!

"But without faith it is impossible to please Him, for he who comes to God must believe that HE IS, and that He is a rewarder of those who diligently seek Him." (Hebrews 11:6)

1. Today I will live in the now! I will live in the now because I understand that God is in the now . . . that He is that "I Am" . . . that He lives in eternity where one day equals a thousand years (and vice versa), so that He is not bound by the limitations of natural time. *Anything* can happen today!

2. Today I make the decision to walk by faith for the next 24 hours, because I know that faith is now and that it is impossible to please God without faith. I will conduct the affairs of my day according to what I believe, rather than by my five natural senses. I will walk by faith today, and not by sight.

3. Today I will not hesitate to approach the Throne of Grace, because it is written that "he who COMES (continually) to God" will have God-pleasing faith. My righteousness consciousness will prevent my heart from condemning me, so that I can make myself comfortable in God's presence and can feel at home there!

4. Today I will diligently seek God and His Kingdom. In every circumstance that occurs today, I will look for the Kingdom truth or principle that is being communicated to me. I will listen diligently for the voice of the Good Shepherd in every conversation that I have. I will be relentless in my pursuit of Him today.

5. Today I will believe that God is a rewarder of those who diligently seek Him. I will be perceptive enough to recognize a reward when it comes to me today, and I will have the boldness to accept it and enjoy it. The discovery of rewards will cause this day to be a great adventure for me. It will be a day of increase for me!

6. Today I will be thankful for what God has done for me previously, but I will pull myself out of the past (where He was), so that I can live my extraordinary "faith-life" where HE IS! I believe that God IS . . . HE IS! . . . HE IS! . . . HE IS!

7. Today I will not miss one miracle that is headed my way. My expectation and faith-filled words will cause me to attract God's best, and to repel what is negative and counterproductive to the Kingdom. I know that I am blessed today because I know that God is, and today I will live in the now!

Father, I come to You today, believing that YOU ARE, and that You are my rewarder because I diligently seek You. Help me to keep my focus on You today. In Jesus' name, amen.

February 10
KEEP SMILING!

". . . the joy of the Lord is your strength." (Nehemiah 8:10)

1. Today I will live in the now! I will live in the now because I have the joy that Jesus Himself has given me to bring me through every circumstance of my day. I "count it all joy," even when I have to deal with negative situations in my life, because the power of supernatural joy always causes me to win!

2. Today I celebrate my Kingdom rights to righteousness, peace and joy in the Holy Ghost! My merry heart will do me good like a medicine and will enable me to partake of a continual feast today.

3. Today I will not be worried or anxious; I will not be fearful or depressed. I know that, regardless of what things may look like right now (in the natural), I actually have a great life and can afford to let myself be happy. I can smile, laugh, sing, and be absolutely positive in my attitude . . . and because I can, I will!

4. Today I will not be in denial of whatever trials I may have to deal with, but I will endure every cross for the joy that is set before me. I can declare the end from the beginning, and call those things that are not as though they are. In my heart I know that everything is going to be all right.

5. Today I will do something to help me maintain a high level of joy . . . take a walk . . . get some fresh air . . . laugh with a friend . . . sing a song . . . accept a compliment . . . help somebody . . . be a blessing . . . get some exercise . . . eat something delicious . . . meditate the Word . . . do something fun . . . praise the Lord . . . be good to myself . . . let go of a grudge . . . learn something new . . . play . . . change my thinking.

6. Today I will expect the best, but will find satisfaction with what I have now. I will be content, without becoming complacent.

7. Today I will be strengthened by joy, even in the midst of a fiery trial, and I will come through that fire without the smell of it on my clothes! I will speak words of life, be proactive in every situation, keep a good attitude, and will, basically, just have a great day because I have His joy. I will overcome today, and today I will live in the now!

Father, help me to keep smiling today,
and to remember that Your joy is my strength. In Jesus' name, amen.

"I call heaven and earth as witnesses against you, that I have set before you life and death, blessing and cursing; therefore CHOOSE LIFE, that both you and your descendants may live." *(Deuteronomy 30:19)*

1. Today I will live in the now! I will live in the now because I have made LIFE my choice, and will demonstrate the power of it today. Today I will **FIND THE FLOW** of life, and will follow it to ultimate success. The flow will bring confirmation to me, as the Peace of God in my heart guides my decisions.

2. Today I will **FACE THE FACTS** of life . . . of my own life. I will accept the reality of my present circumstances, but I will remember that with God nothing is impossible. The law of the Spirit of Life in Christ Jesus has made me free from the law of sin and death! Faith is the victory!

3. Today I will **FORGET THE FAILURES** of my life. I choose to receive forgiveness, learn from my mistakes, change what needs to be changed, and move on with life. " . . . This one thing I do, forgetting those things that are behind . . . ." (Philippians 3:13 – KJV)

4. Today I will **FOLLOW THE FAVOR** in my life. I will go where I am celebrated, instead of where I am tolerated. The path of favor will help to unfold my purpose as His will is done in me as it is in heaven.

5. Today I will **FOSTER THE FRIENDSHIPS** in my life, knowing that God has given me genuine Kingdom connections with others who are significant to my destiny. I will choose life today by doing something to nourish those relationships, and to keep them thriving and healthy.

6. Today I will **FORECAST THE FUTURE** of my life. I will *be* tomorrow what I am *saying* today, so I will *choose life by my words*. Life is in the power of my tongue, and I love the fruit of it. I declare that my latter will be greater than my former! The best is yet to come for me!

7. Today I will **FINISH THE FAITH** in my life. I will cooperate with Jesus, my faith's Author and Finisher, by completing His assignments for me. I will not be a quitter . . . I can see a thing through. It is through faith and patience that I inherit the promises of God, so by faith I choose blessing, prosperity, health, love, peace, joy, contentment, and every good and perfect gift from above. Today I choose life, and today I will live in the now!

Father, help me to make right choices today. In Jesus' name, amen.

February 12
MOVE ON!

"And whoever will not receive you, when you go out of that city, shake off the very dust from your feet as a testimony against them." (Luke 9:5)

1. Today I will live in the now! I will live in the now because I understand the importance of continuing on my path and not letting anything or anyone prevent me from pursuing my purpose. I will **PROCESS THE PAIN FROM MY PAST** by forgiving, letting go, and realizing that everything that has happened to me has worked together for my good.

2. Today I will **BECOME TOO BUSY FOR BITTERNESS**. My proactive response to those around me will take me to a new level of freedom. I am a doer . . . I am active . . . my mind moves me on a positive path to the next chapter of my life.

3. Today I will **CURB MY CRAVING FOR CONTROL**. I will recognize a dead-end street when I see it and will be able to cast all of my care on Him because He cares for me. I will do what only I can do about my situation today, remembering at all times that the government is on His shoulders, and that He is Lord.

4. Today I will **RESIST THE RIGIDITY OF RELIGION**. I will move past dead works and meaningless rituals that I have accepted, and have even initiated in my own life, and will seek the living flow of the river of God. I can move on because I am unencumbered with any tradition that makes the Word ineffective for me.

5. Today I will **DISCERN THE DESIRABILITY OF DIVERSITY**. I welcome change in my life today. I am not afraid to rethink or redo or repent, in an effort to recognize God's unique way of bringing new things to me. Change is good, especially if it enables me to remain mobile and productive.

6. Today I will **REALIZE THE REQUIREMENT OF REST**. I will not wear myself out by warring and wrestling against flesh and blood. I will choose my battles, and fight for what really matters, letting the rest of it all go. Today I can say, "It is well with my soul," as He makes me lie down in green pastures.

7. Today I will **DIRECT MY DESIRES TOWARD MY DESTINY**. I will not waste my time on unimportant things that are contrary to the fulfillment of God's plan for my life. He will put His desires in my heart as I delight in Him today by cooperating with His Spirit. I consider myself free indeed today – free to experience the next thing – and today I will live in the now!

Father, help me to seize the moment and move on today. In Jesus' name, amen.

February 13
BE BLESSED!

"And all these blessings shall come upon you and overtake you, because you obey the voice of the Lord your God." (Deuteronomy 28:2)

1. Today I will live in the now! I will live in the now because I understand the power of the blessing of the Lord. Because I know that God is good, and that His mercy endures forever, I am not ignorant of the blessings available to me today. I will not be destroyed for a lack of knowledge!

2. Today I will do what I need to do to keep myself in the realm of blessing. I will not be lazy, but will maintain a standard of excellence by hard work and diligence. I will keep my heart with all diligence (Proverbs 4:23), because the hand of the diligent makes rich (10:4), and shall bear rule (12:24). I will remember that the soul of the diligent shall be made rich (13:4), and the thoughts and plans of the diligent lead to plenty (21:5); the diligent shall stand before kings (22:29)!

3. Today the BLESSING OF THE LORD WILL MAKE ME RICH, and He will add no sorrow with it (Proverbs 10:22)! But, more importantly, I know that I AM BLESSED WITH EVERY SPIRITUAL BLESSING *today* in the heavenly places in Christ (Ephesians 1:3)!

4. Today I will not allow any bogus feeling of unworthiness to prevent me from receiving my blessings. I am the righteousness of God in Christ, and am blessed because of His grace.

5. Today I will not be satisfied with mediocrity. Because I am so blessed, I can expect the best of myself and strive for excellence in every area of my life. I will not give in to any fear of success, but will act and move like I am the head and not the tail.

6. Today I will not settle for only being blessed, but I will make the effort to be a blessing to those around me. I will be kind, thoughtful, encouraging, giving, generous, and helpful to others. I will salt the earth and light my part of the world today.

7. Today, because I obey the voice of the Lord my God, all these blessings shall come upon me and overtake me! I will be blessed in the city and in the country. The fruit of my body shall be blessed, and I will be blessed in the basket and in the store! I will be blessed when I come in and when I go out, and God will command His blessing on my storehouse, and on everything to which I set my hand! Today will be a blessed day for me, and today I will live in the now!

Father, show me how to receive every blessing that You send today. In Jesus' name, amen.

February 14
GOD'S LOVE!

". . . God is love." (I John 4:8)

Behold what manner of LOVE the Father has bestowed on me, that I should be called a child of God (1 John 3:1)! In this the LOVE of God was manifested toward me, that God has sent His only begotten Son into the world, that I might live through Him. In this is LOVE, not that I LOVED God, but that He LOVED me, and sent His Son to be the propitiation for my sins (1 John 4:9, 10). For God so LOVED me that He gave His only begotten Son, that if I would believe in Him, I would not perish, but would have everlasting life. For God did not send His Son to me to condemn me, but that I, through Him, might be saved (John 3:16, 17). For scarcely for a righteous man will one die; yet perhaps for a good man someone would even dare to die. But God demonstrated His own LOVE toward me, in that while I was still a sinner, Christ died for me (Romans 5:7, 8)!

LOVE has been perfected in me in this: I may have boldness in the Day of Judgment, because as He is, so am I in this world. There is no fear in LOVE, but perfect LOVE casts out fear, because fear involves torment. But he who fears has not been made perfect in LOVE. I LOVE Him because He first LOVED me (1 John 4:17-19).

Therefore, having been justified by faith, I have peace with God through my Lord Jesus Christ, through whom also I have access by faith into this grace in which I stand, and rejoice in hope of the glory of God. And, not only that, but I also glory in tribulations, knowing that tribulation produces perseverance; and perseverance, character; and character, hope. Now hope does not disappoint, because the LOVE OF GOD has been poured out in my heart by the Holy Spirit who has been given to me (Romans 5:1-5).

Today I will LOVE the Lord my God with all my heart, with all my soul, and with all my mind. This is the first and great commandment. And the second is similar to the first . . . Today I will LOVE my neighbor as I LOVE myself. On these two commandments hang all the law and the prophets (Matthew 22:37-40). Because of the LOVE of God in me, I will suffer long, and be kind. I will not envy, will not parade myself, and will not let myself be puffed up. I will not behave rudely, nor look out only for my own best interest. I will not be easily provoked, or think evil about others today. I will not rejoice in iniquity, but will rejoice in the truth . . . will bear all things, believe all things, hope all things, and endure all things. LOVE NEVER FAILS (1 Corinthians 13:4-8)!

Today, by His grace, strength and power, I will LOVE my enemies, bless those who curse me, do good to those who hate me, and pray for those who use me for spite and persecute me (Matthew 5:44). In all these things I am more than a conqueror through Him who LOVES me. For I am convinced that neither death, nor life, nor angels, nor principalities, nor powers, nor things present, nor things to come, nor height, nor depth, nor any other creature shall be able to separate me from the LOVE OF GOD, which is in Christ Jesus my Lord (Romans 8:37-39)! I am LOVED, and today I will live in the now!

February 15
IT'S POSSIBLE!

"But Jesus looked at them and said to them, 'With men this is impossible; but with God all things are possible.'" (Matthew 19:26)

1. Today I will live in the now! I will live in the now because I am a believer whose mind is continually being renewed to think positively, and to abandon all self-defeating and limiting mental images. **ATTITUDE IS EVERYTHING**, so *today I am changing my opinion to take dominion!*

2. Today I will really let myself believe that **ANYTHING IS POSSIBLE!** "Jesus said to him, 'If you can believe, all things are possible to him who believes'" (Mark 9:23). I will not be naïve and unrealistic, but my faith will definitely allow me to visualize the evidence of things not seen and to feel the substance of the things that I hope for!

3. Today I will remember to **NEVER SAY NEVER**. The atmosphere is now so heavy with possibilities that I will not rule out anything or anybody being used by God today to bring miracles into my life. He will even use the foolish things of the world to confound the wise.

4. Today I will TRY, **TRY AGAIN**. I will overcome and move past my failures, and work through the embarrassment of my mistakes. "Many plans are in a man's mind, but it is the Lord's purpose for him that will stand" (Proverbs 19:21 - AMP). My cooperation with God makes my success a possibility.

5. Today I will **THINK WIN/WIN**. I will see obstacles as opportunities, give a good report, and just keep going. "You've all been to the stadium and seen the athletes race. Everyone runs; one wins. Run to win. All good athletes train hard. They do it for a gold medal that tarnishes and fades. You're after one that's gold eternally" (1 Corinthians 9:25 - The Message). Today I see myself as a winner!

6. Today I will demonstrate that **GOD IS GOOD**. I know that His mercy is everlasting, and His truth endures to all generations, so I will seize this day with all the faith, expectation, hope, motivation, energy, and vision that is in me!

7. Today I will confess that **JESUS IS LORD**. I have authority in three worlds through the name of Jesus . . . in heaven, on the earth, and under the earth (Philippians 2:10, 11), so I will see the salvation of the Lord today through my tenacious faith in the power of His might. Because I am seated with Him in the heavenlies, I can see my life from His vantage point and, therefore, am aware that anything is possible with and through Him today. Today I believe that *IT'S ALL GOOD*, and today I will live in the now!

Father, help me to remember that all things are possible today. In Jesus' name, amen.

February 16
LOOK UP!

"And the Lord said . . . 'Lift your eyes NOW and look from the place where you are . . .'"
(Genesis 13:14)

1. Today I will live in the now! I will live in the now because I have the ability to lift up my eyes and look beyond the limitations of my present circumstances. By faith I am able today to observe the unseen things of the spirit realm that are eternal, rather than just the seen things of the visible world that are temporal. I will use my spiritual eyes today to determine what is my reality.

2. Today I will have the courage to be optimistic . . . a nonconformist to the negative majority of people around me. I will exhibit my individuality simply by not going along with the defeatist conversation that I hear. I will not cooperate with those who wallow in doubt and unbelief, even if I make myself unpopular with them.

3. Today I will find my direction through my God-inspired vision, rather than by my natural education. I will allow myself to be led by the Spirit . . . to be "other-worldly" . . . to have the nerve to express my convictions. I will *look up*, and *look beyond* the boundaries of my natural mind to "count the stars" as Abraham did.

4. Today I will have the confidence to look beyond my own perceived weaknesses, and begin to see them as strengths - for in my weakness He is made strong! I consider myself today to be strong in the Lord, and in the power of His might, to the point that I am able to "glory" in my weaknesses and infirmities.

5. Today I have faith . . . today I trust God and have my assurance in Him, which results in my own self-assurance and confidence. Because I can *look up*, I will maintain a spirit of bravery, valor, and boldness to overcome. I can defy danger because I see from my heart instead of from my head. I will have the audacity to keep going when everyone else says I should quit!

6. Today I will look to Jesus, the Author and Finisher of my faith. My spirit will be His candle, and His Word will be a lamp for my feet (in the immediate), and a light for my path (for my destiny). I look to His Word for direction.

7. Today I will not be afraid of any bad news, for my heart is established and fixed. I will be peaceful in the midst of the storm . . . calm, relaxed, stress-free, and centered, because I can see past the chaos. I see the Lord, today, high and lifted up, with His train filling the temple. I "look and live" today, and today I will live in the now!

Father, help me remember to look up today. In Jesus' name, amen.

February 17
LIVIN' LARGE!

"I called upon the LORD in distress: the LORD answered me, and set me in a LARGE PLACE. The LORD is on my side; I will not fear: what can man do unto me? . . . It is better to trust in the LORD than to put confidence in man." (Psalm 118:5, 6, 8 - KJV)

1. Today I will live in the now! I will live in the now because I am free to be myself in God, with no need to try to be something or someone that I am not. No man can **DEFINE MY PERSONALITY.** "Don't set people up as experts over your life, letting them tell you what to do. Save that authority for God; let Him tell you what to do. No one else should carry the title of 'Father'; you have only one Father, and He's in heaven" (Matthew 23:9, The Message).

2. Today I will live in a large place because no man can **DETERMINE MY POTENTIAL!** "It is God Himself who has made us what we are . . . " (Ephesians 2:10 - The Living Bible).

3. Today I will live in a large place because no man can **DETER MY PROGRESS!** "The Lord is my light and my salvation; whom shall I fear? The Lord is the strength of my life; of whom shall I be afraid?" (Psalm 27:1) ". . . If God is for me, who can be against me?" (Romans 8:31)

4. Today I will live in a large place because no man can **DELAY MY PROMOTION!** For promotion comes neither from the east, nor from the west, nor from the south. But God is the judge; He puts down one, and sets up another (Psalm 75:6, 7).

5. Today I will live in a large place because no man can **DECREASE MY PROSPERITY!** "The blessing of the Lord makes one rich, and He adds no sorrow with it." (Proverbs 10:22)

6. Today I will live in a large place because no man can **DESTROY MY POSSIBILITIES!** ". . . With men it is impossible, but with God all things are possible." (Matthew 19:26)

7. Today I will live in a large place because no man can **DEFEAT MY PURPOSE!** "And we know that all things work together for good to those who love God, who are the called according to His PURPOSE" (Romans 8:28). The only person who could stop me today is me – but, since I believe in myself, I will help myself have a true Kingdom day of progress and productivity in Christ. Today is a big day for me, and today I will live in the now!

Father, help me to live the Kingdom life, as You live big in me today. In Jesus' name, amen.

February 18
FORGIVE SOMEBODY!

"For if you forgive people their trespasses [their reckless and willful sins, leaving them, letting them go, and giving up resentment], your heavenly Father will also forgive you. But if you do not forgive others their trespasses . . . neither will your Father forgive you your trespasses." (Matthew 6:14, 15 - AMP)

1   Today I will live in the now! I will live in the now because I will not be tied to the past by the familiarity of my resentments. My ability in Christ to forgive will be a path into the present for me, and a bridge to my better future. Forgiveness will create a world of possibilities for me, enabling me to rise above the fray, and to move on to greatness.

2.   Today I will have a realistic grasp of the definition of forgiveness. I will know what it is, and what it is not. I can forgive without having to condone or accept the actions of someone who has seriously wronged me, with the awareness that, even though I have released them from their debt, things may never be the same between us again.

3.   Today I will manage my time wisely. I will not fall into the trap of going over and over again in my mind or in my words the injustices done to me. I will not waste someone else's time by talking to them about situations over which they have no control or influence. I will be sensitive to the Spirit when He tells me that it is the time for me to be silent.

4.   Today I will experience a sense of relief from the stress caused by the maintenance of a grudge. As I forgive, I set myself free from oppression and negative emotions and will walk in supernatural peace today, knowing that I AM forgiven because I HAVE forgiven. This peace will cause me to be healthier spiritually and even physically – free from the "dis – ease" that causes disease.

5.   Today I will experience a genuine flow in my life as I remove the obstacles and barriers that bitterness has built in me. My mind will be clear today – my thoughts undistracted – my heart free from impurities – which will allow me to be highly productive and effective in my sphere of influence.

6.   Today love will prevail, and Jesus will rule and reign through me as I demonstrate His forgiveness on earth as in heaven. The sins that I remit will be remitted, and His Kingdom will come today!

7.   Today I will be empowered by the ability to forgive . . . even 70 x 7 will be possible to me because faith works by love. The freedom flowing through me by forgiveness will prove that I can do all things through Christ who strengthens me today, and today I will live in the now!

Father, help me to forgive someone today. In Jesus' name, amen.

February 19
HELP SOMEBODY!

"And the King will answer and say to them, 'Assuredly, I say to you, inasmuch as you did it to one of the least of these My brethren, you did it to Me.'" (Matthew 25:40)

1. Today I will live in the now! I will live in the now because of my God-given ability to move beyond the limits of my selfishness, into the universe of usefulness. I will make my life count today by being a blessing . . . translating what I believe into what I do . . . making a positive difference in the surrounding environment.

2. Today I will make a genuine effort to bring Kingdom solutions to the people in the world around me, using my covenant prosperity to be a blessing to mankind. I am a giver . . . a contributor . . . a benefactor . . . a participator in the pursuit of purpose . . . an opener of doors and a builder of bridges.

3. Today I will invest in my future as I sow into relationships that will prove to be part of my destiny. I will lend a helping hand, knowing that I may need help later. "Two are better than one, because they have a good reward for their labor. For if they fall, one will lift up his companion. But woe to him who is alone when he falls, for he has no one to help him up." (Ecclesiastes 4:9, 10)

4. Today I will look beyond the faults of those who need my help, and will supply their need, to the best of my ability, with a spirit of non-judgmental, unconditional love. I will help someone, just because it is the right thing to do.

5. Today my mind will be full of ideas of how to help, and my creativity will give birth to those ideas. I will be a light in the darkness . . . a healer . . . a world changer.

6. Today I will really listen to God, and to the people who need my help. I will follow His leading in how to meet needs, and I will hear with spiritual ears the cries of the hearts of those that He has placed around me. The field is the world, and I will be a laborer in the harvest.

7. Today I will not be overwhelmed by the demands of those who need my help, because the Spirit – the Paraclete – the Helper – will be with me today to help me as I help others. By His grace I will do what I can, but I will also rest in Him, and cast my care on Him, because the government is on His shoulder. Today I will help to make the world a better place in which to live, and today I will live in the now!

Father, show me how to be there today for someone who really needs my help – help me to be helpful. In Jesus' name, amen.

February 20
ULTIMATE WORKOUT!

"Therefore . . . work out your own salvation with fear and trembling; for it is God who works in you both to will and to do for His good pleasure." (Philippians 2:12, 13)

1. Today I will live in the now! I will live in the now because I have the courage to accept the responsibility of taking ownership of my unique and personal salvation, and I will move toward that goal today. I will **MIND MY OWN BUSINESS**, knowing that I can only legitimately compare myself to Jesus, and to no one else - striving to remove the *plank* from *my* eye, instead of attempting to remove the *splinter* from my *brother's*.

2. Today I will **MOVE AT MY OWN PACE**. My "work-out" requires that I flow with my own times and seasons, and allow others the liberty to do the same. Jesus has done what only He can do concerning my salvation, but today I will move in Him toward becoming the best version of me that I can be, as my life in Christ issues from the inside out.

3. Today I will **MAKE MY OWN HAPPINESS**. I will not wait for external things to improve my feelings, but will take the initiative to activate the joy that is already in my heart through the Holy Spirit. As David did, I will encourage myself in the Lord today!

4. Today I will **MINIMIZE MY OWN STRESS**. Working out my own salvation means that it is up to me to "let not my heart be troubled." No matter what happens today, I make the choice to walk in peace. Accepting the fact that I can't control what others do or say to me, I exercise my ability to control how I let what they do or say affect me.

5. Today I will **MEASURE MY OWN PROGRESS**. Whatever strides I make toward success in God today will only be done to please Him, and for my own satisfaction. I will work OUT what God has done IN me, regardless of the praise or criticism of others.

6. Today I will **MANAGE MY OWN PERSONALITY**. He who rules his spirit is greater than he who takes a city (Proverbs 16:32). I will celebrate and accentuate my strengths, with full acceptance and understanding of my limitations.

7. Today I will **MANIFEST MY TRUE SELF**, being who God made me – not who everyone else thinks I am, or should be. The process of working out my own salvation is a joint effort with the Author and Finisher of my faith, and I trust Him to do what I cannot do for myself. Today He and I together will produce the synergy necessary to accomplish His will for my life, and today I will live in the now!

Father, help me to work out my own salvation with godly fear today. In Jesus' name, amen.

February 21
GIVE THANKS!

"Giving thanks always for all things to God the Father in the Name of our Lord Jesus Christ."
(Ephesians 5:20)

1. Today I will live in the now! I will live in the now because of the powerful role that thanksgiving plays in my life, and for all of the **POSSIBILITIES PRESENTED** In and by this 24-hour period. I am thankful for today, that I am alive to live in it, and that I have the ability to live it in the present! This is the day that the Lord has made, and I will be glad and rejoice in all that today holds for me!

2. Today I will be thankful for the **BLESSINGS BESTOWED** upon me – the benefits so bountifully lavished upon me – and will not take for granted the goodness of God. I will show my appreciation today through my attitude of gratitude, and through my authentic worship. I will have a positive outlook, and will give a good report. His praise shall continually be in my mouth!

3. Today I will be thankful for the **LESSONS LEARNED** through my personal experiences in life. Viewing my history through the paradigm of thankfulness will enable me to live beyond regret, believing that all things have worked (and are working) together for my good, because I love God, and am called according to His purpose.

4. Today I will be thankful for the **OBSTACLES OVERCOME** in my life through the grace of God. What I thought was going to kill me has actually served to make me stronger, and in all these things I am more than a conqueror through Him who loves me! Because "He who overcomes shall inherit all things . . ." (Revelation 21:7), I will walk in the confidence of a true heir of God today.

5. Today I will be thankful for the **RELATIONSHIPS REMAINING** in my life – those people who have gone the distance with me, who have believed in me and prayed for me. As I perceive their purpose in playing out God's plan for me, their presence in my world becomes more precious!

6. Today I will be thankful for the **DAY'S DIRECTION**, knowing that a part of my path will unfold for me in the now, if I will stay focused on the big picture of my life. I will not underestimate the importance of this day, but will seize it, making the most of it as I recognize the doors opened up to me, and gain the courage to walk through them.

7. Today I will be thankful for **GOD'S GRACE** poured out in my life, because it makes all things possible for me. Today I will walk in the fullness of that grace, and today I will live in the now!

Father, thanks for everything! In Jesus' name, amen.

February 22
SPEAK FAITH!

"And since we have the same spirit of faith, according to what is written, 'I believed and therefore I spoke,' we also believe and therefore speak." (2 Corinthians 4:13)

1. Today I will live in the now! I will live in the now because I have the creative ability of God in my spirit, in my mind, and in my mouth. As God created His worlds by the words of His mouth, I will help to create my world today by my faith-filled words (Hebrews 11:3).

2. Today I will call those things that are not as though they are (Romans 4:7), looking to the unseen things that are eternal, rather than the seen things that are temporal (2 Corinthians 4:18).

3. Today I will be justified by my words, and not condemned by them (Matthew 12:37). I will only speak about myself in the way that God would speak about me today.

4. Today I will activate the power of life and death in my tongue by speaking life to that which is positive and needs to grow . . . and by speaking death to that which is unfruitful and needs to die (Proverbs 18:21; Mark 11:12-14, 20-23).

5. Today I will try to turn the direction of any negative conversations that I hear around to a positive one (Romans 12:21).

6. Today I will strive to only say what is necessary, gracious and edifying (Ephesians 4:29).

7. Today I will not allow my words to be idle, but will use them to cause my life to be productive and proactive (Matthew 12:26). I will speak faith today, and today I will live in the now!

I confess the Lordship of Jesus over this day, and command it to come under His authority. Because it is the day that He has made, I say that I will walk in joy and gladness today, not in sorrow or depression. I will walk in light and revelation, not in darkness and deception. I will walk in health and wholeness, and not in sickness or disease. I will walk in prosperity and abundance, not in poverty or lack - in liberty and in the Spirit, not in bondage or in the flesh. I will walk in wisdom and knowledge, not in ignorance, and the destruction that it causes. I will walk in success, not in failure – in victory, not in defeat – in power, not in weakness – in favor, not in rejection. Today I will walk in the God-kind of life, and not in the law of sin and death. I declare the end from the beginning, that this is a great, productive, blessed, and enjoyable day. I believe in my heart that what I say with my mouth will come to pass concerning the day's outcome - it is a good day because God is a good God, in the name of the Apostle and High Priest of my confession – Jesus Christ.

PRAY TODAY!

"Pray without ceasing." (1 Thessalonians 5:17)

1. Today I will live in the now! I will live in the now because I have the ability to pray myself into the present (Mark 11:24). I believe I receive WHEN I PRAY, right where I am – in the now!

2. Today I will pray for those in authority, that I may lead a quiet and peaceable life in all godliness and reverence (dignity) today (1 Timothy 2:2, 3). I will pray for my country and its leaders, believing that the heart of the king is in the hand of the Lord. I will pray for those in authority in the Body of Christ, particularly those who have influence over my life and destiny. I will pray for my local church to become everything that it is supposed to become as an embassy of Christ to this planet.

3. Today I will remember that "**the field is the world**," so I will pray for the world around me and that the Lord of the Harvest would send laborers into that field to bring it into the Kingdom of God for His glory. I will loose on earth what is loosed in heaven, praying for the "*restoration of all thing*s" so that Jesus will no longer be held captive there (Acts 3:21).

4. Today I will pray for my community – that His will would be done there, on earth, as it is in heaven. I will not just pray it, but I will LIVE my prayer by doing what only I can do to make my world a better place in which to live. I will let myself actually BECOME this prayer, and in so doing, will salt the earth, and light the world!

5. Today I will pray for the significant people in my life – the ones I love and live with – that they would become who God wants them to be, not what I want them to be. His will for their life will be my will for their life, with no strings attached, and no hidden agenda. My prayer will be mature, rather than manipulative – liberating instead of legislative. The government is on Jesus' shoulders!

6. Today I will pray for my enemies and, in so doing, will free myself from their power to affect me negatively. The love of God poured out in my heart will cause me to conquer in this capacity.

7. Today I will pray about my problems ("Is anyone among you suffering? Let him pray . . . " - James 5:13), instead of worrying about them. My prayers will be effective today, and today I will live in the now!

"Do not fret or have anxiety about anything, but in every circumstance and in everything, by prayer and petition (definite requests), with thanksgiving, continue to make your wants known to God." Philippians 4:6 – AMP)

Father, I thank You that you always hear me. In Jesus' name, amen.

February 24
WORSHIP GOD!

"Oh come, let us worship and bow down;
let us kneel before the Lord our Maker." (Psalm 95:6)

Today I will live in the now! I will live in the now because I am a worshipper of the I AM.

7 Affirmations Of Worship In The Now For Today:

1. "Who is like You, O Lord, among the gods? Who is like You, glorious in holiness, fearful in praises, doing wonders? You in your mercy have led forth the people whom you have redeemed; You have guided them in Your strength to Your holy habitation." (Exodus 15:11, 13)

2. "I know that whatever God does, it endures forever; nothing can be added to it nor anything taken from it. And God does it so that men will [reverently] fear Him [revere and worship Him, knowing that He is]. That which is now already has been, and that which is to be already has been; and God seeks that which has passed by [so that history repeats itself]." (Ecclesiastes 3:14, 15 – AMP)

3. "And in that day you will say: Praise the Lord, call upon His name; declare His deeds among the peoples, make mention that His name is exalted. Sing to the Lord, for He has done excellent things; this is known in all the earth. Cry out and shout, O inhabitant of Zion, for great is the Holy One of Israel in your midst!" (Isaiah 12:4-6)

4. "Ah, Lord God! Behold, You have made the heavens and the earth by Your great power and outstretched arm. There is nothing too hard (difficult) for You. You are great in counsel and mighty in work [deed] . . . You have set signs and wonders in the land of Egypt, to this day . . . and You have made Yourself a name, as it is this day." (Jeremiah 32:17,19,20)

5. "God is sheer being itself – Spirit. Those who worship Him must do it out of their very being, their spirits, their true selves, in adoration." (John 4:24 - The Message)

6. "Now to the King eternal, immortal, invisible, to God who alone is wise, be honor and glory forever and ever. Amen." (1 Timothy 1:17)

7. ". . . Allelujah! For the Lord God Omnipotent reigns! Let us be glad and rejoice and give Him glory . . ." (Revelation 19:6, 7)

Today I rejoice, and today I will live in the now!

February 25
FOLLOW JESUS!

"Then He said to them, 'Follow Me, and I will make you fishers of men.'" *(Matthew 4:19)*

1. Today I will live in the now! I will live in the now because I am following my Good Shepherd, the resurrected Christ, into the green pastures of the present, as He creates in me the charisma necessary to become a fisher of men. I have authority because I am under His authority, and am therefore influential in and for the Kingdom of God.

2. Today I will follow Jesus out of the bondage of guilt from the past as He covers my sins with His own blood, freeing me to be who I really am. Knowing that I am accepted in the Beloved, I can consciously conduct my life in the confidence that comes from a self-esteem cleansed from condemnation! I am the righteousness of God in Christ in the now!

3. Today I will follow Jesus out of the dead-end street that is religion, knowing that He came to destroy the works of the devil, who introduced the religious spirit and mindset to this world. His transforming truth will lead me out of, and deliver me from, the tired traditions that make the true Word of God seem trivial, and into the glorious liberty of the sons of God!

4. Today I will follow Jesus even in the smallest details of my routine, with the awareness that today's decisions will become tomorrow's realities. I will follow Him out of the morass of my mediocrity, and into the arena of accelerated achievement. His Word will be a lamp to my feet (the realization of potential), and a light to my path (the unfolding of destiny).

5. Today I will follow Jesus through the storm. Even though I walk through the valley of the shadow of death, I will fear no evil, for He is with me. When I pass through the waters, He will be with me – and through the rivers, they shall not overflow me. When I walk through the fire, I will not be burned, neither shall the flame scorch me.

6. Today I will follow Jesus to become a fisher of men, becoming *all things to all men*, for the advancement of the Kingdom of God. He will cause me to be relevant and effective. He will give me the answers to the questions that are asked of me — the tongue of the learned — to speak a word in season to him who is weary.

7. Today I will follow Jesus into my blessed future. He is the Lord of who I am, but He is also the Lord of who I am becoming, as I follow Him from glory to glory. I am not worried about what will happen today, and I am not worried about will happen tomorrow, because the "I AM" is going before me, and He cannot fail. I know that everything is under control today as I follow the Leader, and today I will live in the now!

Father, help me to follow Jesus today. In His name, amen.

February 26
BE NICE!

"It is not conceited (arrogant and inflated with pride); it is not rude (unmannerly) and does not act unbecomingly. Love (God's love in us) does not insist on its own rights or its own way, for it is not self-seeking; it is not touchy or fretful or resentful; it takes no account of the evil done to it [it pays no attention to a suffered wrong]." (1 Corinthians 13:5 – AMP)

1. Today I will live in the now! I will live in the now because, in Christ, I have the ability to become the person that I have always wanted to be. Because of the unique work that the Spirit of God is doing in my heart and personality, I can love others unconditionally, treating them respectfully, as God treats me with respect and affectionate kindness. They will not have to suffer because of my unfinished business and unresolved issues, because the character of Christ will enable me to keep my relationships in proper perspective.

2. Today I will allow the river of the Christ-life to flow out from my inner man, into the world around me, so that I can be a blessing to humanity, and a Kingdom world-changer. I will be loving, helpful, friendly, cooperative, empathetic, and understanding today. The fruit of the Spirit operating in my life will feed and satisfy the hungry souls of those who come into contact with me, causing me to be attractive in an authentic, godly, and life-affirming way.

3. Today I will not retaliate where my enemies or accusers are concerned, knowing that vengeance belongs to the Lord, and He will vindicate me. I will experience the power of turning the other cheek, and the soft answer that turns away wrath. I will not wrestle with flesh and blood today, and will agree with my adversary quickly when I am in the way with him. Today I will not be overcome with evil, but will overcome evil with good, my ways pleasing the Lord so that even my enemies will be at peace with me. If God is for me, who can be against me?

4. Today I will be blessed because I am a peacemaker, and will be called a son of God (Matthew 5:9). I will obtain mercy because I will be merciful to others (5:7).

5. Today I will be a bridge-builder, because God has given me the ministry and word of reconciliation. I will endeavor to wage war against hatred, strife, division, bigotry and prejudice when I see evidence of it, by the hidden weapons of the Spirit of God in me.

6. Today Jesus will live big in me, and will even love the unlovable through me. Love never fails, and love will put me over!

7. Today I will win by doing the right thing, and today I will live in the now!

Father, help me to love like You today. In Jesus' name, amen.

February 27
OPEN VISION!

". . . in those days there was no OPEN VISION." (1 Samuel 3:1 - KJV)

1. Today I will live in the now! I will live in the now because I have an open vision – a continuing and increasing revelation of God's Kingdom and power in the earth. Because of the free flow and flexibility of faith in my heart, I am able to embrace my **ACCEPTANCE OF CHANGE**, as revelation knowledge stretches my mind, and transports me to the next level of glory. Vision-inspired change is good and necessary for my growth and well being, and I welcome it into my life today without any fear.

2. Today I will exercise my **ABILITY TO RIGHTLY DIVIDE THE WORD OF GOD**. The Holy Spirit, my mentor, tutor, and guide, writes the true Word on the tablet of my heart daily, as my capacity for vision increases. The Word is not bound, and the knowledge of it continually makes me free from falsehoods and fables concerning the real Jesus.

3. Today I will demonstrate my **ABANDONMENT OF PREJUDICES**. My renewed mind delights in diversity, as vision enables it to proudly wear the coat of many colors today. I am open-minded, enlightened, mature in Christ, and sensitive to God' voice, as I persistently seek the truth that liberates people and promotes the Kingdom of God.

4. Today I will celebrate my **ACCESS TO NEW INFORMATION**. Mentally and spiritually, God is doing a new thing in me, as He makes ways in the wilderness and streams in the desert for my life. I have the Mind of Christ, yet I am eager to learn . . . to grow . . . to rethink a problem . . . to experience a paradigm shift concerning my past.

5. Today I will appreciate the **ABSENCE OF RELIGIOUS CONFINEMENT** in my life. The letter kills, but the Spirit gives life – and I am alive! My mind is free from the limitations of the old wineskins – the old order – the system of rules and regulations that tries to compete with righteousness, peace and joy in the Holy Ghost. Vision and revelation have brought me into a large place, activating me to become a liberator of legalists, an emancipator of elitists, with a platform that persistently provokes the pious.

6. Today I will use my **ACTIVITY IN THE WORLD** to bring glory to God. I will get involved with life today, as a player instead of a spectator, and will make a positive difference when and where I can. My ever-increasing vision demands my "doing!"

7. Today I will show my **APPRECIATION OF NOW**, because today I will live in the now!

Father, keep my vision open today. In Jesus' name, amen.

February 28
ON TIME!

"He has made everything beautiful in its time. He also has planted eternity in men's hearts and mind [a divinely implanted sense of a purpose working through the ages which nothing under the sun but God alone can satisfy], yet so that man cannot find out what God has done from the beginning to the end." (Ecclesiastes 3:11 – AMP)

1. Today I will live in the now! I will live in the now because the God of the NOW, the "I Am," lives in and through me, and He is the Lord of time. One day with Him is as a millennium; because in eternity, where He exists, time is nonexistent . . . eternity is always NOW. Yet He maintains Lordship over time, because in my realm of existence, time is very real, and very important. But, as His will is done in earth as it is in heaven, eternity (now) supersedes and dominates the restraints of earth time, and the workings of His supernatural Kingdom can prevail in my natural life.

2. Today I will see beyond the limits of time, and will draw the strength needed to succeed in my endeavors from the eternal life resident in me.

3. Today I will believe that I receive WHEN I PRAY (Mark 11:24), not having to wait to believe sometime out in the future, when I see the manifestation of the answer to my prayer. "NOW faith is . . ." – hope is in the future, faith is in the now (Hebrews 11:1)!

4. Today I will have otherworldly patience, and when I add that patience to my faith, I will inherit the promises of God (Hebrews 6:12)!

5. Today I will not worry about deadlines – the first shall be last, the last shall be first - if I come to work in the vineyard at the eleventh hour, I will still receive the same wages as those who have labored all day long! He will restore to me the YEARS that the pests in my life have eaten away, and because He is in the now, time is on my side!

6. Today I will appreciate the seasonal work of God in my life, believing that He really has made everything beautiful in its time. I will rest in Him when the pace of my progress is unsatisfactory to me, totally trusting in Him, and in His perfect timing for my life.

7. Today I will water the eternity that God has planted in my heart with the water of the Word, becoming whole by integrating my past, present, and future under the authority of the timeless Christ. I will be right on time today, and today I will live in the now!

Father, help me to stay in sync with Your timing today. In Jesus' name, amen.

February 29
CREATION'S LONGING!

"All around we observe a pregnant creation. The difficult times of pain throughout the world are simply birth pangs. But it's not only around us; it's within us. The Spirit of God is arousing us within. We're also feeling the birth pangs. These sterile and barren bodies of ours are yearning for full deliverance. That is why waiting does not diminish us, any more than waiting diminishes a pregnant mother. We are enlarged in the waiting. We, of course, don't see what is enlarging us. But the longer we wait, the larger we become, and the more joyful our expectancy." (Romans 8:22-25 – The Message)

1. Today I will live in the now! I will live in the now because the Holy Spirit is actively in the process of working to reveal my true identity as a manifested son of God in the earth. I am aware that something is developing and maturing on the inside of me that is real and alive, and it is increasing in the now!

2. Today I will walk in the revelation that the whole creation of irrational creatures has been moaning together in pains of labor until now, and not only the creation, but I, too, groan inwardly. Because I have and enjoy the first fruits of the Spirit, I continually experience a foretaste of blissful things to come that causes me to wait expectantly for the redemption of my body from sensuality and the grave.

3. Today I will not attempt to resist the emergence of the real me, as I begin to finally live my life from the inside out. The concept of existing in the eternal present is becoming less abstract to me, and the infilling of the Holy Spirit is becoming more important and precious to me everyday, as He produces in me the reality of son-ship that cries "Abba! Father!"

4. Today I will communicate a certain confidence that comes from comprehending that I am a child of the Creator, and, therefore, I am His heir, which makes me a fellow heir with Christ. Knowing that I share Christ's inheritance with Him enables me to gladly share His suffering, because I also share His glory!

5. Today I will not allow myself to become frustrated in waiting for my personal manifestation of God's will, because waiting is a necessary part of the birth process. The waiting is not decreasing the quality of my life in any way – on the contrary, I am being increased by it! Through faith and patience I inherit the promises, and while faith is coming to me by hearing the Word, patience is being developed in me by counting it all joy!

6. Today I will walk in the Spirit, and not in the flesh.

7. Today I will intercede harmoniously with the rest of creation for the Kingdom to come, and today I will live in the now!

Father, help me to pray Your will today. In Jesus' name, amen.

March In The Now!

✦M✦A✦R✦C✦H✦

A month to make room for miracles.

Time for a spiritual, mental and emotional "spring-cleaning" . . .

The explosion of color everywhere . . . new life . . . new growth . . .

makes it easy to believe for the impossible . . . to hope again . . . to dream again . . .

Spring-cleaning means opening the windows (of your spirit),

sweeping out the cobwebs (of your mind), and shaking out the dust (of your memories) . . .

March is the time for those who envision the harvest of the future to begin to plant tiny

seeds of the now . . .

the patience to plow . . .

the selflessness to sow . . .

the grace to grow . . .

In just a few days, you'll see miracles start to sprout up all over the place . . .

first the blade . . . then the ear . . . then the full grain in the ear . . .

Spring-cleaning and prophetic planting mean making room for more to come.

It's all about the possibilities of resurrection . . .

Anything can happen in the month of March!

"Through the tender mercy of our God
with which the Dayspring from on high has visited us." (Luke 1:78)

March 1
BE STRONG!

"Finally, my brethren, be strong in the Lord and in the power of His might." (Ephesians 6:10)

1. Today I will live in the now! I will live in the now because I have the very strength of Almighty God resident eternally in me, as a partaker of the divine nature! I can face anything today, knowing that the Greater One dwells in me individually, as He does in the church corporately. I am strong now – today – for such a time as this — to rise to the occasion and overcome every obstacle — to run through a troop, and leap over a wall!

2. Today I will use my words to strengthen myself (". . . Let the weak SAY, 'I am strong.'" - Joel 3:10), believing that I have what I say, as I believe it in my heart. So, I say that I am strengthened with might by His spirit in the inner man, today . . . that in all these things I am more than a conqueror through Him who loves me . . . that the Lord is my light and my salvation, the strength of my life . . . that I can do all things through Christ Who strengthens me!

3. Today I will make the effort to maintain a high level of joy, knowing that the joy of the Lord really is my strength. I will intentionally avoid places, things, words, people, imaginations, memories, or situations that tend to darken my spirit and mood – those things that could make me sad or depressed, causing me to be vulnerable to weakness. I choose to walk in the supernatural joy that is now deep within me, and allow it to build me up, and to empower me from the inside out! With joy I will draw water from the wells of salvation.

4. Today, if I am aware of weaknesses in my life, I will still be strong, because in my weakness He is made strong! I exercise the strength to glory in my infirmities [weakness] (II Corinthians 12:9 - KJV), and this amazing Kingdom principle will create illogical confidence in me, enabling me to slay every giant that I confront. I say to my day, "Bring it on!"

5. Today I will expose myself to knowledge and information that will strengthen me spiritually, intellectually and emotionally. I will also make the effort to do something to increase my physical strength today, to the glory of my Creator.

6. Today I will be self-sufficient in Christ's sufficiency.

7. Today, I will draw strength from the healthy relationships in my life, investing my strength and support into them. I will be strong today, and today I will live in the now!

Father, help me to walk in Your strength today. In Jesus' name, amen.

March 2
PARADIGM SHIFT!

"Don't become so well-adjusted to your culture that you fit into it without even thinking. Instead, fix your attention on God. You'll be changed from the inside out. Readily recognize what He wants from you, and quickly respond to it. Unlike the culture around you, always dragging you down to its level of immaturity, God brings the best out of you, develops well-formed maturity in you." (Romans 12:2 - The Message)

1. Today I will live in the now! I will live in the now because I have the ability to change my life by changing my mind! I am not bound to think like everybody else. I can think beyond my culture and heritage and generation. I can imagine things that exceed my experience, and move beyond my past points of reference. My mind and thoughts are my own, willfully submitted to the Lordship of Jesus, and are bringing my life into the now!

2. Today I will dare to dream, even when the apparent reality in my life shows no promise of changing or improving. I will expose myself to new ideas, and childlike faith . . . to let myself believe that dreams, even illogical and improbable ones, can and do come true!

3. Today I will empathize with someone else. My spirit of understanding will enable me to see the situation through their window, and to stop trying to force them to see through mine. I don't have to be right today – someone else may have a valid point that I will be willing to acknowledge and accept. I will even overcome my fear and dread of letting myself finally see myself the way they see me! The truth will set me free!

4. Today I will allow vigorous discussion and idea-exchange with those who do not necessarily think like I do, and the stimulus will release creative energy in me that will flow from the inside out. In speaking with those who may even disagree with me today, I will remain confidently confrontational, without becoming combatively contentious.

5. Today I will listen, learn, read, talk, inquire, investigate, ask, think, converse, reflect, meditate, study, and pay attention to the world around me, in an effort to keep my mind open . . . vital . . . flexible . . . pliable . . . changeable. I will maintain an attitude of youthfulness and sense of wonder, by refusing to let my mind become petrified in its prejudices.

6. Today I will welcome a mental revolution - a brainstorm - a radical idea - an inspiration!

7. Today I will have a new outlook on my life, and today I will live in the now!

   Father, show me where I need a paradigm shift today. In Jesus' name, amen.

March 3
PROMISES, PROMISES!

*"For all the promises of God in Him are Yes, and in Him Amen
to the glory of God through us." (2 Corinthians 1:20)*

1. Today I will live in the now! I will live in the now because of the power of the promises of God to pull me out of the past, and into the present. He is not a man that He should lie, and by His exceedingly great and precious promises, He has made me a partaker of His divine nature (2 Peter 1:4)! My self-confidence flows from this knowledge today.

2. Today I will maintain the balance between faith and patience, knowing that, through these two forces working together, I am able to inherit the promises of God (Hebrews 6:12). I will let patience have her perfect work in me, so that I may be mature, and whole, lacking nothing (James 1:4).

3. Today I will stand on God's Word, living by everything that proceeds from His mouth.

4. Today I will keep my own promises, demonstrating my dependability, and incorporating my integrity into my individual circumstances. I will do the right thing, regardless of what anyone else may, or may not, do. I am responsible for my own actions. I will be honest, reliable, trustworthy and faithful to the best of my ability today.

5. Today I will:

   P - erceive   the promises, searching the Scriptures to see what is mine.
   R - eceive   the promises, walking by faith, and not by sight.
   O - btain   the promises, speaking of the nonexistent as though it exists.
   M - aintain   the promises, by faithful obedience to God.
   I - nherit   the promises, because I am a world-overcomer.
   S - ecure   the promises, understanding the benefits of righteousness.
   E - njoy   the promises, guiltlessly grateful for the goodness of God!

6. Today I will be thankful for all of the kept promises that have shown God's faithfulness to me. I will bless Him at all times; His praise shall continually be in my mouth!

7. Today I will expect to see some movement toward the fulfillment of God's promises to me for this time in my life. I will not forget His benefits. I will maintain a manifested attitude of expectation today, and today I will live in the now!

Father, help my to appropriate Your promises today. In Jesus' name, amen.

March 4
LOVE YOURSELF!

"Jesus said, 'Love the Lord your God with all your passion and prayer and intelligence.' This is the most important, the first on any list. But there is a second to set alongside it: 'Love others AS WELL AS YOU LOVE YOURSELF.' These two commands are pegs; everything in God's Law and the Prophets hangs from them." (Matthew 22:37-40 – The Message)

". . . he who loves his wife LOVES HIMSELF. For no one ever hated his own flesh, but nourishes and cherishes it, just as the Lord does the church." (Ephesians 5:28, 29)

1. Today I will live in the now! I will live in the now, because the power of God's unconditional love allows and enables me to live my life in the present. Because I am accepted in the Beloved, I can give myself permission to love myself as I am now, knowing that I am improving by continually being conformed to His image.

2. Today I will love myself without being conceited, arrogant, puffed up with pride, or condescending. I will not feel inferior to anyone else, nor will I feel superior to anyone else, but will be balanced and mature in the way that I relate to everyone around me.

3. Today I will love myself, and still maintain a mindset of servitude and humility. I will selflessly consider the needs of others by taking up my cross to follow Jesus.

4. Today I will forgive myself for the ways in which I have disappointed myself. I will stop being angry with myself, and punishing myself for my mistakes, having the same patience with myself that God has with me.

5. Today I will speak well of myself, building a healthy self-esteem with verbal building blocks. I will not sin against my own potential by speaking self-destructive words, but will say about my life what God says about it, because I am in agreement with His word.

6. Today I will be good and kind to myself. I will not feel guilty for doing something nice just for me, with no obligation to any bogus, religious ideas of my own unworthiness.

7. Today I will walk in the God kind of love with the people in my life, and will be a blessing to them. They will see Jesus in me today, and today I will live in the now!

Father, give me the courage to love myself today. In Jesus' name, amen.

March 5
OPPORTUNITY KNOCKS!

"I returned and saw under the sun that – The race is not to the swift, nor the battle to the strong, nor bread to the wise, nor riches to men of understanding, nor favor to men of skill; but time and chance happen to them all." (Ecclesiastes 9:11)

1. Today I will live in the now! I will live in the now because I can discern the importance of this day, and the opportunities for growth that it presents. By walking in the Spirit, my sense of timing will put me in the right place at the right time – not ahead of schedule, nor falling behind – but perfectly in the zone for realizing potential and creating success.

2. Today I will be perceptive to the people that God has placed in my path to help me progress and to prosper. I will be receptive to the results that my relationship with them will allow me to realize, as I rise to a higher realm of revelation!

3. Today I will recognize the remarkable, and consider it confirmation to God's plan for me when things seem to fall into a pattern of perfection, not dismissing the extraordinary events of the day as common coincidence. All things will work together today for my good, as God perfects that which concerns me!

4. Today I will be noticed and commended for my diligence, discipline, determination and drive! I will do what needs to be done for the development of the discovery of my dreams, because faith without works is dead, and I am more than just a hearer of the Word!

5. Today I will prepare for promotion, knowing that it ultimately comes from the Lord, but that I can do my part to facilitate the favor that I need to find it. As I bind mercy and truth around me, I will obtain the favor with God and man that will surround me like a shield.

6. Today I will be sensitive to ministry opportunity around me, looking to the fields that are ripe for harvest. I will redeem the time, and work while I have daylight to illuminate my path. God can and will use me today as his instrument of influence.

7. Today I will turn a corner on my journey, and will discover that I have only just begun! What I have perceived as a closed door will be seen as a new beginning for me. Today will make a difference in my life, and today I will live in the now!

Father, help me to hear the door when opportunity knocks today! In Jesus' name, amen.

March 6
TOP CONDITION!

"You've all been to the stadium and seen the athletes race. Everyone runs; one wins. Run to win. All good athletes train hard. They do it for a gold medal that tarnishes and fades. You're after one that's gold eternally. I don't know about you, but I'm running hard for the finish line. I'm giving it everything I've got. No sloppy living for me! I'm staying alert and in TOP CONDITION. I'm not going to get caught napping, telling everyone else all about it and then missing out myself." (1 Corinthians 9:24-27 – The Message)

1. Today I will live in the now! I will live in the now because I have made the decision to exercise myself toward godliness (1 Timothy 4:7) in everything that I do during this 24-hour period. Through my faith, obedience to God, and meditation of His Word, I will run and not be weary - I will walk and not faint. I will overcome because I am fit and in good spiritual condition.

2. Today I will keep my mind active and productive, not wasting my creative mental energies on nonessential things. I will give my mind over to important pursuits and large ideas that challenge and stretch me . . . that speak to my capacity to take dominion. I will assume leadership roles in my life through my power to be decisive.

3. Today I will be diligently disciplined to be constructively competitive. I have an edge, an advantage – the will to win my own, personal race to the glory of God, as well as for my own satisfaction.

4. Today I will train my thoughts and tame my tongue — I will stay alert, being keenly aware of what is really happening in the world around me. I will strive to make positive changes in my words, actions and routines, especially in the areas in which I am influential to others.

5. Today I will hold myself to a high standard of achievement by the ongoing operation of an organized thought life. I will be willing to withdraw whatever ways are wasting my time by making me maintain a mode of mediocrity in my manner of living.

6. Today I will not settle for second-best in my standards, but will strive for ethical excellence, spiritual superiority, and moral maturity. I am energized for peak performance in the things of God – to maximize my potential in Him for the advancement of His Kingdom authority.

7. Today I will be aggressive in the acquisition of conditioning techniques for my spirit, soul, and body, accepting the responsibility of being an example and an inspiration to those with whom I come into contact. Today I will make my life count, and today I will live in the now!

Father, help me to stay in top condition today. In Jesus' name, amen.

March 7
GO AHEAD!

"Then Caleb quieted the people before Moses, and said, 'Let us go up at once and take possession, for we are well able to overcome it.'" (Numbers 13:30)

1. Today I will live in the now! I will live in the now because I have the attitude of an achiever, the will of a winner, and the heart of a hero! Because God has not given me a spirit of fear, I am eager to encounter the events of this day, energized by my expectancy for the exceptional. Because God is able, I am able!

2. Today I will give a good report as Joshua and Caleb did. Whatever obstacle lies ahead of me in today's path, my constant confession will be that I am "well able to overcome it." There is a miracle in my mouth . . . victory in my voice . . . winning in my words . . . success in my speech . . . creativity in my conversation . . . triumph in my talk!

3. Today I will not be persuaded or influenced by the negative people surrounding me who have no vision or desire for taking the Promised Land — I am of a different spirit! Regardless of what is said in my presence today, I will not allow myself to forget who I am, or what I am called to do. I will go ahead and conquer, even if I have to go alone.

4. Today I will seize the moment ("let us go up AT ONCE . . ." – Numbers 13:30) and make the most of the obvious opportunities ordinarily overlooked by those who are paralyzed by procrastination. When the right door opens for me in the right way, I will be in the right frame of mind to enter it at the right time!

5. Today I will recognize confirmation when I see it, and will have the confidence to act on it, carefully, yet courageously. The Christ in me causes me to be a mover and a shaker . . . a possessor of the promises.

6. Today I will dare to do what has not been done, disregarding the danger, and directing my drive toward taking dominion! I can do all things through Christ who strengthens me, because greater is He who is in me than he who is in the world!

7. Today I will go ahead and do what I can to help facilitate the fulfillment of God's faithfulness to me, inhabiting the land, even if there are giants currently in it. Today I am equipped for every enterprise, and today I will live in the now!

Father, give me the courage today to move forward in my life. In Jesus' name, amen.

March 8
REACH OUT!

"I'm not saying that I have this all together, that I have it made. But I am well on my way, reaching out for Christ, who has so wondrously reached out for me."
(Philippians 3:13 - The Message)

1. Today I will live in the now! I will live in the now because I am moving past my limiting self-beliefs, and reaching toward a revelation of the "new me" in Christ! I am not afraid to be stretched or challenged today. In fact, I welcome whatever thing or event forces me to reach beyond my usual safety zone of comfortably familiar mediocrity for something greater.

2. Today I will be bold enough to reach out to someone in need, because there is no fear in love, and love never fails. I will make the first move, even if it is difficult for me to do so, and will not be intimidated by confrontation, nor deterred by controversy. I am capable of creating an atmosphere for authentic covenant connections today.

3. Today I will do what needs to be done to reach out – I will return phone calls . . . tell the truth . . . do good deeds . . . set an example . . . be a friend . . . solve a problem . . . forgive an offense . . . pay a debt . . . return a favor . . . make someone happy . . . share good news . . . try something new . . . bless an enemy . . . think win/win . . . open my mind . . . open my heart.

4. Today I will reach for my dreams, regardless of how unreachable they currently seem to be. I will believe for the improbable, as well as the impossible, knowing that my mind will not return to its regular dimensions, having been stretched by big, new ideas!

5. Today I will reach out to my environment, being a blessing to my community by my awareness of its needs, and my innovative ways of meeting them through the wisdom of the Mind of Christ. My heart will connect to the world around me in a real and intuitive way, and I will demonstrate my unique abilities as an intercessor to the glory of God.

6. Today I will abandon my preoccupation with myself, and will lay down my life for another, making the attempt to see the world through his/her eyes. My service will initiate new adventures in the love of God, through pure motives, and honest compassion.

7. Today I will live free because I am not afraid to grow and change. I am resolved to do the right thing, and I will not look back . . . my reach propels me into the future. God is reaching out through me today, and today I will live in the now!

Father, give me the boldness to reach out today. In Jesus' name, amen.

March 9
REALITY CHECK!

"And you shall know the truth, and the truth shall make you free." (John 8:32)

1. Today I will live in the now! I will live in the now because I am a real person, experiencing the real God in the real world. I will live truthfully today, understanding the difference between walking by faith instead of by sight, and living in denial of reality. Today I will reconcile my preparation for the worst case, with my expectation of the best case in every situation that arises.

2. Today I will be sober without being sullen – mature, but not morose – levelheaded, yet lighthearted at the same time! Harmony, balance and a genuine sense of serenity will display the peace that passes understanding through my life. The peace of God makes me shockproof today, so that, come what may, I am calm, cool, and collected in every circumstance.

3. Today I will not waste my time trying to be someone or something that I am not. The people in my life will have an authentic sense of trust in me, because my self-truth will give them permission to be who they really are, and to like who they really are.

4. Today I will embrace the inevitable. If I can't change it, I will adapt to it, and will live freely and peaceably, choosing to go with the flow, accepting life as it really is. Today I choose truth-inspired tranquility, and welcome honesty-induced happiness. Parting with illusions will bring great relief to my soul, as I live the liberated life with godly contentment.

5. Today I will tell the truth, plain and simple. My stories will need no embellishment, my memories will remain intact, my ambitions will be realistic. I will see life the way that it is, and call it as I see it. Whatever is built on a lie in my world will fall, because it should fall, and I will have no fear today, because the Lord is my shepherd, and I do not lack or want for anything.

6. Today I will not get involved with the silly games that people play when trying to relate to one another. I will let my "yes" be "yes," and my "no" be "no," providing a safe haven for those, like me, who seek the truth in the world. I will move on from those who refuse to live in authenticity.

7. Today I will get a grip on reality. I will not fear telling the truth, or hearing the truth, taking both praise and criticism in stride. Today I will enjoy the effect of speaking the truth in love, even to myself, and today I will live in the now!

Father, help me to live truthfully today. In Jesus' name, amen.

March 10
FRESH START!

". . . Behold, the fresh and new has come!" (2 Corinthians 5:17 – AMP)

1. Today I will live in the now! I will live in the now because today is a new day, with new vision, and new opportunities for my life. Because His mercies are new every morning, I have a chance to begin again, knowing that I have not exhausted His grace for my life. I can still reach my potential, and fulfill my destiny. It's not too late - I can still make it!

2. Today I will glorify God in my mind and personality by abandoning the old, counterproductive thought processes and negative patterns. It's a new day, and I am walking in a new way because of the freshness of the flow of the Holy Spirit. There is a river of God, and I am finding new ways to move in it effectively.

3. Today I will make room in my life for the bigger picture of my future. I recognize that more is coming – abundance is on the way – increase is on the horizon . . . so I call myself a planner, a doer, a mover and a shaker. I am stirred up today, excited about what is coming. I declare my future as I prophesy to the wind, and call the nonexistent things into existence! I am prepared for the next wave – the new thing in my abundant life.

4. Today I will invest in the next generation, as my own youth is renewed like the eagle's. I am not getting older, but am continually experiencing a re-creation in my spirit that affects my mind and physical body. I have access into the Kingdom, as I remain childlike and child-friendly.

5. Today I will be energized by my faith in the Ancient of Days. I will not let myself be burned-out, cynical or depressed, but I will drink from the fountain of hope that springs eternal, as the Dayspring arises in my heart. Wherever I go today, I will create an atmosphere of anticipation because of the Zoë life of God that flows out of my inner man.

6. Today I will get it together concerning regret. No time for crying over spilled milk for me today – now is all that matters. I redeem the time by my faith and understanding of what is eternal and important.

7. Today is going to be a great day of influence for me. I will be a walking illustration to the world at large of the new creation species, demonstrating "in-Christ realities" to everyone that I encounter. I am believing that today is the first day of the rest of my life, and today I will live in the now!

Thank you, Father, for a fresh start in my life today! In Jesus' name, amen.

March 11
OPEN UP!

". . . These things says He who is holy, He who is true, 'He who has the key of David, He who opens and no one shuts, and shuts and no one opens.'" (Revelation 3:7)

1. Today I will live in the now! I will live in the now because I have Kingdom keys in my possession, and I am using them to unlock my true self – my heart – where the Kingdom of God dwells – releasing the life of God from my inner man into the world around me. My life is an open book to be read by all people to the glory of God!

2. Today I will move beyond my emotional walls – my self-imposed prison of defense mechanisms that I have developed for my natural survival. My realization that I am accepted in Christ, the Beloved, sets me free from the fear of rejection, and produces peace, poise and perfect self-confidence in my personal life.

3. Today I will communicate on a real level, speaking the truth in love. I will really listen to others when they speak, and I will hear the voice of their hearts. I will be touched with the feeling of someone else's weaknesses, and will minister to them without being judgmental. My openness and truthfulness will set the captives free!

4. Today I will have a spirit of understanding – a heightened sense of awareness of my environment. Jesus is made wisdom unto me, and He gives me the sensibility of a sage, the language of the learned, and the temperament of a teacher. I am a helper and a mentor – an asset to those in my life.

5. Today my senses are sharp and keen, and the Word in my heart and mouth acts as a two-edged sword, cutting through the nonsense of pretentious religion. His Word is like a hammer that breaks the rock in pieces, and He will use me today to make a difference!

6. Today I will stop trying to defend myself, giving myself the permission to not always have to be right. I am a human being, capable of making mistakes, who has been made a partaker of the Divine Nature through Christ. I am righteous, but not perfect, so I can relax and be myself, accepting myself for who I am, and for Whose I am.

7. Today I will have an open mind and heart, prepared for whatever comes because God is on my side. Today I will be openly blessed, and today I will live in the now!

Father, help me to open up today. In Jesus' name, amen.

March 12
GOOD NEWS!

"As cold water is to a weary soul, so is good news from a far country." *(Proverbs 25:25)*

1   Today I will live in the now! I will live in the now because my life is built on the foundation of the good news - the gospel of Jesus Christ. God is good, and His will for mankind is that the people of His earth be blessed with genuine well being, living in peace with Him, as well as with one another. Jesus came to manifest that will – to make it possible – to give life, and life more abundantly to all who come to Him.

2.   Today I will give a good report, and will hold others to the standard of excellent speech that I create by my own example. Because my heart is established, I am not afraid of evil tidings, realizing that things are rarely (if ever) as bad as they first appear. My soul is anchored in the God-kind of faith, and my life is centered and balanced by His Word.

3.   Today I will look for the good in every situation, putting a positive spin on each account that I give concerning the day's activities. I will see to it that all of the stories of my personal history will have happy endings, because my faith speaks up for the outcome of my life today.

4.   Today I will not be overcome by evil, but I will overcome evil with good. I will speak words of edification to nourish the hungry souls of those around me. I will build people up with the language of life, instead of tearing them down with gossip, slander and accusation. My lips will produce good fruit today.

5.   Today I will be energized by news that produces a confident and favorable expectation. I have hope because I have good tidings of great joy in my life, every day of the year. I believe that my future is bright!

6.   Today I will tell someone the story of Jesus – not just the One found in the accounts of Matthew, Mark, Luke and John – but the One that represents the gospel that I live every day. My life promotes the proof that the gospel is practical!

7.   Today I will move my life in a positive direction, away from all that is negative and counterproductive to the purposes of the Kingdom. My flow of good news will make the world a better place in which to live today, and today I will live in the now!

Father, help me to share the good news today. In Jesus' name, amen.

March 13
CREATE JOY!

". . . Weeping may endure for a night, but JOY comes in the morning." (Psalm 30:5)

1. Today I will live in the now! I will live in the now because I have access to my unalienable, Kingdom rights to righteousness, peace and JOY in the Holy Ghost! I have joy by the answer of my mouth His strength-giving joy that keeps me young, vibrant, and healthy today. I will use my creative ability to allow the issues of life to flow from my heart, out into the world around me, causing the landscape to lighten up and live!

2. Today I will not have to wait for external things to bring me joy and happiness. I am joyful now! Because Jesus has given me His own supernatural, inward joy – a fruit of the recreated spirit (the fruit of the spirit is joy) – I am able to be genuinely joyful, regardless of outward circumstances or situations. My cup runs over!

3. Today I will use the solid front of Kingdom joy to ward off and repel oppression and depression, sadness and anxiety. My renewed mind is positively hopeful and optimistic in Christ, as I walk in a different dimension from those who dwell in daily drudgery.

4. Today I will create an atmosphere of joy by my words and attitude – my reactions – my laughter – my peace of mind. The joy of the Lord, in cooperation with my own joy, will be influentially inspirational and corporately contagious. It will enable me to help make the world a better place in which to live today.

5. Today I will be radiant with the glory of the Lord – His joy – His praise – will cause me to be attractive and highly favored today. The strength that comes from godly joy will win the day, and bring satisfying success to me as I prosper in relation to the prosperity of my soul.

6. Today I will turn around a long-standing and negative situation through the force of joy. The paradigm shift that I experience will pull down strongholds of despair and hopelessness. The joy of the Lord makes anything possible today.

7. Today I will be a singer, a dancer, a praiser, and a warrior for the Kingdom of God. His praise shall continually be in my mouth, and with joy I will draw water out of the wells of salvation. Victory is mine today, and today I will live in the now!

Father, help me to create joy today. In Jesus' name, amen.

March 14
TAKE HEART!

"Wait on the Lord; be of good courage, and He shall strengthen your heart;
Wait, I say, on the Lord!" (Psalm 27:14)

1. Today I will live in the now! I will live in the now because my heart is strong and resilient – it is the heart of a warrior, a winner, and a world-overcomer. I am more than a survivor, I am a conqueror . . . and in Christ I am *MORE* than a conqueror! He has changed me into a champion, enabling me to do exploits in His Name, waxing strong as I wait on Him! God is my strength, and His strength is my weapon against the enemies of my destiny.

2. Today I will be of good courage, regardless of what I hear. Bad news and negative reports will not affect me today because God is my strength, and His strength is the Life Force that keeps me going in a positive direction.

3. Today I will speak confidently and courageously concerning my current circumstances. God is my strength, and His strength is the source of my confession (". . . Let the weak SAY 'I am strong.'" - Joel 3:10). I say that I am strong in Him, and in my weakness He is made strong!

4. Today I will stay true to my vision, and I will not perish because my life is motivated by it. God is my strength, and His strength is the vision that is written on my heart – the one that I read and run with to His glory!

5. Today I will manifest all the grace that I need to do great things for God, as well as for mankind. His grace is my equipping for service, and is sufficient for me to do the impossible. God is my strength, and His strength graces me in every way today.

6. Today I will rise to the top by my ability to make good decisions. I am strong in the Lord, and in the power of His might, so I decide to overcome weakness and incompetence by exercising my spiritual muscles. God is my strength, and His strength enables me to choose the right path for my life today.

7. Today I will have the charisma that I need to be persuasive and influential. I have the power to salt the earth and light the world – to be a positive force in my community – to hold up a standard of righteousness. God is my strength, and His strength is a gift to be treasured. Today I will share that gift with others, and today I will live in the now!

In Jesus' name, I will be bold and courageous today!

March 15
CELEBRATE LIFE!

". . . I came that they may have and enjoy LIFE, and have it in abundance (to the full, till it overflows)." (John 10:10 - AMP)

1. Today I will live in the now! I will live in the now because I have learned how to appreciate my life – to celebrate all of it – reveling in my victories, learning from my defeats, and simply enjoying the journey. God is good! Life is good! It's all good! I have cause to celebrate just because it's today!

2. Today I will be happy and thankful and positive and light . . . with a good attitude . . . with hope in my heart and strength in my soul. I have nothing to fear or dread, because Christ in me is the hope of glory, and He has won every battle for my life. He is the champion, and I celebrate His conquering life today! He is my hero in everything that happens.

3. Today I will not waste my time for celebration by regarding regrets. I do not regret my past . . . what's done is done, and God and I can deal with it all. I no longer regret my sins, for they are all under the blood of Jesus. I do not regret the time that I have wasted, because I live in the now, and God restores my lost years to me. I do not regret my life choices, my mistakes, my abuses or my problems, because, in the big picture, all things have worked together for my good!

4. Today I will praise the Lord Who is great, and greatly to be praised. I will pitch my tent on Mount Zion, in the presence of the Lord of Hosts, and will find fullness of joy there for me and for my house.

5. Today I will live in the moment . . . I will seize the day . . . I will rejoice and be glad in the day that the Lord has made for me! Today I embrace the world around me, and love it unconditionally.

6. Today I will enjoy abundance and favor and prosperity and success . . . every good and perfect gift that comes down from the Father of Lights. Joy flows out of my heart like a river, bringing life to the desert of depression where so many are dying.

7. Today is a day to thank Jehovah Rapha, the God who heals by making bitter experiences sweet. He has turned for me my mourning into dancing, and has given me the garment of praise for the spirit of heaviness. I celebrate His life in me because He has girded me with gladness and caused my cup to run over. Today He anoints me with the oil of joy above those around me, and today I will live in the now!

In Jesus' name, I will celebrate my life today!

March 16
NO LIMITS!

"Yes, again and again they tempted God, and limited the Holy One of Israel." (Psalm 78: 41)

"Now to Him Who . . . is able to [carry out His purpose and] do superabundantly, far over and above all that we [dare] ask or think [infinitely beyond our highest prayers, desires, thoughts, hopes, or dreams]." (Ephesians 3:20 - AMP)

1. Today I will live in the now! I will live in the now because, in Christ, there are no limits to the possibilities presented to my personal life. Today I will **EXPLORE NEW AREAS OF REVELATION KNOWLEDGE!** God desires to unfold His mysteries to me, so He will reveal the depths of His Word to me as I study and meditate the Scriptures under the anointing of the Holy Spirit.

2. Today I will **EXPOSE MYSELF TO THE SUPERNATURAL!** All nine Gifts of the Spirit are available to any believer who has been baptized in the Holy Spirit, so I will operate in the gift (or gifts) necessary for today's tasks.

3. Today I will **EXPRESS MY FAITH BY A GOOD CONFESSION!** My heartfelt and sincere words of faith will create an atmosphere that is conducive to the miraculous today. I believe, and therefore I speak (2 Corinthians 4:13).

4. Today I will **EXPEL THE WORD "IMPOSSIBLE" FROM MY VOCABULARY!** Since Christ dwells in my heart by faith (Ephesians 3:17), I cannot afford to speak antichrist words such as "I can't;" "It will never work out;" "we can't afford it;" "things just keep getting worse;" "I'm scared to death;" "there is no way" . . . !

5. Today I will **EXPAND MY CAPACITY TO BELIEVE FOR THE MIRACULOUS!** I will wean myself off my dependence on natural things, because such dependence (as Abraham and Sarah depended on the natural womb of Hagar to produce a supernatural seed) only creates an incapacity to believe.

6. Today I will **EXPERIENCE THE DEEP THINGS OF GOD!** I will maintain a high level of praise and worship until my being is flooded with His actual presence.

7. Today I will **EXPECT SIGNS AND WONDERS TO BECOME A WAY OF LIFE!** Today I am prepared for anything and everything, and today I will live in the now!

Father, help me to remember today that there are no limits to Your power and ability in my life. In Jesus' name, amen.

March 17
KEEP BELIEVING!

"[For Abraham, human reason for] hope being gone, hoped on in faith that he should become the father of many nations, as he had been promised . . . ." *(Romans 4:18 - AMP)*

1. Today I will live in the now! I will live in the now because my ability to walk by faith and not by sight enables me to dare to do what hasn't been done before. God has called me to be a pioneer and a visionary, so I must keep believing, no matter what things look like in the natural realm. The testimony of Jesus is the spirit of prophecy, and His witness in my inner man propels me to fulfill all the prophecies spoken over my life!

2. Today I will repent of any religious attitudes that remain in me, refusing to revere the past as I recognize new realms of revelation. I make the decision to live this day in the now, because no matter what report I hear from the religious, who are rebellious to the realities of Christ, I realize that these are the good "new" days, and they are getting better, because the best is yet to come!

3. Today I will not be afraid of the radical change that comes from living in the now. The fire that is shut up in my bones is ignited by the Holy Ghost, and He is effective in all of His endeavors to establish and enlighten me.

4. Today I will keep believing as I see the plan for my life unfold. Even if I don't know the next step to take, I remember that Abraham went out, not knowing where he was going (Hebrews 11:8), so I move with God in faith and trust for His moment-by-moment direction. In Him I *move*.

5. Today I will listen for God's voice, for faith comes by hearing, and hearing by the Word of God!

6. Today I will meditate His Word, in an effort to locate the gifts of faith which He has imparted to me.

7. Today I will be glad that change is on the horizon, and that I am not frozen in time so that I am unable to accept it. Today, when I pray, "Let Your will be done on earth as it is in heaven," I will really mean it from the bottom of my heart – I will pray it in faith! I want heaven to change this earth, and I will continue in my believing to see that God's Word is performed in my surroundings. Even if everybody else in the world gives up on their faith today, I will keep on keeping on, because I have come too far to turn back now! Today my faith will put me over, and today I will live in the now!

By faith, in Jesus' name, I will keep believing today!

March 18
CUTTING EDGE!

"For the Word that God speaks . . . is sharper than any two-edged sword, penetrating to the dividing line of the breath of life (soul) and [the immortal] spirit, and of joints and marrow [of the deepest parts of our nature], exposing and sifting and analyzing and judging the very thoughts and purposes of the heart." (Hebrews 4:12 - AMP)

1. Today I will live in the now! I will live in the now because the true Word of God is cutting through all of my old, dead, religious, self-defeating strongholds and thought patterns, setting me free to develop His picture of my life in this world. The sword of the Lord divides my soul and spirit, bringing health and wholeness to me, by discerning and discovering my genuine self in Christ!

2. Today I will dare to do what hasn't been done as I discover destiny through the door of dreams! The "now" Word is activating me to realize the vision of God for my life, as He makes my dreams come true in order to unfold His purpose and plan for me. The realization that anything is possible continues to dawn on me, increasing steadily as the light of day.

3. Today I will cut through my unnecessary tradition, repenting of any idolatry to the past, in order to discover the pioneering spirit in me that is searching for new frontiers of revelation knowledge. I will think clearly today, because my mind is uncluttered, and my vision is focused.

4. Today I will cut through the fear of failure, and will be free to be faithful to my faith. With God on my side, I will not shy away from the urge to "go out on a limb," "get in over my head," or "bite off more than I can chew!" His Word will be my anchor as I courageously launch out into the deep!

5. Today I will flow with God's ideas, God's dreams, and God's vision, knowing that He finishes whatever He authors. I trust Him completely with my life, destiny, and future.

6. Today I will allow the good fight of faith to bring out the best in me, to develop my character, and to build my confidence as a mighty warrior of God! Because I know that I cannot walk in fear and faith at the same time, any more than I could travel north and south at the same time, I am resolved to move forward with God's sword in my hand and His praise in my mouth (Psalm 149:6).

7. Today I will use His sword to cut out all of the nonsense in my life, refusing to put up any longer with that which is counterproductive to His purposes. I will keep the sword sharp today, and today I will live in the now!

Father, help me to keep my life on the cutting edge today. In Jesus' name, amen.

March 19
HIDDEN ROOMS!

"The spirit of a man is the lamp of the Lord, searching all the inner depths* of his heart."
(Proverbs 20:27) [*literally: "rooms of the belly"]

1. Today I will live in the now! I will live in the now because the events of this day will serve to reveal the treasure within me. I am greater on the inside than I am on the outside, and my destiny is being discovered today through the process of practically prevailing over my personal problems, all things working together for good to identify the hidden rooms of my heart.

2. Today I will be guided by the "lamp of the Lord" by being sensitive to the inward witness, and by listening to the internal voice of His Word that is written on my heart – the Word that is a lamp for my feet and a light for my path. I will use the tools of confirmation and agreement to my advantage, and will find the flow where I can function fearlessly as I face forward in faith!

3. Today I will be aware of those who speak to me on a level where "deep calls unto deep" - those who see my spirit and prophesy to my potential - and will hear what they say to me with spiritual ears, finding the discipline resident in me to be obedient to inspirational and insightful instruction.

4. Today I will find the fruit of my future hidden in a room of the heart. I will know that there is a bigger vision stored somewhere in my internal warehouse, and I will be relentless in my search for it, knowing that, when the times comes to reveal it, I will have the faith to see it to its fruition.

5. Today I will maintain contentment with the present, but will find the motivation to move mountains in preparation for the miracles that are going to be mightily manifested *in* and *through* and *for* me! Today is a great day, but tomorrow will be greater!

6. Today I will believe that the rooms containing greatness really are in me – everything that I need to succeed is here now! I will not be discouraged when I find a room locked, but will search for the Kingdom Key that will release on the earth what is currently a reality in heaven, where I am already seated with Him in power!

7. Today I will talk up my future, and my purpose and my destiny. Today I will be energized by all that I have to look forward to, and today I will live in the now!

Father, help me to discover the hidden rooms of my heart. In Jesus' name, amen.

March 20
DISCOVER DESTINY!

"For those whom He foreknew [of whom He was aware and loved beforehand], He also destined from the beginning [foreordaining them] to be molded into the image of His Son [and share inwardly His likeness], that He might become the first-born among many brethren." (Romans 8:29 – AMP)

1. Today I will live in the now! I will live in the now because, in Christ, I have a great destiny to discover and fulfill, and I will use this God-given day to work toward that end. Through His power working in me, I am able to become the person that I always wanted to be . . . accomplish everything that I ever wanted to accomplish . . . have everything that I ever wanted to have! Today I will **DETERMINE WHAT IT IS THAT I WANT TO DO!**

2. Today I will **DECIDE NOT TO FAIL!** Because God has given me the ability to choose either life or death, I exercise my ability to choose either success or failure . . . and I choose to succeed today! This decision is the driving force of motivation for me, and it ensures my victory in the affairs of life.

3. Today I will **DIRECT MY LIFE FORWARD!** Forgetting what is behind me, I set my face like an arrow toward my future. Now is all that matters to me as I prepare for better days ahead by bringing the direction of my life out of reverse.

4. Today I will **DILIGENTLY PURSUE MY GOAL!** I stand on all the promises that the Scriptures have bestowed upon the diligent, and I realize the benefits as I meet the conditions. It is not in me to quit or to give up in defeat!

5. Today I will **DISCOVER MY VICTORY OVER TIME!** It is never too late for me to win because of my divine right to time-redemption (Ephesians 5:16). Time is not just on my side, it is under my feet as I demonstrate my dominion over it!

6. Today I will **DEPEND UPON THE HOLY SPIRIT!** He is my helper, and He knows my destiny. Because He cannot fail, I cannot fail as long as I continue to be led by Him, obeying His voice of wisdom.

7. Today I will **DO EVERYTHING TO THE GLORY OF GOD!** This day is God's gift to me, and what I do with it will become my gift to Him. I will present Him with something wonderful, because I will never put my "talents" in a hole in the ground! Today is a destiny-day for me, and today I will live in the now!

Father, help me to discover destiny for my life today. In Jesus' name, amen.

March 21
ABOVE ONLY!

"And the Lord will make you the head and not the tail; you shall be ABOVE ONLY, and not be beneath, if you heed the commandments of the Lord your God, which I command you today, and are careful to observe them." (Deuteronomy 28:13)

1. Today I will live in the now! I will live in the now because I am simply above only, so I will get right to the point . . . BECAUSE I AM THE HEAD AND NOT THE TAIL, I MAKE THIS DEMAND ON MYSELF TODAY: *"NO EXCUSES TOLERATED!"* I have the ability to "just do it" in me, so I will not waste time today in trying to explain why something can't be done. With God, all things are possible!

2. Today, BECAUSE I AM THE HEAD AND NOT THE TAIL, I MOVE INTO A DIMENSION OF FREEDOM BY DECLARING: *"NO APOLOGIES NECESSARY!"* I am the righteousness of God in Christ. Period. Today I will behave myself like I am *somebody!*

3. Today, BECAUSE I AM THE HEAD AND NOT THE TAIL, I MAKE THIS DECISION: *"NO FEAR EXALTED!"* I know that it is time to start using the power, love and sound mind that I have been given by God to overcome it all – so I will!

4. Today, BECAUSE I AM THE HEAD AND NOT THE TAIL, *"NO BLAME ALLOWED!"* "Jesus answered, 'Neither this man, nor his parents sinned, but that the works of God should be made manifest in him'" (John 9:3). I am not afraid to give an account of my OWN life today!

5. Today, BECAUSE I AM THE HEAD AND NOT THE TAIL, *"NO SHAME ACCEPTED!"* I am forgiven, accepted, righteous, redeemed, justified, graced, and wholly holy in Christ!

6. Today, BECAUSE I AM THE HEAD AND NOT THE TAIL, *"NO JUDGMENT PASSED!"* I will walk in love, know people after the spirit instead of the flesh, pray for my enemies, and will "live and let live." My life is too busy to spend it in judgment of others, anyway!

7. Today, BECAUSE I AM THE HEAD AND NOT THE TAIL, *"NO QUESTIONS ASKED!"* I will live like a true, obedient disciple today, and today I will live in the now!

Father, help me to live like the head and not the tail today. In Jesus' name, amen.

March 22
ALL AUTHORITY!

"And Jesus came and spoke to them, saying, 'All authority has been given to Me in heaven and on earth. Go therefore . . .'" (Matthew 28:18, 19)

1. Today I will live in the now! I will live in the now because, as a joint-heir with Christ, I have been given His authority to decree the things that need to be established. "You also will DECREE a thing, and it will be established for you; so light will shine on your ways" (Job 22:28). I decree Christ's victory and authority over my life and over every minute of this day!

2. Today I will, by Christ's shared authority, declare unto God by my own right hand. "Gird up thy loins now like a man: I will demand of thee, and DECLARE thou unto me . . . deck thyself now with majesty and excellency; and array thyself with glory and beauty . . . then will I also confess unto thee that thine own right hand can save thee" (Job 40:7, 10, 14 - KJV). I make a demand on God today, according to His Word: "Hear, I beseech thee, and I will speak: I will DEMAND of thee, and declare thou unto me" (Job 42:4 - KJV).

3. Today I will, by Christ's authority, command the works of God's hands. "Thus says the Lord, the Holy One of Israel, and his Maker: Ask Me of things to come concerning My sons; and concerning the work of My hands, you COMMAND me" (Isaiah 45:11).

4. Today I will, through Christ's covenant authority, PROPHESY to the wind and command every dry bone of my vision and life to live again (Ezekiel 37:1-4)!

5. Today I will, through Christ's delegated authority, make effective use of the keys of the Kingdom, BINDING on earth what needs to be bound in heaven, and LOOSING on earth what needs to be loosed (Matthew 16:18, 19, 18:18-20).

6. Today I will, with Christ's authoritative word, CALL those things which are not as though they are (Romans 4:17).

7. Today I will, by the power of Christ's authority, HOLD FAST to my confession of faith in Him (Hebrews 3:1; 4:14; 10:19-23). The faith from my heart, spoken through the words of my mouth, will make positive changes in my world. I sense that there is a new thing – a good thing - a powerful thing - happening in and through me today, and today I will live in the now!

    Father, help me to walk in my authority in Christ today. In Jesus' name, amen.

March 23
FACE FORWARD!

"For the Lord God will help me; Therefore I will not be disgraced; therefore I have set my face like a flint, and I know that I will not be ashamed." (Isaiah 50:7)

1. Today I will live in the now! I will live in the now because I am a winner who realizes that winners do fail. But they get up and try again. And again. And again. Today, by the power vested in me by God, I am going to make every effort to kick the habit of losing, and forsake the fear of failure - to become, in Christ, who and what I've always wanted to be. What I am is God's gift to me, but what I become is my gift to God!

2. Today I will remember that God's will must be done on earth as it is in heaven . . . that my life is not my own. But I have the positive attitude that comes from a healthy self-esteem; the attitude that repeats relentlessly, "You've got to do it for you!" So today I will gladly get going to the glory of God, but I will move mightily toward the manifestation of the miracle of ME!

3. Today I will let go so that I can move forward. I officially release guilt, blame, shame, and all of my collected injustices. In the grand scheme of things, it just doesn't matter to me. "For I consider that the sufferings of this present time are not worthy to be compared with the glory which shall be revealed in us" (Romans 8:18). "For our light affliction, which is but for a moment, is working for us a far more exceeding and eternal weight of glory" (2 Corinthians 4:17)!

4. Today I will kick the block to my successful future by learning to talk to myself in a new way, and by getting myself unstuck through accepting new ideas. God is for me, and no demon can stop me, so I will stop getting in my own way, blocking my own success by disobedience to God's perfect plan for my purpose.

5. Today I will remember that I can't always wait until the "mood hits" to get started. I will be about my Father's business today, regardless of my frame of mind or my emotional status at the moment.

6. Today I will follow the Spirit's leading to put myself in the precise environment where winning is most likely to occur.

7. Today I will follow the frightening arrow, and today I will live in the now!

Father, help me to keep facing forward today. In Jesus' name, amen.

March 24
SURPRISE PARTY!

"For I know the thoughts and plans that I have for you, says the Lord, thoughts and plans for welfare and peace, and not for evil, to give you hope in your final outcome." (Jeremiah 29:11 - AMP)

"You prepare a table before me in the presence of my enemies; you anoint my head with oil; my cup runs over." (Psalm 23:5)

1. Today I will live in the now! I will live in the now because I believe that the day is filled with wonderful surprise events that God has before-ordained for me, and I will arrive at the right place, at the right time, to experience all of them as I follow Him!

2. Today I will delight in the beauty and natural wonders around me. I will enjoy the little things: the laughter of children, the flower ready to burst into bloom, the sweet smell of the air after a rain. God is a good God, and He is good all the time! His goodness is everywhere . . . all around me today . . . overtaking me with His blessings!

3. Today I will enjoy the adventure of locating God's surprises with an upbeat, optimistic attitude. I will channel my thoughts and words into uplifting and encouraging ideas and observations. I will experience the good things that are happening in the present, knowing that the past is a library of information from which to learn, and the future is a happy, inviting land of unlimited promise!

4. Today I will dream winning dreams, and will not be defeated by anyone who attempts to strip away my coat of many colors from me. Those colors have been so internalized that I have unshakeable, child-like faith in happy endings, and I refuse to quit until my dreams are realized.

5. Today I will delight myself in the Lord, and He will give me the desires of my heart . . . and when the desire comes, it is a tree of life!

6. Today I will navigate the uncharted waters of my current circumstances with complete confidence and consistent courage. I will demonstrate boldness by beginning to release the hidden winner within me into the external world.

7. Today I will not miss my window of opportunity. I am present in my present as I stay in His presence! Today is my day, and today I will live in the now!

Father, I thank you for what You are preparing for me today!

March 25
HIS MAJESTY!

" . . . He set it all out before us in Christ, a long-range plan in which everything would be brought together and summed up in Him, everything in deepest heaven, everything on planet earth . . . All this energy issues from Christ: God raised Him from death and set Him on a throne in deep heaven, in charge of running the universe, everything from galaxies to governments, NO NAME AND NO POWER EXEMPT FROM HIS RULE. And not just for the time being, but forever. He is in charge of it all, has the final word on everything. At the center of all this, Christ rules the church. The church, you see, is not peripheral to the world; the world is peripheral to the church. The church is Christ's body, in which He speaks and acts, by which He fills everything with His presence."
(Ephesians 1:10, 19-23 - The Message)

1. Today I will live in the now! I will live in the now because I worship the Creator – the "I Am" - revealed in the person of Jesus Christ. My knees bow, and my tongue confesses, to the glory of God, that Jesus Christ is Lord!

2. Today I recognize Christ's rule of the universe, and I derive confidence from knowing that I am His sibling and His joint-heir, as well as His servant and loyal subject of His Kingdom that reigns over every living thing!

3. Today I decree the rule of King Jesus over every name that names itself in my life **today**. I demonstrate His/my authority in three worlds: the earth, things above the earth, and things beneath the earth!

4. Today I declare the majesty and dominion of Christ the King over every second of every minute of this day. This day must come into divine order, and submit to His/my authority, as His will is done on earth as it is in heaven!

5. Today I will prevail and conquer as someone who is a champion of the chosen generation, a revealer of the royal priesthood and a harbinger of the holy nation (1 Peter 2:9)! Jesus rules and reigns through my life today!

6. Today I will speak the Word only, and will expect to have what I say. "Where the word of a king is, there is power . . ." (Ecclesiastes 8:4). I will not waste my royal vocabulary on the petty and the trivial.

7. Today, as a king in the earth, I willingly worship the King of Kings, and as a lord of the earth, I am eager to exalt the Lord of Lords. His praise shall continually be in my mouth today, and today I will live in the now!

Almighty God, my Father, I worship You in Spirit and in truth.
Help me to recognize Your majesty in my own life today. In Jesus' name, amen.

March 26
TAKE DOMINION!

"Then God blessed them, and God said to them, 'Be fruitful and multiply; fill the earth and subdue it; have DOMINION over the fish of the sea, over the birds of the air, and over every living thing that moves on the earth.'" (Genesis 1:28)

1. Today I will live in the now! I will live in the now because, as I celebrate my dominion in the earth, I progressively perceive my position in Christ. Because I can do all things through Him, I have confidence in my abilities. Because I believe in myself, I try harder, doubling my efforts for Him as I move boldly ahead toward destiny discovery.

2. Today I will dare to question established methods and fixed policies, including the religious systems in the earth, and will fearlessly initiate alternate ways of looking at life and getting things done. When I am thwarted in my efforts, I will discover innovative ways to reach my goals through the Mind of Christ.

3. Today I will not be afraid of facing a crisis, because my dominion mentality forces me to not only work at resolving it, but to try to find something beneficial in the situation. The Christ in me conquers the chaos as I manage to discover that fine vein of positive thinking that can lead to new chances for success!

4. Today I will hang in when the going gets tough, because greater is He who is in me than he who is in the world. I am actively dedicated to surviving, so I have no choice but to continue to struggle with a problem until I either find a solution or uncover new information concerning it. The just shall live by faith, and I am a walking illustration of that fact!

5. Today I will notice my door of opportunity, even if it is slightly ajar, and, if that is the case, I will seize my chance to push it open the rest of the way. If I am rejected, I will try to change the situation and alter the circumstances in my favor. The God who never sleeps or slumbers will be my strength!

6. Today I will exercise the authority resident in the name of Jesus, and will use it to dominate depression, disease, disorder, discouragement, demons, and even death itself. My effectual, fervent prayers will avail much, and the sword of the Lord will enable me to be a gladiator for God!

7. Today I will fulfill God's mandate for covenant dominion, and today I will live in the now!

Father, I decree that, in the name of Jesus, I will walk in dominion today!

PERCEIVING PURPOSE!

"Mortals make elaborate plans, but God has the last word." (Proverbs 16:1 – The Message)

1. Today I will live in the now! I will live in the now because I am tapped in to the reality of my synergistic relationship with God and to the awareness that He and I together are co-creating destiny. "The plans of the mind and orderly thinking belong to man, but from the Lord comes the [wise] answer of the tongue." (Proverbs 16:1 - AMP)

2. Today I will flow with God, recognizing the harmony of our natures, the unity of our purposes, and the manifestation of our mutual creativity. "All the ways of a man are pure in his own eyes, but the Lord weighs the spirits (the thoughts and intents of the heart)." (v. 2)

3. Today I will think with my spiritual, infinite mind, breaking free from an average attitude and a mediocre mentality in order to develop a divine dimension in my daily discipline. "Roll your works upon the Lord [commit and trust them wholly to Him; He will cause your thoughts to become agreeable to His will, and] so shall your plans be established and succeed." (v. 3)

4. Today I will discern the purpose of the dark side, understanding the positive things that are being developed in my life through negative forces. "The Lord has made everything [to accommodate itself and contribute] to its own end and HIS OWN PURPOSE - even the wicked [are fitted for their role] for the day of calamity and evil." (v. 4)

5. Today I will meditate God's Word to develop sensitivity to His Spirit's leading, paving my path with the progressive presentation of His perfect plan! "A man's mind plans his way, but the Lord directs his steps and makes them sure." (v. 9)

6. Today I will exercise my royal right to regulate my life through the revelation of my righteous decrees . . . my purpose is being revealed through the words of my mouth. "Divinely directed decisions are on the lips of the king . . . " (v. 10)

7. Today I will see the big picture of my purpose, by the Spirit, with my visionary eyes of faith. "The lot is cast into the lap, but the decision is wholly of the Lord [even the events that seem accidental are really ordered by Him]" (v.33). I will remember all these things today, and today I will live in the now!

Father, help me to perceive the significance of what is really happening to me today.
In Jesus' name, amen.

March 28
EXPRESS YOURSELF!

". . . out of the abundance of the heart the mouth speaks. A good man out of the good treasure of his heart brings forth good things, and an evil man out of the evil treasure brings forth evil things." (Matthew 12:34, 35)

". . . but, speaking the truth in love, may grow up in all things into Him who is the head – Christ." (Ephesians 4:15)

1. Today I will live in the now! I will live in the now because there is a miracle in my mouth that is ready to be manifested as I move through this day, motivated by the momentum that comes from magnifying the Lord! Out of the heart are the issues of life and, through my words today, I will release God-life into the earth.

2. Today I will tell the truth about myself, meticulously dispelling the myths of mediocrity that I have manufactured in my mind and finding a victorious voice for the verification of my true value as a viable visionary!

3. Today I will make my words work for me. ". . . But only speak a word, and my servant will be healed. For I also am a man under authority, having soldiers under me. And I say to this one, 'Go' and he goes; and to another, 'Come' and he comes; and to my servant, 'Do this' and he does it." (Matthew 8:8, 9)

4. Today I will not deny my feelings, but I will communicate them to others. Because I am secure with my sense of adequacy, I can recognize, acknowledge and share my true experiences and emotions.

5. Today I will speak up when something happens that annoys or frustrates me. As Jesus commanded, I will go directly to the person involved. I won't allow negative reactions to collect, fester and grow. I will speak up and release my anger, when necessary. By speaking the truth in love, I will be able to maintain fellowship and friendships and still be able to discuss and dispel grievances.

6. Today I will release my faith by the words of my mouth, believing that what I say with my mouth - and believe with my heart - will come to pass. This mountain before me will be cast into the sea!

7. Today I will let no corrupt word proceed out of my mouth, but what is good for necessary edification that it may impart grace to the hearers (Ephesians 4:29). Life is in the power of the tongue, so today I will communicate like the true conqueror that I am, expressing myself to God and to the people around me. My words will put me over in all the affairs of life today – living truly – speaking truly – finding victory through vocabulary. Today I will win this round of the game of life, and today I will live in the now!

Father, grant me the courage to effectively express myself today. In Jesus' name, amen.

March 29
IMAGINE POSSIBILITIES!

"And the Lord said, Behold, they are one people and they have all one language; and this is only the beginning of what they will do, and now nothing they have imagined they can do will be impossible to them." (Genesis 11:6 - AMP)

1. Today I will live in the now! I will live in the now because the power of my God-given imagination enlarges me, and allows me to rise above the limitations of the finite world and the rigors of the day's responsibilities. The Mind of Christ is the source of my creativity and intellectual liberty, and today is a good day to just let the river flow! His thoughts are higher than mine, and they elevate me to a higher dimension in Him – revelation and illumination working together.

2. Today I will imagine the possibility of life without the restraints of time – eternal life emanating from the "I Am." I will believe I receive when I pray, inheriting the promises through faith and patience, because I know that, to God, there is no difference between a day and a thousand years!

3. Today I will make the effort to bring my spirit, soul, and body into complete agreement and unity (1 Thessalonians 5:23). In the same way that God declared that the people's unified imagination made anything possible for them, I say that "I am ONE" (whole, unified, interconnected), and that nothing that I imagine to do will be impossible to me because I have ONE LANGUAGE – the Word of God – and it is my final authority!

4. Today I will seek the perspective of someone who is able to think outside of the box, allowing iron to sharpen iron through creative dialogue. I will not consider it coincidence when I connect with someone new who brings me a "now" word.

5. Today I will refuse to be retarded by religious prejudice and archaic thinking. I will not engage in the foolishness of "answering a matter before I hear it," but will listen to the wisdom that cries out to me from the streets.

6. Today I will nourish the prophetic in me, allowing my inner "young man" to see visions, and my inner "old man" to dream dreams. Today I will dream the dreams of God Himself, wearing my coat of many colors with no timidity!

7. Today I will leave my tent as Abram did, and will get out and look up into the night skies, counting the stars to increase my vision. In my heart I believe that there is no problem facing me today that I cannot rise above in my imagination, and my faith will become the substance of the things that I hope for. Today I will remember my supernatural potential for doing great things in this way, and today I will live in the now!

Holy Spirit, help me to imagine possibilities today. In Jesus' name, amen.

March 30
TAKE RISKS!

". . . but the people who know their God shall be strong,
and carry out great exploits." (Daniel 11:32)

1. Today I will live in the now! I will live in the now because the fearless part of my nature is living big in me today. Comfort and caution are low priority to me as I dare to do the dangerous, defying the defeatist mentality while discovering the destiny deposited into me as a disciple through the divine nature!

2. Today, even if I find myself frightened when attempting to solve problems or learn new skills, I will ignore my apprehension and focus on getting the job done. I will turn my anxiety into fuel and will find power in being proactive.

3. Today, if I am faced with an emergency, I will be able to tap into amazing hidden potential. My fear and anxiety will serve as potent sources of energy ("BY FAITH Noah . . . MOVED WITH . . . FEAR, prepared an ark . . . - Hebrews 11:7) that stimulate heroic efforts and enable me to accomplish seemingly impossible tasks.

4. Today I will repent of the traditional thinking that tries to addict me to my comfort zone. I know that experimenting with different approaches to revelation, theology, and walking in the Spirit can result in insights and ideas that I might never know by playing it safe!

5. Today I will obey the voice of the Good Shepherd, even when He asks me to do a hard thing. I am ever ready to move with the cloud of the anointing (*in Him I move*), and will maintain the confidence that He will not ask me to do something without equipping me to do it!

6. Today I will risk exerting every bit of energy that I have, even when I know that increased efforts may not always guarantee success. In the big picture, I know that I will eventually come out ahead as a consequence of hours of time devoted to trying. Nothing I do today will be wasted, because my steps are ordered!

7. Today I will remember that I am blessed when I go out, as well as when I go in. (I can't steal second if I don't take my foot off first!) The rush that I get from walking on the water is worth the risk of sinking beneath the waves. It is more desirable for me to be a wonderful "wet water-walker" than to be a dreary "dry boat-dweller!" Today I walk in the Christ-confidence that carried Him courageously to the cross, and today I will live in the now!

Father, help me to know when to take risks,
and give me the boldness to take them today. In Jesus' name, amen.

March 31
SOMETHING MORE!

". . . my cup runs over." (Psalm 23:5)

". . . good measure, pressed down, shaken together, and running over, will be put into your bosom." (Luke 6:38)

1. Today I will live in the now! I will live in the now because El Shaddai, the God Who is more than enough, is taking the "loaves and fishes" of my life and multiplying them to feed the world around me - leaving twelve baskets full of leftovers! He is using my life experiences for the glory of His Kingdom, and nothing, not even one mistake that I have made, is wasted as far as He is concerned.

2. Today I will rejoice that He is doing exceedingly abundantly above all that I can ask or think, according to the working of my internal, eternal power. I have no choice but to make it because my God is *all that AND a bag of chips!*

3. Today I will not be discouraged when things don't work out the way I thought they would or should, but I will keep looking forward to the next great thing coming my way. The Lord perfects that which concerns me, so, no matter what happens during the day – *it's all good!*

4. Today, through whatever conflict or hardship that I may face, I will reach down deep inside of myself and find untapped resources of strength – strength that I have never even used yet. There is a river flowing in my inner man from the throne of God, and my circumstances will cause me to sing the song that Israel sang in the wilderness: *"Spring up, O well!"*

5. Today I will minister to others out my own overflow. The Lord takes pleasure in the prosperity of His servant, and I will not take my abundance in any area for granted. My God provides seed for the sower and bread for the eater – and He is causing me to become the bread of life for those who are hungry for something real.

6. Today I will let God anoint my head with oil, and overflow my cup, at the very table that He has prepared in my enemy's presence. I will rest in the fact that my enemies are still in my life because I have to be vindicated in front of them. This will enable me to endure the persecution that comes with the 100-fold return, enjoying all the benefits of the God of power and might.

7. Today I will give more because I have more, and today I will live in the now!

Father, help me to reach for something more today. In Jesus' name, amen.

⋄A⋄P⋄R⋄I⋄L⋄

A month to be reminded of the life-giving properties of rain.

Every day is a beautiful day, regardless of the weather . . .

That's why the birds sing every morning, no matter the conditions,

And why Jesus commanded that we consider the birds of the air

to understand how to function in the Kingdom.

The water helps the earth through its times of transition,

And enables the trees of the field to produce their fruit.

Every manifestation of weather is beautiful in its own way . . .

Even the deadliest storm has its own majestic beauty,

as it brings its harsh purging to the stubborn earth.

Don't be afraid of the thunder and lightening above you, for it will soon pass.

Enjoy

the volume of the thunder . . .

the velocity of the lightning . . .

the violence of the winds . . .

and know that your God is a great and mighty God.

"For as the rain comes down, and the snow from heaven, and do not return there, but water the earth, and make it bring forth and bud, that it may give seed to the sower and bread to the eater, so shall My Word be that goes forth from MY mouth; it shall not return to ME void [empty, without fruit], but it shall accomplish what I please, and it shall prosper in the thing for which I sent it." (Isaiah 55:10, 11)

April 1
PURE GOLD!

"The twelve gates were twelve pearls: each individual gate was of one pearl.
And the street of the city was pure gold, like transparent glass." (Revelation 21:21)

1. Today I will live in the now! I will live in the now because my life has been purified by the fire of the Holy Ghost and I am coming forth as gold that is refined to the point of being transparent. Having been purged, I can live this day with no pretense, phoniness or hypocrisy, giving myself permission to be a real person seeking the real God in the real world!

2. Today I will accept the fact that my life has also been purified through tribulation (". . . We must through many tribulations enter the Kingdom of God." - Acts 14:22), so I will make peace with my past, releasing all regrets, walking in the wisdom that comes only by learning from failure and mistakes.

3. Today I will embrace openness, living an honest life before the world – no hidden agenda, no camouflage of religion, no axe to grind. The pure gold within me allows me to walk in harmony with my surroundings, going with the flow, enjoying my Kingdom rights to righteousness, peace, and joy in the Holy Ghost.

4. Today I will accept my acceptance in the Beloved. I will strive to be open about who I am, revealing the many aspects of my personality (my coat of many colors), and will not be afraid to let others see my flaws and shortcomings as well as my winner qualities. My transparency will allow me to admit when I am wrong and to stand up for what I believe when I believe that I am right.

5. Today I will work toward peer Kingdom relationships where the partners are neither "right" or "wrong" – where both are human, make errors, share frailties – and are mutually respectful and loving (love covers a multitude of sins).

6. Today I will realize that perfection is a false image, fostered by religion, and is not only unobtainable, but unhealthy and undesirable. It is only "in Christ" that I can be complete, so I will not demand others to be, individually, what I will not expect myself to be, individually. Only the unified, corporate Body of Christ can achieve His perfection under His headship as it is "fitly joined TOGETHER."

7. Today I will use the pearls of my life (gems evolved through pressure and pain) as gates into the Kingdom. All things will work together for my good today, so I will not try to prevent the process today, and today I will live in the now!

Father, help me to come out of the fire as pure gold today. In Jesus' name, amen.

April 2
KINGDOM KEYS!

"And that's not all. You will have complete and free access to God's kingdom, keys to open any and every door: no more barriers between heaven and earth, earth and heaven. A yes on earth is a yes in heaven. A no on earth is no in heaven." (Matthew 16:19 – The Message)

1. Today I will live in the now! I will live in the now by accepting the responsibility that rests in the reception of the Keys of the Kingdom. There was a transference of authority, and a transition of power that transpired when Jesus transmitted those Keys to His church in the earth and, as a part of that church, I am a shareholder in His authority!

2. Today I will make a positive difference in the world by bringing about positive changes in my life. I cannot alter my world without being willing to alter myself, and I can't change myself until I change my mind! I will, therefore, stop ignoring the obvious Kingdom Keys in my mental and emotional possession today, and will use them to transform my losing patterns into winning skills.

3. Today I will do something significant to improve my attitude, so that I can impact others for good and better the conditions around me. Through my own Kingdom Keys, I have the power within me to make definite demands on heaven that will affect my inner world – my thought processes, my personality, my world-view – causing His will to be done in my mind as it is in heaven!

4. Today I will reject any form of a victim-mentality because I am empowered by His authority. His Kingdom Keys in my mouth will help to advance His rule on the earth in my sphere of influence, so I will talk up my victories in Him and play down my weaknesses. I can do all things through Christ who strengthens me!

5. Today I will believe for the impossible, using the Kingdom Keys of faith and vision. I will take the lid off the box, and let the dreams flow and grow to expand my borders and broaden my horizons. I will see my problems in a whole new way today, and will find a second wind within me that will enable me to easily overcome them. I will run and not be weary – I will walk and not faint!

6. Today I will be a building block in the true church and the gates of hell will not prevail against me in my endeavors to advance the Kingdom. Keys to deliverance and the pulling down of strongholds will be easily accessible to me today.

7. Today I will use the Keys to unlock my destiny as a liberator, a visionary, and a reconciler. A new door is opening for me today, and today I will live in the now!

Father, thank You for the Keys to Your Kingdom.
Help me to use them effectively today. In Jesus' name, amen.

April 3
JESUS RULES!

"Which He worked in Christ when He raised Him from the dead and seated Him at His right hand in the heavenly places, far above all principality and power and might and dominion, and every name that is named, not only in this age but also in that which is to come. And He put all things under His feet, and gave Him to be head over all things to the church, which is His body, the fullness of Him who fills all in all." (Ephesians 1:20-23)

1. Today I will live in the now! I will live in the now because I have confessed with my mouth that Jesus Christ is Lord, to the glory of God the Father, and my knees have bowed in worship before Him, acknowledging that He is the Ruler of all things in the earth, above the earth, and beneath the earth!

2. Today I will proclaim the gospel of the Kingdom in my own, personal way, doing my part to make the kingdoms of this world become the Kingdoms of God and of His Christ in the now. I will do what I can to demonstrate His authority in the earth through my life experiences; I live them out before the world today.

3. Today I will not pray that the cup of difficulty pass from me, but I will invite and welcome God's will to be done instead of mine, confidently assured that He will enable and equip me to do what I cannot do in my own strength. I will emerge triumphant from my personal Garden of Gethsemane, enduring my cross for the joy that is set before me, and I will reign with Him today on His throne!

4. Today I will recognize that Jesus has been made both Lord and Christ, with all authority, rule, rights and privileges of the Kingdom and its blessings, and I will celebrate the fact that I am His joint-heir. My self-confidence today will find its source in Christ's sufficiency, and I will overcome all obstacles and conquer in every circumstance through the Greater One who dwells within me!

5. Today I will remember that His Kingdom does not come by observation, so I will look beyond the natural, finite realm of sight, into the glorious reality of things that are happening in and for me that are unrevealed to the senses. Jesus rules even when I can't see the reach of His domain, so I will have a victorious day, regardless of what I see, hear, or feel.

6. Today I will crown the King with a steady stream of praise and worship, making melody in my thankful heart with the songs of Zion in the courts of the Most High God. My report will be the report of the Lord, no matter what happens today.

7. Today I will live and act and think like a ruler, and today I will live in the now!

I CONFESS THAT JESUS CHRIST IS LORD, TO THE GLORY OF THE FATHER!

April 4
TAKE INVENTORY!

*"Be diligent to know the state of your flocks, and attend to your herds;
for riches are not forever, nor does a crown endure to all generations." (Proverbs 27:23)*

"But let a man examine himself . . . ." (1 Corinthians 11:28)

1. Today I will live in the now! I will live in the now because I am going to pour all of my energy into making this day count! The secret to my success is hidden in my daily routine, so I will honestly look into how my typical day is spent, and, starting today, make whatever changes may be necessary in order to maximize the potential of each day's opportunities.

2. Today I will examine my motives in all things, being willing to forsake any improper, hidden agenda that I may find in my subconscious mind. I will let my "yes" be "yes" and my "no" be "no," speaking the truth in love, abandoning the falsehoods and denials that are counterproductive to my living a full life.

3. Today I will take inventory of the relationships in my life, and will hold myself accountable to the highest standard of being a loving and lovable person. I will take more chances, share more of my feelings with those who care about me, and be open to allow people to safely share their vulnerable selves with me.

4. Today I will make sure that my debts are paid, or are being paid ("Owe no one anything except to love one another . . ." - Romans 13:8), and will pull my own weight and assume my own responsibility. I will be a contributor to the world around me today . . . ethical, generous, liberal, gracious, and full of integrity.

5. Today I will be the first to admit my own mistakes – I will let somebody else be right for a change – I will divorce myself from the desire to always prove my point – I will learn from someone else – I will say "I'm sorry" and "I was wrong" and "Please forgive me." And if I am unable to do and say these things, I will ask the Holy Spirit to reveal to me why, and to help me to repent.

6. Today I will have the heart of David who said, "Who can understand his errors? Cleanse me from secret faults. Keep back your servant also from presumptuous sins; let them not have dominion over me. Then I shall be blameless, and I shall be innocent of great transgression. Let the words of my mouth and the meditation of my heart be acceptable in Your sight, O Lord, my strength and my Redeemer" (Psalm 19:12-14).

7. Today I will take a really good look at me, and today I will live in the now!

Father, give me the courage to take honest inventory of my life today. In Jesus' name, amen.

April 5
FORGIVE YOURSELF!

"For if you forgive men their trespasses, your heavenly Father will also forgive you. But if you do not forgive men their trespasses, neither will your Father forgive your trespasses." (Matthew 6:14, 15)

"If you forgive the sins of any, they are forgiven them; if you retain the sins of any, they are retained." (John 20:23)

1. Today I will live in the now! I will live in the now because I am mature enough to realize that everyone is flawed ("For all have sinned and come short of the glory of God." – Romans 3:23, KJV), that perfection is a false image fostered by religion, and that God's grace is the only hope for humanity.

2. Today I will give myself the same consideration that I am willing to give others. Jesus said that my ability to receive forgiveness was in direct proportion to my willingness to forgive, so I will enter the flow of the river of mercy today – giving mercy and receiving mercy – forgiving myself, as well as others, so that I will be totally forgiven in His sight.

3. Today I will shake off the spirit of condemnation and guilt. I will stop the counterproductive work of blaming myself, and I will let it all go. Today I will be free and confident, unafraid of the faces of people, able to look them in the eye, knowing that I am not perfect, but I AM forgiven!

4. Today I will give somebody a break. Because I am forgiven, I will not feel compelled to nag others or complain about their performance – "free and easy" will be the theme for today - no unreasonable and unrealistic expectations of anybody – including me! No grudges, no finger pointing, just peace and harmony with God and man for me today.

5. Today I will have confidence before God, because my heart does not condemn me (1 John 3:19-21), so, whatever I ask, I will receive from Him (v.22).

6. Today I will stay focused on the big picture because my mind is free from self-condemnation. I will fuel myself with continued optimism and determination because I am undistracted, and the lessons that I have learned from my own mistakes will be an incentive to work even harder.

7. Today I will have a good attitude, knowing that it is well with my soul. My ability to forgive myself will release me from the past today, so today I will live in the now!

Father, give me the grace to forgive myself today. In Jesus' name, amen.

April 6
BE GRATEFUL!

"Praise the Lord! Oh, give thanks to the Lord, for He is good!
For His mercy endures forever." (Psalm 106:1)

1. Today I will live in the now! I will live in the now because I can recognize how much I have to be thankful for. With a heart full of gratitude, I can face the issues that the day brings with a proper perspective and a positive attitude. I am blessed and I *know* that I am blessed, so, today, I will *act* like I know that I am blessed!

2. Today I will be grateful for what God is doing in my life (name three positive things that are happening in your spiritual life right now):

   _____
   _____
   _____

3. Today I will be grateful for the people in my life (name three people who are important to your progress right now):

   _____
   _____
   _____

4. Today I will be grateful for the unexpected blessings that flow out of God's mercy to me (name three good things that have happened to - or for - you lately that were total surprises):

   _____
   _____
   _____

5. Today I will be grateful for the wonderful memories that I always carry with me (name three significant things that have happened in your life that brought you great joy):

   _____
   _____
   _____

6. Today I will be humbly grateful for the things that I have been able to accomplish with my life (name three things that you have done that make you feel proud of yourself):

   _____
   _____
   _____

7. Today I will be grateful for the little things, seeing the glass half-*full* in every situation, and today I will live in the now!

Father, thank You for everything!

April 7
FEAR NOT!

"The Lord is my light and my salvation; whom shall I fear? The Lord is the strength of my life; of whom shall I be afraid?" (Psalm 27:1)

1. Today I will live in the now! I will live in the now because I have the nature of God in me which produces the courage to face all of my fears, and to overcome them. He has not given me a spirit of fear, and there is no fear in love, but perfect love casts out fear! Greater is He that is in me, than he who is in the world!

2. Today I will not be afraid to embrace change. I will not be afraid to tell the truth. I will not be afraid to be myself. I will not be afraid to accept a challenge. I will not be afraid to try something new. I will not be afraid to listen to a different point of view. I will not be afraid to give my opinion. I will not be afraid to fly.

3. Today I will not be afraid to try again after I have failed at trying something. I will not be afraid to admit when I am wrong. I will not be afraid to believe again, even when I have been greatly disappointed. I will not be afraid to be vulnerable. I will not be afraid of rejection. I will not be afraid of bad news.

4. Today I will not be afraid to be great at something. I will not be afraid to believe in myself. I will not be afraid to learn from a mistake. I will not be afraid of the devil or of demons. I will not be afraid of death or of hell. I will not be afraid of the end of the world or "signs of the times." I will not be afraid that I won't make it. I will not be afraid of what I don't understand.

5. Today I will not be afraid to go to the doctor. I will not be afraid of disease. I will not be afraid of the symptoms in my body. I will not be afraid to grow old. I will not be afraid that I am unloved. I will not be afraid of pain. I will not be afraid of being talked about or falsely accused. I will not be afraid of poverty or lack. I will not be afraid that I can't pay my bills. I will not be afraid of tragedy.

6. Today I will not be afraid of added responsibility. I will not be afraid of success. I will not be afraid of promotion. I will not be afraid of having a nervous breakdown or of losing my mind. I will not be afraid of losing a loved one. I will not be afraid to be alone. I will not be afraid of the dark or of nightmares.

7. Today I decide to live fear-free, and what fears I do have remaining I will use as a catalyst to unleash my super-powers (*when I am weak, then I am strong*)! Today I will keep my mind stayed on Him so that He may keep me in perfect peace, and today I will live in the now!

Father, I thank You that I do not have to be afraid of anything today! In Jesus' name, amen.

April 8
FREE YOURSELF!

"No one engaged in warfare entangles himself with the affairs of this life, that he may please him who enlisted him as a soldier." (2 Timothy 2:4)

1. Today I will live in the now! I will live in the now because I will **KEEP THE FAITH,** no matter what I see or hear or feel — today I make a quality decision to be moved solely by what I believe! My walk of faith will liberate me from the trappings of the transitory world and will unite me with the unseen realm.

2. Today I will **KEEP IT REAL**. I will not waste my time on pretense and the silly immaturity of playing mind-games with those with whom I interact today. I officially declare my independence from worrying about what people think about me, strip away all masks, and settle into the freedom of just being me.

3. Today I will **KEEP IT SIMPLE**. Even though I am prosperous, I will not be ensnared by the deceitfulness of riches or the serving of mammon, but will "consider the lilies of the field" and be content with what I have. "And having food and clothing, with these we shall be content." (1 Timothy 6:8)

4. Today I will **KEEP HOPE ALIVE**. Regardless of the pressure around me to be discouraged, I will not allow myself to become fatigued to the point of failing to accomplish my goals. I will remember that anything is possible today and that the atmosphere is full of miracles that are trying to find their way into my life!

5. Today I will **KEEP GOING FORWARD**. I can't look back, and I can't go back, so I will free myself of the illusion that I can change my history. Here I am today, with no regrets, energized by His resurrection power to endure the cross for the joy that is set before me.

6. Today I will **KEEP THE PEACE**. I will let go of stress and worry, and anything, mentally, emotionally or spiritually that causes me to become anxious and unsettled. I choose the peace that passes understanding for my life today, fully assured that He is working all things together for my good as I cast all my care upon Him.

7. Today I will **KEEP LOOKING UP,** because I know that my help comes from the Lord. As Peter walked on the water by fixing His gaze upon Jesus, I will walk on the circumstances of my life today, looking unto Jesus, the Author and Finisher of my faith. I will free myself from the limitations of looking at the natural today, and today I will live in the now!

Father, help me to effectively use the power that You have given me to free myself today. In Jesus' name, amen.

April 9
BORN AGAIN!

"Jesus said, 'You're absolutely right. Take it from me: Unless a person is born from above, it's not possible to see what I'm pointing to – to God's Kingdom.' 'How can anyone,' said Nicodemus, 'be born who has already been born and grown up? You can't re-enter your mother's womb and be born again. What are you saying with this "born-from-above talk?" Jesus said, 'You're not listening. Let me say it again. Unless a person submits to this original creation – the "wind hovering over the water" creation, the invisible moving the visible, a baptism into a new life – it's not possible to enter God's Kingdom.'" (John 3:3-5 - The Message)

1. Today I will live in the now! I will live in the now because I am born from above – supernatural in origin – "other-worldly" – a partaker of the divine nature!

2. Today I will "see" the Kingdom operating in my world. I will be able to perceive and understand the rule and reign of Christ as it is exercised through my God-given authority on this planet.

3. Today I will be renewed in my soul because of the continual process of being re-born – going from glory to glory – so that my life today will not be stale, or boring, or predictable. I am refreshed by the washing of the water of the Word, born again of the incorruptible sperm of God (1 Peter 1:23). I have His nature! I have His life!

4. Today I will not have to wear a "WWJD?" bracelet to remind myself to ask "What would Jesus do?" - because He is doing what He is doing RIGHT NOW through me! In Him I live, and move, and have my being in the now, because the same Spirit that raised Jesus from the dead dwells in me!

5. Today I will be a witness through my words and actions — God's instrument of reconciliation. I will not take eternal life for granted, and will allow the flow of the good news to replenish the dry and thirsty ground within the lives of those around me. I will be a river in the desert today.

6. Today I will anticipate change because I am being conformed to His image. I will reproduce after my own kind, helping to bring many sons to glory as I awaken their spirits to the truth of Jesus, the King.

7. Today I will repent and enter the Kingdom, seeing the world from God's vantage point, and marching to a different drummer. Today I will rejoice that He lives big in me today, and today I will live in the now!

**Father, give me a fresh understanding of what it means to be 'born again' today.
In Jesus' name, amen.**

April 10
STRESS FREE!

"He makes me to lie down in green pastures;
He leads me beside the still waters." (Psalm 23:2)

1. Today I will live in the now! I will live in the now because I have Jesus' peace reigning in my heart — so I am stress-free, laid-back, chilled-out, settled-down, alright, going-with-the-flow — and calm, cool, and collected in Christ! Today is my day to just let all the pressure go and say, *"It's all good!"*

2. Today I will claim this verse: "Do not fret or have any anxiety about anything, but in every circumstance and in everything by prayer and petition (definite requests), with thanksgiving, continue to make your wants known to God" (Philippians 4:6 – AMP).

3. Today I will also claim the next verse: "And God's peace [shall be yours, that tranquil state of a soul assured of its salvation through Christ, and so fearing nothing from God and being content with its earthly lot of whatever sort that is, that peace] which transcends all understanding shall garrison and mount guard over your hearts and minds in Christ Jesus" (Philippians 4:7 – AMP).

4. Today I will go ahead and claim the verse following the other two: "For the rest, brethren, whatever is true, whatever is worthy of reverence and is honorable and seemly, whatever is just, whatever is pure, whatever is lovely and lovable, whatever is kind and winsome and gracious, if there is any virtue and excellence, if there is anything worthy of praise, think on and weigh and take account of these things [fix your minds on them]" (Philippians 4:8 – AMP).

5. Today I will not take everything so seriously. I will find something funny and really laugh at it. I will avoid negative people who drain me and always stress me out. I will have some well-deserved fun today.

6. Today I will take some time for myself and relax and get some quality rest for my spirit, mind and body. I will go with the flow, let the stress go, and learn to say "no" when it is appropriate to do so!

7. Today I will let the Lord be my Shepherd and quietly follow Him wherever He leads me. I will bow before *Him* – not before deadlines and pressure and expectations and demands. This is the day the Lord has made for me and I will rejoice in it today. I will get my stuff done, without making mountains out of molehills. Today I claim calm nerves, regular blood pressure, steady heartbeat, peace of mind, a positive attitude, and an ulcer-free stomach. Today I am seated with Him in heavenly places, and today I will live in the now!

Father, help me to live a stress-free life today. In Jesus' name, amen.

April 11
REVELATION KNOWLEDGE!

"[For I always pray to] the God of our Lord Jesus Christ, the Father of glory, that He may grant you a spirit of wisdom and revelation [of insight into mysteries and secrets] in the [deep and intimate] knowledge of Him, by having the eyes of your heart flooded with light . . ." (Ephesians 1:17, 18 – AMP)

1. Today I will live in the now! I will live in the now because, by the power of the Holy Spirit, I am able to discern the mysteries of God and really see what is going on in my life beyond the veil of the natural realm. I have information available to me that transcends the logic of my five senses; revelation knowledge is my sixth sense, and it taps me into eternal truth and wisdom!

2. Today I will use the gifts of the Spirit when necessary: the word of wisdom, the word of knowledge, the gift of faith, the gifts of healings, the working of miracles, prophecy, the discerning of spirits, different kinds of tongues, and their interpretation (1 Corinthians 12:8-10). I will live a gifted life today, allowing the Holy Spirit to lead me as He wills.

3. Today I will embrace the rhema Word of God, as well as the logos Word. I will be aware of the power of dreams and visions and the interpretation of those dreams and visions. I will endorse the supernatural to the glory of God!

4. Today I will manifest the sevenfold character of God's Spirit: the Spirit of the Lord, the Spirit of wisdom, the Spirit of understanding, the Spirit of counsel, the Spirit of might, the Spirit of knowledge, and the Spirit of the fear of the Lord (Isaiah 11:2).

5. Today I will be sensitive to the inner witness — the "still, small voice" of my spirit — paying attention to a "check" in the spirit when wisdom is crying in the streets to me to avoid something. I will trust in the Lord with all my heart, lean not to my own understanding, in all my ways acknowledge Him, and He will direct my paths! His revelation knowledge will direct my steps today.

6. Today I will not waste my time arguing and contending with those who are motivated by a religious spirit and, therefore, have no revelation. I will not cast my pearls before swine and give that which is holy to the dogs – those who are learning, but never coming to the knowledge of the truth.

7. Today I will remember who I am in Christ and what I have available to me in Him. The eyes of my heart will be flooded with His light today, and today I will live in the now!

Father, help me to live this day, guided by revelation knowledge. In Jesus' name, amen.

April 12
OVERCOMING FAITH!

*"For whatever is born of God OVERCOMES the world.
And this is the victory that has OVERCOME the world – our faith." (1 John 5:4)*

1. Today I will live in the now! I will live in the now because I am an overcomer, not an escapist. "I do not pray that You should take them out of the world, but that You should keep them from the evil one" (John 17:15). I know that the only way "out" is "through," so I make a demand on the grace of God to help me overcome the world today.

2. Today I will live like I am the head and not the tail, receiving the inheritance that only comes by overcoming. "He who overcomes shall inherit all things, and I will be his God and he shall be My son" (Revelation 21:7). By faith I will overcome the world's system and let His Kingdom come through my life today.

3. Today I will face whatever comes, believing that my overcoming prowess will grant me access into a deeper revelation of the Kingdom (". . . we must through many tribulations enter the Kingdom of God" - Acts 14:22). I will come through the fire as pure gold, strengthened with might by His Spirit in the inner man!

4. Today I will overcome setbacks and disappointments . . . bouncing back from the spiritual brutality brought on by the bombardment of beelzebub's battalions, to a better place of believing and blessing in the Body of Christ! What the prince of darkness meant for evil against me, the Father of Lights will turn around for my good!

5. Today I will overcome my inferior past and move toward my superior future, climbing Jacob's ladder/stairway into a new understanding of my place in God. What didn't break me helped to make me, and I continue to move up because I keep looking forward.

6. Today I will overcome negative words that have been spoken against me. "But no weapon that is formed against you shall prosper, and every tongue that shall rise against you in judgment you shall show to be in the wrong . . ." (Isaiah 54:17 – AMP). I will know the truth about myself, and the truth will set me free!

7. Today I will overcome my weaknesses, allowing God to turn them into strengths, and today I will live in the now!

Father, help me to live an overcoming life today. In Jesus' name, amen.

April 13
PROSPEROUS SOUL!

"Beloved, I pray that you may PROSPER in all things and be in health, just as your soul prospers." (3 John 2)

1. Today I will live in the now! I will live in the now because I have a mindset and attitude that is conducive to prosperity, one that attracts good things to my life. My soul (my mind, will, and emotions) is prospering and taking me to a higher level of success and productivity as it unlocks the treasures hidden in the field of my life's potential.

2. Today I will comprehend the definition of true prosperity, which involves more than just my financial status. Peace of mind, excellence of character, sphere of influence, manifestation of leadership ability, and a virtuous life of unselfishness are all viable parts of real prosperity . . . the kind of prosperity that is a blessing to humanity.

3. Today I will not contaminate my prosperous mentality with thoughts of guilt – the useless emotion that kills effectiveness, or worry – which is the mirror refection of guilt. Guilt is past-oriented and worry is future-oriented, and both ensure that absolutely nothing worthwhile will be achieved in the present! A prosperous soul is one that only functions in the now!

4. Today I will remember that my state of mind is affecting my health, and that good health is more than just the absence of sickness and disease in my body. Today I will speak words that encourage my body's natural immune system and re-creative ability to medicate itself from the inside out - but I will also see the big picture of mental and social health, longevity of life, and contribution to the health and improvement of the world, and make that my ultimate goal.

5. Today I will let my prosperous meditation unblock my energy and creativity. "But his delight is in the law of the Lord, and in His law he MEDITATES day and night. He shall be like a tree planted by the rivers of water, that brings forth its fruit in its season, whose leaf also shall not wither; and whatever he does shall PROSPER." (Psalm 1:2, 3)

6. Today I will expose myself to information that bends my attention toward prospering, unlocking hidden rooms of potential within my spirit. I will not lose precious time by letting my problems become obsessions, re-playing painful thoughts and memories, but will be empowered by the will to be proactive. Jesus has already completed His work for me, and nobody else can make me prosper, so I will make the Word work for myself!

7. Today I will get it together in my soul-life. I will do whatever is necessary to change my negative thought patterns and self-destructive inner voices, and today I will live in the now!

Father, help me to live my life today with a prosperous mentality. In Jesus' name, amen.

April 14
BURNING BUSH!

". . . he looked, and behold, the bush was burning with fire, but the bush was not consumed. Then Moses said, 'I will now turn aside and see this great sight, why the bush does not burn.' So when the Lord saw that he turned aside to look, God called to him from the midst of the bush and said, 'Moses, Moses!' And he said, 'Here I am.'" (Exodus 3:2-4)

1. Today I will live in the now! I will live in the now because I have the spiritual sensitivity to realize when God is trying to get my attention through unusual means . . . when wisdom is crying in the streets. I will not be too busy today to "turn aside and see this great sight" as Moses did, and will be prepared to obey His instructions for me no matter how impossible the requirement may seem in the natural

2. Today I will recognize divine confirmation when I see it – those signposts from heaven that let me know that I am on the right track. I will move through this day on the assumption that there are no accidents, coincidences or flukes, and will take to heart the words of the mouth of two or three witnesses. If God is speaking, I will pick up on the message!

3. Today I will not be dull of hearing or as a brute beast before the Lord. My freedom from religious prejudice, willingness to think outside the box, and openness to revelation knowledge will enable me to know how to appropriately respond when faith comes by hearing the rhema Word. My obedience today will be better than sacrifice.

4. Today I will be willing to do the ridiculous, so that God can do the miraculous. I will remember that the "burning bushes" that I observe in my life are God's way of using the foolish things of the world to confound the wise, and that what seems absurd to the logical world makes perfect sense to the Mind of Christ!

5. Today I will be aware of the presence of God in my life and will know when I am on holy ground. I will reverence His name and come before His presence with singing. I will enter His gates with thanksgiving in my heart and go into His courts with praise. Most importantly, when He makes Himself known, I will respond by saying, "Here I am."

6. Today I will be aware that the bush does not burn up, proving God's persistence and purposeful intention. He will not advance me instructions beyond my last act of obedience, so I will not insult Him by my procrastination!

7. Today I will open my eyes and ears to God, and today I will live in the now!

Father, help me to notice the burning bushes in my life today. In Jesus' name, amen.

April 15
FIND FAVOR!

"Let not mercy and truth forsake you; bind them around your neck, write them on the tablet of your heart, and so find favor and high esteem in the sight of God and man." (Proverbs 3:3, 4)

1. Today I will live in the now! I will live in the now because I expect to receive supernatural favor from God and man today. My promotion in the now will come from the Lord ("For exaltation comes neither from the east nor from the west nor from the south. But God is the Judge: He puts down one, and exalts another." - Psalm 75:6, 7), and I will conduct myself with the confidence that comes from the consciousness that He is in my corner!

2. Today I will be competitive only with myself, striving for my own, personal best, without comparing myself to others. I will be inspired by those who are successful – not intimidated by them – knowing that my success is unique to me and that I can do what no one else can do by being true to my own individuality.

3. Today I will humble myself in the sight of the Lord, that He may lift me up (James 4:10), giving God the glory and my gratitude for His guidance and grace! I can do all things through Christ who strengthens me, and I am gaining more strength as I honor Him and give Him the credit due Him.

4. Today I will let the Lord prepare a table before me in the presence of my enemies, knowing that He will anoint me with the oil of joy above my contemporaries. He will vindicate me and set me in a large place as I trust Him. My latter will be greater than my former!

5. Today I will recognize the flow that comes from godly favor. I will only go where I am celebrated – not where I am tolerated. My gift will make room for me today and will bring me before great men (Proverbs 18:16).

6. Today I will accept affirmation (valid compliments) from authentic admirers without argument. I will receive gifts, knowing that I have given to others. I will embrace promotion, and the added responsibility that it brings me, without any fear. I will renounce any bogus feelings of unworthiness, knowing that He has made me worthy and righteous and acceptable in His sight!

7. Today I will walk in the boldness that comes from having God's favor on my life. I will expect good things to happen to me today, because the Lord is good and His mercy endures forever. Today I know that I have an edge, and today I will live in the now!

Father, I thank You that I find favor for my life today. In Jesus' name, amen.

April 16
ROAD TRIP!

"The voice of one crying in the wilderness: 'Prepare the way of the Lord; Make straight in the desert a highway for our God.'" (Isaiah 40:3)

". . . I will even make a road in the wilderness . . . ." (Isaiah 43:19)

1. Today I will live in the now! I will live in the now because today is an important part of my journey . . . the journey of my life that is helping to prepare the way of the Lord into the earth. I will accept the fact that certain aspects of my life will always be in flux, and will make peace with the movement and transition, knowing that it is God's work to create change to conform me into His image and to challenge me to keep going to the next level.

2. Today I will advance in my attitude instead of regressing through my regrets! I know that I must accelerate, looking ahead through the big windshield of vision, instead of gazing at where I have already been in the little rear-view mirror of memory! If I am going to make progress on my personal road, I must avoid idling in neutral and must never put the gear in reverse!

3. Today I will enjoy the ride of life, facing the events of the day with a sense of adventure and hopeful wonder. I will see no situation as hopeless, because God is a way-maker and a road-builder. His Word today is a lamp unto my feet and a light unto my path.

4. Today I will rethink the roadblocks to progress that I have accepted along life's way and will be willing to remove the ones that I can.

5. Today I will regard any movement as positive movement and will not resist making the changes in my thought processes and speech patterns that are necessary. Old habits can be broken, and anything is possible with God!

6. Today I will follow the leading and witness of the Spirit, speeding up when He says to and slowing down when He says to do that. Timing is everything, and I will trust the Lord of Time to keep me in the zone today, helping me to arrive at each stop along the way right on schedule. My steps are ordered of the Lord today.

7. Today I will consult the road map of God's Word, keeping my eyes fixed on my destination. If I lose my way, my Shepherd will help me to get back on track if I only ask Him. As I exalt every valley of my life, and bring every mountain down to ground level, the King of Glory shall come in through me. I will make the crooked places straight for Him today, and today I will live in the now!

Father, help me be a good traveler today. In Jesus' name, amen.

April 17
JESUS REIGNS!

"The Lord reigns, He is clothed with majesty; the Lord is clothed, He has girded Himself with strength. Surely the world is established, so that it cannot be moved." (Psalm 93:1)

1. Today I will live in the now! I will live in the now because I have the authority of Jesus the King — His own stamp of approval and favor – producing in me the ability to reign as a king in this life. I am an overcomer, and overcomers have been invited to sit with Him on His throne. Today I will accept that invitation and successfully rule the circumstances of my life with His oversight and cooperation.

2. Today I will walk in the dominion that God desires for His covenant people to experience on this planet through Christ. Sickness, disease, defeat, depression, destruction and failure are under His feet, and, as a member of His body, they are under me as well. I am above only and not beneath.

3. Today I will worship the King in spirit and in truth, not just with psalms, hymns and spiritual songs, but with words of victory, acts of valor, and a lifestyle that intimidates demons and impresses the heathen. My demeanor and carriage today will reflect to all who see me that *I know who I am . . . and Whose I am!*

4. Today I will remember that I am a joint-heir with the One Who has been given all authority and power in heaven and on earth. I will decree, declare, prophesy, intercede and confess my way into vital oneness with Him, living in the God-class, producing Kingdom results in this dimension.

5. Today I will direct all of my efforts toward helping to make the kingdoms of this world the Kingdoms of our God and of His Christ. The Holy Spirit will be my guide and instructor in following Jesus as my example of authority and righteous self-confidence. I will turn negative situations around for the good in His name, refusing to be victimized in any way because I am more than a conqueror!

6. Today I will let God use me to help make His enemies to be made His footstool. I will not have to wrestle with flesh and blood, but will use my energy, instead, to accomplish the awesome and to exemplify the extraordinary in the spirit!

7. Today I will be aware that I am crowned with glory and honor and am made just a little lower than Elohim (God) Himself. Loving-kindness and tender-mercies crown all of my efforts, enabling me to overcome today, knowing that I shall not be moved because my world is established. Jesus will reign today and so will I, and today I will live in the now!

Be exalted O God, above the heavens . . . let Your glory be above the clouds!

April 18
BE HEALED!

"He sent His word and healed them,
and delivered them from their destructions." (Psalm 107:20)

1. Today I will live in the now! I will live in the now because I have received the healing Word to my whole nature — the inner man, as well as the outer man — the spiritual as well as the physical. I am strong in the Lord and in the power of His might – strengthened with might by His Spirit in the inner man – the Lord is the strength of my life!

2. Today I will boldly confess that by His stripes I am healed, celebrating the triumph of the Atonement! The blood of Jesus has saved me from my transgressions and iniquities, and healed me from my weaknesses and pains – all of my grief and sorrow has been washed away in that red river.

3. Today I will wholeheartedly worship Jehovah Rapha, my Healer — the God Who takes sickness away from my midst — the God Who makes bitter experiences sweet! Every name of disease that is named must bow to the name of Jesus, acknowledging His undisputed Lordship.

4. Today I will see my health spring forth speedily as I keep my meditation in His Word and continue to speak words of life and health with a positive mental outlook. I will not become discouraged on the road to recovery, but will grow in strength as I document my progress and give God the kind of genuine praise that will quicken my mortal body.

5. Today I will be preserved blameless . . . spirit, soul, and body. Death is pushed back and rebuked on my behalf through the working of His mighty power . . . life is mine . . . health is mine . . . wellness is mine . . . wholeness is mine . . . strength is mine . . . soundness is mine . . . the resurrection is mine . . . Jesus is mine!

6. Today I will receive soul healing from the emotional wounds of bad memories by the power of the Holy Spirit. God has not given me a spirit of fear, but of power and of love and of a sound mind, and I have the healed Mind of Christ working effectively in me today, renewing all of my inner being.

7. Today I will receive some manifestation of healing as I reach out to bring healing to someone else (just as the Lord turned the captivity of Job when he prayed for his friends). My loving unselfishness will serve as a Kingdom key to my own deliverance as the law of compassion conquers the cruel consequences of the curse. I will be a conduit of healing, helping to bring restoration to the earth today, and today I will live in the now!

Father, I thank You that I am healed today. In Jesus' name, amen.

April 19
CREATIVE MIRACLES!

"Then God said, 'Let there be light;' and there was light." (Genesis 1:3)

1. Today I will live in the now! I will live in the now because my faith is creating a supernatural environment of possibilities as my vision increases, and the steady but modest manifestation of the miraculous becomes an avalanche of amazing and awe-inspiring acts of the Almighty! The miracle zone is growing wider every day that I walk in it!

2. Today I will demonstrate through my regular routine to the natural world around me that anything is possible as I act out the miraculous before the skeptics and nonbelievers. I will celebrate my separation from the pack as my lifestyle challenges the norm and questions the status quo. Different is good. Different allows for miracles. Different thinks outside the box. Different is God-friendly.

3. Today I will remember that God never creates something out of nothing – He turns water into wine and multiplies a little lunch of bread and fish into a feast for thousands — so I will give Him what I already have in my hand for Him to use today. If Moses' shepherding rod could be used to astound Pharaoh and part the Red Sea, then I believe that God can take what is mundanely mediocre in my life and make it miraculously magnificent!

4. Today I will accept the necessary suspension of natural law as it is enforced by the Creator of all natural law; the one Who created gravity also allows for the wonder of walking on water! The earth-bound circumstances in my life are no indication to me that wonderful, hidden things aren't happening on a grand scale.

5. Today I will think creatively concerning my connection to Jehovah Jireh, the One Who provides for me. Even as I speak, people are looking for me to give into me – good measure, pressed down, shaken together, and running over! Ravens can feed me, if necessary, and money may be in a fish's mouth! I will take no thought of these things in the natural as I make room for monetary miracles.

6. Today I will set no limits on what I can accomplish in the next 24 hours. God believes in me, so I will believe in myself. He and I together will produce prosperity, give birth to blessings, make miracles, and initiate the impossible!

7. Today I will notice even the smallest miracles, will give God the glory for His excellent greatness, and will be grateful for His goodness. I will be attentive and observant of the millions of things around me that are praiseworthy, and will remain hopefully expectant and faithfully optimistic about what is to come. Today is my miracle day, and today I will live in the now!

Father, help me to create an atmosphere for creativity today. In Jesus' name, amen.

April 20
SECRET PLACE!

"He who dwells in the secret place of the Most High shall remain stable and fixed under the shadow of the Almighty [Whose power no foe can withstand]." (Psalm 91:1 - AMP)

1. Today I will live in the now! I will live in the now because I will find where my access to the secret place is today – my rhema word – my unique understanding of God – my way to work out my own salvation – for the secret of the Lord is with them that fear Him. God wants to reveal Himself to me, and I am willing to passionately pursue Him in order to know Him fully.

2. Today I will be prepared for unusual and unprecedented occurrences flowing from the secret place, where God reveals His personality to me. I will embrace the unpredictable, while trusting in the faithfulness of the One Who is the same yesterday, today and forever, yet reveals Himself as the manna from heaven Who can only be experienced one day at a time.

3. Today I will walk in perfect peace, knowing that I am protected by a fortress of faith, sheltered in the shadow of His wings. The reality of the sanctuary of the secret place demands that I walk with no sense of fear whatsoever.

4. Today I will expect to receive restoration in the realm of my hidden reality, for in the secret place I am naked before Him, with no mask or pretense to protect me from His vision. Today there will be healing in my own secret places, the places that no one knows about but God and me, and I will not be afraid to tell Him my truth, for there is no fear in His presence.

5. Today I will claim spiritual stability, therapy for the soul, divine direction, and revelation knowledge – all of which are the by-products of dwelling in His courts. I am at home with Him. I am at peace in Him. I am whole.

6. Today I will experience a rebirth of sorts, as I emerge from His inner sanctum renewed and ready to face the insanity of the outer world. My sense of interior dominion will qualify me to take dominion in the cosmos and bring God's order to the world-system.

7. Today I will enjoy all the benefits of the 91st Psalm, and will personalize them, adapting them to my present circumstances. His truth will be my shield and buckler . . . a thousand shall fall at my side, and ten thousand at my right hand, but it will not come near me . . . He will give His angels charge over me . . . it's all good, and it's all mine. Today I am surrounded by His promises, and today I will live in the now!

Father, help me to find the secret place today. In Jesus' name, amen.

April 21
MERRY HEART!

"A merry heart does good like a medicine,
but a broken spirit dries the bones." (Proverbs 17:22)

1. Today I will live in the now! I will live in the now because I have made the decision to be happy, and to keep putting myself in a position that is predisposed to pleasurable and positive perceptions. Out of my heart are flowing the issues of life, attracting happy people to my environment – people who add and multiply, instead of subtracting and dividing – and we will walk together because we are in agreement.

2. Today I will receive the healing balm of kind words into my broken spirit, and will allow my wounds to make me sensitive to the wounded around me. But we will not fellowship around our sadness; instead, we will provide mutual help and encouragement for moving past the pain. We will laugh together. We will celebrate. We will be strong and resilient, strengthened by our own scars.

3. Today I will guard my emotions and protect my heart without shutting significant people out of my life. I will be wise as a serpent, yet harmless as a dove, because there is no fear in love, but perfect love casts out fear. I can be open, honest and vulnerable today, without giving place to the devices of those who would use me or take advantage of me.

4. Today I will give my undying praise to the One Who has turned my mourning into dancing and has anointed me with the oil of joy. I have on the garment of praise for the spirit of heaviness, and I wear it well — joy becomes me — and with joy I will draw water from the wells of salvation today and water the thirsty souls around me.

5. Today I will be happy and optimistic, even when I am tempted to be depressed and negative. I will create my own happiness, self-medicating with the merriness of my own heart. The joy of the Lord will energize me and renew my youth like the eagle's so that I will feel like I can run through a troop or leap over a wall!

6. Today I will find a new way of looking at an old situation, refreshing my mind with the positive power of a paradigm shift. There is joy in repentance — a relief from the stress of feeling overwhelmed.

7. Today I will be productive and a joy to be around. The fruit of the Spirit – the joy of Jesus Himself – will cause me to rise above the smog of the valley and allow me to breathe in the fresh air of the mountaintop! The atmosphere is charged with possibilities for me today, and today I will live in the now!

Father, help me to release my merry heart today. In Jesus' name, amen.

April 22
LIBERAL SOUL!

"The liberal soul shall be made fat . . . ." (Proverbs 11:25 – KJV)

"The generous soul will be made rich, and he who waters will also be watered himself."
(Proverbs 11:25)

1. Today I will live in the now! I will live in the now because I live a free life — a life without the bondage of selfishness or stinginess. I am blessed when I come in as well as when I go out, and I have received an overflow that makes me want to be a blessing to others. I have received freely, so I want to give freely.

2. Today I will not be afraid to show my generosity, and I will not be ashamed of my prodigal lifestyle. God has blessed me and given me the power to get wealth that He might establish His covenant with me. I will not put my candle under a bushel, but I will embrace a philosophy of life that makes "my profiting appear to all."

3. Today I will not waste my time with jealousy, because I know that there is enough of the goodness of God to go around, and my focused attention is on Him and not on others. Jesus, though He was so rich, became poor that I might be rich (2 Corinthians 8:9), so I will trust Him to take care of my needs, and mind my own business when it comes to the financial status of my neighbor.

4. Today I will not be cheap. My God supplies all of my need according to His riches in glory by Christ Jesus.

5. Today I will enlarge my vision of prosperity and success, for the One Who teaches me to profit is inviting me to live an abundant life with Him.

6. Today I will water the desert around me, investing in the Kingdom of God with all that I have.

7. Today I will give, not grudgingly or of necessity, for God loves a cheerful giver, and today I will live in the now!

"And God is able to make all grace (every favor and earthly blessing) come to you in abundance, so that you may always and under all circumstances and whatever the need be self-sufficient [possessing enough to require no aid or support and furnished in abundance for every good work and charitable donation]." (2 Corinthians 9:8 – AMP)

Father, help me to show Your kind of generosity today. In Jesus' name, amen.

April 23
FAST FORWARD!

"For the Lord God will help Me, therefore I will not be disgraced;
therefore I have set My face like a flint . . . ." (Isaiah 50:7)

1. Today I will live in the now! I will live in the now because my life is like an arrow shot from the bow. There is no turning back for me now . . . I am through the looking glass of self-examination. God is taking me, just as I am . . . no time to change . . . this is the day . . . this is the hour . . . this is the moment . . . for such a time as this . . . the day of the Lord is here . . . the Spirit is moving . . . go . . . go . . . go!

2. Today I will move at God's pace — my steps will be ordered by Him. I trust Him with all of my heart and lean not unto my own understanding. He Himself is directing my path(s) . . . in Him I move . . . the future is now . . . faith is now . . . God is now . . . I am in the now . . . resurrection life is mine . . . Zoë (life) is mine . . . the same Spirit that raised Christ from the dead is mine . . . move . . . move . . . move!

3. Today I will keep up with Him. I will move with the cloud (cloud by day – fire by night) . . . good-bye past . . . good-bye yesterday . . . good-bye comfort zone . . . good-bye tradition . . . good-bye familiar spirits . . . hello new . . . hello now . . . hello transformation . . . hello conformation to His image . . . hello revelation . . . hello rhema word . . . hello Jesus-manna . . . give me this day my daily bread . . . eat . . . eat . . . eat!

4. Today I will fly like an eagle. I will run and not be weary . . . I will walk and not faint . . . walk in the Spirit . . . go with the flow . . . demonstrate dominion when I can . . . relinquish control when I must . . . hold on . . . let go . . . hold on . . . let go . . . from glory to glory to glory . . . flow . . . flow . . . flow!

5. Today I will erase the tapes in my head that keep directing me backwards. I can't go back . . . I remember Lot's wife . . . the Lord is my rear-guard, because there is no armor behind me . . . there is nothing for me in Egypt, so I will make the best of the wilderness, even before I find my promised land . . . forward . . . forward . . . forward!

6. Today I will allow vision to propel me into my future. Vision keeps me going . . . vision keeps me believing . . . where there is no vision, the people perish (where there is no prophetic revelation, the people cast off restraint). Vision keeps me disciplined . . . I am moving . . . I am growing . . . I am climbing . . . I am excelling . . . vision . . . vision . . . vision!

7. Today I will exceed expectations. There is more on the inside than on the outside . . . I am greater, stronger, wiser on the inside. Today I will live from the inside out . . . the real, better me is emerging day by day, and today I will live in the . . . *now . . . now . . . now!*

AMEN!

April 24
KINGDOM LIFESTYLE!

"Therefore I say to you, do not worry about your life, what you will eat or what you will drink; nor about your body, what you will put on. Is not life more than food and the body more than clothing?" (Matthew 6:25)

1. Today I will live in the now! I will live in the now because I am energized by the benefits of my citizenship in the supernatural Kingdom of God. In Him I live and move, and today His presence will go before me and will deliver me from the beggarly elements of the finite, natural realm. Because I am not of this present world-system, I am able to enjoy living a superior life as the head and not the tail!

2. Today I will not compromise my value system by being dishonest. The people around me will know that they can trust my integrity, because I have built a lasting reputation for being reliable and dependable. I believe in God's provision, so I do not have to compromise my moral authority by being manipulative in order to get ahead by the values fostered by the current god of this world.

3. Today I will reject and abandon all tendencies toward worrying. The Kingdom that I seek daily provides for my every need, and, therefore, I do not want for anything as a protected part of God's flock. My God shall supply all of my need – and my one need is His presence in my life.

4. Today I will accept my responsibility in the Kingdom and will be a good steward over the keys that I have been given. I will unlock revelation in the earth and fill it with the mysteries of God. I will open doors of communication to strengthen covenant in my relationships, demonstrating the triumph of unconditional love.

5. Today I will pursue righteousness, peace, and joy in the Holy Ghost in creative and innovative ways. The Mind of Christ is activated in me and Kingdom wisdom and Kingdom knowledge are coming – not as a steady rain, but as a dam that has been broken – watering the desert, and causing it to bloom like a rose!

6. Today I will expose every antichrist spirit that attempts to harness the liberty of the Kingdom by dead, religious practices. The wind blows where it will and, because I am born again, I can see the movement of God's wind with Kingdom eyes of perception and discernment, and can see how to effectively engage in appropriate warfare against fleshly bondage. Let the wind blow today!

7. Today I will stay in the Kingdom zone – the spirit realm – the Christ-life – and I will subdue the part of the earth in which I live. The King will reign through me today, crowning me with glory and honor as I declare His righteousness. Today I will crown Him with every word and action, and today I will live in the now!

Father, help me to demonstrate a Kingdom lifestyle today. In Jesus' name, amen.

April 25
LIVE LONG!

"With long life I will satisfy him, and show him my salvation." (Psalm 91:16)

1. Today I will live in the now! I will live in the now because I am walking in the kind of obedience to God that prolongs life. I will honor my father and mother that it may be well with me and that I might live long on the earth, for this is the first commandment with promise.

2. Today I will enjoy health and vitality because His words "nourish the bones" and "are health to the navel." The law of the spirit of life in Christ Jesus makes me free from the law of sin and death.

3. Today I will maintain an attitude that is conducive to life and longevity . . . positive mental outlook . . . something to look forward to . . . surrounding myself with positive people . . . staying involved . . . continuing to learn, grow and change . . . planning for the future . . . keeping up with the times . . . living in the now!

4. Today I will experience the kind of success that inspires true achievers to keep going, despite the necessary hard work.

5. Today the spirit of death is rebuked in my behalf.

6. Today I will gain insight into the practical application of the promises of God that speak to longevity of life. I will not limit my faith to accepting the "three score and ten years" that God promised the Israelites in the wilderness. I am a partaker of the New Covenant!

7. Today I will make this day count, and today I will live in the now!

"And the Lord said, 'My Spirit shall not strive [abide] with man forever, for he is indeed flesh; yet his days shall be one hundred and twenty years.'" (Genesis 6:3)

"Moses was one hundred and twenty years old when he died. His eyes were not dim nor his natural vigor diminished." (Deuteronomy 34:7)

Father, I thank You for long life today. In Jesus' name, amen.

April 26
CONTINUAL FEAST!

". . . he who is of a merry heart has a continual feast." (Proverbs 15:15)

1. Today I will live in the now! I will live in the now because I have a merry heart, a positive outlook — my glass is always seen by me as half-full, no matter how much has been spilt. I am a proactive praiser, always expecting things to turn around for the better — encouraging myself in the Lord — building myself up on my most holy faith by praying in the Spirit — believing that God is always working everything together for my good, or even for my best!

2. Today I will hope in God. My heart is established, so that I am not afraid of evil tidings . . . I declare the end from the beginning, and call those things that are not as though they are . . . my faith overcomes the world . . . the joy of the Lord is my strength . . . in all these things I am more than a conqueror through Him Who loves me . . . the Lord is good, and His mercy endures forever!

3. Today I will advance on my road to accomplishing my impossible dream, regardless of the tiny vision and empty words of the little people living in the small world. They do not speak my language, and they do not speak for me! I have been called to greatness, so I must dream grand dreams and think high thoughts as I serve my big God in a large place!

4. Today I will enjoy the abundant and bountiful blessings of the Kingdom life that Jesus Himself is lavishing upon me in an amazing display of extravagant grace. He daily loads me with His benefits, and I will not forget to thank Him for any of them today. The greater the blessings, the greater the joy; the greater the joy, the greater the blessings! To them that have will more be given, and there is more on the way for me today!

5. Today I will find the supernatural strength to keep going, even when mental and spiritual fatigue work against me. I will press in and press on, because my vision is increasing in spite of my setbacks, and I must run with it to read it clearly. My merry heart will even move me beyond physical fatigue, satisfying my mouth with good things so that my youth is renewed like the eagle's!

6. Today I will thrive, even in the midst of trouble. The fire of the current trial will bring out the best in me, exposing my true leadership skills and scaling me down to my best fighting weight. My attitude will affect my altitude as I rise to the optimum level — *the sky is the limit!*

7. Today I will flourish like a green olive tree in the courts of God, Word-watered by the King Himself. Today I win, and today I will live in the now!

Father, help me to maintain a merry heart today. In Jesus' name, amen.

April 27
FORGET YESTERDAY!

"I'm not saying that I have this all together, that I have it made. But I am well on my way, reaching out for Christ, who has so wondrously reached out for me. Friends, don't get me wrong: By no means do I count myself an expert in all of this, but I've got my eye on the goal, where God is beckoning us onward – to Jesus. I'm off and running, and I'm not turning back. So let's keep focused on that goal, those of us who want everything God has for us. If any of you have something else in mind, something less than total commitment, God will clear your blurred vision – you'll see it yet! Now that we're on the right track, let's stay on it." (Philippians 3:12-16 – The Message)

1. Today I will live in the now! I will live in the now because the events of yesterday are not ruling my life — THIS is the day the Lord has made, and the accuser will not gain an advantage over me by throwing the past up to me.

2. Today I will get the upper hand in the battle of life, because I know the power of living in the now. This knowledge sets me apart, gives me an edge, and puts me over! Now is all that matters to me.

3. Today I will not beat myself up because of yesterday's performance. I can't change it in the first place and, secondly, I don't need to change it – even if I could. I will focus on today and on how I can make things better by learning from my mistakes. Failure will force me into faith and keep me looking ahead, creating a real desire within me to improve my skills and to be and do better. All the things that I have experienced will work together for my good.

4. Today I will concentrate on making myself motivated to move on mentally, with a momentum that will become the measure for managing my time. I just can't look back, because the memory of yesterday is already fading in His presence.

5. Today I will become a healer of the breach by encouraging those with whom I have influence to move into their own futures. My words will not divide, but will bring health and harmony to those who really hear me.

6. Today I will operate successfully in the ministry of reconciliation by remitting the sins of those who cannot forgive themselves:

   "So Jesus said to them again, 'Peace to you! As the Father has sent Me, I also send you.' And when He had said this, He breathed on them, and said to them, 'Receive the Holy Spirit. If you forgive the sins of any, they are forgiven them; if you retain the sins of any, they are retained.'" (John 20:21-23)

7. Today I will forget what needs to be forgotten, and today I will live in the now!

Father, I forget! In Jesus' name, amen.

April 28
EXPECT MIRACLES!

". . . Lord, I believe; help my unbelief!" (Mark 9:24)

1. Today I will live in the now! I will live in the now because my attitude of expectancy is creating for me today an atmosphere in which miracles can be incubated and birthed! I was born for the miraculous - for the **RESTORING OF ORDER TO A CHAOTIC ENVIRONMENT**. God has placed me in my own, personal Garden of Eden, so that I can subdue my part of the earth. I will, therefore, make a demand on the supernatural to accomplish my Kingdom responsibilities, facing the chaotic disorder around me and taking dominion!

2. Today I will tap into the miraculous for the **RECOVERING OF SIGHT TO THE BLIND**. God has made me a seer so that I can shine His great light on those who sit in gross darkness. He will prove Himself, through me, to those in my world who do not believe, and I will speak the truth to them without fear.

3. Today I will bring supernatural restoration to those who have been disappointed in covenant relationships for the **REPAIRING OF THE BREACH**. I will be willing to be a physician of the soul to those who are disconnected by their own sin-consciousness and self-condemnation. My miraculous words of grace and mercy will set the captives free in ways that will amaze all who are involved.

4. Today I will believe for the impossible for the **REALIZING OF MY OWN HEADSHIP**. Miracles are standard procedure for me because of my royal sonship and position in Christ and, even though I do not take them for granted, I do expect them to occur on a regular basis – including right now!

5. Today I will believe that God has miraculously released me from any sin-debt, and has created a new resumé for me for the **REWRITING OF MY HISTORY**. Because He has not dealt with me according to my sins, nor rewarded me according to my iniquities, He has seen my past in the most positive light possible. I am who He says I am – righteous, holy, above reproach – a miracle!

6. Today I will expect miracles in the mind for the **REPENTING OF CONTINUAL THOUGHT PATTERNS**. I will change my world by changing my mind — and I will start today.

7. Today I will walk in authority while yielding myself to the Holy Spirit, submitting myself to the will of the Father for the **REVEALING OF CHRIST IN ME**. I will demonstrate that this revelation actually is the hope of glory, and will be an instrument to help others find it for themselves. Today I will make the miracle of the God-man a reality to my world, and today I will live in the now!

Father, help me to believe big today. In Jesus' name, amen.

April 29
SANCTIFIED IMAGINATION!

"Woe to those who devise iniquity, and work out [plan] evil on their beds! At morning light they practice it, because it is in the power of their hand." (Micah 2:1)

1. Today I will live in the now! I will live in the now because I am using my God-given power of creative visualization for the positive advancement of the Kingdom of God. The power of life and death are not just in my tongue, but they are also resident in the pictures in my head and in the images in my heart.

2. Today I will reject any internal image of myself that is contrary to God's vision of me or that is beneath His ideal picture of me.

3. Today I will use the power of positive visualization to believe for positive results in my personal world. I embrace the vision of Jacob, who placed the spotted rods before the cows to make them give birth to spotted calves (Genesis 30), and who gave the coat of many colors to his son Joseph to help him realize his dreams (Genesis 37).

4. Today I will understand the reality that visualization produces and how God sees it in His Kingdom. If Jesus said that fantasizing about adultery is the same thing as committing adultery (Matthew 5:27, 28), then today I will believe that visualizing myself as successful and prosperous is the same thing as being successful and prosperous! If this principle works in the negative, it will work in the positive as well!

5. Today I will get it together in my thought-life and not allow myself to think thoughts that cause me to be defeated, or could potentially destroy me.

6. Today I will let the seed of God impregnate the womb of my spirit so that I can give birth to beautiful, bright and blessed things in the Kingdom. I will not permit my mind to be raped by the demonic thoughts of the dark side. My mind is in a monogamous relationship with Jesus Christ!

7. Today I will think on those things that are true and honest and lovely and of a good report . . . if there is any virtue, if there is any praise, I will think on these things (Philippians 4:8). Today I will help to change the world through the Mind of Christ, and today I will live in the now!

Father, help me to use my imagination in a positive and creative way for Your glory today.
In Jesus' name, amen.

April 30
BE WHOLE!

"Now may the God of peace Himself sanctify you completely; and may your whole spirit, soul, and body be preserved blameless at the coming of our Lord Jesus Christ."
(1 Thessalonians 5:23)

1. Today I will live in the now! I will live in the now because I am moving from just being healed, to being made whole! God's restoration process doesn't just bring me back to where I was before - it always brings me to a better place than where I was before I needed the restoration.

2. Today I will accept the wholeness of my spirit because the Last Adam has made me a new creation in Him. He was condemned to justify me; He was made sin so that I could become His righteousness!

3. Today I will believe for the wholeness of my soul because I am being transformed by the renewing of my mind, and I have no sense of rejection. He went to hell so that I could go to heaven – He was cast out of the presence of God so that I could be welcomed there!

4. Today I will have faith for the wholeness of my body because by His stripes I am healed. He was made sick, to make me well; He was made a curse, so that I could be blessed!

5. Today I will move toward being completely restored from the fragmented self-image that has been damaged by heart-break and rejection, and from the arrested development that I have experienced because of the dysfunction of my past surroundings and influences. The power of God is stronger than all the hurt and pain in my life, and He is able to turn the tide of destruction into a river of life for me!

6. Today I will not be distracted or double-minded. My faith is focused.

7. Today I will enjoy healthy relationships because I know that I am complete in Him. I can love and give unselfishly . . . without co-dependence . . . without dysfunction. God has supplied all of my needs, so I do not need to have unrealistic expectations of others. Today I will seek first the whole Kingdom of God, and today I will live in the now!

Father, help me to walk in wholeness today. In Jesus' name, amen.

⋄M⋄A⋄Y⋄

A month for manifestation.

The earth is completely thawed . . . the green globe has come out of hiding . . .

The trees of the field clap their hands in thunderous applause for the perfectly

orchestrated symphony of nature . . .

The warm weather welcomes a winterless world of wonder . . .

As graduates prepare for promotion, they dream their dreams of destiny.

They have their whole lives ahead of them, and opportunity comes knocking.

The atmosphere is charged with possibilities, as the night air begins to be filled with the

fascinating flickering of fireflies

May.

Time to start seeing some growth . . .

Time to begin to make contact . . .

Time to get some answers . . .

Time to ask the question: May I receive now?

Yes, you may!

"The earth produces [acting] by itself - first the blade, then the ear, then the full grain in the ear. But when the grain is ripe and permits, immediately he sends forth [the reapers] and puts in the sickle, because the harvest stands ready." (Mark 4:28, 29 - AMP)

May 1
SUCCESS NOW!

"This Book of the Law shall not depart from your mouth, but you shall meditate in it day and night, that you may observe to do according to all that is written in it. For then you will make your way prosperous, and then you will have good success." (Joshua 1:8)

1. Today I will live in the now! I will live in the now because the power of meditation in the Word of God, and the desire to be a doer of it, is enabling me to create success for myself. My attitude compels me to search for the good aspects in every situation until I find them, regardless of possible major elements of painful disappointment involved.

2. Today I will not succumb to any latent fear of success or of the responsibility that it brings with it. I deserve to be rewarded for my honest, hard work, so I will give God the glory for my accomplishments, but I will enjoy the benefits of them for myself. I can do what I need to do to make it to the top, and what I can't do, He will do through me!

3. Today I will "make my way prosperous" by God's methods. The blessing of the Lord makes rich and He adds no sorrow with it, so I will not serve mammon, nor will I give in to greed or covetousness. I will make it to the promised land of prosperity without compromise, my virtue and integrity intact.

4. Today I will surround myself with successful people. I will listen to their conversations, read their books, observe their lifestyles and attitudes, and I will receive inspiration from them for my own individual and unique journey. Success is a journey, not a destination.

5. Today I will go the distance, succeeding by simply refusing to quit. I will run until I get my second wind, but if it doesn't come, I will finish my race even if I have to crawl across the finish line on bloody hands and knees! The resurrection life of God in me will not permit me to give up – ever!

6. Today I will resist all temptation to believe that I am a failure in any way. I know that winning not only influences the quality of my life in the present, but it transforms my future attitudes as well. So, to build self-confidence and produce high morale, I will believe the best about myself today.

7. Today I will look beyond the current, natural circumstances of my life, and look to God as the ultimate example and source of all success. There is no failure, incompetence or inferiority in Him. Today I will think His thoughts and speak His words, and today I will live in the now!

Father, thank You for helping me to succeed today. In Jesus' name, amen.

May 2
SUPPORT SYSTEM!

"These likewise are the ones sown on stony ground who, when they hear the word, immediately receive it with gladness; and they have no root in themselves, and so endure only for a time. Afterward, when tribulation or persecution arises for the word's sake, immediately they stumble." (Mark 4:16, 17)

1. Today I will live in the now! I will live in the now because I have a solid root system in the Body of Christ to keep me from falling away when I encounter persecution for the Word's sake: pastor/shepherds, mentors, those who have set an example, teachers, intercessors, those who speak prophetically into me, prayer partners, friends, those with whom I am in covenant, the great cloud of witnesses that surrounds me in the spirit realm, angels who minister to and for me. I am not alone. I am connected. I have support. I have roots!

2. Today I will nurture the meaningful relationships in my life with words of appreciation and acts of kindness, and will accept their offer to help me when I find myself in times of trouble.

3. Today I will remember to be appreciative for the safety and protection of the local church for my life, and for the covering that the ministry provides for me. I will support the church, and be a help to it in some way today.

4. Today I will not be defensive when someone who really loves me tells me the truth that I don't necessarily want to hear about myself. I will let iron sharpen iron, even though the process may be painful, and will let the truth be spoken in love, knowing that love never fails! "Faithful are the wounds of a friend, but the kisses of an enemy are deceitful." (Proverbs 27:6)

5. Today I will have confidence in knowing that God is on my side, and that if He is for me, who can be against me? His unconditional love and unfailing support form the foundation for everything that I do today.

6. Today I will agree with the prayer that Jesus, my High Priest, is praying for me as He lives to make intercession on my behalf. His declaration of the end from the beginning concerning me is saving me to the uttermost as all things work together for my good!

7. Today I will rely on the comfort and help of the Holy Spirit. He is the Stand-by, and I will be aware today that He is always with me when I need Him. Knowing that I have the support that I need, I will be effectively supportive for someone else today. I will be a cooperative "team-player" – an asset to the Kingdom and a contributor to the world, and today I will live in the now!

Father, help me to be a part of Your support-system today. In Jesus' name, amen.

May 3
DECISIONS, DECISIONS!

"How long will you falter between two opinions?
If the Lord is God, follow Him." (1 Kings 18:21)

1. Today I will live in the now! I will live in the now because I have decided to live a "now" life from now on. I am responsible for my own choices, and, having already made the ultimate right choice in following my path to a covenant with God in Christ, I can proceed to building a superior lifestyle by making excellent choices in every area of my world.

2. Today I will tap into the resources available to me — the Mind of Christ, the leading of the Holy Spirit, the prophetic word, the confirmation, counsel, and covering of spiritual authority, the mouth of two or three witnesses — to help me in the decision-making process. I will believe that I can hear God speak, and I will have faith in my own faith to carry out His will!

3. Today I will find stability in all my ways because I am not double-minded; there is no conflict between my mind and my subconscious mind (my spirit), even though the spirit and the flesh lust against each other. Ultimately, my life is guided by my God-given will and the power of decision – so I live by what I believe, more than by what I feel. My soul is anchored . . . my heart is fixed . . . my mind is made up . . . my attention is focused!

4. Today I will not speak idle, non-productive words. My conversation will be resolute and declarative, and I will speak as one who has authority. The power of my positive speech will attract the provisions that I need to be productive.

5. Today I will not second-guess the decisions that I have already made that I know are right for me, even if they create a difficult path for me to follow. I know that doing the *right* thing is not always doing the *easy* thing, but I will remain committed to my decisions and will follow through with them to the glory of God.

6. Today I will command clarity into the chaos and confusion around me, causing things to come into order and to cooperate with the Creator's commitment to conformity in the cosmos! Decisiveness will organize my thought-life and help me to make sense of my world. Decisiveness will move me forward!

7. Today I will remember this, "You will also decree a thing, and it will be established for you; so light will shine on your ways" (Job 22:28). I am ready to make my decrees so that light will shine on my ways today, and today I will live in the now!

Father, help me to make the right decisions today. In Jesus' name, amen.

May 4
ANOTHER COMFORTER!

"And I will pray the Father, and He will give you another Helper (Comforter),
that He may abide with you forever – the Spirit of Truth . . . ." (John 14:16, 17)

1. Today I will live in the now! I will live in the now because the Holy Spirit is my trusted friend and valued confidant . . . the One Who helps me and empowers me to be a witness to my generation. He is the Spirit of Truth who will lead me into all truth and reality today, delivering me from all deception, freeing me from every falsehood, and liberating me from any lies that I have believed.

2. Today I will take comfort in His help. Because I know that I am not alone in my fiery trial, I will not become overwhelmed by the enormity of my problems. He is with me every step of the way — protecting, leading, guiding, counseling, instructing, encouraging, edifying, enabling — and His abiding presence is my sanctuary and strong tower of refuge.

3. Today I will be filled with the Spirit, overflowing with His grace and joy as I sing and make melody in my heart to the Lord. This grace will be an oasis in the desert for me today, regardless of the circumstances of my life.

4. Today I will be empowered by the dynamic work of the Helper Who indwells me, ". . . strengthened with might by His Spirit in the inner man" (Ephesians 3:16 - KJV), so that, no matter what huge task is required of me, I know that I can rise to the occasion with His help. I can overcome any obstacle, and deal with any challenge.

5. Today I will have at my disposal the wisdom of God. The Spirit of Wisdom and Knowledge and Counsel and Might will assist me in every decision that I have to make today and will activate the creativity that I need to excel in all of my endeavors.

6. Today I will find success as I go with the flow. "For as many as are led by the Spirit of God, they are the sons of God" (Romans 8:16 - KJV). The Helper will put me over with an outpouring of His favor and promotion, and I will not have to strive to make things happen in the flesh. I will get things done today — not by might, nor by power — but by His Spirit!

7. Today I will not feel alone because Jesus promised that the Helper would abide with me forever. Because of His promise, I do not have to contend with the fear of rejection or deal with abandonment issues, but I can confidently walk in the assurance that I am accepted in the Beloved! Today I will enjoy all the benefits of the Spirit-life: the fruit of the Spirit, the gifts of the Spirit, the power of the Spirit, and the comfort of the Spirit. Today I will celebrate my own, personal Day of Pentecost, and today I will live in the now!

Father, thank You for sending the Comforter!

May 5
COLORFUL COAT!

"Now Israel loved Joseph more than all his children because he was the son of his old age, and he made him a coat of many colors." (Genesis 37:3)

Today I will live in the now! I will live in the now because I am a dreamer, and God has provided a coat of many colors for me to help me discover my destiny. A dreamer needs:

D – irection . . .
Jacob's gift to his son gave Joseph prophetic significance in that it directed him toward his future. The many colors represented the wide array of diverse experiences ahead of him. Today I will look for God's direction for my dreams as He prepares me for the different things that I must encounter.

R – elationship . . .
The coat was a sign of covenant between Joseph and his father. Today I will nurture the Kingdom relationships that God has placed in my life, for they are necessary to my dream fulfillment. No one makes it alone, and I am not alone today.

E – xpression . . .
Joseph's coat allowed for expression of his dreams as an outward manifestation of his inner perception and self-picture. Today I will focus on those things that confirm to me who God says that I am and that help me establish a proper mental image of myself.

A – ffirmation . . .
The coat was a token of Jacob's love and a symbol of his approval and affirmation for Joseph. Today I will pay attention to those significant people who speak into my life, for their words of faith are activating the dreamer in me.

M – entors . . .
The many-colored coat was a touchstone of mentorship, allowing Jacob to prophetically take Joseph to a higher level. Today I will listen to mentors and will receive sage advice and godly wisdom through seasoned, experienced dreamers.

E – nemies . . .
Joseph's coat was a catalyst of provocation for his brothers. Today I will remember that all dreamers need enemies to help them fulfill their destinies. Enemies can be great motivators, so I will allow God to prepare a table for me in the presence of mine today!

R – esponsibility . . .
The coat was a fine gift that required Joseph to take responsibility for it. This helped to prepare him for the great responsibility that lay ahead of him in the preservation of Egypt's food, and for the salvation of his own family and nation.

Father, help me find my coat of many colors today. In Jesus' name, amen.

May 6
SLOW DOWN!

"You have bedded me down in lush meadows, you find me quiet pools to drink from. True to your word, you let me catch my breath and send me in the right direction."
(Psalm 23:1-3)

1. Today I will live in the now! I will live in the now because I hear the voice of the Good Shepherd Who tells me to step out of my frenzied activity and to enter into His rest. In Him I am able to seize the moment, so that I do not allow the beauty of the life that He has provided for me to pass me by. Today is a day to choose the good part and cast all of my care upon Him so I that I can fulfill His will.

2. Today I will re-prioritize my life and will lighten my load if necessary (and if possible). I will make the effort to recognize when I am "straining at gnats and swallowing camels," and will let go of the time-wasters in my life that are absorbing my energy and distracting me from the really important issues that need my attention. I will simplify and scale down for the restoration of my soul.

3. Today I will stop and listen to my spirit, where the still, small voice of God quietly gives me direction, before I rush to judgment or make decisions concerning my life. I will pay attention to warning signals from within, as well as to the wisdom that cries in the streets and, ultimately, I will follow the path of inner peace into the perfect will of God. I will avoid making decisions under pressure or duress, choosing instead to be led by His Spirit.

4. Today I will enjoy some guilt-free and much-deserved relaxation, taking care of myself first (now), so that I can be a blessing to others later. I will let it all go, getting away from it all (if only mentally), so that I can maintain perspective.

5. Today I will take the time to rediscover the beauty of the world around me. The dramatic grandeur of the Creator's vision will not be lost on me as I marvel at the magnificence of His masterpiece and cry out in praise to His mighty power, and in gratitude for His awesome greatness!

6. Today I will listen to what my body is saying to me, and will refresh it and nourish it and rest it when it cries for help. Stress, stomach ulcers, high blood pressure, nervousness, heart trouble, and insomnia are not God's will for my physical well being, so I will choose health and protect my right to walk in it, knowing that I am responsible for my own natural destiny.

7. Today I will stop, look, and listen . . . to my loved ones . . . to children . . . to nature . . . to the Word . . . to my heavenly Father — and will be still and know that He is God. I will take time to make the most of this day, and today I will live in the now!

Father, help me to know when to slow down. In Jesus' name, amen.

May 7
I WILL!

"I will arise . . . " (Luke 15:18)

1. Today I will live in the now! I will live in the now because I will **RECONSIDER THE BUILDING BLOCKS OF MY WORLD-VIEW**. Whatever is in my foundation that is contrary to the wisdom of God, I will reject and repent of. I will begin to see the world the way that God sees it today.

2. Today I will **RECOGNIZE WHEN I AM WALKING IN THE WRONG REALITY**, and I will move back into my proper place, remembering who I am. When I find myself in the pigsty, I will "come to myself" and go back to my Father's house.

3. Today I will **RECLAIM LOST TERRITORY THROUGH REPENTANCE**. I can change my world by changing my mind, so I will not waste today on regrets, but, rather, will get busy with the restoration process of my soul. Whatever part of me has come into the Kingdom at the eleventh hour, will receive the same wages as those parts of me that have already been under His control.

4. Today I will **RESTORE MY CONFIDENCE IN GOD'S VISION FOR MY LIFE**. I am what He says I am, period. So today I will lose the self-doubts and get myself together out of respect for His work in my life. I will be God's success, and He will see the travail of His soul and be satisfied!

5. Today I will **RE-CREATE A PERSONA THAT GLORIFIES GOD**, making the decision to deck myself with majesty and become the person that God believes that I am. I will speak of the non-existent things needed in my personality as though they already existed.

6. Today I will **REINFORCE MY DOMINION THROUGH THE POWER OF DECISION**. I will subdue my part of the earth by the exercise of my God-given will, driving a stake in the ground by my decision to be victorious, and the circumstances around me will cooperate with my decree.

7. Today I will **RECONCILE MY PARALLEL WORLDS IN CHRIST**, refusing to stagger between two opinions. I will choose life, give a Joshua/Caleb report of my promised land, and reconcile all of my possibilities in Him. Today I will be one – spirit, soul, and body — and nothing I imagine to do will be impossible — and today I will live in the now!

Father, help me to exercise my will in a positive way today. In Jesus' name, amen.

WELCOME TOMORROW!

"Now the Lord blessed the latter days of Job more than his beginning . . . ." *(Job 42:12)*

1. Today I will live in the now! I will live in the now because, even though I am living my life with an appreciation for the present, I know that I have so much more to look forward to in the future! I am open to the possibility that tomorrow will be better than today, as I go from glory to glory and grow up in God. I will not let anything negative from yesterday determine the quality of tomorrow!

2. Today I will not dread what I have to face in the future, but I will confidently move toward my goals, regardless of the unpleasant things that I may encounter along the way. I will deal with whatever I have to deal with when the time comes, and will not hide from hardship or run from responsibility.

3. Today I will use my current experiences as a proving ground for future promotion. I will be faithful over a few things, so that I will be qualified to be a ruler over much down the road. Discipline is doable for me because I have a vision; so, I will be a good steward over my regular routine, knowing that I will reap in due season if I do not faint.

4. Today I will plan my work, and work my plan. I will see the big picture everywhere I look, and will lay a foundation through my diligent efforts and godly work ethic in the now for success tomorrow. Because I know that there is no such thing as luck, I will be a doer of the Word with great expectations. I will not be afraid of hard work, but will partner with God in the realization of my own destiny.

5. Today I will not be afraid to be radically optimistic, even if I come across to others as unrealistically idealistic! I will not quit until I find the cloud's silver lining; I will not leave the theatre until my movie has a happy ending. God's picture of Kingdom fulfillment for my life is being painted on the canvas of my heart by the Word and the Holy Spirit, and He will finish what He started!

6. Tonight I will rest well, confident that tomorrow will be a brighter day than today. Joy will come in the morning when and where His mercies are always new for me. I will not just get up tomorrow morning – I will rise up!

7. Today I will patiently pace myself as I persistently prepare for progress, thereby producing a prognosis for prosperity! My adventures in the now will take me to the next level of discovery as I watch for the dawn of a new day. Today I will believe that the best is yet to come, and today I will live in the now!

Father, help me to prophetically prepare myself for tomorrow today. In Jesus' name, amen.

May 9
NO SMOKING!

". . . and they saw these men on whose bodies the fire had no power;
the hair of their head was not singed nor were their garments affected,
and the smell of fire was not on them." (Daniel 3:27)

1. Today I will live in the now! I will live in the now because I have come through the fire without the smell of smoke on my clothes. I am unscathed and untouched, because God is my rock, fortress and deliverer!

2. Today I will graduate with honors from the school of hard knocks. Having been seasoned and matured by the storms of life, I am able to settle down, without bitterness, into a beautiful and grounded state of stability and strength. I will let go of collected injustices and decide, once and for all, to peacefully live my life in the now.

3. Today I will remember that my fiery trial is releasing something wonderful within me for the world to witness, and burning off of me (and out of me) what needed to go anyway. I will emerge healthier and sharper — optimistic and not cynical — being thankful in all things.

4. Today I will find peace in fearlessly facing the furnace, my confidence coming from the commitment to refuse to compromise! No matter how hot the fire, I just absolutely will not bow, bend or burn. I will not give up! I will not give in!

5. Today I will stay protected in the secret place of the Most High, under the shadow of His wings. I will make good use of the whole armor of God as I prevail in every situation, profiting from my experience. The shield of faith will quench every fiery dart aimed at me.

6. Today I will live as a trophy of grace, triumphant in God, causing Him to say "Well done, good and faithful servant." I am a warrior . . . a lion . . . an eagle . . . a winner . . . an overcomer . . . and God will smile on my courage and valor exhibited today!

7. Today I will declare the end from the beginning, holding on to the five wonderful words of wisdom – "*and it came to pass*" – knowing that this, too, shall pass. Today I will walk in the confidence that I need to get to the other side. The world will not cave in on me today, the sky will not fall, God will not exit His throne, and I will not go under. Today I will make it through, and today I will live in the now!

Father, help me to come through the fire today without the smell of smoke!
In Jesus' name, amen.

May 10
I CAN!

"I have strength for all things in Christ Who empowers me [I am ready for anything and equal to anything through Him Who infuses inner strength into me; I am SELF-SUFFICIENT in Christ's sufficiency]." (Philippians 4:13 - AMP)

1. Today I will live in the now! I will live in the now because, even though I am just one member of Christ's Body, I still have individual significance as a person. "Now you [collectively] are Christ's body and [individually] you are members of it, each part severally and distinct [each with his own place and function]" (1 Corinthians 12:27 - AMP). Today I will walk in **SELF-AWARENESS**, being conscious of my own character, feelings and motives, and the role that I play in God's plan for the earth.

2. Today I will walk in **SELF-CONFIDENCE**, assured and courageous, with a genuine sense of **SELF-RELIANCE** and accomplishment ("... in quietness and confidence shall be your strength" – Isaiah 30:5).

3. Today I will walk in the power that comes from a positive **SELF-IMAGE**. I know who I am, regardless of what people may think or say about me. No one has the authority to define me but God and myself.

4. Today I will not feel embarrassed about having a high **SELF-ESTEEM**. I will love my neighbor as I love myself, and love myself as I love my neighbor. I will be good and kind and forgiving to myself today.

5. Today I will practice **SELF-CONTROL**, which is the fruit of the spirit (Galatians 5:23). I can handle the responsibility of monitoring my external reactions and emotions, being self-disciplined in the power of the Holy Spirit – and I will do so without becoming religious or legalistic.

6. Today I will let His Kingdom come through my own **SELF-SACRIFICE**, negating my own interests and wishes in favor of those of others. The Christ in me empowers me to be released to servitude, without losing my sense of identity and importance to the Kingdom of God. I esteem others better than myself (Philippians 2:3).

7. Today I will celebrate my own **SELF-RESPECT** by living as the head and not the tail. Today I will honor myself in dignity and integrity, with **SELF-REGARD** and godly pride, and today I will live in the now!

Father, help me to remember that I can do all things through Christ Who strengthens me today. In Jesus' name, amen.

May 11
FAMILY TIES!

"For this reason I bow my knees to the Father of our Lord Jesus Christ, from Whom the whole family in heaven and earth is named." *(Ephesians 3:14, 15)*

1. Today I will live in the now! I will live in the now because I am a part of the family in heaven and in earth that is named Christ, and in Christ I can do all things! I was predestined to be conformed to His image, that He might be the firstborn among many brethren.

2. Today I will embrace a genuinely global vision for the Kingdom of God, expanding my world-view to see God's family as He sees it. Because the earth is the Lord's, I will love all the peoples of the earth today – and, because the field is the world, I will do my part as a laborer of the harvest.

3. Today I will be empowered by the Kingdom connections that I have made in my life. The support of my extended family will enable me to do things that I could not do on my own. "Who is My mother, or My brothers . . . For whoever does the will of God is My brother and My sister and mother." (Mark 3:33, 35)

4. Today I will maintain a sense of awareness of the "great cloud of witnesses" — those who have gone on before me into the heavenly realm, who cheer me on and encourage me. I am connected to the other side through them, and they help me to loose on earth what is loosed in heaven today!

5. Today I will share the good news with someone as a means to adopting them into the family of God to help bring many sons to glory. I will also make the effort to destroy bigotry, hatred, prejudice and division when I see it, out of my respect for the family of man. I will be a repairer of the breach today.

6. Today I will love and nurture my natural family, honoring my father and mother, that it may be well with me and that I may live long on the earth. I will love those closest to me, choosing to know them after the spirit, in spite of how well I know them according to the flesh.

7. Today I will celebrate the Fatherhood of Abba God, the maternal creativity of the Holy Spirit, and the fellowship of Jesus, my Elder Brother, Who is not ashamed to call us all brethren. Today I will communicate the gospel of the family, especially to the stranger, the orphan, the widow, and the alienated, and today I will live in the now!

Father, help me to promote the family of God today. In Jesus' name, amen.

May 12
NICE TOUCH!

"And Jesus, immediately knowing in Himself that power had gone out of Him, turned around in the crowd and said, 'Who touched my clothes?'" (Mark 5:30)

1. Today I will live in the now! I will live in the now because I am in direct contact with my Source and Creator; God has touched me, and I can touch God! He knows my name, hears me when I pray, and cares about what is happening in my life today. My strength to live this day successfully comes from His unique touch – His hand is on my life, and He is with me in every step I take!

2. Today I will not live an isolated life. Others have touched me, so I will reach out in unselfishness to someone who needs *my* touch today. I will not let the activities of the day cause me to become insensitive to those in my life who may be lonely or hurting. I will take some time out of my schedule, and invest it in a real, personal connection with that one who is in need.

3. Today I will touch someone in a positive way because I know that using negatives, on myself or others, will not get me the results that I'm looking for. Negative interaction and response will only bring a multitude of new problems into my life (like depression, rebellion, division), so I will overcome evil with good today and will walk in the God-kind of love that never fails.

4. Today I will take comfort in the knowledge that Jesus, my High Priest, is touched with the feelings of my humanity and weaknesses. His empathy for me enables me to be emancipated from unrealistic expectations for myself and for others. Today I will live and let live.

5. Today I will not let myself become cynical and unfeeling, but I will remain reachable – in touch with my emotions . . . caring . . . in touch with the real world.

6. Today I will touch the throne of God by praying effective, genuine prayers in line with His Word and His will. My prayers will avail much because I am righteous!

7. Today I will give something back. I will freely give because I have freely received, recognizing the significance of reciprocating — the sowing and reaping principle — leaving something for the next generation — leaving the world in a better condition than the one in which I discovered it. I will do my part. I will do what I can. I will touch someone with my life today, and today I will live in the now!

Father, help me to stay in touch with You today. In Jesus' name, amen.

May 13
HARVEST TIME!

"And let us not lose heart and grow weary and faint in acting nobly and doing right, for in due time and at the appointed season we shall reap, if we do not loosen and relax our courage and faint." (Galatians 6:9 - AMP)

1. Today I will live in the now! I will live in the now because I am ready to receive the first fruits of my harvest, and I will not give up until I have reaped the full manifestation of what is now growing in my field of dreams! I refuse to give up. I will not quit. I will not throw in the towel. I will not let discouragement cause me to doubt. I will not let fatigue cause me to fail. I will not let the waiting cause me to waver!

2. Today I will refuse to give up on the reception of every heavenly blessing in Christ. God is rebuking the devourer for my sake, so I will not be afraid to aggressively defend what belongs to me – the product of my seed sown – the confirmation of the law of Genesis that everything must produce after its own kind.

3. Today I will be energized by the Zoë — the resurrection life of the living God — the same Spirit that raised Jesus from the dead. I am alive and alert, quickened by His two-edged sword. Regardless of what happens today, or how my harvest is threatened, I can handle it — valiantly rising to the occasion!

4. Today I will keep doing what I am doing until the Lord of the Harvest tells me to do something else, or to work in another field — and I will willingly work with a winning attitude, doing what my hand finds to do with all my might. I am strong in the Lord, and in the power of His might, and the sun shall not smite me by day.

5. Today I will be sustained by the living vision within me that produces a second wind, allowing Him to be strong in my weakness. I will not give up. I will never give up. I will in no way give up. I will by no means give up. I will find it impossible to give up. I will be incapable of giving up. I will simply refuse to give up. I will renounce any thought of giving up. I will not listen to those who tell me to give up. I will know that I can't give up. I will admit that I don't know how to give up. I just won't give up. Not now. Not ever.

6. Today I will run and not be weary. I will walk and not faint.

7. Today I will open my spiritual eyes and see the harvest around me . . . no complaining . . . no worrying . . . no intimidation — just believing and receiving today. Today I will know that the field is the world, and the world is the field, and today I will live in the now!

Father, help me to know how to reap in due season today. In Jesus' name, amen.

May 14
JESUS SAVES!

"Therefore He is able to save to the uttermost (completely, perfectly, finally and for all time and eternity) those who come to God through Him, since He is always living to make petition to God and intercede with Him and intervene for them." (Hebrews 7:25 – AMP)

1. Today I will live In the now! I will live in the now because I know that I am absolutely and ultimately saved, since Jesus, the Captain of my salvation, has completed His assignment through His death, burial, resurrection, and intercession for me! He sees the travail of His soul on my behalf and is satisfied!

2. Today I will celebrate the capability that I possess through the cross of Christ, the Conqueror. As an heir of salvation, I am invincible and indestructible!

3. Today I will not take my salvation for granted, but will walk in the revelation that He Who spared not His own Son, but delivered Him up for us all, shall also freely give us all things (Romans 8:32). If I have received the gift of salvation, I believe that I am able to receive any other gift from God.

4. Today I will remember that my life is a river that is fed by two streams: the will of God, which is the part that *only He can do;* and my response to His will, which is the part that *only I can do.* My salvation is synergistic in that Jesus and I are cooperating in its execution. He paid the price for me (the blood of the Lamb) because I couldn't, and I live my own life for Him (the word of my testimony), because He can't live it for me. By the agreement of these two things, I am able to overcome the accuser of the brethren, once and for all.

5. Today I will remember that, even though my salvation is secure, my life is still a work in progress. Jesus is able to save me "to the uttermost" through a process that takes time – He is the Author and the Finisher of my faith, and He who began a good work in me will continue to perform it! Therefore, I will be content with my current walk with Him, confident that the seed of Christ in me must eventually produce after its own kind! Through faith and patience I will inherit this promise.

6. Today I will live in a state of perfect peace because my salvation frees me from any fear of death, hell, or the grave. I will, therefore, face this day fearlessly!

7. Today I will speak the word of reconciliation to others, letting them know that their own salvation has been paid for, and today I will live in the now!

Father, help me to remember that I am saved to the uttermost today. In Jesus' name, amen.

May 15
SET GOALS!

"May He grant you according to your heart's desire,
and fulfill all your purpose . . . may the Lord fulfill all your petitions." (Psalm 20:4, 5)

1. Today I will live in the now! I will live in the now because the goals that I have set for myself are pointing me toward my future and preparing me for prophetic fulfillment. They are designed to dredge up dreams of destiny from deep within me, and to initiate and inspire the necessary incentive to incite them. Today will be a day of accomplishment for me.

2. Today I will be responsible enough to keep my goals realistically reachable, yet radical enough to rise above rational reasoning, and allow the God who makes all things possible to realize untapped resources in me, and to do something really extraordinary through me!

3. Today I will transcend impossibilities as the pressure applied to me personally from striving to reach my goals affects me positively by activating my faith. When things look impossible, I will simply find a miracle, because I will not have an alternative. When push comes to shove, and Pharaoh's army is at my heels, I will use what I have in my hand to part the Red Sea!

4. Today I will learn from others who have reached their goals, but I will remember that my situation is unique to my life. I will remain teachable, without compromising my individuality. Under God's guidance I will do what is right for me alone.

5. Today I will stretch my capabilities, even if I tax my spirit to the limit! I know that there is excellent hidden treasure in the field of my experiences, and the Holy Spirit will help me to excavate it by the expression of His authority and power! He will cause the eagle in me to soar above the boundaries of my emotional baggage and the hindrances of my humanity.

6. Today I will work hard, but still maintain some grace for myself. I will take time to play — to give myself a break — and even forgive myself when I don't reach the goal in the desired way or preferred time frame. I will learn from my mistakes, and keep moving up the ladder with a healthy balance of diligence and joy.

7. Today I will use my God-given mind, will, and resolve to reach my goals, without compromising my ability to walk in the Spirit. I will write them all down, but I will write them in pencil in case "the Boss" wants to make any changes in them today, and today I will live in the now!

Father, help me to reach my goals for Your glory today. In Jesus' name, amen.

May 16
ETERNAL LIFE!

"That which was from the beginning, which we have heard, which we have seen with our eyes, which we have looked upon, and our hands have handled, concerning the Word of Life – the life was manifested, and we have seen, and bear witness, and declare to you . . . ETERNAL LIFE . . . therefore let that abide in you which you heard from the beginning. If what you heard from the beginning abides in you, you also will abide in the Son and in the Father. And this is the promise that He has promised us – ETERNAL LIFE." (1 John 1:1, 2; 2:24, 25)

1. Today I will live in the now! I will live in the now because I am living my life from the inside out: spiritually, first — mentally, second — physically, third. My reality is determined by the eternal part of me where the fullness of the Godhead lives; I am a spirit being trying to find definition in the material world.

2. Today I will let that abide in me which I heard from the beginning — those eternal God-words that I heard when I was in Him at the creation of all things. I will base my knowledge on the speech of the Spirit – those "I Am" concepts that my finite memory has not contained, but are still a reality in my inner man!

3. Today I will be empowered and energized by my awareness of what is eternal in me. The transient events of the day will be trivialized by the triumph of the ever-living, ever-lasting Mind of Christ. The "eternal me" is bigger than the events of this day, so they will not be able to overwhelm or overpower me in any way!

4. Today I will examine the building blocks of my world-view, and whatever I find in my foundation that is not based on the fundamentals of eternal truths will be challenged to change. I will make the choice to begin to receive my information from the voice of my Creator, rather than from the alternative messages that I have received since my earth-birth.

5. Today I will take the concept of seeing the big picture to a whole new level, as I focus on the larger ideas of purpose and destiny. My life is more than my current circumstances — I am here for a reason — my life matters because it is a valid and viable part of the grand scheme of things. I will believe this until I can feel it.

6. Today I will be able to walk through the valley of the shadow of death, and still fear no evil, because I am alive forevermore. Death has no sting for me, because the law of the spirit of life in Christ Jesus liberates me from its grasp, and His eternal love produces fearlessness in me!

7. Today I will really live my real life, and today I will live in the now!

Father, help me to stay connected to my eternal life today. In Jesus' name, amen.

May 17
TIME TRAVEL!

". . . there is a time appointed for every matter and purpose and every work."
(Ecclesiastes 3:17 – AMP)

1. Today I will live in the now! I will live in the now because the power of memory and vision are enabling me to put the now into perspective. With the eye of truth I am able to see into the distant past and solve the mysteries of my life — and with the eye of faith I am able to see into the distant future and declare the end from the beginning.

2. Today I will travel back in my memory to get in touch with my childhood, knowing that Jesus made childlike-ness a requirement for entrance into the Kingdom. The imagination, innocence, playfulness, and sense of wonder of my youth still remain buried in my subconscious (spirit), and the Keys of the Kingdom are unlocking the prophetic imagery that is produced by the positive parts of my past. I will also know when it is time to put away childish things.

3. Today I will listen to the messages that my dreams and night-visions are conveying to me. Instead of being haunted by horrible images from yesterday, I will recognize that my soul is bringing these things to the surface in an effort to help and heal itself for a better tomorrow.

4. Today I will know the difference between what needs to be resurrected and what needs to stay buried. My sense of timing and propriety, under the anointing of the Holy Spirit, will help me to know what to do and say, and what not to do and say.

5. Today I will see my life as a whole entity, and will accept it for what it is. I will not complain, nor slow my progress through the pointlessness of regret, "But by the grace of God I am what I am . . . " (1 Corinthians 15:10).

6. Today I will keep talking myself into my future, propelling my faith to maintain the motivation for mental mobility in a mature manner. I can't afford to get my life stuck in a time warp now, because I know too much and there is too much for me to do. The future is calling me, so I must move forward!

7. Today I will believe that I am not getting older, but that I am getting better as I grow in God and learn my life-lessons. I will embrace the sage-like wisdom and oak-like strength that comes from having lived a full life. Today I will travel the road of life successfully, and today I will live in the now!

Father, help me to appropriately navigate my past and my future today.
In Jesus' name, amen.

May 18
TOUGH LOVE!

"But, speaking the truth in love, may grow up in all things into Him who is the head – Christ . . . Therefore, putting away lying, let each one of you speak truth with his neighbor, for we are members of one another." (Ephesians 4:15, 25)

1. Today I will live in the now! I will live in the now because I am growing up into Christ as I put away the falsehood that comes from a bogus, religious mindset. His true, unpretentious church is emerging, conquering fear as His kingdom comes and as His will is done on earth as it is in heaven!

2. Today I will speak the actual *truth* concerning a situation, not just my opinion or feelings (which may or may not be accurate) on the matter. I will not lie to myself, or let my mind stay in a state of denial. I will not be afraid to face facts, for there is no fear in love! I will love myself enough today to tell myself the truth, and the truth will set me free!

3. Today I will embrace the power of release, loving others to the point that I can let them go, if necessary. I will let go of things – anything that weighs me down and encumbers me. Release will bring relief as I free myself by finding the flow of unselfishness. I will enjoy having *things*, without things having *me!*

4. Today I will love someone enough to speak the truth to them without fear of reprisal or rejection. I will also walk in restraint, letting love prevent me from saying too much, or anything unnecessarily harsh or hurtful. My words of love will be balanced, honest, and productive. I will know when "there is a time to speak" and when "there is a time to be silent."

5. Today I will not compromise my convictions, but will keep drawing a line in the sand no matter how many times the waves of mediocrity come in to wash it away. My tough love will demand my daily discipline as I dare to do the difficult, even dangerous, task of developing a dominion lifestyle!

6. Today I will expect the best of myself, making no apology for my perceived inadequacies. My inner dialogue will be honest, but I will be strong enough to refuse to put myself down.

7. Today I will not *just settle* for the status quo, having the stamina and stability to swim upstream if I have to. I will be the one to say what everyone else is afraid to say, letting the chips fall where they will. My tough love will be godly, and I will not throw in the towel in today's fight, regardless of my fear or fatigue. I will run toward the giant today, and today I will live in the now!

Father, help me to walk in tough love today. In Jesus' name, amen.

May 19
CLASS ACT!

"Love never gives up. Love cares more for others than for self. Love doesn't want what it doesn't have. Love doesn't strut, doesn't have a swelled head – doesn't force itself on others – isn't always "me first" – doesn't fly off the handle – doesn't keep score of the sins of others – doesn't revel when others grovel – takes pleasure in the flowering of truth – puts up with anything – trusts God always – always looks for the best – never looks back, but keeps going to the end." (1 Corinthians 13:4-7 – The Message)

1. Today I will live in the now! I will live in the now because love – the God-kind of love – is "the more excellent way." As I walk in it today, I will exist in excellence as I experience the expression of my expectations to their full extent!

2. Today I will rise above the fray, and will refuse to become entangled with a wrestling match against "flesh and blood." I will take the high road — do the right thing — walk in the Spirit — and love will win the day and put me over the top! Love never fails, so I can be confident that it will not fail today (nor will I)!

3. Today I will overcome evil with good, and will even "heap coals of fire" on the heads of my enemies by my acts of kindness and goodwill. I will do the unexpected, as well as the undeserved, by demonstrating the mercy of Jesus through my life today. I will freely give because I have freely received.

4. Today I will be empowered by the moral authority that comes from turning the other cheek and going the extra mile. I will not stoop to the tactics of retaliation – the "beggarly elements" of the world, and the ways of the flesh – knowing that God is both my judge and my vindicator!

5. Today I will live in a large place — larger than prejudice, indifference, and the shallow, uninformed passing of judgment that accompanies small-mindedness. I will live like I am not of this world — mature, discreet, and balanced in my thought-life. I will be open to changing my mind today, if necessary.

6. Today I will be a Good Samaritan to someone in need, a mentor to one who has lost his way. The Jesus in me will pour oil and wine and mercy and grace into the wounds of the broken and battered around me and will be a very present help in time of trouble. I will owe no man anything but to love him. I will love unconditionally. I will love with no questions asked.

7. Today I will find joy and satisfaction by acting like the person I want to believe that I really am. My winning ways will make a real difference for someone, as I set a good example for them in the now. I will be an inspiration today, and today I will live in the now!

Father, help me to show some "class" today! In Jesus' name, amen.

May 20
GOD'S MASTERPIECE!

"For we are His workmanship . . . ." *(Ephesians 2:10)*

1. Today I will live in the now! I will live in the now because I know who I am in Christ, and that God has designed me to be who I am – just as I am. Because I was predestined to function in the Kingdom of God, I will direct all my efforts today toward accomplishing what is important and necessary for His purposes in the earth. He chose me in Him before the foundation of the world, so I will not disappoint Him today by living beneath my potential for greatness.

2. Today I will make my life count by doing something that will make the world a better place in which to live. I was not born by accident, so – will search for that thing that needs to be done – that thing that I am supposed to do - that person who is waiting for me to help them find their way – and I will make it happen in my own unique way.

3. Today I will remember that I have a personal destiny that only I can fulfill, so I do not need to compete with anyone but myself, compare myself to anyone else, or complain about what I do not have within me. I am complete in the One Who knew me before He formed me in the womb!

4. Today I will rest in the knowledge that my personality is God-given, acknowledging my strengths and accepting my weaknesses. As I recognize my own limitations, I will be able to rely on people who are developed in other areas and, ultimately, will be able to trust the Greater One Who is in me to share His supernatural strength.

5. Today I will rejoice in the realization that my ego does not have to be destroyed in order for me to be humble, servile, or able to demonstrate the character of Christ. As the Holy Spirit sanctifies my ego for God's purposes, I am able to bring my self-image into perspective as He liberates me to *be* myself and to *believe* in myself.

6. Today I will rise above spiritual warfare, knowing that the enemy only attempts to attack me in an effort to distract me from my unique assignment. This information will enable me to remain focused and centered today as I keep my eyes on the Water-Walker Who ever lives to make intercession for me!

7. Today I will walk in the peace that only comes from the process of becoming the person that I was created to be. My life will be fulfilled by this today, and today I will live in the now!

Father, help me to live my life like I am Your work of art today. In Jesus' name, amen.

May 21
BIG IDEAS!

*"And God gave Solomon wisdom and exceedingly great understanding,
and largeness of heart like the sand on the seashore." (I Kings 4:29)*

1. Today I will live in the now! I will live in the now by using the events of this day to help me maximize my potential in God. I will practice effective time management by refusing to waste my day by spending it in worry, fear, strife, unforgiveness, bitterness, pettiness, or human reasoning. My time is precious because I am important to God and have important things to do (". . . Redeeming the time, because the days are evil . . ." - Ephesians 5:14)!

2. Today I will move toward my goal by displaying a winning attitude. I will behave myself in a mature, positive manner, turning every negative situation around for good by my thought processes (". . . Run in such a way that you may win . . ." - 1 Corinthians 9:24), because attitude is everything!

3. Today I will maintain a manner that is proactive and upbeat, regardless of the day's events, by my ability to stay focused on the big picture. "For the things which are seen are temporary, but the things which are not seen are eternal . . ." (2 Corinthians 4:18). I know that things are not always as they appear to be, so I will expect everything to work out just fine for me today.

4. Today I will proceed toward prosperity by the process of a progressive vision. I am growing in my ability to believe for big things everyday, so I will be able to believe for more tomorrow as I see the manifestations of God's vision for my life unfold today. "Where there is no revelation [prophetic vision], the people cast off restraint . . . ." (Proverbs 29:18).

5. Today I will overcome by my own "come-back power" because I have resurrection life working in me. "Do not rejoice over me, my enemy; when I fall, I will arise; when I sit in darkness, the Lord will be a light to me" (Micah 7:8). ". . . For a righteous man may fall seven times and rise again . . . " (Proverbs 24:16). I know that being knocked down does not mean that I am out of the race or that the fight is over!

6. Today I will prevail through positive networking (". . . two are better than one . . ." - Ecclesiastes 4:9), because I know that I am affected by the company that I keep. I will not "walk in the counsel of the ungodly, nor stand in the path of sinners" (Psalm 1:1), but will connect with those who are capable of creating covenant with me. "As iron sharpens iron, so a man sharpens the countenance of his friend" (Proverbs 27:17).

7. Today I will win simply by my determination to stay on top! I am destined for greatness, so I will not settle for anything less today, and today I will live in the now!

Father, help me dream big dreams today. In Jesus' name, amen.

May 22
WALK TALL!

"Lift up your heads, O you gates! And be lifted up, you everlasting doors! And the King of Glory shall come in." (Psalm 24:7)

1. Today I will live in the now! I will live in the now because I know that I am a gate for God to use to gain access into this world, an everlasting door for His passage. Therefore, I will lift up my head today and be somebody! As a gate/door who holds the Keys of the Kingdom that is within me, my demeanor will display my desire to take dominion and my attitude will accentuate my ability to accept authority.

2. Today I will let the King of Glory come in to control my current circumstances. I will be His dwelling place today – His Garden of Eden – where He can find fellowship. Because He is with me, even during trying circumstances or tragedies, I will walk tall enough to dig out the positives, and summon the courage to take the next step and make things better.

3. Today I will assume accountability in acting as His gate and door by busying myself, turning dark situations around toward the Light. I will realize that, as a holder of the Keys, the Kingdom's advancement is my responsibility, and will act accordingly.

4. Today I will pack my schedule with positives, refusing to waste my time agonizing about yesterday — or speculating about tomorrow. Instead, I will broadcast the excellence in which I am walking today. I will speak up and declare my righteousness in Christ, portraying myself in the most self-enhancing manner possible!

5. Today I will make the decision to be happy with my life as it is, while maintaining motivation to improve it. I will keep talking myself into my future, even if I don't fully believe what I'm saying, yet. My conversation will be peppered with prophetic purpose and proactive prayer as I use my ability to affect significant change!

6. Today I will walk tall in my dreams – initiating creativity and activating the faith that will transcend impossibilities. I will walk out of smallness as I put my past in perspective and point myself toward greater purpose. My progressively victorious life will provide a speaking platform for God, as I plainly personalize the power of His gospel before the public!

7. Today I will walk tall enough to overcome obstacles, knowing that "He who overcomes shall inherit all things (Revelation 21:7)!" I will leave a legacy for the next generation by setting an example of greatness. Today I will dare to believe that I can be at my very best so that the King may enter the environment, and today I will live in the now!

Father, help me to walk tall today. In Jesus' name, amen.

May 23
ACCEPT CHANGE!

"To everything there is a season, a time for every purpose under heaven." (Ecclesiastes 3:1)

1. Today I will live in the now! I will live in the now because, even though my life is going through dramatic changes, I remember that I am still who God says I am, I still have what God says that I have, and I can still do what God says I can do! The constancy of His Word in my heart establishes me so that I can navigate the current of transition without spiritual or emotional shipwreck.

2. Today I will maintain the flexibility that only comes by enjoying the power of living in the now. I will realize the positive aspects of change by disconnecting from past regrets and by avoiding fear of the future. My focused allegiance to the now will make change more tolerable — and even enjoyable.

3. Today I will not get bogged down in the details of change, but will, rather, channel my vision to the "big picture" of my life, my purpose, my destiny, my path, my life-goals. I will not allow my perception of the day's events to become exaggerated in my mind, and will not overreact when things seem to be changing too fast. My peace will be found in working toward fulfilling my unique role in the earth.

4. Today I will appropriately manage the relationships in my life which are being affected by my changing seasons. I will build bridges and tear down walls by using God-inspired words and actions to make a positive difference in the people of the world around me, alleviating the fears of those who fear the changes in me.

5. Today I will seek balance and harmony in my life. I will think like a visionary without being impractical, using my intuitive skills without becoming cynical. I will give myself permission to enjoy a healthy self-esteem, while forbidding myself to feel superior to others in any way, loving myself without becoming self-absorbed, allowing for personal change without compromising my essence and true nature.

6. Today I will go with the flow. I will not let my dreams and goals ensnare me with unnecessary rigidity. I will keep an open mind, never say never, and remember that the God Who is in control, makes all things possible!

7. Today I will survive the effects of change by nurturing my spirit, soul, and body – moving toward optimum spiritual, mental, and physical condition in an effort to be and do my best. I will view transition as needful and healthy today. Change is good for me and it is helping me to realize all of my potential. I will remember this today when the ride gets bumpy, and today I will live in the now!

Father, help me to accept change in my life today. In Jesus' name, amen.

May 24
GET BUSY!

"For as the body without the spirit is dead, so faith without works is dead also." (James 2:26)

1. Today I will live in the now! I will live in the now because I am using every bit of my capability to seize the day, doing what my hand finds to do without questioning God's timing, because I know that **DELAY IS NOT DENIAL!** Even if I have fallen behind schedule, or have not seen God move in a certain area yet, I will catch up by doing my best in whatever situation I find myself, and God's timing will still be perfect for my life!

2. Today I will rejoice in the fact that **DISAPPOINTMENT DOESN'T HAVE TO BE DEVASTATING!** Instead of wasting time and missing valuable opportunities by nursing my emotional wounds and wallowing in self-pity, I will find the strength to be proactive and DO something to turn the tide and make myself feel better about my situation today.

3. Today I will be motivated by the knowledge that **DILIGENCE ULTIMATELY PREVAILS OVER DISCOURAGEMENT!** I stand on every promise in the book of Proverbs concerning diligence, and am energized by the rewards of hard work and of commitment to excellence. God blesses the work of my hands, so I am able to keep my hand to the plow and my eye on the prize!

4. Today I will maintain the belief that **DEVELOPING A DIFFERENT ATTITUDE IS DOABLE!** My activity today will elevate my self-esteem and self-confidence, getting me unstuck from a negative mental stronghold. I can *and will* think in a new way today!

5. Today I will hold to the thought that **DISREGARD FOR MAKING DECISIONS IS DANGEROUS!** I understand the peril of passivity, so I will be decisive today, remembering that if I don't decide my direction, someone else will decide it for me.

6. Today I will be encouraged by the revelation that **DESTINY IS DISCOVERED DAILY!** I will do what I can today and will not be anxious about what I am unable to do. I will be patiently "present" in every moment of this day that the Lord has made.

7. Today I will be empowered by the assurance that **DIVINELY DELIVERED DREAMS DON'T DIE!** The fact that the dream in me will not dissipate means that it is God-breathed, so I will not give up on it, even when it takes a different form or shape. Today I will show my faith to the world by my action — writing my own book of "Acts" as a living epistle. Today my delight is in the doing, and today I will live in the now!

   Father, help me to get busy with Your work today. In Jesus' name, amen.

May 25
SHINING LIGHT!

"Everything was created through Him; nothing – not one thing! – came into being without Him. What came into existence was Life, and the Life was Light to live by. The Life-Light blazed out of the darkness; the darkness couldn't put it out." (John 1:3-5 — The Message)

1. Today I will live in the now! I will live in the now because the light of God in me – the light that created every living thing – is living and shining through my life today. I will not be intimidated by any work of darkness that I encounter, because the light is more powerful and it perpetually prevails over the practices of the prince of darkness!

2. Today I will release light through the words of my mouth, shining it into the hearts of those who are oppressed, dispelling the destructive shadows of despair that may be darkening their day. The entrance of His Word gives light, because it is a lamp for the feet and a light for the path.

3. Today I will not be afraid of the exposure that comes from light. Because I trust the Light of the World, I can allow Him to bring out into the open what has been hidden in the shadows of my past, and let Him remove from my life what needs to be removed, as only He can. I can embrace the light because His goodness leads me to repentance.

4. Today I will bring light into the dark places of my world, my culture and my environment, speaking prophetically, and with revelation knowledge, to the principalities and powers – the spiritual wickedness (of hatred, strife, bigotry, unbelief, rebellion and religion) in high places. The mighty, hidden weapons of my warfare will dispel the darkness in the minds of the men and women who communicate with me today.

5. Today I will let MY light shine, celebrating my own uniqueness and individuality by refusing to emulate someone else's light.

6. Today I will be perceptive, intuitive and insightful in matters pertaining to my life. The light enables me to see things clearly, and from God's perspective, so that I will not find myself stumbling through the darkness of adverse circumstances. I am a seer – a visionary – enlightened by the Son of Righteousness Who is made unto me the wisdom of God. I can see where I have come *from* and I can see where I am *going*!

7. Today I will glow and be radiant with the light of God, attracting favor with God and man. Today is a supernatural day for me, and today I will live in the now!

   Father, help me to let my light shine today. In Jesus' name, amen.

May 26
GET REAL!

"For we do not have a High Priest Who is unable to understand and sympathize and have a shared feeling with our weaknesses and infirmities and liability to the assaults of temptation, but One Who has been tempted in every respect as we are, yet without sinning." (Hebrews 4:15 - AMP)

1. Today I will live in the now! I will live in the now because I am a real person experiencing the real God in the real world. I will be honest and open before God today — naked, refusing to search for emotional "fig leaves" with which to hide myself!

2. Today I will remember that faith is not denial. That, even though I believe in the supernatural intervention of God in my life, I am not out of touch with reality. I will call those things that are not as though they are, instead of calling those things that are as though they are not! And when I see the inevitable truth, I will embrace it without reservation.

3. Today I will find confidence in relating to the humanity of Jesus, recognizing that He was/is just as much Son of Man as He was/is Son of God! He felt hunger and pain in His earth-walk, and experienced every human emotion, being tempted in all points, so that He could empathize with my weaknesses!

4. Today I will part with my illusions and tell myself the truth concerning the circumstances of my life. Jesus said that the Spirit of Truth would lead me into all truth, so I will not fear what is real. I welcome truth into my life, knowing that the knowledge of it will always set me free.

5. Today I will be genuine in relating to others. I will not lie. I will not gossip. I will not give compliments that I don't really mean. I will make time to listen. I will value the people in my life enough to tell them the truth, and they will be able to confide in me without fear of breach of confidence.

6. Today I will confront any traces of sham religion that I find remaining in my life, in my own way, and will exalt my true belief system — not just the one that is the most popular, but the one that demonstrates the theology by which I really live. I will make the Word plain, and approach it with genuine faith.

7. Today I will serve others with an attitude that exemplifies works of pure gold – not those of wood, hay and stubble. My motivation to be a blessing will be above reproach and beyond question — full of integrity and good fruits. Today I will not waste my time on what is not authentic and actual, and today I will live in the now!

Father, help me to really be real today. In Jesus' name, amen.

May 27
PERFECT PEACE!

"You will keep him in perfect peace whose mind is stayed on You, because he trusts in You." (Isaiah 26:3)

1. Today I will live in the now! I will live in the now because my mind is fixed on the God of all peace, and His tranquility and serenity are flowing through me like a cool stream in a green meadow on a lazy summer afternoon. Regardless of the turmoil around me today, the secret place of the Most High will be the eye of the storm for me as I walk in the peace that passes understanding.

2. Today I will let the peace of God's Word wash away the worry that wastes my time, and keeps me from walking in a way that is worthy of me, as I welcome its wonderful wealth of wisdom into my world!

3. Today I will enjoy an undisturbed and composed existence, refusing to become unnecessarily agitated over trivial problems and inconveniences in my day. I will "let not my heart be troubled," but will choose the path of peace without frustration and aggravation, remaining calm and collected in Christ.

4. Today I will find some quiet time for myself, removing myself from the stress of striving in the flesh. The Spirit will be a dove for me as I cast all of my care upon Him, laboring to enter into His rest without pressure.

5. Today I will be a peace*maker*, not just a peace*keeper*. I will proactively insist on living in an environment of harmony — doing whatever is necessary to produce peace in my relationships — because where envy and strife are, there is confusion and every evil work (James 3:16).

6. Today I will practice the presence of God by praise, worship and meditation.

7. Today I will walk in my Kingdom rights to peace (along with righteousness and joy in the Holy Ghost), and following that peace in my spirit will guide me into the perfect will of God when I need to make decisions. Today I will settle down, inwardly, and trust God with my life completely. Today I will just chill, and today I will live in the now!

Father, help me to keep my mind stayed on You today. In Jesus' name, amen.

May 28
GRADUATION DAY!

"Blessed (happy, to be envied) is the man who is patient under trial and stands up under temptation, for when he has stood the test and been approved, he will receive [the victor's] crown of life which God has promised to those who love him." (James 1:12 - AMP)

1. Today I will live in the now! I will live in the now because I am passing the current test that I am in, and passing a test always means that promotion is coming. God has given me a strong drive toward accomplishment — I value it and strive toward it — and He is strengthening me to bring to fruition the realization of all my dreams.

2. Today I will take it up a notch, in a determined effort to go the distance — to get all that is coming to me. I will utilize every fiber of my potential, whatever it is, great or small, to stretch to the limit of my capabilities. I will concentrate on doing even the smallest job that faces me, as well as possible!

3. Today I will recognize the present movement that I am making toward the fulfillment of my destiny, encouraging myself to keep going by the inspiration created by my own progress. I can tell that I am growing, even if it is not obvious to those around me.

4. Today I will pass the daily test of covenant relationship. I will go the extra mile. I will turn the other cheek. I will forgive 70 x 7 times. I will be a servant, knowing that promotion comes from the Lord.

5. Today I will maintain a positive attitude toward competition, ultimately competing only with myself. And because I will compete primarily with myself, I am able to avoid being hostile or unfriendly to others, not having to belittle them in an attempt to build up myself.

6. Today I will show a great sense of accountability in the way I respond to testing in my daily circumstances. I do not have to cheat at the game of life; I can take the high road and do the right thing, and still be a winner.

7. Today I will wear the victor's crown — God's badge of honor for those who overcome. Through faith and patience I will inherit the promises today, and today I will live in the now!

Father, help me to pass the test today. In Jesus' name, amen.

May 29
JOYFUL NOISE!

"Make a joyful noise to the Lord all ye lands. Serve the Lord with gladness;
come before His presence with singing." (Psalm 100:1, 2 - KJV)

"On your feet now - Applaud God! Bring a gift of laughter,
sing yourself into His presence." (Psalm 100:1, 2 - The Message)

1.   Today I will live in the now! I will live in the now because I am an instrument of worship, magnifying the Lord with my life and playing songs of deliverance for all the world to hear. I will come before the presence of the Lord in proper order — with a song — and I will serve Him today with gladness.

2.   Today I will penetrate the darkness around me with a joyful sound — *a good report* — a proactive response to the doom and gloom so prevalent in the world, and even in the church! The light in me will shine in the darkness, and the darkness will not be able to overtake it. I will proclaim a gospel of dominion and conquest, overcoming the defeatist theologians who have no vision and who put a negative spin on the good news of the Kingdom.

3.   Today I will send up a shout of triumph, even in the midst of trials — *an explosion of praise* — from the depths of the jail cell, the fiery furnace, the Red Sea, or the lion's den! In all these things I am more than a conqueror through Him Who never leaves me, nor forsakes me.

4.   Today I will sing a new song — *the song of the Lord . . . a song in the night . . . a song of deliverance . . . a song of victory* — to the Lord of the Dance, who invites me to His banquet table and whose banner over me is love! I will celebrate Jesus in all I do and say today.

5.   Today I will advance to the next level of glory through the transportation provided by the high praises of God in my mouth. My list of things to thank God for is not just extensive, it is endless. But my true satisfaction comes from worshipping God, not just because of all that He has done for me, but simply because He is worthy of it. I was created for His pleasure, and it is my highest joy to give Him the praise due Him. God is good, and His mercy endures forever!

6.   Today I will laugh easily and freely, making a joyful noise that removes oppression and lightens up the atmosphere around me. My merry heart will not just medicate me — it will help to set the captives free.

7.   Today I will be a positive participant in the praises that please God, and today I will live in the now!

Father, help me to make a joyful noise today! In Jesus' name, amen.

May 30
YOU'RE SPECIAL!

"For You formed my inward parts; You covered me in my mother's womb. I will praise You, for I am fearfully and wonderfully made; Marvelous are Your works, and that my soul knows very well." (Psalm 139:13, 14)

1. Today I will live in the now! I will live in the now because there is nobody exactly like me anywhere, nor has there ever been.

2. Today I will attract uncommon favor to my life — blessed coming in and going out — as people go out of their way to do for me what is out of the ordinary.

3. Today I will do the rare and unusual, challenging social mores and conventional modes of ministry that attempt to deprive people of their individuality and special-ness. God has called me to confront every system that exalts itself against the knowledge of the God Who encourages creativity and applauds originality.

4. Today I will demonstrate my uniqueness in God by defining my own personal path of destiny, defying the limitations of my ancestral ties, if necessary. My success will openly resist logic as I allow God to do more for me than I can ask or think, in spite of the negative prophecies spoken by those closest to me.

5. Today I will have confidence in the importance of my significant contribution to the world. I am supposed to be here. I need to be here. My accomplishments are notable, and my life matters. I will keep moving toward my goals in my own way, breaking the mold if I have to. I will expect the best of myself as my relationship with my Creator supersedes the traditions of men.

6. Today I will derive a genuine and workable sense of self-worth by knowing that I am the apple of God's eye. Because of His approval, I am able to face my fears, break new ground, and open new doors for myself. I am ready to go beyond the boundaries of what everyone else expects of me, moving onward and upward, because the power of Christ working in me is bigger than religion, politics, culture, philosophy, doctrines, or anything else that could potentially be binding, limiting, discriminating, narrow, or even mediocre! Christ in me is the hope of glory!

7. Today I will do something special because *I am special*, and today I will live in the now!

   Father, thank You for creating me in Your image. In Jesus' name, amen.

May 31
HEART TRANSPLANT!

"Then I will give them a heart to know Me, that I am the Lord; and they shall be My people, and I will be their God, for they shall return to Me with their whole heart." (Jeremiah 24:7)

"But this is the covenant that I will make with the house of Israel after those days says the Lord: I will put my law in their minds, and write it on their hearts; and I will be their God, and they shall be my people. No more shall every man teach his neighbor, and every man his brother saying, 'Know the Lord', for they all shall know Me, from the least of them to the greatest of them, says the Lord. For I will forgive their iniquity, and their sin I will remember no more." (Jeremiah 31:33)

"Then I will give them one heart, and I will put a new spirit within them, and take the stony heart out of their flesh, and give them a heart of flesh, that they may walk in My statutes and keep My judgments and do them; and they shall be My people, and I will be their God." (Ezekiel 11:19, 20)

"Clearly you are an epistle of Christ, ministered by us, written not with ink, but by the Spirit of the living God, not on tablets of stone but on tablets of flesh, that is, of the heart." (2 Corinthians 3:3)

1. Today I will live in the now! I will live in the now because I have been given a new heart in Christ.

2. Today I will think like Christ as He thinks *through* me.

3. Today I will love like Christ as He loves *through* me.

4. Today I will move like Christ as He moves *through* me.

5. Today I will pray like Christ as He prays *through* me.

6. Today I will minister like Christ as He ministers *through* me.

7. Today I will triumph like Christ as He triumphs *through* me! Today I will demonstrate the authority of His heart, and today I will live in the now!

Father, thank You for giving me a new heart - help me to walk in the power of it today. In Jesus' name, amen.

June In The Now!

⋄J⋄U⋄N⋄E⋄

A month to slow down the pace a little.

School's out for the summertime and the livin' is easy . . .

"Consider the lilies, how they do not toil or spin"

Time to take a vacation from your vocation . . .

a rest from your responsibilities . . . a sabbatical from your stress . . .

and find that the Kingdom is alive and well on the beach . . .

in the park . . .

down by the creek bank . . .

or just in the beauty of your own back yard.

The Kingdom is at hand, and Jesus is ready to reveal Himself . . .

in the personal peacefulness of a porch-swing,

or in the corporate communion of a cookout.

Go out and try to count the stars in a summer sky . . .

to find, like Abraham, your midsummer night's dream.

"Then He spoke to them a parable: 'Look at the fig tree, and all the trees. When they are already budding, you see and know for yourselves that summer is now near. So also, when you see these things happening, know that the Kingdom of God is near.'" (Luke 21:29-31)

June 1
NEW ATTITUDE!

"Strip yourselves of your former nature [put off and discard your old unrenewed self] which characterized your previous manner of life and becomes corrupt through lusts and desires that spring from delusion; and be CONSTANTLY RENEWED in the spirit of your mind [having a fresh mental and spiritual ATTITUDE]; and put on the new nature (the regenerate self) created in God's image, [Godlike] in true righteousness and holiness."
(Ephesians 4:22-24 - AMP)

1. Today I will live in the now! I will live in the now because my world-view is "other-worldly," and my attitude transcends the accepted norm of the natural realm. Today I will **RENOUNCE ALL COUNTERPRODUCTIVE ALLEGIANCE TO CULTURAL TRADITION**. I am born-again — not of this cosmos (world system) — and I am not obliged to just go along with the crowd in my opinions and perspectives. Christ has given me the power and authority to go against the tide, and to swim upstream, if necessary.

2. Today I will **RE-EXAMINE ANY BELIEF THAT I HAVE IN STEREOTYPES**, dealing with each individual in my life individually, giving them the benefit of the doubt before prejudging them in any way. My attitude is predisposed to know people after the spirit, and not after the flesh, in honor of Christ's development of the New Creation Species.

3. Today I will **RE-EVALUATE MY CONCEPT OF SUCCESS**, and will attempt to define it from God's vantage point.

4. Today I will **RETHINK MY DEVOTION TO ANCESTRY**. I will praise my parents, be faithful to my family, and honor my heritage, but I will not feel bound to be limited to their level of learning or to the laws leading their lifestyle.

5. Today I will **RECONSIDER THE EXPLANATION THAT I USUALLY GIVE FOR MY LIFE CIRCUMSTANCES**. I will take full responsibility for my own life choices and their consequences, and will accept the appropriate criticism without receiving condemnation, as well as the appropriate praise without becoming puffed up with pride.

6. Today I will **REJECT ANY LATENT FEAR OF CHANGE** that may be resident in my soul, keeping an open mind, and an open heart.

7. Today I will **REINFORCE MY GRASP OF REALITY** by allowing God's Word to be the final authority in my life, and today I will live in the now!

Father, help me to function with a new attitude today. In Jesus' name, amen.

June 2
KINGDOM VIOLENCE!

"And from the days of John the Baptist until now the Kingdom of Heaven suffers violence, and the violent take it by force." (Matthew 11:12)

"And from the days of John the Baptist until the present time the Kingdom of Heaven has endured violent assault, and violent men seize it by force [as a precious prize — a share in the heavenly kingdom is sought for with most ardent zeal and intense exertion]." (Matthew 11:12 - AMP)

1. Today I will live in the now! I will live in the now because I have the heart of a warrior, and a fire in my belly that causes me to want to know the real God and to see the advancement of His Kingdom on the earth in the now!

2. Today I will embrace the spirit of Jacob who wrestled with the Lord, exercising my dominion, without being denied. I will take by force the blessings and benefits that Christ has bestowed upon all those who believe in His Kingdom, and the gates of heaven will open up for me as I make a demand on them to do so!

3. Today I will purpose in my inward parts to please God by purging passivity from my personality and passionately pursuing the Pearl of Great Price – praying for the power to present His Kingdom to all the people with whom I come in contact, in all places, and in all positions of influence!

4. Today I will be aggressive enough to seek the Kingdom FIRST in every situation – before I do anything else . . . before I react emotionally . . . before I worry about it . . . before I complain . . . before I try to figure it out in my natural mind . . . before I do anything else — my first response will be to seek the Kingdom of God and His righteousness. My top priority in every circumstance will be to discern that thing's relationship to the Reign of Christ.

5. Today I will not waste the wonderful weapons of warfare that are in my mouth by engaging in idle, inoperative speech. My words will pull down the walls of division, and pluck up the weeds of doubt, and if I tell the mountain to be relocated into the sea, it will obey me!

6. Today I will be focused in my faith, bold in my believing, and precise in my praise, to achieve my goal of glorifying God.

7. Today I will not succumb to a violent flesh-nature – the kind that creates wars and strife in the natural realm. But I will still be a formidable force to reckon with in the Spirit. Today I will fight faith's good fight, and today I will live in the now!

Father, help me to be aggressive for the advancement of Your Kingdom today.
In Jesus' name, amen.

June 3
STAND UP!

". . . and having done all, to stand. Stand therefore . . ." **(Ephesians 6:13, 14)**

1. Today I will live in the now! I will live in the now because I know how to stand in faith, and faith is now, so I am standing in the now – where God is able to prove Himself to be a very present help in trouble.

2. Today I will be confident in the midst of trials and hardships, knowing that, once the smoke clears and the dust settles, I will always be found upright and on my feet because the Lord perfects that which concerns me! I am more than just a survivor . . . *I am more than a conqueror*!

3. Today I will embrace the posture of a nonconformist who is willing to stand up and be counted, no matter the cost. I will give no place to compromise when it comes to defending what is right, but I will be outspoken, and will refuse to be intimidated by anyone who dares to defy the God in me! If He is for me, who can be against me! Greater is He Who is in me than he who is in the world! The Lord is on my side!

4. Today I will stand up and be noticed, letting my light so shine before men that they may see my good works and glorify my Father in heaven. My gift will make room for me and bring me before great people. I will not be passed by nor overlooked for receiving blessing, favor or promotion.

5. Today I will stand strong in battle, wearing the whole armor of God and effectively using the Sword of the Spirit against religious spirits and antichrist strongholds around me. I will make an open show of principalities and powers of darkness that are rebellious to Jesus, the King.

6. Today, if I fall in any way, I will get up again, for a just man falls seven times and still stands back up. I am justified in Jesus — made righteous by His blood and kept by His intercession on my behalf — so I will always continue to stand, reigning as a king in this life.

7. Today I will be ready for anything, because I am not lying down, but I am *up* and *ready* and *prepared*. When opportunity knocks today, I will be standing at the door. I take my stand in Christ today, and today I will live in the now!

Father, help me to keep standing today. In Jesus name, amen.

June 4
EXCELLENCE NOW!

"Instead of bronze I will bring gold, instead of iron I will bring silver, instead of wood, bronze, and instead of stones, iron." (Isaiah 60:17)

1. Today I will live in the now! I will live in the now because I understand that excellence is an attitude – a state of mind that gradually becomes a lifestyle, and I am developing that lifestyle daily. I know that excellence exists and that successful people live it, so I will not be destroyed by a lack of knowledge in this area. I have seen it in others, and now I will see it work for me!

2. Today I will not be lazy and just assume that excellence will be a natural development in my life, but I will work hard to maintain a high standard for myself and will walk in the required diligence to achieve my goals.

3. Today I will not give in to feelings of unworthiness that would prevent me from expecting the best of myself. I will believe that I deserve to live an excellent life, and will retrain my mind away from lies that I have believed that have damaged my self-esteem.

4. Today I will not be satisfied with "good" or "good enough." God has called me to greatness in my area, so I will be faithful to hone my skills for the development of excellence, and I will do it to be a blessing to the Kingdom.

5. Today I will rid myself of any fear of success that I may still have, realizing that the continued pursuit of excellence ultimately brings undeniable success – and with that success comes added responsibility. But I am preparing myself to take on more, enlarging my capacity for faith and productivity, and, when opportunity knocks, I'll be standing at the door, ready to open it!

6. Today I will not feel like I am an imposter, not living my real, deserved life. I am blessed because God is good, and I am successful because He has allowed me to work His system in the earth for my own benefit, as well as for His. I am not afraid that success will tell on me, revealing that I can't make the grade. On the contrary, with every level of promotion, I will easily rise to the occasion.

7. Today I will see the big picture of my success, increasing in excellence incrementally, patiently progressing and possessing the higher standard of living that I deserve. Today I will give it all I've got, and today I will live in the now!

Father, help me to live a life of excellence today. In Jesus' name, amen.

June 5
I'M EXPECTING!

"Why are you cast down, O my inner self? And why should you moan over me and be disquieted within me? Hope in God and wait EXPECTANTLY for Him, for I shall yet praise Him, Who is the help of my countenance, and my God." (Psalm 42:11 – AMP)

1. Today I will live in the now! I will live in the now because I have an attitude of expectancy that causes me to keep looking forward, no matter how many times I have experienced disappointment. I believe in the probable occurrence or appearance of something good today, because something good is due, and I have an eager anticipation for things to look up, get better, and turn out for the best!

2. Today I will create an atmosphere of expectancy by my words of life and faith, preparing to attract success to myself by my irresistible optimism. I will cultivate this attitude by using my life experiences to teach me as I practice positive responses to personal problems.

3. Today I will not walk in presumption, setting myself up for more disappointment. I will expect the best, prepare for the worst if necessary, and always look at my situation from God's perspective. No matter how things look right now, I will always have a happy ending, eventually.

4. Today I will get in touch with my heart's true desire, releasing my faith for what I really can believe for. Faith comes by hearing a RHEMA word, so I will meditate, listen to the still, small voice, be original in my praying, and ultimately be honest with myself about what I really want.

5. Today I will allow my sense of expectancy to create a feeling of enthusiasm for living. I will let God inspire me, as only He can do, and will not be afraid to be intensely excited about my future. I will be eager to live out this day, and I will do it with a zeal and a fervor that will wake up my potential and cause me to go to the next level.

6. Today I will remember that I can only have significant success with something that is an obsession, so I will give 110% to those things that are conducive to the development of my destiny, and will withdraw from those things that I don't really have a passion for. I will follow my bliss into my blessing!

7. Today I will realize that enthusiasm is an emotion, optimism is an attitude, but faith is a substance – and that I have all three things working on my behalf. Today I say, "It's all good!" and today I will live in the now!

Father, thank You for always giving me something to look forward to.
In Jesus' name, amen.

June 6
BE CREATIVE!

"God spoke: 'Let us make human beings in our image, make them reflecting our nature so they can be responsible for the fish in the sea, the birds in the air, the cattle, and yes, Earth itself, and every animal that moves on the face of Earth.' God created human beings; He created them godlike, reflecting God's nature. He created them male and female. God blessed them: 'Prosper! Reproduce! FIll Earth! Take Charge! Be responsible for fish in the sea and birds in the air, for every living thing that moves on the face of Earth.'" (Genesis 1:26-28 – The Message)

1. Today I will live in the now! I will live in the now because I have God-given creative ability – the spark of the Divine – and my every act of creativity is a manifestation of the nature of God. I am capable because I am cognitive of the Creator's commitment to involving me in His cause of continuing the creative process with co-laborers!

2. Today I will be responsive to the voice of God, and will be intuitive to spiritual things – grasping the abstract, so that I can master the material world.

3. Today I will let myself become emancipated from the world-system that discourages creativity and originality. I will be aware of possibilities that are not obvious to the natural eye, and will walk "circumspectly" (Ephesians 5:15), seeing the cycles of my life correctly and how everything in creativity comes full circle (I will become as a little child again – creative, imaginative, able to see the invisible things).

4. Today I will become transcendent in my thought life, rising above negative thoughts, images and memories, surpassing the sorrow and sadness of past things and moving on to better thoughts . . . to hope against hope . . . to be creative in the solving of my problems.

5. Today I will be confident enough to communicate my concepts to others.

6. Today I will avoid being surrounded by those who diminish my creativity — those who engage in negative speech, complaining, gossiping, doubting — those who are skeptical and cynical — those who are unimaginative and closed to new ideas. Instead, I will seek out those who have vision — those who think out of the box — those who really know God.

7. Today I will allow creative thoughts to flow and evolve into things that will make my life better, make the world a better place, advance the Kingdom of God, and give Him glory. I will meditate like my Maker today, and today I will live in the now!

Father, help me to think like You today. In Jesus' name, amen.

June 7
ROYAL PRIESTHOOD!

"But you are a chosen generation, a royal priesthood,
a holy nation, His own special people,
that you may proclaim the praises of Him Who called you out of darkness
into His marvelous light." (1 Peter 2:9)

1. Today I will live in the now! I will live in the now because I have been called out of darkness, spiritually, emotionally and intellectually – I have the light of Christ! Moreover, I have been called out for a purpose – to live a life that shows forth the praises of God.

2. Today I will walk in the confidence that comes from knowing who I am in Christ and recognizing my royal roots. He has made me a king and a priest, so my life is special and important, and what I do and say matters.

3. Today I will not let myself be defined by my nationality, ethnicity, ancestry, or the color of my skin. I am a part of the new creation species . . . born of God . . . otherworldly . . . supernatural . . . original. I am a citizen of the holy nation, the Kingdom of God, and my life is not dominated by the present world system. I am who God says that I am.

4. Today I will rejoice that I have been chosen. I will not take it lightly, and I will listen for my instructions from the Captain of my Salvation, always being careful to carry out His orders in the way that He desires me to.

5. Today I will shine the light on someone who sits in darkness, patiently illuminating them and broadening their horizons, yet remembering that Jesus said that people love darkness more than they love the light. But I will find courage in the assurance that, when the light shines in darkness, the darkness cannot overtake it, so I will continue to communicate the truth!

6. Today I will let His praise continually be in my mouth, for this is my highest purpose; I was created for His pleasure.

7. Today I will act, speak, move, dress, walk and live like the royalty that I am, making no apologies for my self-awareness. I am special because God made me that way, and by faith I will reproduce after my own kind. Today I will be an inspiration and a light-bearer, and today I will live in the now!

PRAISE THE LORD!

June 8
HAND-DELIVERED!

"God reached out, touched my mouth, and said, 'Look! I've just put my words in your mouth – HAND-DELIVERED! See what I've done? I've given you a job to do among nations and governments – a red-letter day! Your job is to pull up and tear down, take apart and demolish, and then start over, building and planting.'" (Jeremiah 1:10 – The Message)

1. Today I will live in the now! I will live in the now because God has given me something to do that no one can do but me – and God has given me something to say that no one can say but me. Today I will find my voice, and will say the words that He has put in my mouth, without intimidation.

2. Today I will speak to negative strongholds in my community and will do my part to pull them down. Religion must fall. Racism must fall. Rebellion must fall. Every antichrist must be dethroned. The antichrist spirit must be exposed. The kingdoms of this world must become the Kingdoms of our God, and of His Christ! And God's hand-delivered word in my mouth will help to bring these things to pass.

3. Today I will nourish any prophetic tendencies that I may have, encouraging myself in the areas of revelation. I can hear from God, and I can communicate His message.

4. Today I will prophesy to the wind, allowing for a season of change because change is good and necessary. I will not be afraid to take a risk, even in the area of revelation knowledge. I will prophesy confidently, according to the proportion of my faith!

5. Today I will be open to dreams and visions from God, allowing Him to speak directly to my spirit in ways that supersede my intellectual capacity. I will let Him do more than I ask or think!

6. Today I will be submitted to spiritual authority, so that I can have confirmation that I am flowing correctly. I will know the voice of the Good Shepherd, but I will also know the voice of a local shepherd, remembering that in the mouth of two or three witnesses every word is established.

7. Today I will use my influence for positive purposes, and God will take me into a wider sphere of influence as I trust and obey Him. Today is a red-letter day, and today I will live in the now!

Father, give me the courage to proclaim Your Word today. In Jesus' name, amen.

June 9
SOMETHING'S COMING!

"And then God answered, 'Write this. Write what you see. Write it out in big block letters so that it can be read on the run. This vision-message is a witness pointing to what's coming – it can hardly wait! And it doesn't lie. If it seems slow in coming, wait. It's on the way. It will come right on time.'" (Habakkuk 2:2, 3 – The Message)

1. Today I will live in the now! I will live in the now because I have a vision, and a vision from God doesn't lie. It lets me know that something good is on the way, and that I must make room for it in my life.

2. Today I will have faith in my goals and in my ability to reach them. I will write a petition, which will give my faith a focal point, and I will find a Word on which to stand to make that petition come to pass.

3. Today I will have a positive outlook, anticipating the arrival of a long-awaited answer to a prayer. I will not be weary in well doing, knowing that I will reap in due season if I do not faint.

4. Today I will run with the vision, because the vision is alive and growing – mobile and evolving – and running to keep up with it will be good and healthy for me. I will abandon my comfort zone and stretch toward the bigger and better breakthrough that is bound to become mine!

5. Today I will be appreciative of the little things that are a blessing to my life as I increase my capacity for accepting even greater outpourings of God's love and affection for me. God wants me to be blessed even more than I want to be blessed, and He has written a vision on my heart to make sure that I receive all that He has in store for me!

6. Today I will not be moved when it looks like I am having a setback. All things are working together for my good, and God's timing will ultimately be perfect – so I will walk in the faith and patience that enables me to obtain the promises! I will not become discouraged, because I will keep my eyes on the big picture.

7. Today I will keep hope alive by believing for the impossible, seeing the invisible, and feeling the intangible. I will speak of the non-existent things as though they already existed, because the vision in my mind is increasing with the faith in my heart. Something's coming, and it could be here any minute — I will be ready for it *today*, and today I will live in the now!

Father, write Your vision on my heart today. In Jesus' name, amen.

June 10
GOING THROUGH!

"By faith Noah, being divinely warned of things not yet seen, MOVED WITH FEAR, prepared an ark for the saving of his household, by which he condemned the world and became an heir of righteousness which is according to faith." (Hebrews 11:7)

1. Today I will live in the now! I will live in the now because I am going through my present difficulties bravely and I will safely make it to the other side of these circumstances, regardless of how I feel right now. God has not given me a spirit of fear, but even if I am afraid, I will make the fear work for me as Noah did. I will **FEEL THE FEAR AND GO THROUGH ANYWAY!**

2. Today I will **FOCUS ON THE FACT THAT I AM STRONGER THAN MY FEARS, AND MORE COMPETENT THAN MY WORRIES!** Most of my fears are irrational, and the Mind of Christ keeps me centered enough to know what to fear, and what not to fear.

3. Today I will **FREE MY MIND OF MY MOST SELF-DEFEATING BELIEF!**

4. Today I will **FIND MY COMFORT IN THE WORDS OF OTHER FAITH-FILLED BELIEVERS!**

    "Therefore comfort each other and edify one another, just as also you are doing."
    (1 Thessalonians 5:11)

5. Today I will **FIND MY COMFORT IN THE HOLY SPIRIT!**

    "But the Helper (Comforter), the Holy Sprit, whom the Father will send in My Name, He will teach you all things, and bring to your remembrance all things that I said to you." (John 14:26)

6. Today I will **FIND MY COMFORT IN HIS ROD** (for protection) **AND STAFF** (for guidance)!

    "Yea, though I WALK THROUGH the valley of the shadow of death, I will fear no evil; For You are with me; Your rod and your staff they comfort me." (Psalm 23:4)

7. Today I will **FIND MY COMFORT IN THE SECRET PLACE OF THE MOST HIGH!** There is a secret place in God that is uniquely for me – my rhema word – today I will find it, and today I will live in the now!

    "He who dwells in the secret place of the Most High shall abide under the shadow of the Almighty." (Psalm 91:1)

    Father, help me to go through today! In Jesus' name, amen.

June 11
ALL CONFIDENCE!

"Then Paul dwelt two whole years in his own rented house, and received all who came to him, preaching the Kingdom of God and teaching the things which concern the Lord Jesus Christ with ALL CONFIDENCE, no one forbidding him." (Acts 28:30, 31)

1. Today I will live in the now! I will live in the now because I am walking in the confidence that only comes by walking in my calling. Being in the flow of the will of God for my life gives me the **C**ourage to **O**ptimistically be a **N**onconformist, **F**inding my **I**ndividuality and **D**irection in **E**xpressing myself, having the **N**erve to share my **C**onvictions **E**ffectively! *That's confidence!*

2. Today I will find confidence in the fact that my weaknesses actually allow me to be strong in Christ, for His strength is made perfect in my weakness. I will be energized by the (natural) absurdity of this fact that — when I am weak, I am *strong*!

3. Today I will find confidence in the knowledge that I am strong in the Lord and in the power of His might, strengthened with might by His Spirit in the inner man. I will not have to pray for strength – I will simply *be strong* – for this is a commandment in scripture (Ephesians 6:10)!

4. Today I will find confidence in facing my infirmities (weaknesses), and "glorying" in them as Paul gloried in his. As I do this, I gain the dominion over these things.

5. Today I will put my trust in God and have faith in His ability to deliver me. This feeling of assurance causes me to be secure in myself, with a virtual absence of fear in my heart. In God I am courageous and brave, boldly daring to believe His Word, even when things around me look hopeless in the natural realm.

6. Today I will be audacious in my faith, deriving confidence from doing the thing that I am called to do . . . finding my message . . . finding my place of fulfillment . . . finding my audience. I will preach with all confidence, no one forbidding me!

7. Today I will have the confidence to be patient and endure hardships and trials with great fortitude. Walking in this confidence forces things in my life to come into divine order and helps to reveal my destiny. I will be as bold and courageous as a lion today, and today I will live in the now!

Father, help me walk in godly confidence today. In Jesus' name, amen.

June 12
ARISE, SHINE!

"Arise [from the depression and prostration in which circumstances have kept you — rise to new life]! Shine (be radiant with the glory of the Lord); for your light is come, and the glory of the Lord is risen upon you!" (Isaiah 60:1 – AMP)

1. Today I will live in the now! I will live in the now because the light of God is shining on me, in me and through me, so I have an incentive to arise – to release resurrection life from my inner man – to rise from the pit of gloom and make my way to the palace of glory! My entire life is illuminated by the excellence of the absolute and perfect light of God . . . the light that is pure and complete in quality . . . not limited by restrictions or exceptions . . . unconditionally qualified in extent or degree . . . total and whole! This light is mine, and I will not hide it under a bushel of doubt or under a bed of depression.

2. Today I will rise to meet the day with the confidence that comes from knowing that God has smiled on me. My path is paved with His favor, so I have every reason to get up and fearlessly face the challenges that lie ahead of me.

3. Today I will demonstrate the dominion of the glory of God, the glory which Isaiah prophesied that all flesh would see together (Isaiah 40:5). I will go to where the people (the flesh) are, and show them the real Jesus — the real Light of the World!

4. Today I will protect the light in me, and will not allow anyone to put it out. I will give no person or spirit or demon or thing the right to dim my light in any way. My light is important, and it must stay visible on a lamp stand so that it can eventually become a city set on a hill that cannot be hidden.

5. Today I will expand my vision as the light of revelation increases in my heart and mind. God is *showing* me more, so that I can *receive* more!

6. Today I will make a decision to rise above anything that tries to keep me down. Nothing will prevent me from arising and shining: no voice from the past, no religious false doctrine, no accusation, no misunderstanding. My decision to arise will create events in my life that will promote me and illuminate me even more.

7. Today I will see things clearly by the light from heaven that shines around me. My mental images, ideas and emotions will be under the supervision and authority of the Light, and darkness will have no control over me or influence in my life. Today I will arise and shine, and today I will live in the now!

Father, help me shine for You today. In Jesus' name, amen.

June 13
FUTURE NOW!

"That which is now, already has been; and that which is to be, already has been; and God seeks out that which has passed by so that history repeats itself." (Ecclesiastes 3:15)

1. Today I will live in the now! I will live in the now because God is the I AM, and He has created me to be an eternal being who lives and moves in the now.

2. Today I will celebrate my triumph over time. It is not too late to receive the miracle that I need, and God is showing me how to redeem my time as He restores to me the years that have been eaten away from my life! My personal "Lazarus" can still be raised from the dead, four days after the funeral!

3. Today I will declare the end from the beginning as I forget yesterday and move into my future. I will not allow the distraction of looking at the past cause me to miss enjoying the adventure of NOW!

4. Today I will free myself from the stress of time limitations and restraints, and I will escape the trap of being dominated by deadlines: "My eyes are ever toward the Lord, for He shall pluck my feet out of the net" (Psalm 25:15).

5. Today I will flow spontaneously in the river of eternity that transcends the time-bound world-system. Going with the flow will take me to where I need to be as I am led by the timeless Holy Spirit.

6. Today I will explore the possibilities presented to me by believing that I receive WHEN I PRAY — not waiting to believe *when I see* the manifestation later. Walking in faith is all about living in the now, and I live my life by my faith!

7. Today I will harmonize my past, present and future into the wholeness of the eternal life provided for me by the I AM, seeing the picture of my life start to take shape and make sense. Today I will gain a new appreciation for my eternal life, and today I will live in the now!

Father, I thank You that the future is now! In Jesus' name, amen.

June 14
BUILT UP!

"Let each one of us make it a practice to please (make happy) his neighbor for his good and for his true welfare, to edify him [to strengthen him and build him up spiritually]." (Romans 15:2 – AMP)

1. Today I will live in the now! I will live in the now because I am a builder in the Kingdom; one who encourages and enlightens others so as to edify them intellectually, morally or spiritually. Edification in the church takes priority over rules and regulations ("let all things be done unto edifying . . . "), so I will be about the building up of the church — a Christ Body-Builder!

2. Today I will surround myself with others who are builders: those who can edify me and not tear me down; those who do not expect me to join them in tearing down others; those who have a blueprint for their own lives and a vision to build, even after having counted the cost of construction.

3. Today I will refuse to waste my time by involving myself with the cancers of bitterness, unforgiveness and pettiness, and anything else that is destructive and detrimental to my walking in abundant life.

4. Today I will only speak positively of myself and of others, and, if there is nothing positive to say about someone else, I will remain silent! My faith-filled words of encouragement will be the building blocks for the edification of the part of Christ's Body with which I have influence – not empty compliments, but powerful, prophetic words that point to the fulfillment of potential.

5. Today I will reinforce my belief in the possibility of rebuilding after a set-back, and, if my world gets knocked down today, I will not procrastinate when it comes to getting started on building an even better one in its place.

6. Today I will make peace with the fact that I will always be in a building program, so I cannot allow myself to become weary in well doing. I will make the decision to run and not be weary – to walk and not faint!

7. Today I will build myself up on my most holy faith by praying in the Spirit (Jude 20), cooperating with Jesus, the Master-Builder and Divine Architect, Who is the Author and Finisher of my faith. Today is a good day for building, and today I will live in the now!

Father, help me to build Your Kingdom in the earth today. In Jesus' name, amen.

June 15
ISAIAH'S PATTERN!

1. STAY PREPARED FOR THE NEW THING!

"Do not [earnestly] remember the former things; neither consider the things of old. Behold, I am doing a new thing. Now it shall spring forth; do you not perceive it and will you not give heed to it? I will even make a way in the wilderness and rivers in the desert." (Isaiah 43:18, 19 – AMP)

2. STATE YOUR CASE!

"Put Me in remembrance [remind Me of your merits]; let us plead and argue together. Set forth your case, that you may be justified (proved right)." (Isaiah 43:26 – AMP)

3. STAND ON THE WORD! (Isaiah 44:21-28*)

". . . Who confirms the word of His servant, and performs the counsel of His messengers . . ." (v. 26)

4. STAKE YOUR CLAIM!

"Thus says the Lord, the Holy One of Israel, and his Maker: 'Ask Me of things to come concerning My sons; and concerning the work of My hands, you command me.'" (Isaiah 45:11)

5. STRETCH YOUR VISION!

"Declaring the end from the beginning, and from ancient times things that are not yet done, saying, 'My counsel shall stand, and I will do all my pleasure.'" (Isaiah 46:10)

6. STRENGTHEN YOUR ABILITY TO PROFIT!

"Thus says the Lord, your Redeemer, the Holy One of Israel: 'I am the Lord your God, Who teaches you to profit, Who leads you by the way you should go.'" (Isaiah 48:17)

7. STAY PREPARED FOR THE GRAND FINALE! (Isaiah 49:19-26)

Today I will live in the now! I will live in the now because I will follow this pattern laid out by the Prophet Isaiah, and it will bring me into the realm of success in God. Today God's Word will be a lamp to my feet and a light to my path. I will walk in the fullness of it today, and today I will live in the now!

Father, help me to walk in Your Word today. In Jesus' name, amen.

June 16
GOOD FIGHT!

"Fight the good fight of faith, lay hold on eternal life, to which you were also called and have confessed the good confession in the presence of many witnesses." (1 Timothy 6:12)

1. Today I will live in the now! I will live in the now because I am a fighter, and today is a good day for a good fight!

2. Today I will fight for my Kingdom rights to righteousness, peace, and joy in the Holy Ghost, because the Kingdom suffers violence and the violent take it by force!

3. Today I will lay hold of the eternal life to which I have been summoned, making my awareness of the eternal (the "now") work for me.

4. Today I will confess a good confession in the presence of many witnesses, using the verbal weapons of warfare with which I have been equipped to wage war in the spiritual world – to wrestle with wickedness in high places.

5. Today I will not allow myself to be drawn into a battle with flesh and blood. I will keep my spiritual eyes and ears open so that I can stay aware of who the real enemy is.

6. Today I will remember that my waist is girded with the belt of truth, so I can fight religious lies and false doctrines effectively. I will use the breastplate of righteousness to prevail over any illusions of condemnation that I retain in my mind, and will walk the road of authentic ministry to the tormented by wearing the shoes of the gospel of peace. For my personal well-being, my shield of faith will quench any fiery darts aimed at me from hell - long before they are able to bring any destruction to my life, and the sword of the Spirit will enable me to be a champion today, because God's Word will not return to Him empty or void!

7. Today I will call my spiritual fight good (whatever it may be today, even before I engage in it, because I have what I say, and I say that I am a winner. Today I will be dangerous to demonic powers, and today I will live in the now!

Father, help me to fight the good fight of faith today. In Jesus' name, amen.

June 17
REAL WORLD!

"This is how much God loved the world: He gave His Son, His one and only Son. And this is why: so that no one need be destroyed; by believing in Him, anyone can have a whole and lasting life. God didn't go to all the trouble of sending His Son merely to point an accusing finger, telling the world how bad it was. He came to help, to put the world right again." (John 3:16, 17 – The Message)

1. Today I will live in the now! I will live in the now because I know the real God, revealed through the real Jesus Christ, and I know that there is a very real world out there, full of real people with very real problems who really need Him! They don't need the phoniness and irrelevance of dead religion; they need a real Jesus, and I will do what I can today to make Him real to my world.

2. Today I will not let myself become out of touch with the genuine issues that the people around me are dealing with, but I will be empathetic, touched with the feeling of their weaknesses as Jesus is.

3. Today I will remember that the field is the world, and I will volunteer once again to be a laborer in the ripe harvest of the earth.

4. Today I will be understanding and non-judgmental in my relationships, accepting people and receiving them just as they are.

5. Today I will be a good listener, and a safe place for the wounded to find help.

6. Today I will intercede for the lost, the hurting, the rejected, the disenfranchised and the broken. I will love with the agape of God and will fulfill my duties as an ambassador of Christ to my community.

7. Today I will speak the word of reconciliation in an effort to bring many sons to glory. I will not do or say anything that would make anyone feel alienated from God. I will be sensitive to the leading of the Holy Spirit in this area today, and today I will live in the now!

Father, love Your world through me today. In Jesus' name, amen.

June 18
SUFFICIENT GRACE!

"And He said to me, 'My grace is sufficient for you,
for My strength is made perfect in weakness . . . .'" (2 Corinthians 12:9)

1. Today I will live in the now! I will live in the now because I am living in the grace of God, and His grace is sufficient for the equipping that I need today to overcome any thorn in the flesh that I may encounter.

2. Today I will not be afraid of my weaknesses, for when I am weak, then I am strong, because His strength is made to be seen perfect in, and through, the weaknesses of my imperfections.

3. Today I will supernaturally carry on, despite hardships, able to bear with tolerance the things that would destroy those who do not walk in this grace. Through Christ I will exhibit a quality today that shows my inner power to withstand stress and to persevere with a continued existence of courage under fire.

4. Today I will count it all joy when I find myself enveloped in, or encounter trials of any sort, that I may be perfect and entire (mature and complete), wanting for nothing and abundantly supplied. I will stand the test in my time of tribulation, and as my faith is put on the defense, it will pass the cross-examination with flying colors.

5. Today I will endure hardness as a good soldier, thriving in the midst of afflictions and keeping my head about me in times of persecution.

6. Today I will respond appropriately to the chastisement (correction, instruction) of my heavenly Father, knowing that, even though Jesus has borne my punishment, I still need to be corrected!

7. Today I will boldly take up my own cross and follow Jesus Who, though He was a son, learned obedience through the things that He suffered. Today I will learn what I need to learn, and today I will live in the now!

Father, let Your grace work in me today. In Jesus' name, amen.

June 19
YOKE-BREAKER!

". . . and the yoke will be destroyed because of the ANOINTING . . . ." (Isaiah 10:27)

"But you have been anointed by [you hold a sacred appointment from, you have been given an unction from] the Holy One, and you all know [the Truth] or you know all things." (1 John 2:20 – AMP)

"But as for you, the anointing (the sacred appointment, the unction) which you received from Him abides [permanently] in you; [so] then you have no need that anyone should instruct you. But just as His anointing teaches you concerning everything and is true and is no falsehood, so you must abide in (live in, never depart from) Him [being rooted in Him, knit to Him] just as [His anointing] has taught you [to do]." (I John 2:27 – AMP)

1. Today I will live in the now! I will live in the now because I have an anointing that abides in me, teaches me everything that I need to know, and breaks every yoke of bondage in my life.

2. Today the anointing will lead me into new areas of revelation knowledge, enabling me to explore and comprehend the width and length and depth and height of the love and character of God.

3. Today the anointing will lead me into new areas of information, natural knowledge, and wisdom that will give me an edge and will promote me to the front of the line. The earth is filled with the knowledge of the glory of the Lord, and the anointing will help me make contact with everything that I need to know.

4. Today the Spirit of the Lord God is upon me because He has anointed me to preach good tidings to the poor and to recover sight to the blind. God has anointed me in Christ to go about doing good and to heal all those who are oppressed of the devil.

5. Today my steps will be directed by God as I go wherever the flow of the anointing takes me. He will not allow the foot of the righteous to slip.

6. Today I will find unprecedented liberty in my life through the breaking of the yoke, and He whom the Son sets free is free indeed!

7. Today I will have a fresh realization of and reawakening to the anointing in my life. My anointing is Christ's anointing because I am His joint-heir and co-laborer and, therefore, I can do all things through Him! Today I will make good use of our joint-unction, and today I will live in the now!

Father, help me to walk in my anointing today. In Jesus' name, amen.

June 20
THREEFOLD CORD!

"Two are better than one, because they have a good [more satisfying] reward for their labor; for if they fall, the one will lift up his fellow. But woe to him who is alone when he falls and has not another to lift him up! Again, if two lie together, then they have warmth; but how can one be warm alone? And though a man might prevail against him who is alone, two will withstand him. A threefold cord is not easily broken." (Ecclesiastes 4:9-12 – AMP)

1. Today I will live in the now! I will live in the now because I have invested in covenant relationships. I have been there for others when they have needed me, and they are there for me when I need them.

2. Today I will reach out to help someone unselfishly and with no hidden agenda or ulterior motive, because he who would have friends must show himself friendly.

3. Today I will be a support and encouragement for one who is disconnected and alone.

4. Today I will celebrate the power of agreement in prayer, for when any two or more agree as touching anything, it shall be done.

5. Today I will guard myself against strife and division with others, so that my cord is not broken. I will forgive freely, and will not let the sun go down on my wrath.

6. Today I will welcome the third party of the threefold cord, the Holy Spirit, into all of my lateral relationships. As we agree with one another, He agrees with us (". . . for it seemed good to the Holy Ghost, and to us . . ." - Acts 15:28), and as we help each other, He helps us to be helpful.

7. Today I will be open to forming new relationships, for there is safety in numbers and in the multitude of counsel. I will be strengthened by the people in my life who already love and care for me today, and today I will live in the now!

Father, help me to form a successful threefold cord with You and someone else today. In Jesus' name, amen.

June 21
BE STILL!

"Be still and know that I am God; I will be exalted among the nations, I will be exalted in the earth!" (Psalm 46:10)

1. Today I will live in the now! I will live in the now because I recognize the importance today of just being still before God and not making any unnecessary movement. I will not allow the activity around me to alienate me from the Almighty's shadow.

2. Today I will wait.

3. Today I will be quiet.

4. Today I will not make any petition.

5. Today I will not spend time in intercession.

6. Today I will do no warfare.

7. Today I will just be . . . and I will just know . . . and today I will live in the now!

BE EXALTED AMONG THE NATIONS . . . BE EXALTED IN THE EARTH!

June 22
BREAK OUT!

"Out of my distress I called upon the Lord; the Lord answered me, and set me free and in a large place. The Lord is on my side; I will not fear. What can man do to me? The Lord is on my side and takes my part, He is among those who help me; therefore shall I see my desire established upon those who hate me. It is better to trust and take refuge in the Lord than to put confidence in man. It is better to trust and take refuge in the Lord than to put confidence in princes." (Psalm 118:5-9 - AMP)

1. Today I will live in the now! I will live in the now because God has set me in a large place where people cannot limit my progress or diminish my gifts and talents; a place where they cannot dilute the force of my life, nor prohibit me from realizing all of my possibilities. No one can confine me to their vision of me, or make me be something that I am not. I will not let anyone put me in a box by their words, opinions, or beliefs about me. I am who God says I am, and that's all that matters!

2. Today I will bow my knees to Jesus and let Him tell me what to do in the authority of the Father, by the power of the Holy Sprit, as He commanded: "Don't set people up as experts over your life, letting them tell you what to do. Save that authority for God; let Him tell you what to do . . ." (Matthew 23:9 – The Message).

3. Today I will let no one define my personality nor determine my potential. They cannot deter my progress, delay my promotion, or defeat my purpose. I am God's workmanship — He is the potter and I am the clay!

4. Today I will let no one choose the right path for me. I will be teachable, submitted to spiritual authority, and will wait for the confirmation of two or three witnesses; but, ultimately, I must choose for myself the way that I should go. I will be solely responsible for my own decisions.

5. Today I will get a bigger picture in my head of who I am and what I am supposed to do, than what I have settled for up to this point.

6. Today I will break out of the mold that has been set for me (or that I have set for myself), not so that I can be seen as a rebellious maverick, but so that I can be the individual that God created in His own image, submitted to His unique will for my life.

7. Today I will just generally live a bigger life, and today I will live in the now!

Father, let Your will be done in me, on earth as it is in heaven today. In Jesus' name, amen.

June 23
TOTAL RESTORATION!

"Repent therefore . . . so that times of refreshing may come from the presence of the Lord, and that He may send Jesus Christ, who was preached to you before, whom heaven must receive until the times of RESTORATION OF ALL THINGS, which God has spoken by the mouth of all His holy prophets since the world began." (Acts 3:19-21)

1. Today I will live in the now! I will live in the now because I recognize my own, personal season of restoration and how it relates to the big picture of the returning of the earth to God's original purposes for it. This Kingdom vision gives me a **REASON TO BELIEVE IN THE IMPOSSIBLE**. If I believe in the possibility of the "restoration of all things," then I must also believe in the restoration of all things in my own life!

2. Today I will exercise my **RIGHT TO EXPECT A SOLUTION TO MY PROBLEMS**. God is restoring me by working all things together for my good, and there are Kingdom Keys available to me today that will unlock mysteries and help me to bring solutions to my world.

3. Today I will accept my **REQUIREMENT TO KEEP GETTING UP**. No matter how many times I fall or miss the mark, I must continue to arise, because God cannot restore me if I refuse to cooperate with Him. He will forgive and redirect me, but I must dust myself off, take up my own bed and walk, and rise to an even higher level by my own faith!

4. Today I will acknowledge the **REALITY OF LIFE AND DEATH**. The ability to choose between these two is an enormous part of the restoration process, so today I will make choices that I can live with, opting for life in every situation.

5. Today I will embrace the vision of having a **REPUTATION FOR WINNING**. God is restoring me to success so that my life can be a testimonial to His excellent greatness!

6. Today I will accept the **RESPONSIBILITY FOR PREACHING THE GOOD NEWS**. God is restoring me so that I can bring restoration to others, especially those who have had similar experiences to mine. I will see my sphere of influence as my own, personal pulpit, and will salt the earth where I live.

7. Today I will find peace in the belief that I have a **RESIDENCE IN HEAVEN**. My eternal life resides in the heavenly realm, and even now I am seated with Him in heavenly places. Today I will loose on earth what is loosed in heaven, and today I will live in the now!

Father, help me to be restored as I bring restoration to the earth. In Jesus' name, amen.

June 24
BRIGHT FUTURE!

"Give your entire attention to what God is doing right now, and don't get worked up about what may or may not happen tomorrow. God will help you deal with whatever hard things come up when the times comes." (Matthew 6:34 – The Message)

1. Today I will live in the now! I will live in the now because my attention is on the Kingdom, and the Kingdom is always in the now.

2. Today I will not worry about what's coming up, because the things that I am dreading may not even happen, and the unknown things are impossible to prepare for. But, regardless of what tomorrow brings, I will face it with the confident assurance that the Lord perfects all that concerns me.

3. Today I will run toward the giants that intimidate me, the way David ran toward Goliath. I will not give place to cowardice, but will be aggressive enough to intimidate the thing that is trying to intimidate me!

4. Today I will have no fear of the unknown, but will anticipate the adventure with appreciation for the attitude of authority that I have attained through accepting the Word of God as an absolute anchor for the soul!

5. Today I will start making plans to go to a higher level, preparing myself for new responsibilities.

6. Today I will believe that my latter is going to be greater than my former as I go from glory to glory.

7. Today I will enjoy the day, believing that tomorrow will be even better. I will protect my dreams and visions today, and today I will live in the now!

*Father, help me be ready for what's ahead, and thank You, in advance,
for how good it's all going to turn out for me. In Jesus' name, amen.*

June 25
DECREE IT!

"You shall also decide and decree a thing and it shall be established for you; and the light [of God's favor] shall shine upon your ways." (Job 22:28 – AMP)

1. Today I will live in the now! I will live in the now because I know that life is a series of decisions and choices, and I am making good and right choices for my life today. Everything that I am presently doing will either benefit my present or my future, so I choose to do things that will help me in the long run and will complement the big picture.

2. Today I will be willing to make decisions that bring me temporary discomfort in the present, if I know that they will pay off for me in the future. Today's decisions are tomorrow's realities, and I plan to have a very good tomorrow!

3. Today I will remember that destiny is not a matter of chance, it is a matter of choice, so I will listen and think and meditate and pray, being careful and wise with the power of my will.

4. Today I will create events and change circumstances with my decisions, knowing that the people in my life respond to the decisions that I make. I am not alone in my life; my life affects and influences others, and so do my decisions. The quality of my decisions will determine the quality of my relationships, so I will think before I act, and I will act responsibly.

5. Today I will remember that God deals with me according to my decisions, and He acknowledges my decrees as the Apostle and High Priest of my confession.

6. Today I will express my desires and dreams by my decisions, and will dedicate myself to the discipline of being diligent enough to dare to make them come true!

7. Today I will walk in the Spirit, for as many as are led by the Spirit of God are the sons of God. Even though I understand the power that I have over my own destiny, I will always acknowledge that it is not by might, nor by power, but by His Spirit. I will trust God with my life today, and today I will live in the now!

Father, help me to make good decisions and to decree them in faith today.
In Jesus' name, amen.

June 26
DON'T QUIT!

*"And let us not lose heart and grow weary and faint in acting nobly and doing right,
for in due time and at the appointed season we shall reap,
if we do not loosen and relax our courage and faint." (Galatians 6:9 – AMP)*

1. Today I will live in the now! I will live in the now because I will not quit!

2. Today I will not quit!

3. Today I will not quit!

4. Today I will not quit!

5. Today I will not quit!

6. Today I will not quit!

7. Today I will not quit, and today I will live in the now!

   Father, help me hang in there today! In Jesus' name, amen.

June 27
BREACH REPAIRERS!

". . . And you shall be called the Repairer of the Breach,
The Restorer of Streets to Dwell In." (Isaiah 58:12)

1. Today I will live in the now! I will live in the now because I am a peacemaker and a bridge-builder, helping people to open lines of communication, because life is in the power of the tongue.

2. Today I will practice the Ministry of Reconciliation, fulfilling this: "Brethren, if any person is overtaken in misconduct or sin of any sort, you who are spiritual [who are responsive to and controlled by the Spirit] should set him right and restore and reinstate him, without any sense of superiority, and with all gentleness, keeping an attentive eye on yourself, lest you should be tempted also." (Galatians 6:1 – AMP)

3. Today I will never say never when it comes to repairing relationships, because anything is possible, whether it is restoration between God and someone who has rebelled against Him, or between two other people whose relationship has been severed, or even between someone else and me. Love never fails, and miracles still happen!

4. Today I will forgive and restore someone, fulfilling this: "[My] brethren, if any one among you strays from the Truth and falls into error, and another [person] brings him back [to God], let the [latter] one be sure that whoever turns a sinner from his evil course will save [that one's] soul from death and will cover a multitude of sins [procure the pardon of the many sins committed by the convert]" (James 5:19, 20 – AMP). I will *remit* sins — not retain them.

5. Today I will speak words of reconciliation to someone and will open the door to the opportunity for repentance for them. I will not judge, but will see them after the spirit, instead of after the flesh.

6. Today I will be sensitive to the feelings of others and will show compassion and empathy to those who need it.

7. Today, if presented with the opportunity, I will help to repair breaches between family members (including those in my own family), help to close generation gaps, help to improve race relations, help to strengthen marriages, help to promote harmony in the community, help to make peace in the church, and do what I can to heal the wounded Body of Christ in the earth. Today I will overcome evil with good, and today I will live in the now!

Father, help me to be a repairer of the breach today. In Jesus' name, amen.

June 28
REDEEMED TIME!

*"See then that you walk circumspectly, not as fools but as wise,
redeeming the time because the days are evil." (Ephesians 5:15, 16)*

1. Today I will live in the now! I will live in the now because I have the ability to walk circumspectly (to see in a circle), observing my past, present and future from one vantage point – the now!

2. Today I will refuse to occupy my mind with regrets – no crying over spilt milk in my life! My life is what it is, what has happened has happened, God is still good, God is still on His throne, and I am still His child!

3. Today I will do what I can to restore broken fellowship with a loved one in attempt to make up for lost time.

4. Today I will be content with things as they are now, even though I am working to make things better. I will not wait until things improve to be happy — I will make the decision to be happy *now*.

5. Today I will reconcile the truth of my life, making no pretense about why my life is like it is. I will redeem the time by taking full responsibility for my life now, and in so doing will be able to triumph over the nagging thoughts that tempt me to wonder what might have been.

6. Today I will make the most of my time, recognizing important windows of opportunity when I see them.

7. Today I will not procrastinate in getting around to doing unpleasant tasks. My time is too valuable to spend in regret or dread, so I will do what I have to do, get it over with, and move on. Today I will enjoy my time, and today I will live in the now!

Father, help me to redeem the time today. In Jesus' name, amen.

June 29
KINGDOM RIGHTEOUSNESS!

"... for the Kingdom of God is ... righteousness ..." (Romans 14:17)

1. Today I will live in the now! I will live in the now because I am the righteousness of God in Christ. Righteousness is a free gift that I have received — purchased by the blood of Jesus — and it gives me the ability to stand in the presence of God with no sense of guilt, shame, condemnation or inferiority. Righteousness is one-third of the Kingdom of God, and it belongs to me!

2. Today I will enjoy my right standing with the Father, being accepted in the Beloved, Jesus, the first-born Son. With my heart I believe unto the righteousness that gives me confidence before God (my heart does not condemn me) and, ultimately, creates confidence before everybody.

3. Today I will expect my prayers to be answered, for the effectual, fervent prayer of a righteous person avails much! I have a regular audience with God and, in Christ, I have clout with Him. My prayers have weight – not because I am perfect – but because He has made me righteous!

4. Today I will have peace with other people because I am at peace with myself as a direct result of having peace with God. This Kingdom flow of peace makes my life worth living.

5. Today I will use the force of righteousness in my life to overcome doubt and fear, as well as weaknesses and insecurities produced by the circumstances of my life. Because I am righteous in Christ, I am able to see opposition as a well-received challenge. Because I am righteous in Christ, I can view failure as an opportunity for growth and learning. Because I am righteous in Christ, I can admit when I am wrong – because, even when I am wrong, I am still righteous!

6. Today I will move beyond bitterness, excelling in my calm, mature attitude and sense of well-being. Because I do not have to fear the wrath of God, I can overcome any other fear in my life — I can live and let live, because I have no sense of rejection! Because Jesus has accepted me as I am, I can accept myself as I am.

7. Today I will be bold before God, before men, and before the devil. "The wicked flee when no man pursues, but the righteous are as bold as a lion" (Proverbs 28:1). I will stand on this Word today, and today I will live in the now!

   Father, thank You for the gift of righteousness. In Jesus' name, amen.

June 30
BE HAPPY!

"Happy are the people who are in such a state;
happy are the people whose God is the Lord." (Psalm 144:15)

1. Today I will live in the now! I will live in the now because I have a right to be happy, and I have been given the power to create happiness! I will not waste the opportunities presented in this day with continual references to tragedies from the past. I will not miss the beauty of living in the moment by bemoaning all the hard times in the present. And I will not let myself become dangerously distracted from prophetically planning my future by predicting calamities ahead!

2. Today I will rejoice that my sins are forgiven, that God knows me and cares about what happens to me today, and that things are getting better for me as I go from glory to glory. I will make the choice to be unaffected by negative forces or bad news.

3. Today I will laugh at my mistakes and problems, not letting them dominate my mind or make me feel inadequate or overwhelmed. I will not take things too seriously today, choosing Jesus' easy burden and light yoke for my life, instead of the pressure, stress, and oppression that comes from being too hard on myself or too anxious about my current state of affairs.

4. Today I will celebrate the goodness of the Lord, counting my blessings and remembering to be thankful for them all. I will not forget His benefits – how He forgives all of my iniquities and heals all of my diseases.

5. Today I will sing a song of victory even before the battle is over. The joy of the Lord will strengthen me to defeat every foe, give me supernatural energy and cause me to get stronger with every fight!

6. Today I will enjoy the company of happy people, and if I can't find any, *I* will try to make some unhappy people feel better about their situations. And if I can't make anybody else happy, I will enjoy being happy alone, because I have that much to be happy about!

7. Today I will make it a point to smile . . . to laugh . . . to think positive thoughts . . . to praise the Lord . . . to cheer up someone . . . to pray for the happiness of others . . . to avoid things that depress me . . . to avoid music or images that darken my mood . . . to speak words of edification to those that I care for . . . to be a blessing . . . to sing . . . to worship God in spirit and in truth . . . to do something positive for the Kingdom. Today will be a day of happiness for me, regardless of the circumstances, and today I will live in the now!

Father, help me do things that make You happy today. In Jesus' name, amen.

July In The Now!

⋄J⋄U⋄L⋄Y⋄

A month for celebration!

Red, white, and blue banners to brighten things up . . .

Marching bands to move you . . .

Parades to pick up your spirits . . .

A dazzlingly deafening display of light, color and noise

To excite you as it explodes above your head in the heat of the summer night . . .

Celebrate it all - all that the summer brings . . .

Baseball games, barbecued ribs, and bare feet . . .

Cotton candy, carnivals, and convertibles . . .

Hamburgers, hot dogs, and homemade ice cream . . .

Long, lazy afternoons, lemonade, and laughing out loud!

Put the top down and go to a drive-in movie . . .

Remember to ride a roller coaster . . .

And celebrate life!

Make a joyful noise all the earth!

"When you win, we plan to raise the roof and lead the parade with our banners. May all your wishes come true!" (Psalm 20:5 – The Message)

July 1
WORLD OVERCOMER!

*"For whatever is born of God overcomes the world.
And this is the victory that has overcome the world – our faith."* *(I John 5:4)*

1. Today I will live in the now! I will live in the now because the God-kind of faith is working overtime, in and through me, enabling me to overcome the present antichrist world system and all of its negative influences. Jesus said that in the world I would have tribulation, but that I should be of good cheer because He has overcome the world — and if He could overcome it, then I can overcome it *through Him*. Therefore, today I will be of good cheer, regardless of what I am going through or how I am being tested!

2. Today I will remember that there is much sadness, suffering and sorrow in the world, that people are in pain, and that evil exists everywhere. I will do what I can to alleviate the suffering, and vanquish the evil, but I will not become overwhelmed by the task or oppressed by the reality of the darkness around me. I will also see the beauty of the earth, and will enjoy guilt-free happiness today, because the light in me will shine in the darkness, and the darkness will not overtake it! From my point of view, the world is a beautiful place, and I will partake of its fullness . . . the earth is the Lord's!

3. Today I will live by my own rules, under the authority of the Lord Jesus. The definition of my destiny will not be dictated to me by the rules of the natural world — in Christ I will write new definitions of who I am and what I am here to do. The mission statement of my life will be penned by the Paraclete (the Helper, the Holy Spirit).

4. Today I will not limit myself to the world's expectations of me.

5. Today I will rise above the level of my own history, breaking out of the bondages that I have imposed upon myself by creating my own little world of self-preservation. My highly developed defense mechanisms will not become the parameters of my present reality.

6. Today I will walk in the kind of faith that truly overcomes the world – faith that has been tried in the fire seven times – faith that grows stronger through conflict and confrontation. Everything that I have been through has served to better equip me to walk in the faith that sets an example, and prevails over principalities and powers.

7. Today I will overcome - moment by moment, step by step, issue by issue — and today I will live in the now!

Father, help me to overcome the world in my life today. In Jesus' name, amen.

July 2
SATISFACTION GUARANTEED!

"Jesus said, 'If? There are no "ifs" among believers.
Anything can happen.'" (Mark 9:23 – The Message)

1. Today I will live in the now! I will live in the now because I am a believer, and I live and think and act like one. I refuse to spend this day in a discontented and unsettled manner, because I am complete in Christ. I am satisfied with Jesus as my portion, because Jesus, the manifestation of El Shaddai, is more than enough!

2. Today I will be empowered by having the ability to see things correctly, and in the proper perspective. By faith, I have a fixed vision of God always being on my side, so that I never have to see myself as a victim - never have to see other people after the flesh – never have to see any situation as being hopeless! I am satisfied because I see no evil!

3. Today I will flow with a vision of limitless possibilities presented to me today, even in the middle of a fiery trial. I am satisfied by my faith to the point that I simply cannot take a negative report seriously. I do not doubt God's ability or His willingness to help me, and in the big picture, everything is working for my good. I am satisfied because I hear no evil!

4. Today I will use the words "will" and "shall" and "know," instead of "hope so," "maybe so" and "I think so." In Christ I am definite, decisive and determined to be a doer of the word instead of a spectator - a hearer only! My ears are just not tuned in to a negative wavelength, and my words are confident words of life! I am satisfied because I speak no evil!

5. Today I will trust in the Lord with all my heart, instead of relying on my own intellect. In Him I move. I do not have to settle for survival by living by my own wits. I am satisfied because I walk in the Spirit!

6. Today I will be generous with my praise to God . . . I will not stifle words of exaltation that are due Him. The Lord is good, and He satisfies my mouth with good things, so that my youth is renewed like the eagle's. With long life He satisfies me, and shows me His salvation! I was created for His pleasure, and I am satisfied because I am walking in my purpose to please Him.

7. Today I will think and speak and do things that improve the atmosphere around me, and make the world a better place. I will be the bread of life, broken for those who are hungry for God, because I am an earth-salter and a world-lighter — one who meets the needs of the people around me. Jesus will see the travail of His soul for me and be satisfied today, and today I will live in the now!

Father, be satisfied with my life today. In Jesus' name, amen.

July 3
GOD'S FRIEND

"Steep yourself in God-reality, God-initiative, God-provisions. You'll find all your everyday human concerns will be met. Don't be afraid of missing out. You're my dearest friends! The Father wants to give you the very Kingdom itself." (Luke 12:31, 32 – The Message)

1. Today I will live in the now! I will live in the now because my ministry to God is more important to me than my ministry to anyone else. As Christ is being formed in me, I am discovering a whole universe of revelation within myself that I didn't even know existed before now, and all of it is drawing me into a deeper, more mature relationship with my Creator.

2. Today I will enjoy intimate and spontaneous communication with my "Abba" revealed to me through my elder brother, Jesus, by the fellowship of the Helper Who stands by to aid and assist me, and Who never testifies of Himself, but always promotes Christ and lifts Him up.

3. Today I will pray to learn the secrets of Abraham, who was called the friend of God in his earth-walk. I will follow his example of unwavering faith, for without faith it is impossible to please God.

4. Today I will walk with Him in the cool of the day as Adam did, innocently naked before Him, with no presence of fear or sense of shameful unrighteousness. I have no need to sew together fig leaves of religion, for I have nothing to hide from the One who chose me in Him before the foundation of the world!

5. Today I will not engage in the friendship with the world that is enmity against God. Our relationship takes priority over culture, tradition, philosophy, self-perception, world-view, theology or attitude. He is a jealous God, Who will have no other Gods before Him, and I am glad that He is jealous over me because it reinforces to me how important I am to Him. I am the apple of His eye!

6. Today I will be able to be a better friend to someone because I am a friend to God. For the same reason, I will even be a better friend to myself, because as God is revealed, I have self-revelation of who I am in Him.

7. Today I will rejoice that nothing – death, life, angels, principalities, powers, present things, future things or any other creature – can separate me from the love of God which is in Christ Jesus. Because I have undisturbed peace with God, I will be at peace with myself and with the world around me today. My friendship with the Originator of all things will produce a tangible confidence in my life today, and today I will live in the now!

Father, show me how to be a good friend to You today. In Jesus' name, amen.

July 4
INDEPENDENCE DAY!

"Then Jesus turned to the Jews who had claimed to believe in Him. 'If you stick with this, living out what I tell you, you are my disciples for sure. Then you will experience for yourselves the truth, and the truth will free you. So if the Son sets you free, you are free through and through.'" (John 8:31, 32, 36 – The Message)

1. Today I will live in the now! I will live in the now because I am making it my personal goal to become the freest person who ever lived! I will stand on the eternal word for my freedom: "And you shall know the truth, and the truth shall make you free" (John 8:32); "Therefore is the Son makes you free, you shall be free indeed" (John 8:36); " . . . where the Spirit of the Lord is, there is liberty" (II Corinthians 3:16); " . . . He shall pluck my feet out of the net" (Psalm 25:25); "Stand fast therefore in the liberty by which Christ has made us free, and do not be entangled again with the yoke of bondage" (Galations 5:1); "For you . . . have been called to liberty . . . ." (Galations 5:13)

2. Today I will celebrate my emancipation from the personal parameters of my own comfort zones, freeing myself emotionally and mentally to discover a whole new (and very real) world of faith. The freedom available to me today is worth striving for, and I am willing to take a risk for it knowing that I can survive taking a possible fall better than I can tolerate living a limited life!

3. Today I will free my mind to dream, making room for change as I plan for tomorrow. I will be free to think outside the box, allowing for the messiness of a brainstorm. The power that works in me enabling Him to do exceeding, abundantly above all that I can ask or think.

4. Today I will be free to think for myself. I will be free from prejudice and intolerance. I will be free to hope, regardless of past disappointments. I make the choice to set my mind in a large place.

5. Today I will say yes to life. All of the promises of God are "yes" and "amen." God is not on a budget. He is free to daily load me with benefits, even after I have exhausted all other opportunities, so I will be free to embrace the blessings of His freedom today. Yes! Yes! Yes! He has made me worthy to receive, so I say an eternal "YES" to Him!

6. Today I will be free to walk away from the traps that have been set for me. He has delivered me from the snare of the fowler, so I can fearlessly face forward in faith as I find freedom that I never knew existed before.

7. Today I will be free to be me – God's workmanship – just as I am – a work in progress, but a masterpiece, nonetheless. I celebrate freedom and liberty in my country and in my life today, and today I will live in the now!

Father, help me to really walk in freedom today. In Jesus' name, amen.

July 5
THE WAY!

"Jesus said to him, 'I am the way . . . .'" **(John 14:6)**

1. Today I will live in the now! I will live in the now because I know that Jesus is the way to salvation for all people because of His finished work in the atonement, the triumph of His blood sacrifice, the victorious confirmation of His resurrection from the dead, and His ascension to the right hand (undisputed place of authority) of the Father. I also know that I have a certain, individual mandate to seek my own unique path – my own "way" - to my personal destiny in Him. Jesus is THE way, and He has an unfolding plan for my life that will be clear to me today!

2. Today I will seek out the right and appropriate counsel that I need to help me find the wisdom to maintain my direction on my path. Psalm 103:7 says that God made his *ACTS* known to the children of Israel, but He made His *WAYS* known to Moses. Today I will be grateful for the mighty *acts* performed by the Creator, but I will make it my ultimate goal to seek to know His *ways*!

3. Today I will seek to discern my true, original identity in God — my one and only place in the Body of Christ, which God has designed as it has pleased Him. Flowing in my function will facilitate my being able to focus on finding my way in a free and freshly unprecedented fashion!

4. Today I will seek the Mind of Christ within myself, trusting the anointing that abides in me and teaches me all things, to reveal the way that this day should go, and to help me to define the decisions that I should make in it. Jesus, the Way, lives in my heart, and He has mapped it all out for me.

5. Today I will seek the divine direction of Adonai, the Lord of my destiny, so that I may better understand the steps that I need to take today to find my own way. I am not lost, disoriented, misguided or unsure of my steps. I am a pilgrim, not a rambler – a stranger, but not an orphan. I am finding the way to my Father's house, one step at a time.

6. Today I will seek the wisdom that is beyond that of the present, cosmetic world system, to bring me out of a shallow existence into a deep walk with God. I know that "there is a way that seems *right to a man*, but the end of it is destruction" (Proverbs 16:25), but I am seeking the way that seems *right to God*!

7. Today I will seek the approval of God alone, and then accept His righteous (and merciful) judgment for my life. I trust in the Lord with all my heart, and acknowledge Him in all my ways. Today I will manifest the spirit of the seeker, and today I will live in the now!

Father, help me to walk in Your way today. In Jesus' name, amen.

July 6
THE TRUTH!

"Jesus said to him, 'I am the . . . truth . . . .'" (John 14:6)

1. Today I will live in the now! I will live in the now because Jesus is the truth, and I love and embrace truth, for knowing it is the only way to find freedom! I will face my own truth today, and **INVESTIGATE MY PRESENT SITUATION HONESTLY.** I will not be a pessimist and only look at my problems; instead, I will be productively optimistic by seeing the problem AND the solution as co-existent. The truth will empower me to take a proactive stance in all matters pertaining to solving the mysteries of life.

2. Today I will truthfully **INDICATE MY AVAILABLE SEED,** realizing that God will always require me to use what I already have in my hand to carry out His will for my life. The One who provides seed for the sower never creates something out of nothing, and He has abundantly invested me with everything that I need to receive a great harvest.

3. Today I will **IMPROVE MY BELIEF SYSTEM** by admitting to myself what I really have faith for, and then standing on what is actual and genuine in my spirit. The truth will enable me to believe with my heart instead of believing with my head, so that my faith can produce something real for a real world.

4. Today I will **IDENTIFY MY REAL HUNGER** so that I can free myself from having to search for answers in things that I know will not satisfy me. It is written, "The satisfied soul loathes the honeycomb, but to the hungry soul, every bitter thing is sweet." (Proverbs 27:7). Because I know that Jesus is ultimately my truth, I do not have to feed myself with bitter things. He is my portion. He is not just sufficient - He is more than enough!

5. Today I will **INTERPRET MY SPIRITUAL JOURNEY** and honestly assess where I am located on it. By telling myself the truth, I will discover what I need to change about my relationship with God and with my life as it now is.

6. Today I will **INSPIRE MY OWN SPIRIT BY THE TRUE SPIRIT OF GOD.** I will nourish my inner man by exposing myself to the true manna – Jesus, the Truth – the Word made flesh. My prayer will be "give us this day our daily bread," but my meaning will be "give me my daily Jesus!"

7. Today I will **INVEST MY WHOLE LIFE** into the Kingdom of God, living truly and authentically as I lay down my life for others. I will live this day wholly, fully and completely by walking in the truth. I will be set free today, and today I will live in the now!

Father, help me to walk in Your truth today. In Jesus' name, amen.

July 7
THE LIFE!

"Jesus said to him, 'I am the . . . life.
No one comes to the Father except through Me.'" **(John 14:6)**

1. Today I will live in the now! I will live in the now because Christ is my life, and I am alive in Him forevermore! Today I will live a **CONFIDENT LIFE,** fully persuaded that God has called and purposed me to fulfill a specific destiny in the earth. I am confident in the fact that I was predestined to be conformed to His (Christ's) image, that He might be the firstborn among many brethren. I am confident that I can get through the fiery trial of this day without the smell of smoke on my clothes!

2. Today I will live a **CHALLENGED LIFE,** rising to every demanding occasion to become a greater asset to the Kingdom of God, and accepting the responsibility for my own prosperity, success and happiness. I will view any problem facing me today as a challenge, letting it energize me and not intimidate me!

3. Today I will live a **CREATIVE LIFE,** speaking into existence the world in which I want to live as God spoke His worlds into existence in the beginning. My living faith will create an atmosphere today that will be conducive to the kind of discipline that causes productivity.

4. Today I will live a **CONQUERING LIFE,** confronting my fears one by one, and overcoming any spirit of laziness or procrastination that would prevent me from rising to the top. The life of God in me demands my devout discipline and displays a deep desire to dare to take dominion!

5. Today I will live a **COMPLETE LIFE,** bringing closure to old, unresolved issues, and putting to rest, once and for all, my fear of familiar strongholds. My spiritual journey will bring me full circle, and create a sense of wholeness in me as I live in the now and overcome one day at a time.

6. Today I will live a **COMPETITIVE LIFE,** competing only with myself, but holding myself to the highest standard possible. I can improve. I can grow. I can stretch. I can progress. I can excel! I will run my own, unique race like a champion today, and I will "run that I may win!"

7. Today I will live a **CHANGED LIFE.** If something that I am doing is not working, I will change it – change my thought patterns – change my direction. Change is possible because I have life, and my ongoing repentance keeps regenerating me. Today I will let Jesus live His life through me, and today I will live in the now!

Father, show me how to live the Christ-life today. In Jesus' name, amen.

July 8
OPEN HOUSE!

"In my Father's house are many rooms . . . ." (John 14:2 - NIV)

1. Today I will live in the now! I will live in the now because Jesus has made room for me in the Father's house, and there is a place for me in the purposes and plans of God! I will not let my heart be troubled concerning my habitation in Him or my place in the ministry, because Christ has declared the end from the beginning. He knows that, even if I deny Him three times out of fear or external pressure, I can still receive forgiveness, and can be trusted to feed His sheep because I love Him, and am called according to His purpose!

2. Today I will make myself at home in His presence, where there is fullness of joy. Jesus has made me worthy there, so I will relax in my righteousness, resting in the revelation of His receptiveness to me. I will freely and confidently partake of the Lord's Table in remembrance of Him, discerning the Body of Christ and adding years to my earth-life in the process.

3. Today I will invite others to come and go with me to my Father's house, assuring them that there are enough robes, rings, shoes, and fatted calves to go around – one for every returning prodigal son or daughter! I will be confident that my Father will see us all coming from a great distance, and will run to meet us, greeting us with a paternal kiss. There will be room for everyone in the house, and they/we all will receive heart-help, healing hope and holy hospitality!

4. Today I will maintain a welcoming atmosphere in my heart – Christ's home. The fullness of the godhead will enjoy residence within my inner being, and I will house the very presence of God today, fulfilling my destiny in becoming a Spirit-temple in the material world.

5. Today I will keep an open mind to the manifestation of revelation, and an open heart to the ministry of reconciliation. My spiritual house will maintain an open door policy, allowing the King of Glory to come in to the world around me, and accepting those who come to me for help just as they are.

6. Today I will promote unity with other believers who are "living stones" – those who are building the true church of the living God with their own testimonies. Together, we will pattern our lives after Jesus, the Chief Cornerstone – the standard by which every other stone is measured – and the gates of hell itself will not prevail against what He is building with and through us!

7. Today I will be a creative architect for the Kingdom of God, and today I will live in the now!

Father, help me to be a vessel of honor in Your house today. In Jesus' name, amen.

July 9
BE CONTENT!

"Now godliness with contentment is great gain. For we brought nothing into this world, and it is certain we can carry nothing out. And having food and clothing, with these we shall be content." (1 Timothy 6:6-8)

1. Today I will live in the now! I will live in the now because I am seeking first the Kingdom of God, and everything that I need is being added to me as the need arises. God knows what I have need of, even before I ask, and He supplies all of my need, according to His riches in glory by Christ Jesus!

2. Today I will choose to be happy – right here, right now. I am not looking for "that" because I have "this!" "This" is whatever I have right now that God has given me and I will be content with it in Christ, because, ultimately, He is all that I need! Jesus said, ". . . THIS is my body . . ." (I Corinthians 11:24), so I will look for a revelation of the omnipresent Body of Christ in the ordinary things around me — the bread, the wine, the table, those familiar faces around the table — Christ is here, and Christ is now!

3. Today I will enjoy simple things, being thankful for the millions of little miracles that surround me everyday — the ones that I rarely notice. I will count my blessings today. I will take nothing for granted, and my thankful heart will give me a heightened sense of awareness of all the beauty that is in my life.

4. Today I will not be afraid to have and enjoy money or things, but I will not let them have me. My prosperous soul will bring me material prosperity, as it should, but I remember that I am not my own, that I am bought with a price, and that everything in my life belongs to God because I have given my life to Him.

5. Today I will be ALIVE while I am alive. I will seize the day, and be in the moment, enjoying my current circumstances, no matter what they are. My happiness will come from within – from my own creative ability. I will not waste my opportunities in the now, and will focus on what God is doing in my life, presently.

6. Today I will tap into the awesome power of pacing myself with the patience that is resident in me through the fruit of the Spirit. I am content because I can endure anything, and my endurance will cause me to be perfect (mature) and entire, lacking nothing! Patience rules!

7. Today I will be content with who I am and with what I have, knowing that I am increasing always because increase is a natural process for me. My contentment will cause me to overcome today, and today I will live in the now!

Father, help me be content in You today. In Jesus' name, amen.

July 10
OVERCOMER'S INHERITANCE!

"He who overcomes shall inherit all things, and I will be his God and he shall be My son."
(Revelation 21:7)

1. Today I will live in the now! I will live in the now because I am an overcomer whose spirit is fed by the fruit of the tree of life, instead of the tree of the knowledge of good and evil! It is written: "He who is able to hear, let him listen to and give heed to what the Spirit says to the assemblies (churches). To him who overcomes (is victorious), I will grant to eat [of the fruit] of the tree of life, which is in the paradise of God." (Revelation 2:7 - AMP)

2. Today I will overcome the second death by walking in the power of my second birth! It is written: "He who is able to hear, let him listen to and heed what the Spirit says to the assemblies (churches). He who overcomes (is victorious) shall in no way be injured by the second death." (Revelation 2:11 - AMP)

3. Today I will overcome by knowing, by the Spirit, who I really am, allowing no one other than God Himself to define my life or persona. It is written: ". . . to him who overcomes (conquers) I will give to eat of the manna that is hidden, and I will give him a white stone with a new name engraved on the stone, which no one knows or understands except he who receives it." (Revelation 2:17 - AMP)

4. Today I will not be reluctant to rule, but I will accept my authority in Christ! It is written: "And he who overcomes . . . I will give authority and power over the nations; and he shall rule them with a scepter (rod) of iron, as when earthen pots are broken in pieces, and [his power over them shall be] like that which I Myself have received from My Father; and I will give him the Morning Star." (Revelation 2:26-28 - AMP)

5. Today I will recognize and appreciate the garments of righteousness that clothe me, and I will be serenely secure in my salvation. It is written: "Thus shall he who conquers (is victorious) be clad in white garments, and I will not erase or blot out his name from the Book of Life; I will acknowledge him [as Mine], and I will confess his name openly before My Father and before His angels." (Revelation 3:5 - AMP)

6. Today I will walk in the strength of the Almighty, knowing that I am a pillar in His eternal temple. It is written: "He who overcomes . . . I will make him a pillar in the sanctuary of My God; he shall never be put out of it or go out of it, and I will write on him the name of My God and the name of the City of My God, the new Jerusalem, which descends from My God out of heaven, and My own new name." (Revelation 3:12 - AMP)

7. Today I will sit beside Christ, and rule with Him! It is written: "He who overcomes . . . I will grant him to sit beside Me on My throne, as I Myself overcame (was victorious) and sat down beside My Father on His throne" (Revelation 3:21 – AMP). I will overcome today, and today I will live in the now!

Father, help me to walk in my inheritance today. In Jesus' name, amen.

July 11
STAY ALERT!

"I went by the field of the lazy man, and by the vineyard of the man devoid of understanding; and there it was, all overgrown with thorns; Its surface was covered with nettles; Its stone wall was broken down. When I saw it, I considered it well; I looked on it and received instruction: A little sleep, a little slumber, a little folding of the hands to rest; so shall your poverty come like a prowler, and your need like an armed man." (Proverbs 24:30-34)

1. Today I will live in the now! I will live in the now because I am actively involved in my world and on top of every situation facing me. The names of laziness, procrastination and foolishness must bow to the name of Jesus in my life!

2. Today I will be sober and vigilant – a watchman on the wall. I will pay attention to what is happening around me, and will trust the Holy Spirit to show me things to come. I will keep my eyes and ears open in the natural realm, as well as in the spiritual realm, and will be a doer of the word, so as not to deceive myself.

3. Today I will remember that the only person who is going to be with me for my entire life is me, so I will befriend myself by taking responsibility for my own productivity. I will enjoy my hard-earned successes and victories, and face up to the unfortunate consequences of my lapses in judgment and poor choices. But, even though I take full responsibility for my life and actions, I will still count on goodness and mercy to follow me all the days of my life and to turn around for the good every negative situation that I have brought on myself. The buck will stop with me, but the government will be on Christ's shoulder!

4. Today I will enjoy the blessing of hard work, and the benefits that accompany it.

5. Today I will choose how I start and finish my day, knowing that attitude is everything, and that I have control over my feelings and reactions to what happens around me.

6. Today I will really listen when people talk. Out of the abundance of the heart the mouth speaks, and I will use my ability to wisely hear the hearts of those with whom I communicate.

7. Today I will "look well to the state of my flocks," and will recognize a wake-up call when I hear it and a reality check when I see it. I will not be clueless and taken unaware by circumstances. I will not let myself be blind-sided by the snare of the fowler. I will be on top of my game today, and today I will live in the now!

Father, help me to stay alert today. In Jesus' name, amen.

July 12
BOTTOM LINE!

"In a word, what I'm saying is, Grow up!
You're Kingdom subjects. Now live like it. Live out your God-created identity. Live
generously and graciously toward others, the way God lives toward you."
(Matthew 5:48 – The Message)

1. Today I will live in the now! I will live in the now because I am maturing in the Kingdom of God today – putting away childish things – growing up into Him Who is the Head of all things. The growth that I am experiencing is causing me to dream big, and to start now; to keep going when I feel tired, and to try again when I fail; to shake off the spirit of heaviness, and willfully put on the garment of praise, even in the midst of intense warfare; to give thanks and keep smiling; to get a grip when I feel like giving up!

2. Today I will stop worrying about what other people think about me. I will be myself, and lighten up about my expectations of myself, which may or may not be realistic. I will let go when I need to, and hold on when I have to, but whatever the case, I will work hard at trying to enjoy today.

3. Today I will realize that tears happen, but that I have the ability to endure – to grieve if I have to – and then to move on. I don't have the time or the need for self-pity, oppression, or even a simple bad mood.

4. Today I will improve the quality of my life by the words of my mouth by engaging in mature communication with others. When I say something, I will try to understand how the other person will hear and interpret it, because their life experiences and subsequent world-view may cause them to hear something different from what I am actually saying. I will remember that people communicate the way that they want to hear, so I will be swift to hear and slow to speak (James 1:19).

5. Today I will improve the quality of my life by making a mature confession of faith, creating my world today by the words of my mouth.

6. Today I will pray maturely, making a solid connection with the One Who supplies all of my needs. I will have the confidence that, if I ask anything according to His will, He will hear me and will grant me the petitions that I desire of Him!

7. Today I will live generously and graciously toward others, operating with no hidden agenda, and no impure motive. I will not wrestle with flesh and blood, but will wage a good warfare in the spirit. I will maintain the ability to be childlike without being childish, walking in the full stature of Kingdom adulthood. Today I will do the world some good, and today I will live in the now!

Father, help me to grow up today. In Jesus' name, amen.

July 13
LOVE CONNECTION!

"Jesus said, 'Love the Lord your God with all your passion and prayer and intelligence.' This is the most important, the first on any list. But there is a second to set alongside it: 'Love others as well as you love yourself.' These two commands are pegs; everything in God's Law and the Prophets hangs from them." (Matthew 22:37-40 – The Message)

1. Today I will live in the now! I will live in the now because love always wins, and the love of God is abundantly deposited in my heart by the Holy Spirit (Romans 5:5). Faith will be a major part of my day, as will hope and love. These three will abide and remain, but the greatest of these will be love!

2. Today I will love audibly, telling the people I love that I love them at every given opportunity, knowing that I may not have the chance to say it tomorrow. But I will not limit my expression of love to words only. I will love visibly as well, by confirming what I say with what I do, because sometimes actions speak louder than words.

3. Today I will love unselfishly, remembering that I do not own the people who are in my life. I will accept and receive people as they are, releasing my desire to control or change them for my own purposes or pleasure. I will pray that God's will be done in their lives, rather than imposing my will on them in the flesh, and will act accordingly.

4. Today I will love tangibly. When it is possible and appropriate, I will not be reluctant to reach out and touch someone, without the fear of rejection on my part. I will let Jesus bring healing to someone through me today by letting *Him* touch *them* through *me*.

5. Today I will love aggressively, going the extra mile to reach those who have been hurt, and have put up a wall of protection around themselves. I will not give up easily, but will manifest my true belief in the ministry of reconciliation by being persistent. "A brother offended is harder to win than a strong city . . ." (Proverbs 18:19), but I can do all things through Christ Who strengthens me!

6. Today I will love maturely, doing what is right for the ones I love, rather than doing what is easy. If tough love is required, then tough love will be given. Faith works by love, and love works by faith, and faith without works is dead!

7. Today I will love truly. I will be loyal and forgiving, even with the ones who don't deserve it, because of the unconditional love and grace that God has poured into me. I will walk in supernatural love today, and today I will live in the now!

Father, help me to love like You today. In Jesus' name, amen.

July 14
KINGDOM REVOLUTION!

"I've come to change everything, turn everything rightside up
– how I long for it to be finished!" (Luke 12:50 - The Message)

1. Today I will live in the now! I will live in the now because Jesus, the King, is reigning in and with and through me, changing me from the inside out – in my mind, in my heart, and in my faith - so that I can change the world around me, and make it a better place in which to live for future generations. I am changing my mind today – learning to think in a new way – so that I can enter the Kingdom, and bring necessary revolution through the revelation of repentance from my present reality into the realm of righteous rebirth! There is a new world coming, and Christ is already reigning from there.

2. Today I will disassociate myself from demonic strongholds that are resistant to authority and to change. I will do what I can to expose the death that is religion.

3. Today I will make room for the new thing that God is doing in my interior world. I will throw out the non-essential numbers that usually define me, including age, weight, and height, and will adopt a new way of seeing myself (then we shall know even as also we are known – I Corinthians 13:12). A new definition of my personhood is being written on my heart and in my imagination. The Kingdom within is causing changes without, and is creating within me a vision for real revolution!

4. Today I will preserve what is good in my world, and will change what needs improvement. If what needs to be changed is beyond my ability to improve it, I will get help, knowing that revolution requires a responsible team effort.

5. Today I will embrace the excitement and adventure of transition, even the frightening kind, knowing that life is not measured by the number of breaths we take, but by the moments that take our breath away! The violent take the Kingdom by force, and today I will welcome the shaking of God in my life, not fearing the violence around me. In all these things I am more than a conqueror through Him Who loves me!

6. Today I will overcome the seduction of staying with the familiar and the temptation to let tradition go unchallenged and unchecked. I will outgrow my comfort zone today, and will move into the next chapter of the book of my life, knowing that the ending of the story will be a portrayal of my personal triumph!

7. Today I will run with the vision that is written on my heart by Jesus, the Revolutionary, and I will be changed for the better because of it. Today is the day for my miracle, and today I will live in the now!

Father, let Your Kingdom come, and revolutionize my life today! In Jesus' name, amen.

July 15
ABSOLUTE CONFIDENCE!

"Do not, therefore, fling away your fearless confidence, for it carries a great and glorious compensation of reward. For you have need of steadfast patience and endurance, so that you may perform and fully accomplish the will of God, and thus receive and carry away [and enjoy to the full] what is promised." (Hebrews 10:35, 36 – AMP)

1. Today I will live in the now! I will live in the now because I walk in the confidence that comes from knowing who I am in Christ, that He has made me righteous, and that He wants me to be involved with His plan of redemption for the earth. My heart does not condemn me ("For if our heart condemns us, God is greater than our heart, and knows all things. Beloved, if our heart does not condemn us, we have confidence toward God." - 1 John 3:20, 21), so I have confidence before God and, therefore, I have confidence before the people in my world.

2. Today I will rise above any sense of inadequacy that attempts to paralyze me emotionally, refusing to be intimidated by phony feelings of inferiority that come from needlessly comparing myself with others. I will welcome the creative tension that is a necessary part of the development of a unique vision for my life, instead of just coping with the random and meaningless stress brought about by choosing to live my life according to someone else's vision for my destiny.

3. Today I will hold my head high ("But You, O Lord, are a shield for me, my glory and the One Who lifts up my head." - Psalm 3:3). I will carry myself with confidence, speak like someone who is successful, walk like a winner, and present myself to the public as one who has a sense of purpose.

4. Today I will face up to the consequences of my mistakes. I will not run and hide from them like a coward, but I will have the confidence to deal with them head on, doing what I have to do to correct them. If I have done irreparable damage in an area, I will learn from the mistake that I have made, do what I can to contain it, and then move forward to something better and greater.

5. Today I will have the confidence to admit when I am wrong, making allowances for error without compromising greatness. Greatness is not perfection, and confidence that comes from a false sense of perfection is not real confidence – it is deception. My confidence today will flow from a sense of understanding who I am, knowing my strengths and weaknesses . . . virtues and flaws . . . potential and limitations.

6. Today I will find the balance between Christ-consciousness and self-confidence.

7. Today I will be strong in the Lord, and today I will live in the now!

Father, help me walk in confidence today. In Jesus' name, amen.

July 16
LIVING WATER!

"Jesus answered, 'If you knew the generosity of God and who I am, you would be asking me for a drink, and I would give you fresh, living water.'" (John 4:10 – The Message)

"Jesus said, 'Everyone who drinks this water will get thirsty again and again. Anyone who drinks the water I give will never thirst – not ever. The water I give will be an artesian spring within, gushing fountains of endless life.'" (John 4:14 – The Message)

1. Today I will live in the now! I will live in the now because I know that I have received living water – a river of life springing up from the root of Christ in me, and flowing out of my inner man, watering the desert of doubt, and causing it to bloom like a rose. Eternal life is my reality, and it causes me to be able to face all of the works of the spirit of death, and rebuke them with no fear or intimidation.

2. Today I will draw water out of the wells of salvation with joy. A broken spirit dries the bones, so I will pursue every outlet of joy that I can, giving no place to depression or sadness by my words, thoughts or actions. The joy of the Lord is my strength, and I make a decision to walk in Kingdom joy all day today, regardless of circumstances!

3. Today I will receive resuscitation, and be revived, refreshed and renewed by the rejuvenating properties and restorative realities of the rain and latter rain together! Every dry bone in the valley of my broken dreams will live again as the rain comes down from heaven and waters them, and does not return void or empty.

4. Today I will embrace the work of the Holy Spirit, so that out of my belly will flow living rivers of prayer and praise. I am in the river of God today – the supernatural place of life and healing provided by the Creator of every living thing – and miracles are flowing freely for me as the river runs rampant!

5. Today I will rejoice that God satisfies my mouth with good things, so that my youth is renewed like the eagle's. I am like a well-watered garden – a thriving, green olive tree in the house of God!

6. Today I will minister the good news – the washing of water by the word - to those who are discouraged and spiritually dried out from their bleak, arid and fruitless existence – those dwelling in a weary land where there is no water.

7. Today I will go with the flow! The Captain of my salvation is leading me today by signs and wonders – many infallible proofs - by confirmation to His word, and the reliability of His still, small voice. I will follow Him anywhere today, and today I will live in the now!

Father, let Your living water flow out of me today. In Jesus' name, amen.

July 17
UNTAPPED RESOURCES!

"And my God will liberally supply (fill to the full) your every need according to His riches in glory in Christ Jesus." (Philippians 4:19 – AMP)

1. Today I will live in the now! I will live in the now because my need – my one, singular need - is Christ, and in Him I have all of my need(s) abundantly supplied. Every necessary thing is being added to my life as I seek the Kingdom first. The Father knows what I have need of, even before I ask – but today I just ask for a revelation of the Christ being formed in me, for the full stature of Christ is the measuring stick by which I am supplied in the material world ("according to His riches in glory by Christ Jesus") — the "glory" is in me! Christ *IN* me, the hope of glory! Everything that I need is in Christ, and Christ is in me – and I am in Christ!

2. Today I will recognize the process by which He daily loads me with His benefits, and I will not forget them. He forgives all of my iniquities in the now! He heals all of my diseases in the now! He renews my youth in the now!

3. Today I will make good use of the prosperity available to me in the New Covenant - released into my life in direct proportion to the prosperity of my soul. The unsearchable riches of the Kingdom flow from the inside out so that I don't have to depend on the outside world to meet my needs – *I* provide prosperity to the outside world!

4. Today I will enjoy abundant life, with no sense of poverty, lack, shame or guilt. God is good, and I will not hide the presence of His goodness in my life today!

5. Today I will remember that God is my source. It is written: "And [God] who provides seed for the sower and bread for eating will also provide and multiply your [resources for] sowing and increase the fruits of your righteousness [which manifests itself in active goodness, kindness and charity]" (2 Corinthians 9:10 - AMP). All promotion, opportunity, flow of wealth and material success comes from the Father of Lights, Who gives all good gifts!

6. Today I will give and receive – good measure, pressed down, shaken together, and running over! I will *give* outside the box because I *think* outside the box!

7. Today I will cooperate with God's work in my life to multiply my resources. The same God who sends ravens to feed His prophets and puts tax money in the mouth of a fish, will show extravagant creativity in giving me what I need, exactly when I need it. I have everything that I need in the now! I won't miss a thing today, and today I will live in the now!

Father, help me to tap in to Your resources today. In Jesus' name, amen.

July 18
PAIN RELIEVER!

"I'm leaving you well and whole. That's my parting gift to you. Peace. I don't leave you the way you're used to being left – feeling abandoned, bereft. So don't be upset. Don't be distraught." (John 14:27 – The Message)

1. Today I will live in the now! I will live in the now because I positively possess the peace that passes the process of natural perception. The stripes of Jesus provide healing for me in three dimensions – spiritual healing, emotional healing, and healing that manifests itself to the material world through my natural body.

2. Today I will be strong in my heart ("Wait on the Lord . . . and He shall strengthen your heart . . ." – Psalm 27:14), for out of the heart are the issues of life. The Word of God is my anchor on the tumultuous and turbulent sea of life, so I will meditate on it until I bring myself into calm stability. No word spoken to me can weaken my stance as I walk on the water of circumstances by keeping my gaze fixed on Jesus!

3. Today I will officially decline any invitation offered to me to take a guilt trip. I may take many journeys today, but I will NOT go where the guilt is! The Christ of the now removes the pain of the past, and provides forgiveness and absolution, the healing of memories, and an ability to attain a paradigm shift concerning my problems, which are actually strengthening me today! So I will not hesitate to deal with them head on, assuming no guilt or spirit of condemnation.

4. Today I will be made whole as I pray for others. The Lord turned the captivity of Job when he prayed for his friends, so I will take a cue from him in this area. I will not be so self-absorbed that I become insensitive to the needs of those around me, and I will channel the energy of my own hurt into fervent intercession for them. I will pray with power because I will pray with passion!

5. Today I will trust the Divine Physician of the soul to administer His thoroughly thought-cleansing therapy to me in ways that may be higher than what I am able to comprehend with the natural mind. I will travel the rocky road to recovery without restraint because the Good Shepherd knows where He is leading me.

6. Today I will envelope myself with the things that I love, allowing my surroundings to become a refuge for me and a sanctuary for my spirit man. I will use my creative abilities to build an environment for myself that is conducive to healing, and I will find within it a passageway to the secret place of the Most High, where I will be able to abide under the shadow of the Almighty!

7. Today I will make the decision to walk freed from pain, giving up the familiarity and shallow comfort of self-pity, and today I will live in the now!

Father, help me to be a pain reliever for someone else today. In Jesus' name, amen.

July 19
SPIRITUAL AUTHORITY!

"Remember your leaders and superiors in authority, [for it was they] who brought to you the Word of God. Observe attentively and consider their manner of living (the outcome of their well-spent lives) and imitate their faith . . . Obey your spiritual leaders and submit to them [continually recognizing their authority over you]; for they are constantly keeping watch over your souls and guarding your spiritual welfare, as men who will have to render an account [of their trust]. [Do your part to] let them do this with gladness, and not with sighing and groaning, for that would not be profitable to you [either]." (Hebrews 13:7, 17 – AMP)

1. Today I will live in the now! I will live in the now because I understand the principle of finding liberty in submission. I know that, in God, the way up is down, so I will let this mind be in me that was in Christ (Philippians 2:5) by humbling myself under the mighty hand of God, that He may exalt me in due season.

2. Today I will lead a quiet and peaceable life in all godliness and reverence, by making supplication, praying, interceding, and giving thanks for those in authority over me (1 Timothy 2:1, 2).

3. Today I will walk in the kind of faith that causes Jesus to marvel, knowing that I only have authority because I am under authority (Matthew 8:5-13).

4. Today I will practice the law of love, allowing true humility and servitude to promote me, not only in the Kingdom, but also in the natural world around me.

5. Today I will make peace with the inevitability that the greatest in the Kingdom must be the servant of all. Pride will not prevent me from practicing the precepts and principles of this promise for promotion!

6. Today I will respect the fivefold ministry – Apostles, Prophets, Evangelists, Pastors, and Teachers – knowing that they are not perfect, but that they ARE called, and that they are gifts, given to the church by Jesus Himself! I will appreciate them as such, and welcome their input into my life.

7. Today I will walk in a new understanding of spiritual authority and how it provides confirmation to my destiny. I will pray for those over me, promote their vision, and be obedient to them as unto Christ by my words, thoughts, and actions. I will not sow discord among the brethren. I will not rob God by withholding the tithe that He has commanded be received by the Levites (fivefold ministry). I will not practice the witchcraft of rebellion (1 Samuel 15:23). Today I will live my life the Kingdom way, and today I will live in the now!

Father, help me to submit to spiritual authority today. In Jesus' name, amen.

July 20
PUMPED UP!

". . . exercise yourself toward godliness." (1 Timothy 4:7)

"But you, beloved, BUILDING YOURSELVES UP on your most holy faith, praying in the Holy Spirit." (Jude 20)

1. Today I will live in the now! I will live in the now because I am building myself up spiritually by working out my own salvation and by exercising myself unto godliness, becoming strong in the Lord and in the power of His might! It is written, ". . . Let the weak say 'I am strong'" (Joel 3:10), so today I proclaim and profess my mighty power in God by His Spirit!

2. Today I will grow in grace as I am strengthened with might by His Spirit in the inner man. As I grow in grace, I will grow in understanding, which will, in turn, enable me to deal with the relationships in my life in a positive and mature manner, as I overcome strife and every evil work that accompanies it.

3. Today I will glory in my tribulations, knowing that the trials of life make me stronger, for His strength is made perfect in my weakness! What doesn't break me or shake me will *make* me, and take me to a higher level of supernatural strength from the God Who will never forsake me!

4. Today I will be energized by the Zoë of God – the resurrection life in me that always overcomes death. The zeal of the house of the Lord will consume me with a fiery passion for the deep things of God, and will create a drive in me to do exploits in His name!

5. Today I will run and not be weary. I will walk and not faint. My attitude will keep taking me to the top as I gain new confidence by remembering all the battles that I have already won, and by giving God the glory for each of them.

6. Today I will practice the principles of good health – I will eat right (spiritually, emotionally and physically), exercise (spiritually, emotionally and physically), get plenty of rest (spiritually, emotionally and physically) and drink plenty of water (spiritually, emotionally and physically). I will be preserved blameless, spirit, soul, and body (2 Thessalonians 5:23), and will experience wholeness and divine life through my Kingdom efforts to build myself up.

7. Today I will be ready to face any giant without fear. I am "pumped up" today, and today I will live in the now!

Father, help me to achieve my personal best in every area of my life today. In Jesus' name, amen.

July 21
RESURRECTION POWER!

"It stands to reason, doesn't it, that if the alive-and-present God Who raised Jesus from the dead moves into your life, He'll do the same thing in you that He did in Jesus, bringing you alive to Himself? When God lives and breathes in you (and He does, as surely as He did in Jesus), you are delivered from that dead life. With His Spirit living in you, your body will be as alive as Christ's!" (Romans 8:11 – The Message)

1. Today I will live in the now! I will live in the now because Jesus is real, alive, and He lives in me! I am empowered by His emergence from the grave, regenerated by His resurrection from death, and animated by His anointing!

2. Today I will be fully alive in my life, allowing my natural senses to be quickened by God, so as to heighten my awareness of His beautiful creation surrounding me. By the Spirit I will hear the trees of the field clap their hands in adoration to the Most High, and I will declare with the Psalmist, "Let everything that has breath praise the Lord!" (Psalm 150:6).

3. Today I will not be afraid when I walk through the valley of the shadow of death, because I know for a fact that He is with me and that His rod (to protect) and His staff (to guide) aid and equip me to walk out of that valley today, and to successfully climb the mountain of the Lord!

4. Today I will be energized by the positive input of the people in my life. Words of encouragement, shared laughter, prophetic insights, inspirational fellowship as iron sharpens iron . . . all of these things will influence and invigorate my inner man to new life.

5. Today I will listen for the word of the Lord to me, specifically. I know that I cannot live by bread alone, but by every word that proceeds out of the mouth of God, so I will make every effort to find my rhema word in the now. His words will create an eternally living fountain within me, producing an effect that will be obvious to all who come into contact with me, including the ones who have no spiritual sensitivity. Even the heathen will sense that there is something different and life-giving about me today! The living word in and to me will recreate me to be a living epistle written on their human hearts, and I will become a manifested confirmation to them that the word works!

6. Today I will rebuke the spirit of death in Jesus' name.

7. Today I will allow the law of the spirit of life in Christ Jesus to make me free from the law of sin and death. I will enjoy the resurrection today, and today I will live in the now!

Father, help me to be really alive today. In Jesus' name, amen.

July 22
GETTING AHEAD!

"Don't look for shortcuts to God.   The market is flooded with surefire, easygoing formulas for a successful life that can be practiced in your spare time. Don't fall for that stuff, even though crowds of people do.   The way to life – to God! – is vigorous and requires total attention." (Matthew 7:13, 14 – The Message)

1. Today I will live in the now! I will live in the now because my ambition, drive and desire to achieve greatness is submitted to the Lordship of Jesus. Knowing Him is my greatest and highest aim, and yet He has encouraged me to pursue my own goals, and to accomplish things in the natural world that will promote and prosper me. In Christ I am able to seek the Kingdom, and still strive to be the best that I can be!

2. Today I will experience true success – God's idea of success – the kind that comes by simply being obedient to Him in every thing. Obedience is better than sacrifice, and I will walk in "better things" today because I have been called to live the life of the head and not the tail.

3. Today I will be smart, listen to the voice of my spirit, make good decisions, and do business wisely. I will associate myself with successful people, and will learn from them. I will hone my leadership skills, and will develop a grasp of my strengths and weaknesses that will bring harmony and balance to my pursuit of excellence.

4. Today I will believe the Word that says: This book of the Law shall not depart out of my mouth, but I will meditate in it day and night, that I may observe to do all that is written in it, for then I will make my way prosperous, and then I will have good success (Joshua 1:8) – Promotion comes from the Lord (Psalm 75:7) – He compasses the righteous with favor as with a shield (Psalms 5:12) – He will bless the work of my hands –(Deuteronomy 2:7) – My leaf also shall not wither, and whatever I do will prosper, (Psalm 1:3) – "I can do all things through Christ Who strengthens me!" (Phillippians 4:13)

5. Today I will think, act, talk, walk, and package myself like the winner that I am!

6. Today I will walk in the God-kind of love, because love never fails (1 Corinthians 13:8).

7. Today I will believe in myself, and will show my belief in others by helping them realize their own dreams. Today I will enjoy life at the top, and today I will live in the now!

Father, help me to be successful for the advancement of Your Kingdom today.
In Jesus' name, amen.

EXTRA MILE!

"And whoever compels you to go one mile, go with him two." (Matthew 5:41)

1. Today I will live in the now! I will live in the now because I am energized to go the extra mile if I have to. The God Who is more than enough enables me to do more than I ever thought I could – more than I can ask or think – and because I can do more, I can believe for more!

2. Today I will give 110%, rising to the top by trying harder . . . doing more . . . challenging myself to go the distance . . . giving my all, and then some . . . understanding my limitations, and compensating for them . . . being willing to do the right thing . . . loving hard work . . . being a team player . . . having a love for excellence . . . managing my time and money well . . . thinking positive thoughts . . . dreaming big dreams, and then working hard to make them come true!

3. Today I will go the extra mile in relationships, knowing that love always wins. I will not be afraid to make the first move . . . to admit when I'm wrong . . . to apologize if I need to . . . to ask for forgiveness if I should . . . to reach out to someone who has been hurt . . . to be persistent in my attempts to develop a rapport with someone who is lonely . . . to be vulnerable . . . to let someone know that I love them . . . to stay in touch . . . to lay my life down for another . . . to be interested in them more than I am interested in me!

4. Today I will not be afraid to turn the other cheek.

5. Today I will not be afraid to also give someone my cloak, if they ask for my coat.

6. Today I will pray for somebody other than myself.

7. Today I will be unselfish and uninhibited in my praise for someone else's accomplishments. I will prefer my brother, and will be a peacemaker if I can. I will invest myself fully in this day, working hard, loving freely, and giving of myself completely. It is written: "There is no fear in love, but perfect love casts out fear" (I John 4:18), so today I will not be afraid of the demands of commitment. I am not afraid that someone will take advantage of me. I am a winner because I am a giver! Today I will do more than I ever thought I could, by the power of God resident in me. Doing more will come naturally to me today, and today I will live in the now!

Father, give me the grace to go the extra mile today. In Jesus' name, amen.

July 24
FRESH OUTLOOK!

"You're blessed when you get your inside world – your mind and heart – put right. Then you can see God in the outside world." (Matthew 5:8 – The Message)

1. Today I will live in the now! I will live in the now because I am experiencing a daily revelation of repentance. I am changing my world by changing my mind, progressing through paradigm shifts that point me in new directions, promoting the perception of my purpose, and painting a permanent picture of unlimited possibilities for me.

2. Today I will practice the power of positive reinforcement, and will re-program my mind with the living word of God – His incorruptible seed. I will reward myself when I excel, training my mind to think the right way, so that I can do the right thing.

3. Today I will rethink my history, and will make the effort to see it in a totally positive light. No matter what has happened (or is happening) to me, all things are working together for my good because God perfects that which concerns me. The way I *see* it causes me to say, "It's ALL good!"

4. Today I will run with the vision, even if I don't understand every detail of it at this point in time. I will not have to wait until I fill in all the blanks before I start making genuine strides toward my goal, because I walk by faith and not by sight!

5. Today I will renew my faith in my faith. I have the ability to believe myself into greatness, so I will not underestimate my innate powers, bequeathed to me by the Author of the New Covenant Himself, to call things into existence that are currently invisible or intangible!

6. Today I will change my opinion to take dominion. My life is not controlling me – I am controlling my life, as I follow Christ. Today I will take charge of my emotions and passions because the fruit of the Spirit Who lives in me is self-control. In Him I am organized, disciplined and firmly focused on fulfilling my destiny!

7. Today I will experience the beauty of a whole new world by thinking a whole new way. My positive mindset will be a magnet for magnificent miracles and mighty moves of God. Today I will see the world from God's perspective, and today I will live in the now!

Father, freshen up my outlook on life today. In Jesus' name, amen.

July 25
STAND OUT!

"Do you want to stand out? Then step down. Be a servant. If you puff yourself up, you'll get the wind knocked out of you. But if you're content to simply be yourself, your life will count for plenty." (Matthew 23:11, 12 – The Message)

1. Today I will live in the now! I will live in the now because I am an original – the workmanship of God Himself! And because I know and like who I am, I will be able to unselfishly help someone else become a better version of himself/herself, knowing that I will reap a harvest for my own life in this area by the seeds of kindness that I sow today.

2. Today I will let my light so shine before men that they may see my good works, and glorify my Father Who is in heaven. I will not hide my lamp stand under a bushel of intimidation.

3. Today I will not waste my time on some bogus, religious version of false humility. If I can do something well, I will let it be known, so that I can be a blessing to humanity. I will speak well of myself, and will encourage others by speaking good things to them about their own lives.

4. Today I will remember that in the seemingly backward Kingdom of God, the way up is down. I will humble myself under the mighty hand of God, that He may exalt me in due season. In Christ I am a king and a servant, and I enjoy filling both roles because they complement one another perfectly.

5. Today I will not have to vie for the attention of others by being untrue to myself. Being myself is not just a good idea - it is absolutely necessary and essential to achieving greatness in God!

6. Today I will be confident enough to stay true to my vision.

7. Today I will not have to be validated by the praise of others or paralyzed by their criticism. I am who I am by the grace of God, and I will follow the right path simply because it is the right thing to do! Today I will receive promotion by the power of servitude, and today I will live in the now!

Father, help me to stand out for You today. In Jesus' name, amen.

July 26
STRAIGHT TALK!

"Let me tell you something: Every one of these careless words is going to come back to haunt you. There will be a time of Reckoning. Words are powerful; take them seriously. Words can be your salvation. Words can also be your damnation."
(Matthew 12:36, 37 – The Message)

1. Today I will live in the now! I will live in the now because I know that I have what I say, and that the creative power that God used to speak the worlds into existence has been deposited into my spirit, so that I am creating the world that I inhabit today by my words. There is a miracle in my mouth, and I will not abort it today by any words of unbelief that I may be tempted to speak.

2. Today I will use my power of positive profession (confession) to proclaim the purposes of God in my personal life, and He will watch over His word - housed in my words - to perform it in the earth!

3. Today I will speak as one who has authority. My words will put me over, and cause people to see me in a positive light. I will not regret anything that I say today because I will not say anything regrettable.

4. Today I will pray that the Holy Spirit will put a watch over my mouth, and will convict me to use my words in a constructive way only - no gossip, no whining, no complaining, no doubt and unbelief, no tearing myself down, and no passing on rumors that I have heard. My tongue will not be set on fire from hell.

5. Today I will take dominion over demonic devices by declaring definite words of deliverance to the kingdom of darkness.

6. Today I will call those things which are not as though they are – speaking of the nonexistent things as though they already existed.

7. Today I will renew myself with new conversation – a new way of expressing myself. Through repentance today, I will break old patterns of speech that have held me back, and today I will live in the now!

"For we all often stumble and fall and offend in many things. And if any one does not offend in speech [never says the wrong things], he is a fully developed character and a perfect man, able to control his whole body and to curb his entire nature." (James 3:2 – AMP)

Father, help me to watch my words today. In Jesus' name, amen.

July 27
SAVING GRACE!

"For it is by free grace (God's unmerited favor) that you are saved (delivered from judgment and made partakers of Christ's salvation) through [your] faith. And this [salvation] is not of yourselves [of your own doing, it did not come through your own striving], but it is the gift of God." (Ephesians 2:8 – AMP)

1. Today I will live in the now! I will live in the now because I am saved! I confess with my mouth that Jesus Christ is Lord, and I believe in my heart that God raised Him from the dead . . . with my heart I believe unto righteousness, and with my mouth confession is made unto salvation! I have called on the name of the Lord, and, by believing in the power of it, I have been given the authority to become a son of God. By these exceedingly great and precious promises I have been made a partaker of the divine nature.

2. Today I will have no fear of death or hell or of the wrath of God on my life. Jesus was wounded for my transgressions and bruised for my iniquities. The chastisement needful for me to obtain peace with God was upon Him, and by His stripes I am healed!

3. Today I will face every circumstance with the confidence and calm assurance that comes from knowing that Jesus ever lives to make intercession for me, in order to save me to the uttermost (Hebrews 7:25). Jesus is actually praying for me today, so all things are possible to me as I agree with His prayer of faith for my life!

4. Today I will be equipped and empowered by grace – God's unmerited favor. The same grace that saved me spiritually will also save my soul – helping me to become transformed by the renewing of my mind. It will also cause His strength to show up in my weakness, His grace is sufficient, and I can do all things through Christ Who strengthens me!

5. Today I will have grace for someone else. I will forgive and restore others because I have been freely and fully forgiven and radically restored to right-standing with God! The grace of God releases me to operate effectively in the ministry of reconciliation, repairing the breach for those who have cut themselves off, and enlightening those who are alienated from God in their minds.

6. Today I will not perform good works to obtain righteousness, but I will perform them because I already HAVE righteousness – I already AM righteous!

7. Today I will give God the glory for everything. He deserves all the praise, and He will receive all of it. I will boast in the Lord. I will glory in the cross. I will enjoy my salvation today, and today I will live in the now!

Father, help me to manifest Your grace in my life today. In Jesus' name, amen.

July 28
TRUE IDENTITY!

"But by the grace of God I am what I am . . . ." **(1 Corinthians 15:10)**

"You're blessed when you're content with just who you are – no more, no less. That's the moment you find yourselves proud owners of everything that can't be bought." **(Matthew 5:5 – The Message)**

1. Today I will live in the now! I will live in the now because I know that God desires truth in the inward parts (Psalm 51:6), and I realize that I desire that same truth for my own self-perception, and self-awareness. The God Who lives in me cannot lie, and His merciful compassion is safely leading me out of the dark valley of deception into the sunshine of liberty by giving me the courage to tell myself the truth about myself.

2. Today I will be real in my interaction with others because I am true to myself. Because I am content with my true identity, I don't need anyone else to validate me. I know who I am, and Whose I am. I can love with no ulterior motive – no strings attached – because I love myself as Jesus commanded (to love your neighbor as you love yourself).

3. Today I will overcome the self-deception that comes from thinking that I must be like someone else. I will accept the fact that God made me who I am – just as I am - and will be content with the gifting that He has seen fit to place within me.

4. Today I will not waver from my position of believing that I am who God says that I am . . . His workmanship . . . His righteousness . . . a son and an heir . . . a joint-heir with Christ . . . a partaker of His divine nature . . . the head and not the tail, above only and not beneath . . . more than a conqueror . . . a member of the Body of Christ, placed there by God Himself.

5. Today I will not have to embellish the truth about my accomplishments to gain someone's approval. In fact, I can let my accomplishments, whatever they are, speak for themselves concerning my abilities. I know that my integrity can't be proven, it must be discerned, so I will not blame myself when others reject or misunderstand me. It's their problem – not mine!

6. Today I will accept the people that I encounter as they are, allowing them the liberty to accept themselves — my unconditional love being an oasis for those dying in the desert of self-loathing and self-doubt. Love never fails, and it won't fail today!

7. Today I will help the earth find its true identity as the property of the Lord. I will make God real to the real world today, and today I will live in the now!

Father, help me to manifest my true identity today. In Jesus' name, amen.

July 29
GET VISIBLE!

"Here's another way to put it: You're here to be light, bringing out the God-colors in the world. God is not a secret to be kept. We're going public with this, as public as a city on a hill. If I make you light-bearers, you don't think I'm going to hide you under a bucket, do you? I'm putting you on a light stand. Now that I've put you there on a hilltop, on a light stand – shine! Keep open house; be generous with your lives. By opening up to others, you'll prompt people to open up to God, this generous Father in heaven." (Matthew 5:14-16 – The Message)

1. Today I will live in the now! I will live in the now because I have been commanded to let my light – my personal, individual and unique light - shine before people in such a way that I would attract them to God's light. In the same way that the moon reflects the light of the sun, and ultimately draws attention to it, I have a purpose in showing my good works – my light – to show that it is God who enables and empowers me to do what I do!

2. Today I will accept the promotion that only comes from the Lord, with no sense of inadequacy, and no thought that I might not deserve it. God has a need to show me off to the world (". . . that your progress may be evident to all" - 1 Timothy 4:15), and even though I know that gain is not godliness, I also know that it gives my Father good pleasure to give me the Kingdom, and all of the benefits that come with it! The better I look to the world, the better He looks to the world, and that is why He has made me His ambassador – His representative in the earth.

3. Today I will let the favor of God on my life take me to a higher level of success.

4. Today I will operate as a mover and a shaker. While everyone else sits around talking about what they would like to accomplish someday, I will get going on gaining ground for my personal project that promotes God's purpose for me. Any step toward my goal is positive, no matter how small it may seem in the natural. I will not "despise the day of small things," but will plant seeds, speak words, meet people, learn lessons, and move toward the mark of achievement.

5. Today I will share the good news of salvation with someone, telling them what Jesus has done for me, proclaiming the purpose of His atonement, and the power of His resurrection. My testimony will make Him real to that one that is not a theologian . . . the one who needs a visual aid. God, through me, will tell a story in pictures - the story of *my* life – but the message will be the glorious gospel!

6. Today I will not withdraw myself from the people who need to hear and see me.

7. Today I will let my light shine, and today I will live in the now!

Father, help me to be visible today. In Jesus' name, amen.

July 30
HIGH PRIEST!

"For we do not have a High Priest Who is unable to understand and sympathize and have a shared feeling with our weaknesses and infirmities and liability to the assaults of temptation, but One Who has been tempted in every respect as we are, yet without sinning." (Hebrews 4:15 – AMP)

1. Today I will live in the now! I will live in the now because I have the assurance that my compassionate and empathetic High Priest is interceding for me today. It is written: "For God did not send His Son into the world to condemn the world, but that the world through Him might be saved" (John 3:17); Jesus has not come to condemn me, but to bring me personal salvation on every level of my life!

2. Today I will remember that Jesus is praying for me, ever living to make intercession on my behalf in an effort to save me to the uttermost (Hebrews 7:25).

3. Today I will be honest and transparent before Him, knowing that His love covers a multitude of my sins. All things are naked and open to His eyes (Hebrews 4:13), and Christ Himself has born my shame by hanging naked on the cross for me. He Who knew no sin became sin for me. In Him I am forgiven! In Him I am righteous! In Him I am justified! In Him I am blameless! In Him I am holy! In Him I am complete!

4. Today I will trust the Apostle and High Priest of my confession (Hebrews 3:1) to watch over my words, to anoint them with His own creative ability and to present them to the Father as a worthy sacrifice of praise.

5. Today I will effectively overcome temptation because He will, with the temptation, make a way of escape for me (1 Corinthians 10:13). Sin will not have dominion over me as I walk in the Spirit and not in the flesh.

6. Today I will honestly worship the Son Who was and is a faithful High Priest over all His house (Hebrews 3:2-6). I will embrace Christ - the Prophet, Christ - the Priest, and Christ - the King, knowing that I will receive blessings from all of the facets of His superior and versatile anointing today.

7. Today I will stand in a priestly ministry for someone else, remitting their sins instead of retaining them (John 20:23), and offering up a sacrifice of intercession in their behalf. Freely I have received the priesthood, and freely I will offer it up. Today is a day for me to witness and partake in a great flow of mercy, and today I will live in the now!

    Father, help me to stand in Jesus' priestly ministry today. In His name, amen.

July 31
SENIOR PARTNER!

"We are assured and know that [GOD BEING A PARTNER IN THEIR LABOR] all things work together and are [fitting into a plan] for good to and for those who love God and are called according to [His] design and purpose." (Romans 8:28 – AMP)

1. Today I will live in the now! I will live in the now because God and I are both involved with my life and, as His partner, I am presently privileged to partake in the presentation of my personal destiny, according to His plans and purposes for all people!

2. Today I will remember that Christ is the True Vine, and that I am the branch. Apart from Him I can do nothing, but, with Him, I can do all things because His life is my life, and my life is His!

3. Today I will take my responsibilities as a co-laborer and a fellow-worker with God seriously. I cannot do what needs to be done without Him, but He cannot do what needs to be done without me, since He has given me the keys of His Kingdom.

4. Today I will discipline myself with the awareness that obedience is better than sacrifice. He is my mentor and example, so I will not do anything that I do not see the Father do, and I will not say anything that I do not hear the Father say today!

5. Today I will carry myself with the confidence that comes from knowing that I am an heir of God, and a joint-heir with Christ. I know where I came from, and I know where I am going. I know what I can and can't do, and I know what God can and can't do – He CAN work through me, and He CAN'T fail!

6. Today I will remember that God brought the animals to Adam to see what he would name them, and that whatever Adam called the animals is what God called them. In the same way, God has brought this day to me to see what I will name it, and I whatever I call it is what He will call it. He has involved me in the creative process for His own glory, and I call this day blessed, anointed, successful, and productive!

7. Today I will enjoy the fruits of my own labor, but I will give God all the glory, for He makes all things possible for me. God and I together form a majority – if He is for me, who can be against me? I am not stranded alone in the desert today, but I am with Him, working in His beautiful vineyard that is watered by His life-giving words. His words will be my words today, and His victory will be my victory. I can overcome anything today, and today I will live in the now!

Father, help me to walk in real partnership with You today. In Jesus' name, amen.

◇A◇U◇G◇U◇S◇T◇

A month to be restored and refreshed . . .

The heat is on, but help is on the way!

These dog-day afternoons are the days that the Lord, your Shepherd has made.

He is faithful to lead you to where the cool, green pastures are,

and to cause you to lie down beside the peaceful, still waters . . .

"Like the cold of snow in time of harvest, is a faithful messenger to those who send him,

for he refreshes the soul of his masters." (Proverbs 25:13)

No sweat . . .

Be cool . . .

Chill out . . .

Get ready . . .

Good news is coming like an unexpected arctic breeze from the north.

A miracle is in the making . . .

Welcome the surprise of a summer snow!

"The Lord is your keeper; the Lord is your shade at your right hand.
The sun shall not strike you by day, nor the moon at night." (Psalm 121:5, 6)

August 1
CREATIVITY NOW!

"God said, Let Us [Father, Son, and Holy Spirit], make mankind in Our image, after Our likeness, and let them have complete authority . . . So God created man in His own image, in the image and likeness of God He created him; male and female He created them. And God blessed them and said to them, Be fruitful, multiply, and fill the earth, and subdue it [using all its vast resources . . .] and have dominion . . . ." (Genesis 1:26-28 – AMP)

1. Today I will live in the now! I will live in the now because I know that God performed the ultimate act of creativity when He created after His own kind – the Creator creating creators! Every act of creativity is a manifestation of the nature of God because the divine spark is resident in all of God's creation, especially in human beings, whether they are in the family of God (through salvation) or not.

   The creative person is:

C - ognitive	(Hosea 4:6)
R - esponsive	(Psalm 118:17)
E - mancipated	(Matthew 15:6)
A - ware	(Ephesians 5:15)
T - ranscendant	(Isaiah 55:8, 9)
I - maginative	(Genesis 11:6)
V - isionary	(Proverbs 29:18)
E - volved	(2 Corinthians 3:12-18)

2. Today I will exercise my cognitive skills, apprehending, sensing and perceiving knowledge by the supernatural Mind of Christ in me.

3. Today I will be responsive to the spiritual impulses and messages that I am receiving from the Helper, the One Who shows me things to come. My ability to receive revelation knowledge will free me from the restraints of the tradition that makes the word of God ineffective.

4. Today I will rise above, surpass, and function outside the range of natural skill. The One Who gives the ". . . knowledge of witty inventions" (Proverbs 8:12 – KJV) will enable me to produce and develop ideas, independent of my experiential knowledge.

5. Today I will allow my imagination to be inspired by the Holy Spirit, and will manifest the images that He produces in my mind and spirit into the tangible, natural world.

6. Today I will not believe the report of those who tell me it can't be done.

7. Today I will dream the big dreams of God, and today I will live in the now!

Father, help me to be creative like You today. In Jesus' name, amen.

August 2
ABSOLUTE FAITH!

"[For Abraham, human reason for] hope being gone, hoped on in faith that he should become the father of many nations, as he had been promised, so [numberless] shall your descendants be." (Romans 4:18 – AMP)

1. Today I will live in the now! I will live in the now because I live by the kind of faith that pleases God – absolute faith - the type of faith that shapes the seen world by changing the unseen things first. The definition of *ABSOLUTE* is: Perfect in nature or quality; complete; not mixed; pure; not limited by restrictions or exceptions; unconditional; unqualified in extent or degree; total. Today my faith will manifest itself as **ENTIRE FAITH** as I continue to look to Jesus Who is the Author *AND* Finisher of it!

2. Today my faith will operate as **EXTREME FAITH** – faith that goes the distance and dares to defy logic. This operation of faith will show itself to be time-tested because it declares, "It's never too late for a miracle!"

3. Today I will flow in **EXCEPTIONAL FAITH** – the kind of faith that caused Jesus to marvel at the Centurion who said, "ONLY speak a word, and my servant will be healed!" (Matthew 8:8). I will walk in this kind of authority because I am under authority, and because I have the utmost confidence in the integrity of God's word!

4. Today I will stand in **ESTABLISHED FAITH**, refusing to be moved regardless of circumstances or the information processed through my five natural senses! ("But let him ask in faith, with no doubting, for he who doubts is like a wave of the sea driven and tossed by the wind." - James 1:6)

5. Today I will embrace an **EXPANDED FAITH** that comes by hearing the word, and grows as a tree that is planted in seed form, and then nurtured to maturity. ("And the apostles said to the Lord, 'Increase our faith'" – Luke 17:5.) The test of faith that I experience today will push it to its maximum potential!

6. Today I will move with **EXPEDIENT FAITH** – the kind that gets results NOW ("NOW Faith is . . ." - Hebrews 11:1). I believe I receive when I pray, and even though I know that it is through faith *AND* patience that I inherit the promises, my faith can do a quick work, today, in the case of a pressing need or emergency.

7. Today I will make the world a better place by the working of my **EXCELLENT FAITH** – faith that puts its total trust in God – faith that produces after its own kind. I will build myself up on my *most holy faith* by praying in the Spirit (Jude 20), and my faith will move mountains! Today I will believe God for the impossible, and today I will live in the now!

Father, be pleased with my faith today. In Jesus' name, amen.

August 3
'NUFF SAID!

". . . but one thing I do, forgetting those things which are behind . . ." **(Philippians 3:13)**

"To everything there is a season . . . a time to keep silence . . ." **(Ecclesiastes 3:1, 7)**

1. Today I will live in the now! I will live in the now because I am breaking the ties with my past by ceasing to speak of things that are over and done with. My conversation today will be in the now . . . what God is doing NOW . . . where I am on my journey NOW . . . the truth and revelation that I am walking in NOW!

2. Today I will stop bringing up incidents that remind me of the offenses of the past. I will release myself from the hurt and pain caused by others by forgiving them – everyone who has wronged me, whether they have asked for my forgiveness or not. What's done is done, and there is no point in my continuing to speak of negative things that are only going to bring oppression into my life. By forgiving others, even my enemies, I break any power or control that they may have over me emotionally or spiritually.

3. Today I will stop advertising for my weaknesses and failures. I will be real, humble and transparent. I will even admit when I am wrong and apologize when necessary, but I will not continue to harp on negative things that I have done or said that cause me to blame myself and bring my mind under a cloud of self-condemnation. If Jesus is faithful and just to forgive me and cleanse me from all unrighteousness, then I will have the good taste to honor His justification by shutting up about my shortcomings!

4. Today I will break any familiar patterns of negative conversation that I am apt to fall into with those who are close to me. I will address the issue head on, for my own good, as well as for the good of the person to whom I am speaking.

5. Today I will stop letting down my ethical defenses and allowing myself to fall into gossip, verbally judging others or speaking things that will snare me and cause trouble in my life. I am responsible for what I say, so I will use my Holy Spirit-produced fruit of self-control to help me stop and think before I speak. I will walk away from the temptation to engage in hell-ignited talk with others, and I will finish up every conversation today with no feeling of regret and no fear that my words are going to come back to haunt me.

6. Today I will be sensitive to the voice of the Spirit when He tells me to be quiet.

7. Today I will speak words that are like apples of gold in settings of silver, and today I will live in the now!

Father, help me to know when I've said enough today. In Jesus' name, amen.

August 4
ENCOURAGE YOURSELF!

"Why are you down in the dumps, dear soul? Why are you crying the blues?
Fix my eyes on God – soon I'll be praising again. He puts a smile on my face. He's my God."
(Psalm 42:11 – The Message)

". . . But David encouraged and strengthened himself in the Lord his God."
(1 Samuel 30:6 – AMP)

1. Today I will live in the now! I will live in the now because I have learned from David's example how to encourage myself in the Lord by speaking prophetically to my own soul. ("Bless the Lord, O my soul; and all that is within me, bless His holy name! Bless the Lord, O my soul, and forget not all His benefits." – Psalm 103:1, 2)

2. Today I will not feel sorry for myself for any reason. If God is for me, who can be against me?

3. Today I will not let myself fall into sadness or depression. The joy of the Lord is my strength!

4. Today I will not act like a big baby. When I was a child I spoke as a child, but now that I am an adult, I will put away childish things, and act and speak like the mature person that I am.

5. Today I will not be negative in my thoughts or words. I can do all things through Christ Who strengthens me!

6. Today I will not be afraid of anything. God has not given me a spirit of fear, but of power, and of love, and of a sound mind.

7. Today I will speak the word only . . . keep a positive outlook on life . . . respond proactively to all circumstances . . . forgive my offenders . . . pray for my enemies . . . see the glass half full . . . surround myself with positive people . . . count my blessings, and be grateful for all of them . . . forgive myself for my failures . . . refuse to live with regret . . . learn from my mistakes . . . keep smiling . . . look forward to my future . . . face my fears . . . keep moving in the right direction . . . be a blessing to someone . . . reward myself for my accomplishments . . . pray without ceasing . . . in everything give thanks . . . get up when I fall down . . . overcome evil with good . . . do the right thing . . . let yesterday go . . . speak well of myself . . . accept change . . . stay true to my vision . . . believe in my dreams . . . imagine possibilities . . . give myself a break . . . see the big picture . . . put my trust in God . . . keep my eyes on Jesus . . . rely on the help of the Holy Spirit . . . get it together for the sake of the Kingdom! Today I will encourage myself in the Lord, and today I will live in the now!

SELAH!

August 5
PRO WRESTLING!

"For we are not wrestling with flesh and blood [contending only with physical opponents] but against the despotisms, against the powers, against [the master spirits who are] the world rulers of this present darkness, against the spirit forces of wickedness in the heavenly (supernatural) sphere." (Ephesians 6:12 – AMP)

"For our fight is not against human foes, but against cosmic powers, against the authorities and potentates of this dark world, against the superhuman forces of evil in the heavens." (Ephesians 6:12 – New English Bible)

1. Today I will live in the now! I will live in the now because I am strong in the Lord, and in the power of His might. I have on the whole armor of God, and am skillfully using the hidden weapons of the Spirit, which are mighty in God for the pulling down of strongholds.

2. Today I will use my Christ-given authority to tread on serpents and scorpions, and over all the power of the enemy, and nothing shall by any means hurt me (Luke 10:19). I will tread upon the lion and the cobra – the young lion and the serpent I will trample under foot (Psalm 91:13).

3. Today I will give no place to the devil by giving him permission to use my power or to access my authority. Instead, I will cause him to flee from me by simply resisting him.

4. Today I will have no fear, because greater is He who is in me than he who is in the world.

5. Today I will overcome every work of darkness by the blood of the Lamb (which has already been shed for me), and by the word of my testimony (which I am walking out today).

6. Today I will keep it all in perspective - I will not rejoice that demon spirits are subject to me, but that my name is written in heaven (Luke 10:20)! I know that I have dominion in Christ on the earth, and will not struggle with accepting my rightful authority.

7. Today I will remember who the real enemy is, before I get myself entangled in a flesh and blood altercation. I will fight a good fight today, and win it, and today I will live in the now!

Father, help me wage a good warfare today. In Jesus' name, amen.

August 6
ULTIMATE VICTORY!

"So, my dear brothers, since future victory is sure, be strong and steady, always abounding in the Lord's work, for you know that nothing you do for the Lord is ever wasted as it would be if there were no resurrection." (1 Corinthians 15:58 – Living Bible)

1. Today I will live in the now! I will live in the now because I have come through the fire without the smell of smoke on my clothes, and I know that He Who began a good work in me will continue to perform it in my life, regardless of how many times I have missed the mark. I know the voice of the Good Shepherd Who always leads me into victory, and I will not follow the voice of a stranger who tries to drag me down to destruction by reminding me of my past mistakes and exaggerating my failures in my mind.

2. Today I will remember that, in Christ, all things are new for me!

3. Today I will refuse to give up, knowing that maturity cannot be obtained by any means other than growing gradually while facing forward – the process of learning life's lessons through long-suffering, and looking for the larger meaning in the laborious occurrences of low-impact living! I will not give in to the temptation to take the easy way – settling for a shortcut to something that God has already promised to me in His own timing.

4. Today I will be energized by the promises of God that speak prophetically to my potential and help me to perceive my purpose. Knowing who I am in Christ, and what I am inevitably becoming in Him, will produce an unshakable confidence in me ("Beloved, NOW we are children of God; and it has not yet been revealed what we SHALL BE . . . ." - 1 John 3:2). The seed of Christ deposited into my spirit will produce after its own kind, ultimately conforming me to His image!

5. Today I will access the whole armor of God that empowers me to excel in battle. I will fight the good fight of faith, and my faith will be the victory that overcomes the world for me! The people around me today will know that I am a champion!

6. Today I will not be weary in well-doing. My efforts for the Kingdom of God are not wasted, but they are an asset to God's plan for man. I will fulfill my divine assignment today with a good attitude and an unshakable energy, because I have read the back of the Book and I know that I (we) have won!

7. Today I will do something positive to change the world because I realize that I am on the winning team! God is for me, so who can be against me? My current situation will have a happy ending today, and today I will live in the now!

   Father, help me to abound in Your victorious work today. In Jesus' name, amen.

August 7
GOOD SPORT!

"Love endures long and is patient and kind; love never is envious nor boils over with jealousy, it is not boastful or vainglorious, does not display itself haughtily. It is not conceited (arrogant and inflated with pride), it is not rude (unmannerly) and does not act unbecomingly. Love (God's love in us) does not insist on its own rights or its own way, for it is not self-seeking; it is not touchy or fretful or resentful; it takes no account of the evil done to it [it pays no attention to a suffered wrong]." (1 Corinthians 13:4, 5 – AMP)

1. Today I will live in the now! I will live in the now because the agape love of God that has been deposited into my heart enables me to be a good friend and a mature team-player . . . someone who is a pleasure to be around . . . someone who is helpful, kind and generous to people everywhere.

2. Today I will not take myself too seriously. I will lighten up and laugh at myself when I make a mistake. I will not set myself up to try to be perfect. I will do my best, and encourage others to do the same.

3. Today I will not gloat when I hear a bad report concerning the circumstances in the life of an enemy ("Do not rejoice when your enemy falls, and do not let your heart be glad when he stumbles, lest the Lord see it, and it displease Him, and he turn away His wrath from him." - Proverbs 24:17,18). I will pray for my enemies and be good to them, knowing that vengeance belongs *only* to the Lord.

4. Today I will be low-maintenance in my personal relationships. I will be easy to get along with and will not add to the stress of those whose plates are already full by forcing them to have to deal with my unresolved issues. I have a faithful High Priest Whom I can talk to anytime about my problems.

5. Today I will let bitterness go, because being bitter just isn't worth the effort that it takes to maintain it or the hard feelings that accompany it.

6. Today I will be a peacemaker and I will be called a son of God because of it (Matthew 5:9)! I will play fair in relationships and will promote team spirit whenever and wherever I can.

7. Today I will bring joy into the lives of those around me. I will make this day a productive one, and today I will live in the now!

Father, help me to be a good sport in the game of life today. In Jesus' name, amen.

August 8
CHILL OUT!

"Casting the whole of your care [all your anxieties, all your worries, all your concerns, once and for all] on Him, for He cares for you affectionately and cares about you watchfully." **(1 Peter 5:7 – AMP)**

"Cast your burden on the Lord, and He shall sustain you; He shall never permit the righteous to be moved." **(Psalm 55:22)**

"Peace I leave with you, My peace I give to you; not as the world gives do I give to you. Let not your heart be troubled, neither let it be afraid." **(John 14:27)**

"Do not fret or have any anxiety about anything, but in every circumstance and in everything by prayer and petition (definite requests), with thanksgiving, continue to make your wants known to God. And God's peace [shall be yours, that tranquil state of a soul assured of its salvation through Christ, and so fearing nothing from God and being content with its earthly lot of whatever sort that is, that peace] which transcends all understanding shall garrison and mount guard over your hearts and minds in Christ Jesus." (Philippians 4:6, 7 – AMP)

1. Today I will live in the now! I will live in the now because I believe the word of God that tells me that I possess supernatural peace, given to me by Jesus Himself – in fact, it is actually His own, personal peace that He desires to share with me!

2. Today I will not worry about tomorrow. The Kingdom is in the NOW (Matthew 6:33, 34).

3. Today I will relax, casting all of my care on Him.

4. Today I will believe I receive when I pray. I can't worry *and* believe at the same time.

5. Today I will let go of the stress and pressure. The government is on Jesus' shoulder.

6. Today I will respond to whatever comes my way with these three words: "It's all good!" God is perfecting that which concerns me so I know that everything will always, ultimately, turn out all right with His help.

7. Today I will choose the good part and sit down with "laid-back Mary" at the feet of Jesus, instead of working up a sweat in the kitchen trying to help "stressed-out Martha" get her dinner ready! I don't have to worry about preparing a meal because Jesus is the Bread of Life – the Manna from Heaven! Today I will walk in the peace that passes understanding, and today I will live in the now!

Father, help me to keep it all in perspective today. In Jesus' name, amen.

August 9
ACQUIRE WEALTH!

"And you shall remember the Lord your God, for it is He Who gives you power to get wealth, that He may establish His covenant which He swore to your fathers, as it is this day." (Deuteronomy 8:18)

1. Today I will live in the now! I will live in the now because I have a Kingdom paradigm concerning prosperity, seeing it, from God's viewpoint, as an important and necessary multidimensional blessing, encompassing the prospering of my spirit, soul, and body! My God is supplying all of my need, on every level, according to His riches in glory by Christ Jesus. I prosper, and am in health, even as my soul prospers, so I will think about the acquisition of wealth in a godly manner, and from a spiritual perspective, knowing that heaven is sending it to me so that I can be a blessing to humanity here on the earth.

2. Today I will keep a lookout for men and women who are pursuing me for the purpose of giving into my life – good measure, pressed down, shaken together, and running over - those who have been activated in the spirit realm by my obedience, in the natural, in this area. I will be sensitive to the leading of the Holy Spirit as He directs key people to cross my path for Kingdom reasons.

3. Today I will walk in the assurance that comes from having laid up treasure where moth and rust cannot corrupt. When the need arises, I am able to make necessary withdrawals from my heavenly account because I have consistently made deposits into it. I can claim all of the promises of Psalm 112 because I have met the conditions stated in that chapter: ". . . He is gracious, and full of compassion, and righteous. A good man deals graciously and lends; he will guide his affairs with discretion . . . He has dispersed abroad, he has given to the poor; his righteousness endures forever . . ." (Psalm 112:4, 5, 9). My descendants will be mighty on the earth and wealth and riches will be in my house!

4. Today I will remember that Jesus, though He was so rich, became poor, that through His poverty I might be rich (2 Corinthians 8:9). His blessing will make me rich in every dimension today and He will add no sorrow with it.

5. Today I will derive confidence from knowing that I am an obedient tither/giver. I am the head and not the tail, with a liberal soul – one who has given to the poor and, therefore, has lent to the Lord. I will also discipline myself to present a worthy, verbal sacrifice to the Apostle and High Priest of my confession.

6. Today I will enjoy hard work, knowing that the Lord will bless my hands' labor.

7. Today I will promote a poverty-free mentality, and today I will live in the now!

Father, thank You for giving me the power to get wealth today. In Jesus' name, amen.

August 10
CHRIST-MINDED!

"For who has known or understood the mind (the counsels and purposes) of the Lord so as to guide and instruct Him and give Him knowledge? But we have the MIND OF CHRIST (the Messiah) and do hold the thoughts (feelings and purposes) of His heart." *(1 Corinthians 2:16 - AMP)*

1. Today I will live in the now! I will live in the now because I am walking in a greater understanding and appreciation of the Mind of Christ than I ever have before. I am beginning to comprehend its many facets:

    M - emory   (John 14:26)
    I - ntuition   (Isaiah 11:1-3)
    N - ewness   (Romans 6:4; 7:6)
    D - ecisiveness   (1 John 3:8)

    O - ptimism   (Hebrews 12:1, 2)
    F - oresight   (John 16:13)

    C - reativity   (Philippians 2:13)
    H - umility   (Philippians 2:5)
    R - evelation   (Ephesians 3:1-7)
    I - magination   (Ephesians 3:14-21)
    S - ensitivity   (Matthew 9:35, 36)
    T - ruth   (Ephesians 4:17-21; John 14:6)

2. Today I will have an edge in decision-making by using my Christ-centered intuition. I will enjoy the ability to know, without the use of rational process. I will have immediate cognition and acute insight for every important matter.

3. Today I will by motivated by maintaining a mentality that exists beyond all doubt.

4. Today I will be disposed to expect the best possible outcome in every situation and will emphasize its most positive aspects.

5. Today I will be compassionate beyond my understanding, having a sympathetic concern for the suffering of others, together with the inclination to give them aid, support or to show them mercy.

6. Today I will *walk* in truth and *speak* the truth.

7. Today I will courageously confront every challenge with complete confidence, and today I will live in the now!

Father, help me to walk in the fullness of the Mind of Christ today. In Jesus' name, amen.

August 11
SELF-SUFFICIENT!

"Let each one [give] as he has made up his own mind and purposed in his heart, not reluctantly or sorrowfully or under compulsion, for God loves (He takes pleasure in, prizes above other things, and is unwilling to abandon or to do without) a cheerful [joyous, "prompt-to-do-it"] giver [whose heart is in his giving]. And God is able to make all grace (every favor and earthly blessing) come to you in abundance, so that you may always and under all circumstances and whatever the need, be SELF-SUFFICIENT [possessing enough to require no aid or support and furnished in abundance for every good work and charitable donation]." (2 Corinthians 9:7, 8 – AMP)

"I have strength for all things in Christ Who empowers me [I am ready for anything and equal to anything through Him Who infuses inner strength into me; I AM SELF-SUFFICIENT IN CHRIST'S SUFFICIENCY]." (Philippians 4:13 – AMP)

1. Today I will live in the now! I will live in the now because I have learned how to depend on the Christ in me to bring me through the events of the day with obvious success.

2. Today I will appreciate the power of the prayer of agreement, but I will remain confident in the fact that I can pray *for* myself – *by* myself – if I have to.

3. Today I will take to heart words of encouragement from others, but I will remember that I can encourage myself if no one else is around to edify me.

4. Today I will be blessed and honored by the support of my peers, but, ultimately, I will believe in myself whether anyone else believes in me or not.

5. Today I will enjoy the company of friends and loved ones if possible, but I will equally enjoy my own company if they are not available.

6. Today I will participate in the anointing of corporate worship if the situation presents itself, but I will singularly worship the Lord in spirit and in truth if it doesn't.

7. Today I will remember that I am never alone because Jesus has promised to be with me always, even to the ends of the earth. I can depend on *myself* because I depend on *Him*. I will expect this day to be great, whether I am in a crowd or by myself, and today I will live in the now!

   Father, help me to be self-sufficient in You today. In Jesus' name, amen.

August 12
ORDINARY PEOPLE!

"Remember, our Message is not about ourselves; we're proclaiming Jesus Christ, the Master. All we are is messengers, errand runners from Jesus for you. It started when God said, 'Light up the darkness!' and our lives filled up with light as we saw and understood God in the face of Christ, all bright and beautiful. If you only look at us, you might well miss the brightness. We carry this precious Message around in the unadorned clay pots of our ordinary lives. That's to prevent anyone from confusing God's incomparable power with us." (2 Corinthians 4:5-7 – The Message)

1. Today I will live in the now! I will live in the now because I know that God uses ordinary people like me to do extraordinary things!

2. Today I will remember that the Kingdom is "at hand" — it is within my reach, in my everyday experiences. It is here, where I am, and God wants to take what I already have in my hand, and turn it into a key of the Kingdom!

3. Today I will look for the significant and profound things to be revealed within the context of the familiar and recognizable ("And He took bread, gave thanks and broke it, and gave it to them, saying, 'THIS is My body' . . . likewise He also took the cup after supper, saying, 'THIS cup is . . . My blood' . . ." Luke 22:19, 20). I will seek a revelation today of the power of understanding what "THIS" is for me in the now.

4. Today I will lay my little limited lunch of loaves and fish at the feet of Jesus so that He can feed thousands by multiplying my finite resources! He uses the foolish things of the world to confound the wise, and, as I follow Him closely, He will turn the water in my life into the finest wine! And if it seems that He is taking too long in the manifestation of the miracle, it is simply because he is saving the best for last!

5. Today I will be myself because God wants to use me just as I am!

6. Today I will not complain about what I don't have, but I will plant seeds of faith, with a vision for the future, expecting a great harvest in my life. God is increasing me as I enter my season of maturity and manifestation.

7. Today I will allow God to supernaturally make something special out of my simple life. I will do great things today, and today I will live in the now!

Father, use what I have in my hand today for Your Kingdom. In Jesus' name, amen.

August 13
MY HEALER!

"He was despised and rejected and forsaken by men, a Man of sorrows and pains, and acquainted with grief and sickness; and like One from Whom men hide their faces. He was despised, and we did not appreciate His worth or have any esteem for Him. Surely He has borne our griefs (sickness, weakness, and distress) and carried our sorrows and pain [of punishment], yet we [ignorantly] considered Him stricken, smitten, and afflicted by God [as if with leprosy]. But He was wounded for our transgressions, He was bruised for our guilt and iniquities; the chastisement [needful to obtain peace] and well-being for us was upon Him, and WITH THE STRIPES [THAT WOUNDED] HIM WE ARE HEALED AND MADE WHOLE." (Isaiah 53:3-5 – AMP)*

"He was looked down on and passed over, a man who suffered, who knew pain firsthand. One look at Him and people turned away. We looked down on Him, thought He was scum. But the fact is, it was our pains He carried – our disfigurements, all the things wrong with us. We thought He brought it on Himself, that God was punishing Him for His own failures. But it was our sins that did that to Him – our sins! He took the punishment, and that made us whole. THROUGH HIS BRUISES WE GET HEALED." (Isaiah 53:3-5 – The Message)*

1. Today I will live in the now! I will live in the now because I am healed – spiritually, emotionally, and physically – by the stripes of Jesus, the Christ!

2. Today I will believe with my whole, redeemed heart that by His stripes I am healed!

3. Today I will meditate with my whole, renewed mind the Scripture that says, by His stripes I am healed!

4. Today I will confess with my mouth that by His stripes I am healed!

5. Today I will be thankful in my attitude that by His stripes I am healed!

6. Today I will receive in my body the confirmation that by His stripes I am healed!

7. Today I will overcome by the blood of the Lamb and by the word of my testimony — and my testimony is BY HIS STRIPES I AM HEALED! Today I will believe it and receive it, and today I will live in the now!

   Father, watch over Your word to perform it today. In Jesus' name, amen.

August 14
MIRACLE MOUTH!

"Death and life are in the power of the tongue,
and those who love it will eat its fruit." (Proverbs 18:21)

1. Today I will live in the now! I will live in the now because my mouth has the power to help me COME THROUGH trouble! "The wicked is ensnared by the transgression of his lips, but the righteous will COME THROUGH trouble. A man will be satisfied with good by the fruit of his mouth, and the recompense of a man's hands will be rendered to him" (Proverbs 12:13, 14).

2. Today I will depend on the words of my mouth to preserve my life! "He who guards his mouth preserves his life, but he who opens wide his lips shall have destruction" (Proverbs 13:3).

3. Today I will escape destruction by the power of my words! "A fool's mouth is his destruction, and his lips are the snare of his soul" (Proverbs 18:7).

4. Today I will avoid trouble altogether by using the power of my words correctly! "Whoever guards his mouth and tongue keeps his soul from troubles" (Proverbs 21:23).

5. Today I will overcome condemnation by the words of my mouth! "For by your words you will be justified, and by your words you will be condemned" (Matthew 12:37).

6. Today I will use the power of words to dominate the physical realm! "For we all stumble in many things. If anyone does not stumble in word, he is a perfect man, able also to bridle the whole body" (James 3:2).

7. Today I will see a good day by speaking good things, and today I will live in the now! "He who would love life and see good days, let him refrain his tongue from evil, and his lips from speaking deceit" (1 Peter 3:10).

Father, help me say the right things today. In Jesus' name, amen.

August 15
CELEBRATE DIVERSITY!

*"In this new life one's nationality or race or education or social position
is unimportant; such things mean nothing.
Whether a person has Christ is what matters,
and He is equally available to all." (Colossians 3:11 – The Living Bible)*

1. Today I will live in the now! I will live in the now because I can confidently celebrate my complete freedom from prejudice, bigotry and all forms of narrow-mindedness. Because I understand the beauty of the diversity of the people of the earth – the spectrum of individuality that God has created for His world – I can enjoy life to the fullest. Diversity is a part of the natural order of things – as natural as the colors of the rainbow or the infinite number of shapes, shadows, and shades of spring flowers or autumn leaves. God is good, and so is His creation.

2. Today I will recognize that diversity brings new solutions – Kingdom solutions – to the ever-transient environment. I will appreciate the individuality of others, as well as that of my own, because God has called us all to rise above the uninteresting and limiting parameters of sameness. "Now you are the body of Christ, and members individually" (1 Corinthians 12:27).

3. Today I will exalt life by exalting diversity, with all of the opportunities that it presents. I will do what I can to pull down the strongholds of intolerance and division when and where I can, taking dominion, and overcoming evil with good!

4. Today, when I look at people, I will be able to see beyond their natural, fleshly appearance. "Therefore, from now on, we regard no one according to the flesh. Even though we have known Christ according to the flesh, yet now we know Him thus no longer" (2 Corinthians 5:16). Man looks on the outward appearance, but God looks on the heart, so today I will choose to see things in the world from God's perspective.

5. Today I will live and let live, look for the best in others, and will love people unconditionally because there is no fear in love. Perfect love casts out fear!

6. Today I will treat everyone with the respect that they deserve. I will do unto others as I would have them do unto me and, in so doing, I will show respect for myself and, ultimately, for the Creator of all the people of the earth.

7. Today I will show the real Jesus to the real world, and today I will live in the now!

Father, help me to be a bridge-builder today. In Jesus' name, amen.

August 16
SCHOOL'S OUT!

"My counsel for you is simple and straightforward: Just go ahead with what you've been given. You received Christ Jesus, the Master; now live Him. You're deeply rooted in Him. You're well constructed upon Him. You know your way around the faith. Now do what you've been taught. SCHOOL'S OUT; quit studying the subject and start living it! And let your living spill over into thanksgiving. Watch out for people who try to dazzle you with big words and intellectual double-talk. They want to drag you off into endless arguments that never amount to anything. They spread their ideas through empty traditions of human beings and the empty superstitions of spirit beings. But that's not the way of Christ. Everything of God gets expressed in Him, so you can see and hear Him clearly. You don't need a telescope, a microscope, or a horoscope to realize the fullness of Christ, and the emptiness of the universe without Him. When you come to Him, that fullness comes together for you, too. His power extends over everything."
(Colossians 2:5-10 – The Message)

1. Today I will live in the now! I will live in the now because I have the Mind of Christ, and am being instructed daily by the Holy Spirit, Who has written the laws of God on my heart. He is helping me to remember the deep, eternal things resident in me from the foundations of the world as I let that abide in me which I heard from the beginning (1 John 2:24).

2. Today I will make it my goal to walk in all the light that I currently have.

3. Today I will be willing to part with traditional, religious illusions that war against my revelation, so that I may know Christ and the power of His resurrection!

4. Today I will embrace, with my whole heart and mind, the spirit of wisdom and the spirit of knowledge (Isaiah 11:2).

5. Today I will see to it that I do not fall into the category of those who are "ever learning, and never coming to the knowledge of the truth" (2 Timothy 3:7 - KJV). I am open-minded and hungry for righteous reality, so today I will exalt Wisdom so that she may promote me to the next level of learning.

6. Today I will trust the still, small voice of God to be my inner guidance system ("Though He give you the bread of adversity and water of affliction, yet He will be with you to teach you – with your own eyes you will see your Teacher. And if you leave God's paths and go astray, you will hear a Voice behind you say, 'No, this is the way; walk here.'" Isaiah 30:20, 21 – Living Bible).

7. Today Jesus will be made unto me wisdom (1 Corinthians 1:30), and today I will live in the now!

Father, help me walk in revelation knowledge today. In Jesus' name, amen.

August 17
MENTAL HEALTH!

"For God has not given us a spirit of fear,
but of power and of love and of a SOUND MIND." (2 Timothy 1:7)

1. Today I will live in the now! I will live in the now because the God Who has recreated my spirit is renewing my mind and restoring my soul. It is written: "Fear not, for you shall not be ashamed; neither be confounded and depressed, for you shall not be put to shame. For you shall forget the shame of your youth, and you shall not [seriously] remember the reproach of your widowhood anymore." (Isaiah 54:4 – AMP)

2. Today I will be far from oppression or any other dark thing that tries to come against my mind. It is written: "You shall establish yourself in righteousness (rightness, in conformity with God's will and order): you shall be far even from the thought of oppression or destruction, for you shall not fear, and from terror, for it shall not come near you." (Isaiah 54:14 – AMP)

3. Today I will walk in the light of the glory of God, and that light will shine into every remote corner of my mind and will bring revelation, clarity and understanding to me concerning my circumstances. It is written: "ARISE [from the depression and prostration in which circumstances have kept you — rise to new life]! Shine (be radiant with the glory of the Lord), for your light has come, and the glory of the Lord is risen upon you!" (Isaiah 60:1 – AMP)

4. Today I will remain stable, settled and stress-free, even in the midst of confusion and insanity all around me, by keeping my mind stayed on God. It is written: "You will guard him and keep him in perfect and constant peace whose mind [both its inclination and its character] is stayed on You, because he commits himself to You, leans on You, and hopes confidently in You." (Isaiah 26:3 – AMP)

5. Today I will meditate the Word of God, and whatever is good and edifying, I will "think on these things." (Philippians 4:8 - KJV)

6. Today I will think positively and remain optimistic, regardless of the influence of negative people in my life.

7. Today I will walk in the blessings of the Mind of Christ, and today I will live in the now!

Father, help me to hold it together today. In Jesus' name, amen.

August 18
APPRECIATE LIFE!

"What I'm trying to do here is get you to relax,
not be so preoccupied with getting so you can respond to God's giving."
(Luke 12:29 – The Message)

"In everything give thanks;
for this is the will of God in Christ Jesus for you." (I Thessalonians 5:18)

1. Today I will live in the now! I will live in the now because I am aware that I inhabit a wonderful world that my Father has created for me to enjoy, and I am thankful for everything that He continues to do to make my stay here a pleasurable one. I am counting my blessings today because I am blessed when I go out, and I am blessed when I come in!

2. Today I will be thankful for the little things . . . a bird singing in a tree in my yard . . . hearing the laughter of children . . . sharing a joke with a good friend . . . finding money in a pocket of a coat that I haven't worn in a while . . . receiving a compliment . . . watching a sunset . . . hearing good news from an old acquaintance . . . eating something that's not necessarily good for me . . . knowing that someone is praying for me . . . the comfort of home . . .

3. Today I will live without regrets, because regrets tie me to the past and limit my abundant life in the now. I will see my problems as opportunities for God to work miracles, and I will view my mistakes as educational tools that prepare me for a better future. In my vocabulary, I will replace the words "if only" with the more positive words "next time!"

4. Today I will enjoy what I have available to me in this day. Tomorrow will take care of itself, and, even though I have things to look forward to, I will not allow my anticipation of future events to rob me of my appreciation of the wonderful NOW! I will make the decision to believe that today is the best day of my life!

5. Today I will remember to thank the people in my life who are a blessing to me – those who are reliable and dependable – those who go to the effort every day to make my life what it is. I will not take what they do for me for granted, and I will do and say things that will let them know it!

6. Today I will be in the moment, and will walk in godly contentment, being satisfied with what I have. I will consider the lifestyle of the lilies of the field.

7. Today I will remember to really thank the Lord for all of the blessings with which He regularly overtakes me. I will be loaded with unforgettable benefits in Christ today, and today I will live in the now!

Father, help me to realize what I have to be thankful for today. In Jesus' name, amen.

August 19
COMMAND PERFORMANCE!

"Applause, everyone. Bravo, bravissimo!
Shout God-songs at the top of your lungs!
God Most High is stunning, astride land and ocean.
He crushes hostile people, puts nations at our feet.
He set us at the head of the line, prize-winning Jacob, his favorite.
Loud cheers as God climbs the mountain, a ram's horn blast at the summit.
Sing songs to God, sing out!
Sing to our King, sing praise!
He's Lord over earth, so sing your best songs to God.
God is Lord of godless nations – sovereign, he's King of the mountain.
Princes from all over are gathered, people of Abraham's God.
The powers of earth are God's – He soars over all."
(Psalm 47 – The Message)

1. Today I will live in the now! I will live in the now because I know that God reigns, and as His offspring and heir, I am reigning today as well!

2. Today I will join with all creation in singing uninhibited praise to the Almighty! His throne and Kingdom are established forever! Long live the King!

3. Today I will cheer for the Sovereign Potentate Who rules over godless nations. The earth is the Lord's, and all of its fullness!

4. Today I will publish His mighty acts, declaring them to the heathen nations – magnifying His great name among the saints!

5. Today I will give Him my best and highest praise. I will bless the Lord with all that is within me!

6. Today I will ride on the high places of the earth with the God Who soars over all!

7. Today I will declare that my destiny is in Him, and today I will live in the now!

God, You are great, and greatly to be praised! Amen!

August 20
DIVINE ROMANCE!

"[She said,] 'I am only a little rose or autumn crocus of the Plain of Sharon, or a [humble] lily of the valleys [that grows in deep and difficult places].' But Solomon replied, 'Like the lily among thorns, so are you, my love, among the daughters. Like an apple tree among the trees of the wood, so is my beloved [shepherd] among the sons! [cried the girl]. Under his shadow I delighted to sit, and his fruit was sweet to my taste. He brought me to the banqueting house, and his banner over me was love [for love waved as a protecting and comforting banner over my head when I was near him].'" (Song of Solomon 2:1-4 – AMP)

1. Today I will live in the now! I will live in the now because God and I share a deeply committed and passionate relationship.

2. Today I will hear Him say to me, ". . . Arise, my love, my fair one, and come away" (v.13), and I will find a time and a place, even in the middle of a busy day, to be alone with Him to seek His face and to let Him speak words of intimacy and affection to me.

3. Today I will be totally secure in the solidarity of our relationship (". . . My beloved is mine and I am his! . . ." - v. 16). My confidence and high self-esteem will come from knowing that I am greatly loved and greatly desired by One Who is completely committed to keeping covenant with me.

4. Today I will walk in love with others because I love God. ("If someone says, 'I love God' and hates his brother, he is a liar; for he who does not love his brother whom he has seen, how can he love God whom he has not seen?" - 1 John 4:20)

5. Today I will keep the first commandment of the New Testament — I will love God with all my heart, with all my soul, and with all my mind.

6. Today I will keep the second commandment of the New Testament, as well — I will love my neighbor as I love myself.

7. Today I will succeed because love never fails (1 Corinthians 13:8), and today I will live in the now!

Father, show me how to love You more today. In Jesus' name, amen.

August 21
MAKE CONTACT!

"Then He turned to the host. 'The next time you put on a dinner, don't just invite your friends and family and rich neighbors, the kind of people who will return the favor. Invite some people who never get invited out, the misfits from the wrong side of the tracks. You'll be – and experience – a blessing. They won't be able to return the favor, but the favor will be returned – oh, how it will be returned! – at the resurrection of God's people.'" (Luke 14:12-14 – The Message)

1. Today I will live in the now! I will live in the now because the love of God in me is enlarging my heart to such a size that it is having to break out (and break free) of the little fortress of selfish interests that I have built around it in a vain attempt to protect it from harm. My enlarged heart will reach out to make contact with someone, even if it is risky . . . even if it is dangerous . . . because there is no fear in love, but perfect love casts out fear!

2. Today I will love the unlovable and touch the untouchable. The Christ in me will flow like a river of reconciliation to those who have been rejected and refused. I will gladly fill the role of a good Samaritan when the opportunity presents itself and, in so doing, the Kingdom will come and the will of the Father will be done on earth as it is in heaven.

3. Today I will not be overly and unnecessarily concerned with protecting my reputation when it comes to reaching out to someone who really needs my help. I will lay down my life for them, by the grace of God and the power of the Holy Spirit.

4. Today I will make time for people and will show a genuine interest in what is happening in their lives. I will show respect for others and make the people around me feel important and special — by making eye contact when we speak; by a firm handshake; by listening and reacting appropriately; by calling people by their names; by displaying good manners; by being thoughtful and considerate; by being helpful and generous; by showing them the real Jesus.

5. Today I will pray for someone else's needs, taking them as seriously as I would take my own.

6. Today I will communicate to others on their level – relating to them in a real way. I will not be insensitive or judgmental, accepting people as they are and ushering them to the mercy seat of the Christ Who loves them unconditionally.

7. Today I will be kind to strangers, knowing that I may be unwittingly entertaining angels (Hebrews 13:2), and today I will live in the now!

   Father, help me to make the right contacts today. In Jesus' name, amen.

August 22
GOOD CONFESSION!

"Fight the good fight of faith, lay hold on eternal life, to which you were also called and have CONFESSED THE GOOD CONFESSION in the presence of many witnesses."
(1 Timothy 6:12)

1. Today I will live in the now! I will live in the now because I understand the power of confession – the avowal of my beliefs - the declaration of the creed by which I live. Jesus said that if I say with my mouth what I believe in my heart, that I would have what I say (Mark 11:23). Today I confess the Word of God over my life, and over every situation that I am facing.

2. Today I will confess that Jesus Christ is Lord! It is written: "That if you CONFESS with your mouth the Lord Jesus, and believe in your heart that God has raised Him from the dead, you will be saved. For with the heart one believes unto righteousness, and with the mouth CONFESSION is made unto salvation" (Romans 10:9, 10). "And that every tongue should CONFESS that Jesus Christ is Lord, to the glory of God the Father." (Philippians 2:11)

3. Today I will consider Jesus, and offer up to Him a worthy sacrifice of my lips. It is written: "Therefore, holy brethren, partakers of the heavenly calling, consider the Apostle and High Priest of our CONFESSION, Christ Jesus." (Hebrews 3:1)

4. Today I will be consistent in my confession, regardless of transient circumstances. It is written: "Seeing then that we have a great High Priest Who has passed through the heavens, Jesus the Son of God, let us hold fast our CONFESSION." (Hebrews 4:14)

5. Today I will not waver in my faith, even if I receive a negative report, because I have hope and my faith gives substance to the things that I hope for. It is written: "Let us hold fast the CONFESSION of our hope without wavering, for He who promised is faithful." (Hebrews 10:23)

6. Today I will confess the word concerning my spirit, soul and body . . . my past, present and future.

7. Today I will be creative and authoritative in my speech, for life and death are in the power of my tongue. I will use the power of my words wisely today, and today I will live in the now!

"Let the words of my mouth and the meditation of my heart be acceptable in Your sight, O Lord, my strength and my redeemer." (Psalm 19:14) Amen.

August 23
SPREAD OUT!

"'Sing, barren woman, who has never had a baby. Fill the air with song, you who've never experienced childbirth! You're ending up with far more children than all those childbearing women.' God says so! 'Clear lots of ground for your tents! Make your tents large. Spread out! Think big! Use plenty of rope, drive the tent pegs deep. You're going to need lots of elbow room for your growing family. You're going to take over whole nations; you're going to resettle abandoned cities.'" (Isaiah 54:1-3 – The Message)

1. Today I will live in the now! I will live in the now because God is enlarging my life by placing within my mind a big vision and by depositing within my heart a big dream!

2. Today I will think big – outside the box. I will color my picture outside the lines, knowing that God will do more than I ask or think, in direct proportion to the power that works in me! (Ephesians 3:20)

3. Today I will prepare to expand to the right and to the left in expectation of the new thing that God is bringing into my life. I will "lengthen my cords" by running with the vision, and I will "strengthen my stakes" by grounding myself deeply in the Word of God.

4. Today I will expect to be challenged to change!

5. Today I will expect to be groomed for growth!

6. Today I will expect to be inspired to increase!

7. Today I will expect to be prepared for promotion! Today I say, "Bring it on!" - and today I will live in the now!

Father, help me to pitch a big-enough tent today. In Jesus' name, amen.

August 24
TRUE RICHES!

"Let your character or moral disposition be free from love of money [including greed, avarice, lust and craving for earthly possessions] and be satisfied with your present [circumstances and with what you a have]; for He [God] Himself has said, I will not in any way fail you nor give you up nor leave you without support. [I will] not, [I will] not, [I will] not in any degree leave you helpless nor forsake nor let [you] down (relax my hold on you). [Assuredly not!]" (Hebrews 13:5 – AMP)

1. Today I will live in the now! I will live in the now because I am absolutely confident that God will never leave me, nor forsake me. If my father and mother forsake me, then the Lord will take me up because He is a friend who sticks closer than a brother. Even if I make my bed in hell, He will come and find me!

2. Today I will be satisfied with solely seeking spiritual success, seeing myself safely and securely standing on the solid soil of soul salvation! In other words, as I seek the Kingdom first, everything that I need will be added to me, and I will prosper as my soul prospers! The most important thing is knowing that I am in Christ — for what does it profit a man to gain the whole world, and then lose his own soul?

3. Today I will serve God, and not mammon (money), for no one can serve two masters – he will love the one, and hate the other. But part of refusing to serve mammon is acknowledging that I do not have to ask mammon's permission to do anything! I never have to say, "I can't do this — or go there — or buy that, because 'I can't afford it.'" Money doesn't dictate or define the parameters of my life. Instead, I will say, "If the Lord wills, I will do whatever — or go wherever — or buy whatever." And my God shall supply all of my need, according to His riches in glory by Christ Jesus!

4. Today I will remember that I am bought with a price! I'm in! I'm connected! I have a covenant! I have a relationship! I am a son of the God Who owns the cattle of a thousand hills, an heir of the God Who gives me all things that pertain unto life and godliness, richly to enjoy ("He who did not spare His own Son, but delivered Him up for us all, how shall He not with Him also freely give us all things?" Romans 8:32), and a joint-heir with the Christ who willingly and voluntarily shed His own blood for me! *No one can pluck me from God's hand!*

5. Today I will feel like a million bucks!

6. Today I will have a prosperous mentality!

7. Today I will enjoy being in Christ, and today I will live in the now!

    Father, help me to realize how rich I am today. In Jesus' name, amen.

LISTEN UP!

". . . Do you think all God wants are sacrifices – empty rituals just for show?
He wants you to listen to Him!
Plain listening is the thing, not staging a lavish religious production.
Not doing what God tells you is far worse than fooling around in the occult.
Getting self-important around God is far worse than making deals with your dead ancestors."
(I Samuel 15:22, 23 – The Message)

1. Today I will live in the now! I will live in the now because I have spiritual ears to hear what God is saying to me – I know His voice, and I will not follow a stranger! Whether He speaks to me from heaven or from the depths of my inner man (the still, small voice) . . . by anointed preaching and teaching . . . by prophecy, tongues and interpretation of tongues, a word of knowledge or a word of wisdom . . . with a rhema word or a logos word . . . through the Scriptures . . . by the foolish things of the world . . . out of the mouth of babes . . . in the mouth of two or three witnesses . . . through an angel or by a dream or a vision . . . however He chooses to communicate with me, I am all ears today!

2. Today faith will come to me by hearing, and hearing by the word of God.

3. Today I will be still and know that He is God.

4. Today I will spend time in the secret place of the Most High.

5. Today I will study to show myself approved unto God – a workman who does not need to be ashamed, rightly dividing the word of truth.

6 Today I will recognize when God speaks, for His voice will make my spiritual baby leap in my spiritual womb.

7. Today I will pay attention to creation, for the heavens declare the glory of God! Today I will hear, *and obey*, and today I will live in the now!

Speak, Lord.

What God is saying to me in the now:

_____

_____

_____

_____

_____

August 26
FIRST CLASS!

". . . and yet I will show you a still more excellent way
[one that is better by far and the highest of them all] . . . ."
(1 Corinthians 12:31 – AMP)

1. Today I will live in the now! I will live in the now because God is continually improving the quality of my life by showing me a more excellent way in which to live it. Today I will operate in the systematic superiority of always embracing the NOW. I will **REACH FOR THE PRESENT** where God eternally exists, and will bring my thoughts, perceptions and paradigms into an understanding of what is currently happening in my life, and who I presently am in Christ.

2. Today I will ascend to a higher altitude in life, advancing by the acquisition of an attitude of aggressive faith! I will **REFUSE TO FEAR THE UNKNOWN**, walking by faith, one step at a time.

3. Today I will **REJOICE CONTINUALLY**, putting up a solid front of joy that will conform negative circumstances in my life into things that work together for my good! My positive attitude will promote me to the front of the line every time!

4. Today I will **RECEIVE MY DAILY SUPPLY OF MERCY**. God's mercies are new every morning (Lamentations 3:23), and they give me a sense of rightness with God that produces success-building confidence in me.

5. Today I will **RESPOND APPROPRIATELY TO THE VOICE OF THE LORD**. My prosperous and excellent lifestyle is not a fluke or the product of luck. I live a first-class life simply because I listen to God and do what He tells me to do.

6. Today I will **REMEMBER THE WORKS OF THE LORD**. I am humbled by God's goodness to me . . . always thankful, and ever grateful. I would consider it to be beneath me – and in very bad taste - to whine, murmur or complain about the abundant life that I enjoy on a daily basis.

7. Today I will **REST IN GOD**. He is my sanctuary. He is my Sabbath. I don't have to struggle with the symptoms of stress in my life because I have the peace of God! How excellent is His name in all the earth! He does all things well! He is an awesome God in Whom I put my trust today, and today I will live in the now!

Father, help me to make a good impression on the world today,
so that I can bring glory to You. In Jesus' name, amen.

August 27
FAST LANE!

"[Oh, I know, I have been rash to talk out plainly this way to God!] I will [in my thinking] stand upon my post of observation, and station myself on the tower or fortress, and will watch to see what He will say within me and what answer I will make [as His mouthpiece] to the perplexities of my complaint against Him. And the Lord answered me and said, 'Write the vision, and engrave it so plainly upon tablets that every one who passes may [be able to] read [it EASILY AND QUICKLY] AS HE HASTENS BY. For the vision is yet for an appointed time and it HASTENS to the end [fulfillment]; it will not deceive or disappoint. Though it tarry, wait [earnestly] for it, because it will surely come; IT WILL NOT BE BEHINDHAND ON ITS APPOINTED DAY.'" (Habakkuk 2:1-3 – AMP)

1. Today I will live in the now! I will live in the now because I am running with the vision, and the vision is changing everything in my life! Today I will run and not be weary; I will walk and not faint. I will keep up with the mobility of my ever-increasing vision by remembering that in Him I live, and in Him I *move!*

2. Today I will run **AGGRESSIVELY** with the vision!

3. Today I will run **CONSISTENTLY** with the vision!

4. Today I will run **COURAGEOUSLY** with the vision!

5. Today I will run **FAITHFULLY** with the vision!

6. Today I will run **FAST** with the vision!

7. Today I will run **WELL** with the vision, and today I will live in the now!

"The Lord God is my strength, my personal bravery, and my invincible army; he makes my feet like hinds' feet, and will make me to walk [not stand still in terror, but to walk] and make [spiritual] progress upon my high places [of trouble, suffering, or responsibility]!" (Habakkuk 3:19 - AMP)

Father, help me to keep up with You. In Jesus' name, amen.

August 28
REJOICE EVERMORE!

"Be happy [in your faith] and rejoice and be glad-hearted continually (always)."
(1 Thessalonians 5:16 – AMP)

"Rejoice in the Lord always [delight, gladden yourselves in Him];
again I say, Rejoice! (Philippians 4:4 – AMP)

1. Today I will live in the now! I will live in the now because the joy of the Lord is my strength, I have a song in my heart and a good report in my mouth. I am cheerful, positive, optimistic and full of faith for the future. I have too much to be happy about – too much to be thankful for – to allow myself to succumb to a bad mood, much less a spirit of depression. Today is a great day to be alive . . . a great day to praise the Lord . . . a great day for the Kingdom to come! Today is the day that the Lord has made and I will REJOICE and be glad in it!

2. Today I will remember that the sun is shining up above the clouds, even during the darkest thunderstorm. The sky is blue above the clouds every day. The weather is beautiful above the clouds every day. Today I will know where to look for the sunshine, and I will find it!

3. Today I will locate my joy and return to an internal place of happiness. It is written: "[The Lord God says,] And the redeemed of the Lord shall RETURN and come with singing to Zion; everlasting joy shall be upon their heads. They shall obtain joy and gladness, and sorrow and sighing shall flee away." (Isaiah 51:11 – AMP)

4. Today I will exercise dominion in the interior world by choosing to be happy regardless of outward circumstances. ". . . He who has a merry heart has a continual feast" (Proverbs 15:15), so I will set my own table and serve my own banquet, living the Kingdom life from the inside out. The joy of the Lord is my strength!

5. Today I will rejoice with those who rejoice, and weep with those who weep.

6. Today I will encourage myself in the Lord.

7. Today I will rejoice that my sins are forgiven and I am at peace with God. It is written: "The Lord your God is in the midst of you, a mighty One, a Savior [Who saves]! He will REJOICE over you with joy; He will rest [in silent satisfaction], and in His love He will be silent and make no mention [of past sins, or even recall them]; He will exult over you with singing" (Zephaniah 3:17 – AMP). I sing because I'm happy today, and today I will live in the now!

Father, sing for joy over me today. In Jesus' name, amen.

August 29
BUSINESS SENSE!

"Not slothful in business; fervent in spirit; serving the Lord." (Romans 12:11 - KJV)

"Servants, obey in everything those who are your earthly masters, not only when their eyes are on you as pleasers of men, but in simplicity of purpose [with all your heart] because of your reverence for the Lord and as a sincere expression of your devotion to Him. Whatever may be your task, work at it heartily (from the soul), as [something done] for the Lord and not for men, knowing [with all certainty] that it is from the Lord [and not from men] that you will receive the inheritance which is your [real] reward. [The One Whom] you are actually serving [is] the Lord Christ (the Messiah)." (Colossians 3: 22-24 – AMP)

1. Today I will live in the now! I will live in the now because I can see my vocation and employment from God's perspective.

2. Today I will be diligent in the work of my hands.

3. Today I will remember that I am working for the Lord, not for men, so I will have a good attitude concerning my labor.

4. Today I will walk in authority because I am under authority (Matthew 8:9).

5. Today I will be honest and will characterize integrity — doing the right thing, whether anyone else does or not — taking responsibility for my own actions and for the quality of my own work.

6. Today I will be thankful that God has given me a way to make money. He gives me the power to get wealth that He may establish His covenant with me (Deuteronomy 8:18).

7. Today I will be successful and will achieve my goals in life by being a hard working Kingdom–seeker with a vision for excellence! I can do all things through Christ who strengthens me. I will put my hand to the plow and not look back today, and today I will live in the now!

Father, help me to do a good job today. In Jesus' name, amen.

August 30
YOU PASS!

"The words of the Lord are pure words,
like silver tried in a furnace of earth, purified seven times." (Psalm 12:6)

1. Today I will live in the now! I will live in the now because I am passing the seven trials of the Word of God in my life – the test of my divinely inspired dreams that define a door through which I am able to discover my destiny. Today I will pass the **TRIAL OF SIGHT**, believing that my dreams are coming true, even if I can't see progress toward that end. I walk by faith and not by sight because faith is the evidence of things not seen!

2. Today I will pass the **TRIAL OF SELF-ESTEEM** by believing that I am worthy to receive answers to prayers, and the fulfillment of vision, because Christ has made me worthy! I will not lose out because of some bogus idea that I don't deserve the best in my life.

3. Today I will pass the **TEST OF SOCIETY**. If God requires me to do the ridiculous so that He can do the miraculous, I will gladly obey Him. I will not worry about what people will think or say about me. God uses the foolish things of the world to confound the wise, and I will walk in His logic concerning the confirmation of His Word!

4. Today I will pass the **TEST OF SUBMISSION**, being willing to submit my dreams to the Lordship of Jesus. In Him I live, and my personal desires must always come under the umbrella of these words: "let *YOUR* Kingdom come, let *YOUR* will be done on earth as it is in heaven."

5. Today I will pass the **TEST OF SEPARATION**, knowing that success will potentially separate me from others who may be jealous of it or intimidated by it. The hundredfold return comes with persecutions, so I will be prepared to deal with the transition that may come from my being promoted and favored of the Lord.

6. Today I will pass the **TEST OF SEASONS**, refusing to be time conscious while remembering that timing is everything. Because I know that "to everything there is a season . . ." (Ecclesiastes 3:1 – KJV), I will content myself to enjoy living in the now, regardless of the present, natural state of my dream.

7. Today I will pass the **TEST OF SURRENDER**. I will believe in the dream confirmed by the Word of the Lord to me with my whole heart, but, as Abraham was willing to sacrifice Isaac, I will be willing to lay the dream down if I have to. In any case, I will see the goodness of God today, and today I will live in the now!

Father, help me to pass all of my tests today. In Jesus' name, amen.

August 31
MISSION ACCOMPLISHED!

"And don't for a minute let this Book of The Revelation be out of mind. Ponder and meditate on it day and night, making sure you practice everything written in it. Then you'll get where you're going; then you'll SUCCEED. Haven't I commanded you? Strength! Courage! Don't be timid; don't get discouraged. God, your God, is with you every step you take." (Joshua 1:8, 9 – The Message)

"This Book of the Law shall not depart out of your mouth, but you shall meditate on it day and night, that you may observe and do according to all that is written in it. For then you shall make your way prosperous, and then you shall deal wisely and have good SUCCESS. Have I not commanded you? Be strong, vigorous and very courageous. Be not afraid, neither be dismayed, for the Lord your God is with you wherever you go." (Joshua 1:8, 9 – AMP)

1. Today I will live in the now! I will live in the now because I know the importance of meditation in the Word of God – the kind of meditation that progressively produces prosperity and sends supernatural success ("But his delight is in the law of the Lord, and in His law he meditates day and night. He shall be like a tree planted by the rivers of water, that brings forth its fruit in season, whose leaf also shall not wither; and whatever he does shall PROSPER." - Psalm 1:2, 3). Today I will get the job done, successfully, and in excellence – finishing what I start, and bringing things to their completion!

2. Today I will stay focused on my mission by forgetting what lies behind, and pressing diligently toward what lies ahead. My eye is on the prize!

3. Today I will avoid unnecessary distractions – the "little foxes that spoil the vine" – and will be able to differentiate between what is important and what is vital.

4. Today I will keep it real. I will think outside the box without sacrificing my practicality. I will stay grounded and centered by anchoring my thought-life in the word of God.

5. Today I will take seriously the tackling of the tasks that I must accomplish – pacing myself, step by step – staying in the moment, so that I don't let myself become overwhelmed.

6. Today I will take pride in my work.

7. Today I will be an inspiration to others. I will be dependable and confident that I can accomplish amazing things today, and today I will live in the now!

Father, help me do what I've got to do today. In Jesus' name, amen.

⋄S⋄E⋄P⋄T⋄E⋄M⋄B⋄E⋄R⋄

A month for wisdom and knowledge.

Back to school . . .

Back to basics . . .

Back to the Bible . . .

The strength to study, the longing to learn, the promise of promotion . . .

All working together to bring out the best in you!

Study to show yourself approved . . .

Learn your lessons well . . .

Welcome to a wonderful world of walking in well-informed,
well-grounded, and well-timed wisdom . . .

Work well, without wavering . . .

Work without wasting the wealth of information available to you!

Study to be a "workman that does not need to be ashamed, rightly dividing the word of truth."

September: A Pursuit of the Proverbs . . .

September 1
WISDOM'S HOUSE!

"Wisdom has built her house . . . hewn out and set up her seven [perfect number of] pillars. She has killed her beasts . . . mixed her [spiritual] wine . . . set her table . . . sent out her maids to cry . . . 'Whoever is simple . . . turn in here!' . . . [God's] Wisdom says to him, 'Come, eat of my bread, and drink of the [spiritual] wine which I have mixed . . . [forsake the foolish and simple-minded] and live! . . . Walk in the way of insight and understanding.'" (Proverbs 9:1-6 – AMP)

1. Today I will live in the now! I will live in the now because I have the spirit of wisdom (Isaiah 11:2): the ability to use knowledge correctly. Jesus is made unto me wisdom (1 Corinthians 1:30) and I am daily growing in it and in revelation ("For I always pray . . . that He may grant you a spirit of wisdom and revelation [of insight into mysteries and secrets] in the [deep and intimate] knowledge of Him . . . " Ephesians 1:17 – AMP). Wisdom has built her house on seven pillars and I embrace all of them. Today I will walk in the **KNOWLEDGE OF GOD** (2 Peter 1:2; Philippians 3:3-10)!

2. Today I will walk in the **KNOWLEDGE OF GOD'S PLANS AND PURPOSES**. He made his *ACTS* known to the children of Israel, but He made His *WAYS* known to Moses (Psalm 103:7). Today I will have insight into the ways of God, because I love Him more than I love what He does for me!

3. Today I will walk in the **KNOWLEDGE OF THE SCRIPTURES**. I will study to show myself approved unto God as a workman that does not need to be ashamed of his ignorance, because I have learned to rightly divide the logos Word so that I am able to receive the rhema word (2 Timothy 2:15).

4. Today I will walk in the **KNOWLEDGE OF LIFE**, the kind that only comes by experience — learning by trial and error — from mistakes — graduating, maturely and soberly, from the school of hard knocks. Jesus LEARNED obedience through the things He suffered (Hebrews 5:8); Paul LEARNED how to be abased and how to abound (Philippians 4:11); I will seek to LEARN something about real life today.

5. Today I will seek to grasp a **KNOWLEDGE OF PEOPLE** so that I can deal wisely with them. ("But Jesus [for His part] did not trust Himself to them, because He knew all men . . . He Himself knew what was in human nature. [He could read men's hearts.]" - John 2:24, 25 – AMP) Today I will be people-smart!

6. Today I will embrace the **KNOWLEDGE OF SELF**, the truth that God desires in the inward parts (Psalm 51:6). I will find my true self in the revelation of Christ.

7. Today I will love **PRACTICAL KNOWLEDGE** — to be, like Moses, "mighty in words and deeds" (Acts 7:22). Today I will wisely live knowledgably in the now!

Father, help me live in Wisdom's house today. In Jesus' name, amen.

September 2
TREASURE HUNT!

"Good friend, take to heart what I'm telling you; collect my counsels and guard them with your life. Tune your ears to the world of Wisdom; set your heart on a life of Understanding. That's right – if you make Insight your priority, and won't take no for an answer, searching for it like a prospector panning for gold, like an adventurer on a TREASURE HUNT, believe me, before you know it Fear-of-God will be yours; you'll have come upon the Knowledge of God." (Proverbs 2:1-5 – The Message)

1. Today I will live in the now! I will live in the now because I know that there is great treasure buried in the field of my life experiences, and the Word of God is my treasure map that will lead me to it and will enable me to unearth it! Today I will search for the wisdom of God for every situation, refusing to rely solely on natural logic or on the information that I have processed through my five natural senses.

2. Today I will dig deep for understanding. I will not be satisfied with surface explanations for the mysteries of life. "But the spiritual man tries all things [he examines, investigates, inquires into, questions and discerns all things]; yet is himself to be put on trial and judged by no one [he can read the meaning of everything, but no one can properly discern or appraise or get an insight into him]" (1 Corinthians 2:15 – AMP).

3. Today I will embrace the power of godly insight, relying on my spiritual instincts and trusting them to guide me in the right direction. I will be sensitive to the inward witness as it responds to the promptings of the Holy Spirit.

4. Today I will tap into the knowledge of the God Who wants to make Himself known. His ways are higher than mine, but they are not past finding out! The secret of the Lord is with them that fear Him (Psalm 25:14), and I will walk close enough to hear Him speak in whispers today.

5. Today I will pan for the gold in my life that has been tried and purified in the fire. I will glory in my infirmities and thank God that He has caused all things – even the negative, dark and painful things – to work together for my good!

6. Today I will enjoy the adventure of hunting for buried treasure, without fear that I will uncover the things of the past that are under the blood of Christ. God has not dealt with me according to my iniquities, nor has He appointed me unto wrath. I will search without fear today, knowing that He has made me His righteousness!

7. Today I will fear the Lord and be wise, and today I will live in the now!

    Father, help me to find where the treasure is today. In Jesus' name, amen.

September 3
ENCOURAGING WORD!

*"Anxiety in the heart of man causes depression,
but a good word makes it glad." (Proverbs 12:25)*

*"Anxiety in a man's heart weighs it down,
but an ENCOURAGING WORD makes it glad." (Proverbs 12:25 – AMP)*

1. Today I will live in the now! I will live in the now because I am receptive and attentive to words of encouragement coming from God Himself, communicated through my spirit, and processed in my mind — words that will incite me to acts of bravery and valor — words that dispel discouragement and dare me to defy the darkness of depression. I will be made glad by a good word today ("I rejoice at Your word as one who finds great treasure." – Psalm 119:162).

2. Today I will plant seeds of encouragement into the life of someone else in order to receive my own harvest of encouragement.

3. Today I will derive confidence from knowing that God has spoken to my situation. My confidence is in the Word of the Lord and is manifested in my life in many ways and on many levels. This kind of CONFIDENCE is:

C – ourage	(2 Timothy 1:7)	
O – ptimism	(Jeremiah 29:11; Psalm 42:5, 11)	
N – onconformity	(Romans 12:1, 2)	
F – avor	(Proverbs 3:4; Psalm 5:12)	
I – ndividuality	(1 Corinthians 12:14-21, 27)	
D – irection	(1 John 3:8)	
E – ducation	(2 Timothy 2:15)	
N – erve	(Proverbs 28:1)	
C – onviction	(2 Corinthians 4:13)	
E – ffectiveness	(Matthew 5:13-16)	

4. Today I will look at my current circumstances *from God's perspective.*

5. Today I will not be passive when I hear negative news. I will refuse to just accept a bad report, by aggressively affirming the authority of the Word of God.

6. Today I will disconnect myself emotionally from people or things that produce anxiety in my life.

7. Today I will be enlightened, because the entrance of His Word gives light! I will walk in that light today, and today I will live in the now!

Father, help me to agree with Your Word today. In Jesus' name, amen.

September 4
MAKE ROOM!

"A man's gift makes room for him,
and brings him before great men." (Proverbs 18:16)

1. Today I will live in the now! I will live in the now because God has prophetically placed practical gifts within me that will, when properly cultivated and prioritized, progressively procure for me promotion, prosperity and prolonged success!

2. Today I will walk in the favor of God – the favor that will open doors for me that no man can close.

3. Today I will be significantly noticed for my diligence and excellent work ethic ("Do you see a man diligent and skillful in business? He will stand before kings; he will not stand before obscure men" - Proverbs 22:29 - AMP).

4. Today I will remember that promotion comes from the Lord (Psalm 75:6), but that I must co-labor with Him in wisdom and works of righteousness in order to receive that promotion in due season.

5. Today I will expect my gift to bring me before great men, but I will not act proud or arrogant about it. I will not feel superior to anyone else, remembering that I am a servant in the Kingdom. "Live in harmony with one another; do not be haughty (snobbish, high-minded, exclusive), but readily adjust yourself to [people and things] and give yourselves to humble tasks. Never overestimate yourself or be wise in your own conceits" (Romans 12:16 - AMP). I have learned how to be abased and how to abound, and I can do ALL things through Christ who strengthens me!

6. Today I will remember the Lord in relation to my prosperity, for it is He Who gives me the power to get wealth (Deuteronomy 8:18).

7. Today I will expect supernatural intervention in the affairs of my life. As I have given, men will give to me today – good measure, pressed down, shaken together and running over! I am anticipating something good happening to me today, and today I will live in the now!

Father, use my gifts for Your glory today. In Jesus' name, amen.

September 5
LOVE LEARNING!

"If you love learning, you love the discipline that goes with it –
how shortsighted to refuse correction!" (Proverbs 12:1 – The Message)

1. Today I will live in the now! I will live in the now because I love education and do not want to be destroyed, in any area of my life, because of a lack of knowledge. Knowledge is power, and discipline activates it. Today I will follow the example of Daniel and his friends who were "Young men in whom there was no blemish, but good-looking, gifted in all wisdom, possessing knowledge and quick to understand, who had ability to serve in the king's palace, and whom they might teach the language and literature of the Chaldeans" (Daniel 1:4).

2. Today I will make the decision to finish any course of study that I have started, knowing that I am able to run and not be weary – to walk and not faint. For this reason I will be able to reap, in due season, a harvest of higher learning.

3. Today I will expose myself to information – by reading good books, newspaper and magazine articles, listening to informative or inspirational tapes – anything that positively stimulates my brain and exercises my intellectual muscles.

4. Today I will engage in some healthy dialogue and lofty conversation with somebody intelligent – someone who knows something that I don't know – someone with the capability of broadening my horizons.

5. Today I will not be afraid or hesitant to ask questions. It is written: "If any of you lacks wisdom, let him ASK . . ." (James 1:5), and "For everyone who ASKS receives . . . " (Luke 11:10). I will admit when I don't know something.

6. Today I will not underestimate my mental abilities. I have the Mind of Christ and I can do all things through Him. It is written: "So Moses was EDUCATED in all the wisdom and culture of the Egyptians,* and he was mighty (powerful) in his speech and deeds" (Acts 7:22 – AMP). [*The wisdom and culture of the Egyptians consisted of the mysteries of the Egyptian religion, arithmetic, geometry, poetry, music, medicine, and hieroglyphics.] Today I will embrace natural knowledge, as well as spiritual knowledge, because the earth is filled with the knowledge of the Lord as the waters cover the sea!

7. Today I will resolve to never lose my love for learning – regardless of my age, circumstances or responsibilities. Continuing to learn will help to renew my youth, and keep me vitally involved with my world. Today I will keep an open mind, and today I will live in the now!

Father, help me to be a good student of life today. In Jesus' name, amen.

September 6
SELF-HELP!

"He who is loose and slack in his work is brother to him who is a destroyer and he who does not use his endeavors to heal himself is brother to him who commits suicide." (Proverbs 18:9 – AMP)

1. Today I will live in the now! I will live in the now because I know that God has given me real and tangible ways to help myself. I am dependent on Him, but He has not left me helpless!

2. Today I will make my own way prosperous and will possess my promised land by observing God's commandment to Joshua. It is written: "This Book of the Law shall not depart from your mouth, but you shall meditate in it day and night, that you may observe to do according to all that is written in it. For then YOU WILL MAKE YOUR [OWN] WAY PROSPEROUS, and then you will have good success." (Joshua 1:8)

3. Today I will take up my bed and walk concerning my own health and healing.

4. Today I will get busy with accomplishing the task of making my dreams come true. God will do what only He can do concerning my dream, but I will do what only I can do about it — faith without works is dead!

5. Today I will not waste valuable time by being jealous of others or by feeling sorry for myself for any reason. My life is unique to me and I, alone, am responsible for the quality of it.

6. Today I will make my words work for me ("A man's [moral] self shall be filled with the fruit of his mouth; and with the consequence of his words he must be satisfied [whether good or evil]. Death and life are in the power of the tongue, and they who indulge it shall eat the fruit of it for death or life." Proverbs 18:20, 21 – AMP). I will take full responsibility for my words and for their consequences today. I am what I say that I am.

7. Today I will work hard, with a good attitude, and a positive self-image. I will do something to make my life better today, and today I will live in the now!

Father, help me to help myself today. In Jesus' name, amen.

September 7
PLEASING GOD!

"These six things the Lord hates, yes, seven are an abomination* to Him: a proud look, a lying tongue, hands that shed innocent blood, a heart that devises wicked plans, feet that are swift in running to evil, a false witness who speaks lies, and one who sows discord among brethren." (Proverbs 6:16-19)

[*Abomination: extreme dislike or abhorrence; something that elicits extreme dislike.]

1. Today I will live in the now! I will live in the now because I do not desire to do anything that the Lord hates. Today I will not have a "proud look" — I will not feel or act like I am superior to anyone else, nor will I be religiously judgmental of someone whose life or actions may not meet with my approval. I am not God, so I will leave the judging to Him, and will walk humbly before Him in grace.

2. Today I will demonstrate my integrity by refusing to have a "lying tongue." I will speak the truth in love, knowing that the truth is liberating to those who really know it. I will be true to myself and say what I really mean, with no pretense, falsehood or hypocrisy.

3. Today I will not intentionally bring harm to anyone, nor will I have ill will toward them – not even my enemies. I will not "shed innocent blood" — literally, figuratively or theoretically.

4. Today I will not use my creative powers of visualization to "devise wicked plans." Instead, I will only practice the power of positive imaging for the purposes of promoting Kingdom principles!

5. Today I will not have "feet that are swift in running to evil." My true, inner self will awaken to righteousness, with a genuine desire to only do good and to be a positive influence on my world.

6. Today I will not be a "false witness who speaks lies." I will not gossip about others or talk about things that are none of my business . . . things that are beyond the scope of my understanding or authority.

7. Today I will refuse to play any part in "sowing discord among brethren" because I understand the extreme importance of unity. I will do everything within my power to promote it — to be a bridge-building peacemaker who operates fully in the ministry of reconciliation for the good of the Body of Christ and the Kingdom of God. Today I will live a life that brings pleasure to Him, and today I will live in the now!

Father, make my life pleasing to You today. In Jesus' name, amen.

September 8
MY CONFIDENCE!

"My son, let them not depart from your eyes – keep sound wisdom and discretion; so they will be life to your soul and grace to your neck. Then you will walk safely in your way, and your foot will not stumble. When you lie down, you will not be afraid; Yes, you will lie down and your sleep will be sweet. Do not be afraid of sudden terror, nor of trouble from the wicked when it comes; FOR THE LORD WILL BE YOUR CONFIDENCE, and will keep your foot from being caught."
(Proverbs 3:21-26)

1. Today I will live in the now! I will live in the now because I have the promise that the Lord is my confidence!

2. Today I will walk in safety, with no fear of accident or calamity, for the Lord is my confidence!

3. Today I will walk in progress on the path of my purpose — the Lord will not allow my foot to stumble! I will not fear failure or defeat, for the Lord is my confidence!

4. Today I will walk in peace. Tonight when I sleep, my sleep will be sweet ("I will both lie down in peace and sleep; For You alone, O Lord, make me dwell in safety" - Psalm 4:8), for the Lord is my confidence!

5. Today, in the event of a crisis, I will not fall apart – I will have the peace that passes understanding, and will keep my head about me — knowing what to do and what not to do. My heart is established, so I am not afraid of bad news, remembering that things are a rarely, if ever, as bad as they first appear. Today I will be a rock, for the Lord is my confidence!

6. Today I will walk in liberty. The Lord will keep my foot from being caught in the snare of the fowler. I will stay free by staying smart, remembering that the Lord is my confidence!

7. Today I will take on any challenge and will do more than I am actually capable of doing, because the Lord is my confidence. I will make His power known today, and today I will live in the now!

Father, help me walk in Your confidence today. In Jesus' name, amen.

September 9
ADDED YEARS!

"My son, forget not my law or teaching, but let your heart keep my commandments; for LENGTH OF DAYS and YEARS of a life [worth living], and tranquility [inward and outward and continuing through old age till death] these SHALL THEY ADD TO YOU."
(Proverbs 3:1, 2 – AMP)

1. Today I will live in the now! I will live in the now because I am walking in the kind of wisdom that adds quality years to a life lived in obedience to God. It is written: "Happy . . . is the man who finds skillful and godly Wisdom, and the man who gets understanding [drawing it forth from God's word and life's experiences]. For the gaining of it is better than the gaining of silver . . . and fine gold. Skillful and godly Wisdom is more precious than rubies; and nothing you can wish for is to be compared to her. LENGTH OF DAYS is in her right hand, and in her left hand are riches and honor" - Proverbs 3:13-16 - AMP. The wisdom of God will not just give me a long life, but a prosperous one, as well!

2. Today I will receive instruction and recognize good, sound advice when I hear it. It is written: "Hear, my son, and receive my sayings, and THE YEARS OF YOUR LIFE WILL BE MANY." (Proverbs 4:10)

3. Today I will worship the Lord in reverence and awe, respecting His commandments and loving Him with all of my heart. It is written: "The fear of the Lord is the beginning of wisdom, and the knowledge of the Holy One is understanding. For by me your DAYS WILL BE MULTIPLIED, and YEARS OF LIFE WILL BE ADDED TO YOU." (Proverbs 9:10, 11)

4. Today I will realize the importance of this day and will invest myself in it, totally. Every day of my life is important and special and significant. I will not take the gift of this day for granted.

5. Today I will make the decision to be satisfied with my life as it is. "With LONG LIFE I will SATISFY him, and show him my salvation" (Psalm 91:16). There is great confidence that comes from a life of contentment without complacency, so I will walk in that confidence by an act of my will. Life is good! God is good! Today is good!

6. Today I will make the effort to walk in health and safety. The name of sickness, disease, accident, calamity or any other potentially life-threatening thing must bow to the name of Jesus!

7. Today I will celebrate all that life has to offer, acknowledging, in all my ways, the God Who adds years to mine. Today I will LIVE, and today I will live in the now!

Father, help me to keep Your commandments today. In Jesus' name, amen.

September 10
TRUST GOD!

"Trust God from the bottom of your heart; don't try to figure out everything on your own. Listen for God's voice in everything you do, everywhere you go; he's the one Who will keep you on track. Don't assume that you know it all. Run to God! Run from evil! Your body will glow with health, your very bones will vibrate with life! Honor God with everything you own; give Him the first and best. Your barns will burst, your wine vats will brim over. But don't, dear friend, resent God's discipline; don't sulk under His loving correction. It's the child He loves that God corrects; a father's delight is behind all this." (Proverbs 3:5-12 – The Message)

1. Today I will live in the now! I will live in the now because I absolutely trust in the Lord with all of my heart. I trust in His power and ability, and in His unfailing goodness and faithfulness to me!

2. Today I will trust the Lord with my finances – with the whole concept of my prosperity. He will put me first with His guidance because I put Him first with my giving!

3. Today I will trust God with my health. The One Who created a miraculous, physical body for me to live in (I am fearfully and wonderfully made), has the power and the knowledge to fix whatever is wrong with it!

4. Today I will trust God with my relationships. He is the source of all favor.

5. Today I will trust God with my emotional needs. He knows what I need better than I do.

6. Today I will trust God with this day, and will not fear anything in it or any person that I encounter during it.

7. Today I will trust God with the fulfillment of my destiny. He is Lord over all of me – spirit, soul, body – past, present, future. Today I will not walk in fear, worry or anxiety of any kind (the Lord perfects that which concerns me!), and today I will live in the now!

Father help me to trust You completely with my life today. In Jesus' name, amen.

September 11
STRONG TOWER!

"The name of the Lord is a STRONG TOWER;
the righteous run to it and are safe." (Proverbs 18:10)

1. Today I will live in the now! I will live in the now because I have the confident assurance that God is my refuge and strength – a very present help in time of trouble! His name is my fortress and protection . . . I will not fear . . . what can man do to me? I dwell in the secret place of the Most High and, therefore, I remain stable and fixed under the shadow of the Almighty today, knowing that no foe can withstand Him! He has not given me a spirit of fear, but of power and of love and of a sound mind.

2. Today I will walk in perfect peace – the peace produced by possessing the promise that God is personally watching over His Word to perform it in my behalf – preserving and protecting me in the private pavilion of the power of His name!

3. Today I will boldly decree and declare that no weapon formed against me can prosper, and that every tongue that rises against me today will be shown to be in the wrong (Isaiah 54:17)!

4. Today I will be strong in the Lord and in the power of His might – strengthened with might by His Spirit in the inner man. The joy of the Lord is my strength. The Lord is my light and my salvation – whom shall I fear? The Lord is the strength of my life — of whom then shall I be afraid? Let the weak say I am strong (Joel 3:10), so in all of my weaknesses today, I say that God is my strength, and *I am strong in Him*!

5. Today I will rejoice in my righteousness, for the righteous run into God's tower and find real safety.

6. Today I will be kept free from all harm – spiritually, emotionally and physically. The angel of the Lord encamps around me – the angels bear me up in their hands, so that I do not injure my foot (my path of destiny) against a stone (of crisis, calamity or consequences of the curse).

7. Today I will enjoy the view from atop the strong tower of the Lord, and today I will live in the now!

Father, keep me safe in You today. In Jesus' name, amen.

September 12
INNER LIGHT!

"The light of the [uncompromisingly] righteous [is within him — it grows brighter and] rejoices but the lamp of the wicked [furnishes only a derived, temporary light and] shall be put out shortly." (Proverbs 13:9 – AMP)

1. Today I will live in the now! I will live in the now because the eternal light of God in me is growing brighter daily, bringing me into a larger realm of revelation and dispelling any darkness designed to defeat or discourage me! God is in me, and there is no darkness in Him!

2. Today I will let MY light – my own personal light - shine publicly for the purpose of presenting the power of God to the people Who properly perceive my place in His Kingdom. "Let your light so shine before men that they may see your moral excellence and your praiseworthy, noble, and good deeds and recognize and honor and praise and glorify your Father who is in heaven" (Matthew 5:16 – AMP).

3. Today I will enlighten others with bright ideas, inspired by the Father of Lights, expressed through words of encouragement that will ignite a fire of hope and creativity in them.

4. Today I will speak the Word of God over my life, and it will go before me, illuminating my path. I say to every area in my mind that is still under construction, "Let there be light!"

5. Today I will see things around me clearly, because Jesus said that if my *eye* is healthy, my *whole body* will be filled with light!

6. Today I will think of myself as a city set on a hill – a brightly lit city that cannot be hidden. Favor, promotion, success, prosperity and every good and perfect gift will be evident in the streets of my life's metropolis, and Jesus will reign from the center of it all!

7. Today I will arise and shine, because my light has come and the glory of the Lord is risen upon me. I will spread the glory around today, and today I will live in the now!

Father, help me to shine my inner light on the outside world today. In Jesus' name, amen.

September 13
OPEN EYES!

"Where there is no vision, the people perish . . . ."
(Proverbs 29:18 – KJV)

"Where there is no revelation*, the people cast off restraint . . . ."
(Proverbs 29:18 - NKJV) [*prophetic vision]

"Where there is no vision [no redemptive revelations of God], the people perish . . . ."
(Proverbs 29:18 – AMP)

"If people can't see what God is doing, they stumble all over themselves . . . ."
(Proverbs 29:18 – The Message)

1. Today I will live in the now! I will live in the now because I can see! Jesus said, "Blessed are the pure in heart, for they shall SEE God" (Matthew 5:8) and, because my heart has been purified from dead works, empty religion and irrelevant traditions of men, I am able to see the real God more clearly than I ever imagined that I could!

2. Today I will see the Kingdom. Jesus said that unless a man is born again, he will not SEE the Kingdom of God, so, because I am a recipient of the new birth, eternal life has entered my eyes, producing eternal vision of the eternal "I Am!"

3. Today I will be able to see what God is doing, in the now, in my life and in my generation. I will walk in godly insight, counsel, and discernment, having the spirit of the sons of Issachar (". . . the sons of Issachar, who had UNDERSTANDING OF THE TIMES, to know what Israel ought to do . . . " – 1 Chronicles 12:32). I will SEE my world, and will understand it by the Spirit so that I will be able to do my part in effectively reconciling it to God. I will heed Jesus' rebuke: " . . . for the sons of this age are shrewder and more prudent and wiser in [relation to] their own generation [to their own age and kind] than are the sons of light" (Luke 16:8 – AMP), and I will walk in Kingdom vision – the vision that will enable me rise above the level of those who cannot see God's plan for the earth — and will empower me to light up my world!

4. Today I will walk in the necessary discipline to fulfill my immediate vision.

5. Today I will walk in the necessary discipline to fulfill my long-range vision.

6. Today I will not perish, and I will not cast off restraint.

7. Today I will look and live, and today I will live in the now!

Father, let me see You today. In Jesus' name, amen.

September 14
STREET LIGHTS!

"But the path of the [uncompromisingly] just and righteous is like the light of dawn,
that shines more and more (brighter and clearer)
until [it reaches its full strength and glory in] the perfect day . . . ."
(Proverbs 4:18 – AMP)

1. Today I will live in the now! I will live in the now because I know that I have a personal path to pursue – a lifelong, spiritual journey of Christ-revelation and self-discovery – that is growing brighter and clearer every day!

2. Today I will trust the Word of God to be a lamp for my faith-following feet (I walk by faith, and not by sight!), and a light for my purpose-paved path (I was predestined to be conformed to His image, that He might be the firstborn among many brethren!).

3. Today I will remember that the spirit of man is the candle of the Lord searching the hidden rooms of the heart, so I will walk by the light of my recreated spirit, under the authority of the Lordship of Jesus, eternally crowned in the Kingdom of my heart, to reveal the internal dreams, visions, and prophetic revelations that have not yet been brought to light! The light will reveal the next part of the path that lies ahead. Turn up the lights! Let the adventure begin!

4. Today I will not be disoriented. I will pray. I will decree. I will worship. I will confess the Scriptures. I will be quiet before the Lord. I will meditate His Word . . . until I get my bearings . . . until I am centered in the center of His perfect will . . . until I find the flow where God makes a way in the wilderness and a stream in the desert!

5. Today I will walk in the Spirit and not in the flesh, for as many as are led by the Spirit of God are the sons of God (Romans 8:14).

6. Today I will seek wisdom and confirmation from those who are pursuing their own paths, but I will not judge them for their position or place on *their* path by *my* own, *personal* standard. My path is my path. My brother's path is my brother's path.

7. Today my steps will be ordered of the Lord — no accidents — no mistakes — no bad timing — no running ahead of God — no lagging behind God. Today I will run with the vision, and today I will live in the now!

Father, light my path today. In Jesus' name, amen.

September 15
STRONG SPIRIT!

"The strong spirit of a man will sustain him in bodily pain or trouble, but a weak and broken spirit who can raise up or bear?" (Proverbs 18: 14 – AMP)

1. Today I will live in the now! I will live in the now because my life is controlled and sustained from the inside out. My recreated spirit is the ascended part of my whole nature, and it is ruling my soul-life today and maintaining the quality of my physical body by the throne of Christ that is established in my heart! I will invest myself completely in this day, inspired by the incontestable insight that no infirmity can infiltrate or injure the infrastructure of my invincible inner fortress!

2. Today I will be rejuvenated by rejoicing as a result of the joy of the Lord resiliently resident in my re-born heart. It is written: "A merry heart makes a cheerful countenance, but by sorrow of the heart the spirit is broken. All the days of the afflicted are evil, but he who is of a merry heart has a continual feast" (Proverbs 15:13, 15). I choose joy for myself today and, in so doing, I choose well-being for every area of my life!

3. Today I will exercise myself unto godliness by choosing to do the right thing – walking in a works-free, nonreligious holiness, without legalism – finding spiritual strength through the true holiness that is simply an *outworking* of the divine nature *through* me.

4. Today I will medicate myself with the merriness of my own heart. "A merry heart does good like medicine . . ." (Proverbs 17:22). I will enjoy experiencing ecstatic laughter, releasing endorphins to elevate me emotionally, enabling me to feel encouraged and enthusiastic about exemplifying an ever-excellent attitude!

5. Today I will stand on the Word – the Word of the written page, and especially the Word written on the tablets of my mind and heart by the Holy Spirit. I will run my current course today with courage and confidence as I command the circumstances of life to conform to Christ's law. Because of the words "It is written . . . ," I will prevail!

6. Today I will cooperate with the Spirit of God as He uses prophetic people to help mend whatever brokenness there may be in my spirit that would weaken me.

7. Today I will encourage others to embrace their own strength by my example of empowerment emanating from the inner man. God's strength will be made perfect in any weakness that I may have. I can get through anything today, and today I will live in the now!

Father, keep me strong in my spirit today. In Jesus' name, amen.

September 16
SMART MOUTH!

"Don't jump to conclusions – there may be a perfectly good explanation for what you just saw."
(Proverbs 25:8 – The Message)

"He who answers a matter before he hears the facts — it is folly and shame to him."
(Proverbs 18:13 – AMP)

1. Today I will live in the now! I will live in the now because I am motivated to manage any manifestation of malignity toward others by moving in the mental maturity manifested in the Mind of Christ! I will not have to tear down someone else in order to make myself look good. I will remember that love "rejoices not in iniquity, but rejoices in the truth" (I Corinthians 13:6). I will not believe everything that I hear, especially when I hear something negative about someone else

2. Today I will not put my foot in my mouth by foolishly speaking of things about which I am ill-informed or of which I am ignorant.

3. Today I will know when to shut up. It is written: "A fool vents all his feelings, but a wise man holds them back" (Proverbs 29:11), and again: "Even a fool is counted wise when he holds his peace; when he shuts his lips, he is considered perceptive" (Proverbs 17:28). Today I will comprehend the meaning of the old adage "Silence is golden."

4. Today I will not say too much or too little. I will not need to impress anyone by making them think that I know more than I actually do. I will be smart enough to be myself. In the words of the great King David, "Lord, my heart is not haughty, nor my eyes lofty. Neither do I concern myself with great matters, nor with things too profound for me" (Psalm 131:1). I will believe in myself, expect the best of myself, walk in confidence and godly counsel – but I will keep it all in perspective. I will realize that I don't know everything. I will not have to always be right today!

5. Today I will think before I speak.

6. Today I will ask the Lord to put a watch over my mouth, relying on the spiritual fruit of temperance and self-control to assist me in this matter.

7. Today I will speak positive and constructive words of discernment and insight, and if I don't have any thoughts worth putting into words (if I don't have anything good to say) I will let my thoughts die unborn. Today I will walk in spiritual intelligence, and today I will live in the now!

Father, help me to speak like a wise person today. In Jesus' name, amen.

September 17
GET WISDOM!

"Get skillful and godly Wisdom, get understanding (discernment, comprehension, and interpretation) . . . forsake not [Wisdom] and she will keep, defend and protect you; love her, and she will guard you. The beginning of Wisdom is: get Wisdom (skillful and godly Wisdom)! [For skillful and godly Wisdom is the principal thing]. And with all you have gotten, get understanding (discernment comprehension, and interpretation). Prize Wisdom and highly exalt her, and she will exalt and promote you; she will bring you to honor when you embrace her. She shall give to your head a wreath of gracefulness; a crown of beauty and glory will she deliver to you." (Proverbs 4:5-9 – AMP)

1. Today I will live in the now! I will live in the now because the wisdom of God is bringing me into a whole new dimension of insight and understanding. I clearly am not clueless – I am clothed in the clean fear of the Lord, which is the beginning of wisdom (". . . the fear of the Lord is clean, enduring forever . . ." – Psalm 19:9)!

2. Today I will be defended by Wisdom. She will see to it that no weapon formed against me will prosper, and that every tongue that rises against me in judgment will be shown to be in the wrong!

3. Today I will be protected by Wisdom. She will lead me to the name of the Lord, which is a strong tower – the righteous run into it and are safe!

4. Today I will be exalted by Wisdom. She will show me how the Lord will compass the righteous with favor as with a shield!

5. Today I will be promoted by Wisdom. She will remind me that promotion does not come from the east, nor the west, nor the south, but God is the judge Who puts down one and exalts another!

6. Today I will be honored by Wisdom. She will crown me with loving-kindness and tender-mercies, and make me the head and not the tail!

7. Today I will embrace and highly prize Wisdom, gravitating toward sages, mentors, seers and visionaries — and fleeing from fools! Today I will wear the crown of beauty and glory given to me by her, and today I will live in the now!

Father, help me to "get it" today. In Jesus' name, amen.

September 18
UNDERSTANDING ALL!

"Evil men do not understand justice, but those who seek the Lord UNDERSTAND ALL."
(Proverbs 28:5)

1. Today I will live in the now! I will live in the now because I seek the Lord, and in seeking Him I seek the truth, because He is the source of all truth. Today I will begin to awaken to the understanding of all things resident in me through the power of the Holy Spirit ("However, when He, the Spirit of Truth, has come, He will guide you into ALL truth . . . " - John 16:13). By the power of the Paraclete, I will trust my own instincts and will rely on His voice communicating with my inner voice to bring about solutions to every problem that arises today.

2. Today I will embrace my own, unique spirituality, and will trust its powers of perception to produce the practical direction that I need for today for my walk of faith in the now. "But the spiritual man tries ALL things . . . and discerns ALL things . . . he can read the meaning of EVERYTHING . . . " (1 Corinthians 2:15 – AMP).

3. Today I will celebrate the charisma of the anointing in and on my life, and will concentrate on cooperating with its creative flow. "But you have an anointing from the Holy One, and you know ALL things" (1 John 2:20).

4. Today I will welcome the Teacher into every area of my life, and will allow Him to conform me to His own image through the distillation of His thoughts into my mind. "But the anointing which you have received from Him abides in you, and you do not need that anyone teach you; but as the same anointing teaches you concerning ALL things . . . you will abide in Him" (1 John 2:27).

5. Today I will realize that I know more than I think I know — letting that abide in me which I heard from the beginning — reading the Word written on the tablets of my heart — becoming the oracle of God.

6. Today I will rise to every occasion, having the right answer, at the right time, for the right situation – speaking beautiful, well-timed and appropriate words that are apples of gold in settings of silver.

7. Today I will seek God in new, unconventional ways. I will flow spontaneously with the Creator through the course of the day, seeking Him in places where I have not previously thought to look for Him – passionately praising Him in spirit and in truth. I will embrace His omnipresence and know that Christ is ALL! Today I will know that I know, and today I will live in the now!

Father, help me to walk in it ALL today. In Jesus' name, amen.

September 19
SOLVING RIDDLES!

"To know wisdom and instruction, to perceive the words of understanding, to receive the instruction of wisdom, justice, judgment and equity; to give prudence to the simple, to the young man knowledge and discretion – a wise man will hear and increase learning, and a man of understanding will attain wise counsel, to understand a proverb and an enigma, the words of the wise and their RIDDLES. The fear of the Lord is the beginning of knowledge, but fools despise wisdom and instruction." (Proverbs 1:2-7)

1. Today I will live in the now! I will live in the now because my ears are open and attentive to hear what God is saying to me. I am sensitive to His voice echoing throughout all creation. The heavens are declaring the glory of God!

2. Today I will do what I can to increase in learning, and to acquire skill, and attain to sound counsels, so that I may be able to steer my course rightly.

3. Today I will embrace prophecy – the word of the Lord that creatively speaks to my potential — for the testimony of Jesus is the spirit of prophecy. Speak, Lord! I will not "despise prophesyings" (1 Thessalonians 5:20) — your words that edify, exhort and comfort me. I will judge prophecy — however it comes to me — by the previously spoken word of the Lord, for I live by every word that PROCEEDS out of the mouth of God, and His words will solve my mysteries and bring me peaceful satisfaction.

4. Today I will empathize with someone . . . I will see another viewpoint . . . I will pray for a spirit of understanding to know why the other person did what he or she did . . . I will try to look at the situation through *their* window.

5. Today I will study to show myself approved. I will be a theologian and a scholar, walking in the light that I have, understanding and accepting my limitations. I will pray that the Word will be revealed to my heart and my mind — His ways are not past finding out — God wants to be discovered!

6. Today I will dialogue with others to gain understanding. I will deeply listen. I will not be intent to prove my point or vindicate myself – I will focus on finding truth.

7. Today I will search the Scriptures, pay attention, observe life, heed good advice, notice confirmation when I see it, pray in the Spirit, pray with the spirit and with the understanding, listen to the wisdom of young children (for ". . . a little child shall lead them" - Isaiah 11:6 — "out of the mouth of babes . . . " - I Psalm 8:2), ask questions, and receive revelation knowledge. Today I will solve a mystery in my life, and today I will live in the now!

Father, teach me Your ways today. In Jesus' name, amen.

September 20
CALM DOWN!

"A soft answer turns away wrath, but a harsh word stirs up anger." *(Proverbs 15:1)*

"Good sense makes a man restrain his anger,
and it is his glory to overlook a transgression or an offense." *(Proverbs 19:11 – AMP)*

"By long forbearing and calmness of spirit a judge or ruler is persuaded,
and soft speech breaks down the most bonelike resistance." *(Proverbs 25:15 – AMP)*

1. Today I will live in the now! I will live in the now because I have the peace of God and am, therefore, at peace with my environment and in harmony with my peers.

2. Today I will manage my emotions – particularly my anger. I will learn what it means to be angry and sin not. I will be Christ-controlled, and wise in choosing my battles. I will be passionate and righteously indignant over things that merit it, but I will not give place to the devil – and I will not wrestle with flesh and blood!

3. Today I will avoid unnecessary stress in my life by learning to let things go, and knowing when to walk away from a situation. I will cast all of my care on Jesus, because He cares for me!

4. Today I will remember that where envy and strife is, there is confusion and every evil work (James 3:16) — and that God is not the Author of confusion (I Corinthians 14:33).

5. Today I will remember to take deep breaths . . . to relax . . . to laugh . . . to turn the other cheek when appropriate . . . to forgive . . . to not take life too seriously . . . to not let my enemies "get to me" . . . to keep everything in perspective . . . to not worry so much . . . to trust in God!

6. Today I will not be overcome with evil, but I will overcome evil with good! My proactive manner and "soft answers" will turn negative situations around for me today. My ways will please the Lord, and I will make even my enemies to be at peace with me.

7. Today I will remain calm by seeing the big picture and by keeping my eye on the prize. I will keep it real today, and today I will live in the now!

Father, help me stay cool today. In Jesus' name, amen.

September 21
GOOD COMPANY!

"He who walks with wise men will be wise,
but the companion of fools will be destroyed." (Proverbs 13:20)

1. Today I will live in the now! I will live in the now because I do not walk in the counsel of the ungodly, nor stand in the way of sinners, nor sit in the seat of the scornful. My delight is in the Law of the Lord, and in His law I meditate day and night.

2. Today I will listen to wise people — I will read their books and observe their lives. I will spend my valuable time wisely. I will respect myself enough to surround myself with quality people who have a vision and a goal for their lives.

3. Today I will plan my escape from relationships with people who are just dragging me down to the pit! I will pray that God will expose the fools in my life and will show me how to deal with them properly.

4. Today I will rid myself of the influence of people who do not have my best interest at heart. How can two walk together unless they are in agreement? I want the best for my life, so I must be in covenant with people who have the same incentive.

5. Today I will abort any plans that I have that will not produce the right things for my future or take me to the next level of excellence. I will recognize a really bad idea when I hear it, and I will abandon it if it has to do with me!

6. Today I will be relentless in my search for wise people to connect with. I know they're out there, and I will not quit until I find them!

7. Today I will begin a new chapter in the book of my life. My steps will be ordered to the right people for the right reasons. I will be in the flow today, and today I will live in the now!

"He who walks [as a companion] with wise men shall be wise, but he who associates with [self-confident] fools [is a fool himself and] shall smart for it." (Proverbs 13:20 - AMP)

"For the fool speaks folly and his mind plans iniquity: practicing profane ungodliness and speaking error concerning the Lord, leaving the craving of the hungry unsatisfied, and causing the drink of the thirsty to fail." (Isaiah 32:6 - AMP)

Father, surround me with wisdom today. In Jesus' name, amen.

September 22
GET RICH!

"Sloth makes you poor; diligence brings wealth." *(Proverbs 10:4 – The Message)*

*"He becomes poor who works with a slack and idle hand,
but the hand of the diligent makes rich."* *(Proverbs 10:4 – AMP)*

1. Today I will live in the now! I will live in the now because I am persistently applying myself to the fulfillment of my destiny, while being content where I currently am. I am putting forth the effort to do what my hand finds to do with all of my might – and to do it well. The fruits of my labor will result in a natural flow of affluence – godly prosperity for the propagation of the gospel of the Kingdom of God!

2. Today I will persevere in my painstaking efforts to promote progress!

3. Today I will discipline myself to produce a pattern of behavior in my life that will bring self-improvement. I can DO better, and I can BE better! I will discipline my thoughts by meditating on the Word of God, because my thoughts eventually become my words, which, in turn, become my deeds, which naturally result in evolving into my habits, which ultimately become my character! I will discipline myself to endure hardships if I must. I will discipline myself to reject the world-system of acquiring wealth. I will discipline myself to train legally and fairly. I will discipline myself to avoid cheating or taking the easy way. I will discipline myself to sow financial seed, even in famine. I will discipline myself to always tithe the first fruits. I will discipline myself to study. I will discipline myself to reject any foolishness that tends to poverty. I will discipline myself to take the moral high road. I will discipline myself to get rich God's way, for the blessing of the Lord makes rich, and He adds no sorrow with it (Proverbs 10:22)!

4. Today I will decide my daily routine, for my daily routine is determining my future!

5. Today I will walk in a prosperous mentality (3 John 2).

6. Today I will tap into the energy of the resurrected Christ – the Zoë life of God – the same Spirit that raised Jesus from the dead – to help me work hard and well.

7. Today I will be enthusiastic about diligence and discipline. I know where I'm going today, and today I will live in the now!

Father, help me to do my part today. In Jesus' name, amen.

September 23
SEEK GOOD!

"He who earnestly seeks good finds favor,
but trouble will come to him who seeks evil." (Proverbs 11:27)

1. Today I will live in the now! I will live in the now because I am finding favor by seeking the good in the world. I will see every glass half full — rather than half empty!

2. Today I will seek to see the good in others – friends and enemies alike!

3. Today I will seek to find the good in what seems to be a bad situation — I will look for the blessings in disguise.

4. Today I will seek the good things that are small, and seemingly insignificant. I will not despise the day of small things, but I will be thankful for every good thing that comes my way today, not taking anything for granted.

5. Today I will seek the good in nature, and will see the hand of God in all His creation.

6. Today I will seek the good in myself, accentuating what is most positive about my nature and personality. I will do good deeds – with no ulterior motive or hidden agenda.

7. Today I will seek the goodness of God, and I will easily find it, for His goodness extends to children's children - to a thousand generations. The Lord is good and His mercy endures forever! I will walk in His goodness today, and today I will live in the now!

Father, help me to find favor today. In Jesus' name, amen.

September 24
IN CHARGE!

"The hand of the diligent will rule,
but the lazy man will be put to forced labor." (Proverbs 12:24)

1. Today I will live in the now! I will live in the now because I have a dream that produces diligence in me, and it is written that the hand of the diligent will RULE! My dream manifests itself in:

   D - esire   (I delight in the Lord, and He gives me my heart's desires - Psalm 37:4)
   R - esolve   (I am steadfast, setting my face like a flint – Isaiah 50:7)
   E - xpansion (I am stretching myself by thinking God's higher thoughts – Isaiah 55:8, 9)
   A - mbition   (I have a strong desire to achieve – Proverbs 19:21)
   M- otivation (I am motivated to get busy - It is written:

   "The plans of the mind and orderly thinking belong to man, but from the Lord comes the [wise] answer of the tongue. All the ways of a man are pure in his own eyes, but the Lord weighs the spirits (the thoughts and intents of the heart). Roll your works upon the Lord [commit and trust them wholly to Him; He will cause your thoughts to become agreeable to his will, and] so shall your plans be established and succeed." (Proverbs 16:1-3 – AMP)

2. Today I will demonstrate the qualities of a true leader.

3. Today I will take responsibility for my own actions and for the quality of my own work.

4. Today I will be true to myself. I will BE myself. I will dream MY dreams!

5. Today I will refuse to quit. I will not be lazy. I will not lose my edge.

6. Today I will prepare to rule, and will adapt my lifestyle accordingly.

7. Today I will take dominion, and today I will live in the now!

   Father, help me to be a worthy ruler today. In Jesus' name, amen.

September 25
PRECIOUS POSSESSIONS!

"The slothful man will not catch his game, or roast it if he should kill it, but the diligent man will get PRECIOUS POSSESSIONS." (Proverbs 12:27 – AMP)

1. Today I will live in the now! I will live in the now because I am able to possess precious and rare things as a result of the outworking of the spirit of diligence resident in me. I have a mind to work, accompanied by a supernatural ability to keep going, even when I am tempted to stop! In Christ I have a second wind always available to me that energizes and inspires me to get up when I fall down, to move forward when everyone else is in retreat mode, and to feel the fear and do it anyway!

2. Today my diligence will give me greater influence in my world. I will make myself indispensable to the operation of my immediate environment, and I will be recompensed because I legitimately fill a valid need.

3. Today I will stay focused on my goal, always remembering that rewards are waiting for me down the road. It is written: "And let us not lose heart and grow weary and faint in acting nobly and doing right, for in due time and at the appointed season we shall reap, if we do not loosen and relax our courage and faint." (Galatians 6:9 – AMP)

4. Today I will have a vision for abundance that will help me maintain my dedication to the things that I really believe in. My purpose will consume me today and will make abundant life a reality to me!

5. Today I will re-examine my priorities and will pay attention to what is occupying my thoughts, words and time. I will reinforce my commitment to prospering in and for the Kingdom of God for all the right reasons.

6. Today I will graciously, humbly and thankfully receive from someone who wants to bless me. I will not be afraid to enjoy things – nice things – knowing that my real life is hidden with Christ and God.

7. Today I will repent of and abandon any slothful attitude that may surface in me today. I will make the most of my time, and will seize every opportunity to do something important and worthwhile with my life. I will get moving today, and today I will live in the now!

Father, help me prepare to receive precious possessions today. In Jesus' name, amen.

September 26
SOUL FOOD!

"The soul of a lazy man desires, and has nothing;
but the soul of the diligent shall be made rich." (Proverbs 13:4)

1. Today I will live in the now! I will live in the now because my soul (my mind, will and emotions) is prospering from being regularly nourished by the sincere meat of the Word of God. My mind is being changed and renewed by the incorruptible seed — it is being washed clean by the water of the word — and the process is progressively and steadily transforming my life into a life of greatness and fulfilled destiny! It is written: "Do not be conformed to this world (this age), [fashioned after and adapted to its external, superficial customs], but be TRANSFORMED (changed) by the [entire] renewal of your mind [by its new ideals and its new attitude] so that you may prove [for yourselves] what is the good and acceptable and perfect will of God, even the thing which is good and acceptable and perfect [in his sight for you]." (Romans 12:2 - AMP)

2. Today I will feed my *mind* with helpful and useful information.

3. Today I will feed my *will* with good and productive decisions.

4. Today I will feed my *emotions* with love and thoughts conducive to a high self-esteem.

5. Today I will feed my *memories* with a healthy perspective and a desire to learn from the past.

6. Today I will feed my *personality* with character and virtue.

7. Today I will feed my *entire inner man* with the rhema word, with every word that is proceeding today from the mouth of God, for that is my true, life-giving bread! I will make myself at home at the table of the Lord today, and today I will live in the now!

Father, help me to feed my soul good things today. In Jesus' name, amen.

September 27
NEW IDEAS!

"The thoughts of the [steadily] diligent tend only to plenteousness,
but every one who is impatient and hasty hastens only to want." (Proverbs 21:5 – AMP)

1. Today I will live in the now! I will live in the now because my thoughts are established, and they are bringing me into a new dimension of Kingdom authority in the area of wealth and finance. God is giving me a clear plan of action that will meet my needs, relieve me of debt, and enable me to be a tangible blessing to the Body of Christ. He is unfolding it to me through my progressive acts of obedience (when I am faithful over a few things, He will make me a ruler over much!), so that I am able to patiently pace myself in my pursuit of purposeful prosperity!

2. Today I will be receptive to new (and realistic) moneymaking ideas that are coming to me.

3. Today I will walk in a new paradigm concerning my current financial situation.

4. Today I will see a new way to get an old thing done more effectively.

5. Today I will speak of myself and my position in life in a new, more positive, way.

6. Today I will think differently about my present job description and the task that is at hand.

7. Today I will dialogue with someone who may have another piece of the prosperity puzzle. Iron will sharpen iron as we brainstorm and help each other to think outside the box. Today I will expect a total brain overhaul and attitude adjustment, and today I will live in the now!

"This is God's word on the subject . . . 'I'll show up and take care of you as I promised . . . I know what I'm doing. I have it all planned out – plans to take care of you, not abandon you, plans to give you the future you hope for.'" (Jeremiah 29:11 – The Message)

"I wisdom dwell with prudence, and find out knowledge of witty inventions."
(Proverbs 8:12 - KJV)

Father, give me fresh and new ideas today. In Jesus' name, amen.

September 28
CLEAR THINKING!

"Dear friend, guard CLEAR THINKING and Common Sense with your life; don't for a minute lose sight of them. They'll keep your soul alive and well, they'll keep you fit and attractive. You'll travel safely, you'll neither tire nor trip. You'll take afternoon naps without a worry, you'll enjoy a good night's sleep. No need to panic over alarms or surprises, or predictions that doomsday's just around the corner, because God will be right there with you; He'll keep you safe and sound." (Proverbs 3:21-26 – The Message)

1. Today I will live in the now! I will live in the now because my mind is disciplined and organized by the Word of God, controlled and tempered by the Holy Spirit, and voluntarily submitted to the Lordship and authority of Jesus. I am not confused by religious tradition, because the sword of the Lord is cutting through the underbrush and defining a clear-cut road in the wilderness for me to travel on.

2. Today I will not let myself be distracted by the "little foxes that spoil the vine" – the tedious and obnoxious things that occupy too much of my time. I will know when to say "no," and I will control and manage my time, staying mentally connected to the more weighty matters at hand!

3. Today I will not let the cares of this world, the deceitfulness of riches, and the desires for other things enter in and choke the Word sown in my heart, making it unfruitful in my life (Mark 4:19).

4. Today I will tell the truth because it is the right thing to do, and because it is easier than trying to maintain a lie. Speaking truly will help me to think clearly, and will keep me from saying things that could impede the Mind of Christ.

5. Today I will pay attention to what I am doing when I am working, driving my car, or doing anything else at home or elsewhere. I will not give place to negative things by my carelessness or by being distracted from maintaining a plate that is too full. If I need to simplify my life in an area in order to free my mind from distraction, then I will do what I have to do.

6. Today I will not let unbridled passions or undisciplined emotions cloud my judgment or compromise my focus. I will think soberly, maturely, and responsibly about every choice that I make today.

7. Today I will maintain my spirituality, without abandoning my common sense. I will tap into the logic that God has invested in the universe, and will ultimately do the right thing. Today I will get it together and make this day count, and today I will live in the now!

Father, help me to think clearly today. In Jesus' name, amen.

September 29
ANIMAL INSTINCTS!

"There are . . . things which are too wonderful for me . . . the way of an eagle in the air, the way of a serpent on a rock . . . four things which are little on the earth, but they are exceedingly wise . . . the ants . . . the rock badgers . . . the locusts . . . the spider . . . three things which are majestic in pace . . . a lion . . . a greyhound . . . a male goat . . . ." (Proverbs 30:18, 24-31)

1. Today I will live in the now! I will live in the now because I am aware of the examples of strength and ability that God has set for me in the animal kingdom. Today I will obey the words of Jesus who commanded that I look at the birds of the air (Matthew 6:26), to see how they fly, and how they rely on God to feed them.

2. Today I will heed His warning not to cast my pearls before swine, nor give that which is holy to the dogs (Matthew 7:6). I will believe in my gift and in my testimony, even if it is not properly discerned by others. I will go where I am celebrated, not where I am tolerated!

3. Today I will remember that He said that the foxes have holes and the birds have nests, but He had no place to lay His head (Matthew 8:18-20). I will interpret this to mean that living in the now is always somewhat uncomfortable, that constant repentance (paradigm shifting) is required for Kingdom entrance, and that following the living Jesus will always challenge my tradition and keep my theology in flux.

4. Today I will know that He has sent me out as a sheep among wolves (Matthew 10:16), and that real, groundbreaking ministry always has the potential to be dangerous.

5. Today I will embrace Christ's concept of being wise as a serpent and harmless as a dove (Matthew 10:16). I will think like a snake if I have to (to beat the devil at his own game), and I will not be gullible or let myself be taken advantage of — but I will maintain the character of the dove-like Holy Spirit, always walking in love and grace.

6. Today I will remember Jesus' admonition to not strain at gnats and swallow camels (Matthew 23:23, 24). I will prioritize intelligently, see things from God's perspective, and separate the *important* things from the *vital* things.

7. Today I will be bold as a lion and will mount up with wings as an eagle. I will run and not be weary today, and today I will live in the now!

Father, help me live a dynamic life today. In Jesus' name, amen.

September 30
LIFE'S ISSUES!

"Keep your heart with all diligence, for out of it spring the issues of life." (Proverbs 4:23)

1. Today I will live in the now! I will live in the now because I am maintaining and guarding my heart, which is the source of my life, with godly diligence and the desire to cultivate it into a beautiful and productive garden.

2. Today I will go with the flow, remembering that things in the natural never stay the same. I will not fight the natural function of transition in my life, but will use the force of life pouring out of my heart to move the circumstances in a positive direction.

3. Today I will let go, and let God . . .

4. Today I will be led by the Holy Spirit and will operate in the manifestation of His fruit in my life.

5. Today I will release the flow of creativity from my inner resources to make the world around me a better place in which to live.

6. Today I will guard my emotions, and keep my mind stayed on God.

7. Today I will allow my spirit to dominate my soul and my body. I will be a blessing to humanity, because a river of life is flowing out of me today. I say, "Spring up, O well!" — and today I will live in the now!

Father, help me guard my heart, and control what flows out of it today.
In Jesus' name, amen.

October In The Now!

⋄O⋄C⋄T⋄O⋄B⋄E⋄R⋄

A month to dream different dreams . . .

As creation makes its demand for diversity,

The hills and mountains abandon their

Usually unvaried uniformity,

And come alive with ornate originality . . .

The plummeting temperatures conduct a

Symphony of color . . .

Falling flaming foliage

Make the landscape

Resonate with rust-toned rainbows of

Glorious golds . . .

Radiant reds . . .

Brilliant browns accented by

Occasional ostentatious oranges . . .

Sleep deeply in the clean crispness of the cool and chilly nights,

And dream your dreams in living color!

". . . behold, I will set your stones in fair colors . . ." (Isaiah 54:11 – AMP)

October 1
FIRST FRUITS!

"And it shall be, when you come into the land which the Lord your God is giving you as an inheritance, and you possess it and dwell in it, that you shall take some of the FIRST of all the produce of the ground, which you shall bring from your land that the Lord your God is giving you, and put it in a basket and go to the place where the Lord your God chooses to make His name abide. And you shall go to one who is priest in those days, and SAY to him, 'I DECLARE today to the Lord your God that I have come to the country which the Lord swore to our fathers to give us.' Then the priest shall take the basket out of your hand and set it down before the altar of the Lord your God. And you shall ANSWER and SAY before the Lord your God . . . 'the Lord brought us out of Egypt with a mighty hand and with an outstretched arm, with great terror and with signs and wonders. He has brought us to this place and has given us . . . a land flowing with milk and honey, and now, behold, I have brought the FIRST FRUITS of the land which You, O lord, have given me.' Then you shall set it before the Lord your God, and worship before the Lord your God. So shall you rejoice in every good thing which the Lord you God has given you . . . ." (Deuteronomy 26:1-5, 8-11)

1. Today I will live in the now! I will live in the now because my tithe, the first fruits of my increase (income), is a living memorial to the delivering work of God in my life. It enables me to acknowledge, on a continual basis, where God has brought me from and to remember why I have so much for which to be grateful!

2. Today I will be aware that the "the tithe" is the tenth of my personal harvest but that "tithing" is what I SAY about that harvest. The Scripture instructs me to declare directionally, and answer appropriately, so I will not allow it to be said of me by the Lord, "Your words have been harsh against Me . . ." (Malachi 3:13). I will watch my words today and make sure that they cooperate with my actions.

3. Today I will seek FIRST the Kingdom of God, and His righteousness, with the confident assurance that everything that I need will be added to me as a result.

4. Today I will appreciate the fact that the tithe and tithing allows me to think outside the box financially, and forces me to regard my prosperity from a spiritual and supernatural paradigm.

5. Today I will explore new territory in the area of ideas, inventions and intuitive inspiration because I am in covenant with the Creator. As a tither I will have the confidence to do what has not been done before!

6. Today I will praise and worship the Lord my God, my Father, and my deliverer.

7. Today I will bear much fruit, and today I will live in the now!

Father, receive my first fruits today. In Jesus' name, amen.

October 2
CHRIST EXALTED!

"Let this same attitude and purpose and [humble] mind be in you which was in Christ Jesus: [Let Him be your example in humility:] Who, although being essentially one with God and in the form of God [possessing the fullness of the attributes which make God God], did not think this equality with God was a thing to be eagerly grasped or retained, But stripped Himself [of all privileges and rightful dignity] so as to assume the guise of a servant (slave), in that he became like men and was born a human being. And after he had appeared in human form, He abased and humbled Himself [still further] and carried His obedience to the extreme of death, even the death of the cross! Therefore [because He stooped so low], God has highly exalted him and has freely bestowed on him the name that is above every name, that in (at) the name of Jesus every knee should (must) bow, in heaven and on earth and under the earth, and every tongue [frankly and openly] confess and acknowledge that Jesus Christ is Lord, to the glory of God the Father." (Philippians 2:5-11 – AMP)

1. Today I will live in the now! I will live in the now because Jesus is Lord.

2. Today I will accept and embrace, without religious prejudice, the humanity of Jesus as being equal with His divinity . . . the mystery of the knowledge that the Son of Man was, and is, the (firstborn) Son of God, and that the (firstborn) Son of God was, and is, the Son of Man – 100% God – 100% man – the amazing Christ!

3. Today I will willingly bow my own knees to His Lordship.

4. Today I will openly confess with my own tongue that He is exalted.

5. Today I will exercise my authority in the name of Jesus . . . in heaven . . . on earth . . . under the earth! His authority is my authority, and my authority is His authority. We are one. We are joint-heirs. He is the vine and I am the branch. I am a partaker of the divine nature!

6. Today I will be a servant to all, humbling myself under the mighty hand of God that He may exalt me in due time! I will take up my cross. I will lay down my life.

7. Today I will walk in the reality of the Mind of Christ, and today I will live in the now!

Father, exalt Jesus through my life today, in His name, amen.

October 3
POSSESSING PLENTY!

"Honor the Lord with your capital and sufficiency [from righteous labors], and with the first fruits of all your income; so shall your storage places be filled with PLENTY, and your vats be overflowing with new wine." (Proverbs 3:9, 10 – AMP)

1. Today I will live in the now! I will live in the now because I recognize the preeminence of God's supernatural supply in my life and circumstances.

2. Today I will not be afraid to face the fact that God is requiring me to do more than I can actually do, as He did with all of the heroes of the Bible. Along with that, He is requiring me to give more than I have to give, as He did with the widow of Zarephath, so that He can take me into a higher level of provision and prosperity. Today I will seek to understand the purpose in His requirements (I know that He is neither unreasonable nor unfair), and I will recognize the treasure hidden in my own earthen vessel, that the excellency of the power may be of God, and not of me!

3. Today I will honor the Lord with my capital because it, ultimately, represents my life. My money and substance are the product of my labor – how I spend my time, so, in giving the Lord what I have, I am able to give Him what (and who) I really am!

4. Today I will not be afraid of any evil tiding or negative report concerning the economy, the stock market, the government, inflation or taxes. I have laid up treasure in heaven, investing in the Kingdom of God, and He supplies all of my need according to His riches in glory, by Christ Jesus! I am not of this world (system), and neither is my money, or my success or my future! God is my source!

5. Today I will not be cheap, or stingy or tight with my money. I will guide my affairs with discretion through the Spirit-fruit of self-control, but I will walk in liberty concerning my finances because I have a perception of the purpose of prevailing over poverty and possessing plenty by proving the power of God!

6. Today I will repent of any mental, emotional or spiritual stronghold that limits the work of the Holy One of Israel in my life (Psalm 78:41), and will allow Him to do more than I can ask or think, in direct proportion to the power that works in me (Ephesians 3:20)!

7. Today my storage places (my home, checking and savings accounts, my income and investments, etc.) will be filled with plenty, and today I will live in the now!

   Father, help me to honor You today with my first fruits. In Jesus' name, amen.

October 4
BE FAITHFUL!

"Today, please listen; don't turn a deaf ear as in 'the bitter uprising,' that time of wilderness testing! Even though they watched me at work for forty years, your ancestors refused to let me do it my way; over and over they tried my patience. And I was provoked, oh, so provoked! I said, 'They'll never keep their minds on God; they refuse to walk down my road.' Exasperated, I vowed, 'They'll never get where they're going, never be able to sit down and rest.' So watch your step, friends. Make sure there's no evil unbelief lying around that will trip you up and throw you off course, diverting you from the living God. For as long as it's still God's Today, keep each other on your toes so sin doesn't slow down your reflexes. If we can only keep our grip on the sure thing we started out with, we're in this with Christ for the long haul. These words keep ringing in our ears: Today, please listen; don't turn a deaf ear as in the bitter uprising." (Hebrews 3:7-15 - The Message)

1. Today I will live in the now! I will live in the now because I am listening for God to speak directly to me *today*.

2. Today I will rely on my Redeemer to renew a right spirit in me, resolving to renounce, reject and rid myself of any rebellion resident in the recesses of my mind, and to respond rightly, without resistance, to His righteous requisitions!

3. Today I will keep my heart soft before God. I will not let bitterness make me calloused to the movement of His Spirit or the manifestation of His presence.

4. Today I will not allow unbelief to enter my life in any way.

5. Today I will be obedient to God, even in the smallest detail.

6. Today I will submit to God in heaven, through my submission to spiritual authority here on earth.

7. Today I will go the distance in Christ, and today I will live in the now!

Father, help me to be faithful to You today. In Jesus' name, amen.

October 5
OPENLY REWARDED!

". . . and your Father who sees in secret will Himself reward you openly." (Matthew 6:4)

"Be especially careful when you are trying to be good so that you don't make a performance out of it. It might be good theatre, but the God who made you won't be applauding. When you do something for someone else, don't call attention to yourself. You've seen them in action, I'm sure – 'playactors' I call them – treating prayer meeting and street corner alike as a stage, acting compassionate as long as someone is watching, playing to the crowds. They get applause, true, but that's all they get. When you help someone out, don't think about how it looks. Just do it – quietly and unobtrusively. That is the way your God, who conceived you in love, working behind the scenes, helps you out." (Matthew 6:1-4 – The Message)

1. Today I will live in the now! I will live in the now because I am making a statement of faith by my actions toward others – a statement that declares that God is my source – my provider – my El Shaddai Who is more than enough! I can be helpful to the people around me with no ulterior motive or hidden agenda, because I know that it is God Who repays me for my efforts and rewards me for my benevolence and acts of mercy. When I do something good "unto the least of these," I am doing it unto Christ Himself and He will recompense me for my deeds.

2. Today I will sow toward my future by my acts of kindness today.

3. Today I will expect an outward manifestation of the Kingdom's inward reality in my life and, when I am rewarded openly, I will not display a false sense of humility or unworthiness. I am not ashamed or afraid to reap what I have sown.

4. Today I will be perceptive enough to use what I already have in my hand.

5. Today I will be confident enough to show my love toward others without the fear of rejection or of being misunderstood. There is no fear in love, but perfect love casts out fear.

6. Today I will do unto others as I would have them do unto me.

7. Today I will invest in covenant relationships which will, in turn, cause me to invest eternally in the Kingdom of God. I will walk worthy of the rewards that are coming to me today, and today I will live in the now!

   Father, I thank You in advance for Your open rewards. In Jesus' name, amen.

October 6
GET GOING!

"Later He appeared to the eleven as they sat at the table; and He rebuked their unbelief and hardness of heart, because they did not believe those who had seen Him after He had risen. And He said to them, 'GO into all the world and preach the gospel to every creature. He who believes and is baptized will be saved; but he who does not believe will be condemned. And these signs will follow those who believe: In My name they will cast out demons; they will speak with new tongues; they will take up serpents; and if they drink anything deadly, it will by no means hurt them; they will lay hands on the sick, and they will recover.'" (Mark 16:14-18)

1. Today I will live in the now! I will live in the now because I have a command to GO into all the world – into every part of the *worlds* of every man, woman, boy and girl – into every culture and counterculture – into every mindset and philosophy – into every system and network — and preach the good news, without the preferential treatment of anyone!

2. Today I will embrace the call of Christ. Even though I may be rebuked for my unbelief or hardness of heart as the first disciples were, I have still been mandated to go — to go anyway — in spite of my weaknesses and vulnerabilities. The gifts and callings of God are irrevocable and, regardless of what I have or haven't done, Jesus is still depending on me to give the inhabitants of His world some good news!

3. Today I will go to where the people are – not just where they are geographically, but to where they are mentally, spiritually, emotionally and philosophically. I will speak with the tongue of the learned (Isaiah 50:4), becoming all things to all men (1 Corinthians 9:22).

4. Today I will make *some* movement, knowing that my steps are ordered of the Lord and that God blesses whatever I put my hand to.

5. Today I will not preach religious tradition, or anything that could possibly make people feel alienated from God. My declaration of the Kingdom ("The Kingdom is at hand!") will make Jesus accessible to those who have been disconnected in their minds. I will go to where the breaches are — and I will repair them!

6. Today I will be a witness, telling my story, finding my voice.

7. Today I will be followed by supernatural signs confirming my words. God will bless my efforts because I believe. My faith will be irresistible to Him today, and today I will live in the now!

Father, help me to get up and get going today. In Jesus' name, amen.

October 7
HIDDEN TREASURE!

"Again, the Kingdom of Heaven is like treasure hidden in a field, which a man found and hid; and for joy over it he goes and sells all that he has and buys that field." (Matthew 13:44)

1. Today I will live in the now! I will live in the now because I am learning to think of myself in a whole new way by the illumination of the Word of God as it dawns on my consciousness and renews my spirit. I am in a phase of realization – the realization of the role that I alone play in the function and reception of the Kingdom of God on this planet – God's great drama, written before the foundation of the world, executed in the 21st century. I am a major player in the unfolding theme, which is the exaltation of Jesus, the Christ, and His dominion through believers (like me) over all cosmic powers and rebel world rulers.

2. Today I will fight for the hidden treasure in my life with the hidden weapons of spiritual warfare (2 Corinthians 10:4) that are mine to use whenever and wherever I need them.

3. Today I will not give up my hunt for the treasure in my own personal field of life and experience, no matter how many people tell me that there is no treasure there. I will not listen to the voices of memory that would try to reach into the now and attempt to influence me to surrender the search. I know that hidden treasure (talents, callings, ability, anointing, success, accomplishment) is there and, in Christ, I have the resolve and the energy to dig up every bit of it and to display it for all the world to see!

4. Today I am willing to sell everything that I have to buy the field where the treasure is buried (Matthew 13:44). Nothing is more important to me today than seeking the Kingdom FIRST — God is top priority, and Jesus is Lord!

5. Today I will believe in the wealth that God has invested in me, and in the value that He has placed on my life and ministry.

6. Today I will uncover mysteries by the word of knowledge and the word of wisdom. The Charismata – the Gifts of the Spirit – will function at a high level of precision and accuracy in my life today. I have the Mind of Christ. I have the wisdom of the Ancient of Days. I have revelation, illumination and an actively growing gift of faith!

7. Today I will ask myself the real and important questions. I will not be afraid to dig deep today, and today I will live in the now!

Father, help me to discover and uncover all of my hidden treasure today.
In Jesus' name, amen.

October 8
CONFIDENT COMMUNICATION!

"And this is the CONFIDENCE (the assurance, the privilege of boldness) which we have in Him: [we are sure] that if we ask anything (make any request) according to His will (in agreement with His own plan), He listens to and hears us. And if (since) we [positively] know that He listens to us in whatever we ask, we also know [with settled and absolute knowledge] that we have [granted us as our present possessions] the requests made of Him." (1 John 5:14, 15 – AMP)

1. Today I will live in the now! I will live in the now because I have the confident assurance that God wants to help me and that He listens to me when I speak. Today I celebrate the awesome power of prayer! I will pray without ceasing (1 Thessalonians 5:17), because Jesus said that men ought always to pray and not to faint or lose heart (Luke 18:1). My effectual, fervent prayer will avail much for me today (James 5:16), so I will be careful for nothing, but in everything by prayer and supplication will make my requests known to God (Philippians 4:6).

2. Today I will pray in the Spirit when I don't know what or how to pray (Romans 8:26). I will build myself up on my most holy faith by praying in the Spirit (Jude 20), but I will pray with both the spirit and with the understanding (1 Corinthians 14:15), in order to exercise my mind, as well as my heart. I will believe that I receive the things that I desire when I pray (Mark 11:24)!

3. Today I will ask in faith, knowing that a double-minded man is unstable in all his ways (James 1:5-8). God knows what I have need of even before I ask (Matthew 6:8), but He has said that I do *not have* what I *have not* asked for (James 4:2), so I will ask, seek and knock today (Matthew 7:7, 8), using the keys of the Kingdom to unlock heaven on the earth (Matthew 16:19)!

4. Today I will pray in line with the Word of God, for His Word is alive and powerful, and sharper than any two-edged sword (Hebrews 4:12).

5. Today I will respond to God's invitation to come and reason with Him (Isaiah 1:18), and I will change part of the world today by my intercessory negotiation.

6. Today I will pray for those in authority, that I may lead a quiet and peaceable life in all godliness and reverence (1 Timothy 2:1, 2).

7. Today I will remember that prayer is conversational, so I will be quiet and listen after I have spoken. All things will be possible to me in prayer today, and today I will live in the now!

Father, help me to pray the right things today. In Jesus' name, amen.

October 9
WILDERNESS ADVENTURE!

"In those days John the Baptist came preaching in the WILDERNESS . . ." (Matthew 3:1)

"While Jesus was living in the Galilean hills, John, called 'the Baptizer,' was preaching in the desert country of Judea. His message was simple and austere, like his desert surroundings: 'Change your life. God's kingdom is here.' John and his message were authorized by Isaiah's prophecy: Thunder in the desert! Prepare for God's arrival! Make the road smooth and straight!" (Matthew 3:1-3 - The Message)

"Then Jesus was led up by the Spirit into the WILDERNESS . . . From that time Jesus began to preach and to say, 'Repent, for the Kingdom of Heaven is at hand." (Matthew 4:1, 17)

1. Today I will live in the now! I will live in the now because I am not afraid of the wilderness experience, for the preaching of the Kingdom always begins in the wilderness . . . away from the organized paths and paved roads . . . away from the structure of the world system . . . in a place where I must walk by the faith that relies entirely on God's ability to make ways in the wilderness, and streams in the desert (Isaiah 43:19).

2. Today I will repent of long-held paradigms of my personal wilderness, rethinking my present position as Jacob did when he had the vision of heaven's gate ("Then Jacob awoke from his sleep and said, 'Surely the Lord is in this place, and I did not know it.' And he was afraid and said, 'How awesome is this place! This is none other than the house of God . . . the gate of heaven!'" – Genesis 28:16, 17). Awaking from my sleep today, I will see my salvation, right where I am in the now, embracing my own wilderness, and saying, "*How awesome is THIS place!*"

3. Today I will recognize the power and potential that is present in what I have in my hand, for that is where the Kingdom is. The Kingdom is not just *at hand*, it is *at MY hand* – it is "handy" — so I will do what I know to do today with excellence and with all of my might (Ecclesiastes 9:10)!

4. Today I will find a river of life in the wilderness as John the Baptist did, and I will follow his example and get busy with the work of the Kingdom . . . where I am . . . with what I have to work with . . . just as I am.

5. Today I will preach (prophetically) that the Kingdom is here (Matthew 4:17).

6. Today I will say (conversationally) that the Kingdom is here (Matthew 4:17).

7. Today I will be happy in the wilderness, and today I will live in the now!

Father, help me to discern why I am in the wilderness today. In Jesus' name, amen.

October 10
PUBLIC SPECTACLE!

*"[God] disarmed the principalities and powers ranged against us
and made a bold display and public example of them,
in triumphing over them in Him and in it [the cross]." (Colossians 2:15 - AMP)*

1. Today I will live in the now! I will live in the now because Jesus declared that He saw satan fall like lightning from heaven, and then He defeated him on the cross, humiliating him in the process and making an open show of his demonic principalities and powers.

2. Today I will give no place to the devil in my words or actions. He will flee from me at the smallest act of resistance, because I am submitted to God.

3. Today I will not buy into the bogus exaggeration of *religionized* Christian theology that denies the defeat of the devil. I will not take Scriptures referring to him out of context. I will rightly divide the Word, and will exercise my Kingdom dominion and authority over all the works of darkness by the power of the Greater One Who indwells me!

4. Today I will take responsibility for my own life, including my mistakes and failures, refusing to take the coward's route of blaming the devil for every negative thing that happens to me. I am in control of my life, and I accept the fact that I must give an account, before the judgment seat of Christ, of how I choose to live it.

5. Today I will not walk in any fear.

6. Today I will rejoice that I am completely covered by the covenant blood of Christ which is alive in the now through the eternal Spirit.

7. Today I will recognize that I serve a big, powerful God, and that I am invincible in Him! In all these things I am more than a conqueror today, and today I will live in the now!

Father, help me to keep it all in perspective today. In Jesus' name, amen.

October 11
FULLY RESTORED!

"Fear not, O land; Be glad and rejoice, for the Lord has done marvelous things!" *(Joel 2:21)*

1. Today I will live in the now! I will live in the now because I am experiencing **PROPHETIC RESTORATION**. As God spoke through Joel (Joel 2:18-20) that the land would be refreshed, I believe that there is a refreshing coming to MY land today! I call those things that are not as though they are and say that I am, by faith, fully restored to flourish and to function in the fullness of fruitfulness in Christ!

2. Today I will believe for **PRACTICAL RESTORATION** (Joel 2:21-24). God is PROVIDING everything that I need to PROSPER in the material world – for His glory and for the advancement of His Kingdom.

3. Today I will be grateful for **PRESERVING RESTORATION** ("So I will RESTORE to you the years . . ." – Joel 2:25). In Christ I am getting my lost time back! THIS is the day of the Lord, and I will rejoice and be glad in it. It's not too late for the manifestation of my miracle!

4. Today I will rejoice at having **PROLiFIC RESTORATION** (Joel 2:26-29). The definition of "prolific" is: producing offspring or fruit in abundance; fertile; producing abundant works or results. The Christ in me is enabling me to create after my own kind. I am growing, enlarging and expanding in every area of the Kingdom today!

5. Today I will walk in **PRODUCTIVE RESTORATION**, knowing that God has restored me so that I can restore others. Freely I have received, so freely I will give. Today I will impart the life of the Kingdom to those who have not received it yet.

6. Today I will be patient in receiving **PROGRESSIVE RESTORATION** — first the blade, then the ear, then the full corn in the ear — some thirty, some sixty, some one hundredfold. I will pace myself to receive from God intelligently, for it is through faith AND patience that I am able to inherit the promises.

7. Today I will celebrate **PRESENT RESTORATION**. When God restores, He makes the latter greater than the former, so I will open my spiritual eyes today to see that I am PRESENTLY in the PROCESS of being restored . . . my health . . . my vision . . . my youth . . . my ideals . . . my hope . . . my energy . . . I am being restored IN THE NOW – spirit, soul, body, past present, future. Today I will see God's Spirit poured out on all flesh, and today I will live in the now!

Father, restore me today in the way that You see fit. In Jesus' name, amen.

October 12
TOTALLY BLESSED!

"Now it shall come to pass, if you diligently obey the voice of the Lord your God, to observe carefully all His commandments which I command you today, that the Lord your God will set you high above all nations of the earth. And all these BLESSINGS shall come upon you and overtake you, because you obey the voice of the Lord your God:

BLESSED shall you be in the city, and
BLESSED shall you be in the country.
BLESSED shall be fruit of your body, the produce of your ground
and the increase of your herds,
the increase of your cattle and the offspring of your flocks.
BLESSED shall be your basket and you kneading bowl.
BLESSED shall you be when you come in, and
BLESSED shall you be when you go out.

The Lord will cause your enemies who rise against you to be defeated before your face; they shall come out against you one way and flee before you seven ways. The Lord will command the BLESSING on you in your storehouses and in all to which you set your hand, and He will BLESS you in the land which the Lord your God is giving you." *(Deuteronomy 28:1-8)*

1. Today I will live in the now! I will live in the now because I am blessed as a direct result of obeying the voice of the Lord.

2. Today I will be blessed when I go in to the routine of my day, and when I come out of it.

3. Today I will be blessed in the city and in the country (and in the mall and the bank and at work and at school - in the car - at the grocery store - at the post office - in court - at the neighbor's house - on the street - in the yard - on the expressway - at a meeting - in a crowd - by myself - at church - at the dry cleaners - on the phone - online - in cyberspace - on a jet - at the health club - on vacation - uptown or downtown, and anywhere and everywhere that I go)!

4. Today I will realize that God is commanding His blessing on me, so I do not have anything to feel bad about. His big blessings far outweigh my little problems!

5. Today I will not just be blessed – I will BE a blessing!

6. Today I will speak blessings over my life and over the lives of those I love.

7. Today the blessings of the Lord will make my life an adventure. I will enjoy the ride today, and today I will live in the now!

Father, help me to obey You today. In Jesus' name, amen.

October 13
KINGDOM BLUEPRINT!

"Pray, therefore, like this: Our Father Who is in heaven, hallowed (kept holy) be Your name. Your Kingdom come, Your will be done on earth as it is in heaven. Give us this day our daily bread. And forgive us our debts, as we also have forgiven (left, remitted, and let go the debts, and given up resentment against) our debtors. And lead (bring) us not into temptation, but deliver us from the evil one. For Yours is the Kingdom and the power and the glory forever. Amen." (Matthew 6:9-13 – AMP)

". . . Father in heaven,
Reveal Who You are.
Set the world right;
Do what's best –
As above, so below.
Keep us alive with three square meals.
Keep us forgiven with You and forgiving others.
Keep us safe from ourselves and the devil.
You're in charge!
You can do anything You want!
You're ablaze in beauty!
Yes. Yes. Yes."
(Matthew 6:9-13 – The Message)

1. Today I will live in the now! I will live in the now because the blueprint of the Kingdom is drawn on my heart, and I will walk out its reality today.

2. Today I will be who I am in Christ, reconciling myself with who I have always been. I will not regret my past, for my past has made me what I am today.

3. Today I will believe for the impossible, but be satisfied with my daily bread.

4. Today I will remember that at the heart of all matter is the Kingdom of God – the presence of Christ.

5. Today I will acknowledge that at the base of everything that is real, is the truth of the Kingdom, laid out in the Lord's Prayer.

6. Today I will be aware that there is only one energy vibrating within every atom (" . . . upholding ALL THINGS by the word of His power . . . " – Hebrews 1:3). As the nucleus of every cell contains a blueprint for life, so the words of Jesus contain the blueprint of the Kingdom, activated for my *life* by my *faith*.

7. Today I will give God all the glory, and today I will live in the now!

Let Your Kingdom come. Let Your will be done on earth as it is in heaven!
In Jesus' name, amen.

October 14
HOT TICKET!

"For the eyes of the Lord run to and fro throughout the whole earth, to show Himself strong on behalf of those whose heart is loyal to Him . . . ." (2 Chronicles 16:9)

1. Today I will live in the now! I will live in the now because God is showing His power through my life – every day is "Show Time" with Him! He is watching like a hawk for opportunities to invade my life with supernatural blessings and awe-inspiring miracles. My life is on display to the principalities and powers ("To me, who am less than the least of all the saints, this grace was given, that I should preach among the Gentiles the unsearchable riches of Christ, and to make all SEE what is the fellowship of the mystery, which from the beginning of the ages has been hidden in God who created all things through Jesus Christ; to the intent that now the manifold wisdom of God might be made known by the church to the principalities and powers in the heavenly places, according to the eternal purpose which He accomplished in Christ Jesus our Lord" – Ephesians 3:8-11).

2. Today God will show the heathen His mighty power through my life. They will have a front row seat in the theatre of my triumph, and gnash with their teeth at how good God is to His chosen ones. But those who have an open heart will see what God is doing - in and for and through me - and will be drawn into the Kingdom as they are "provoked to jealousy" (Romans 11:11). The show of God's might and dominion in my behalf will be the hottest ticket in town!

3. Today I will show by example how to live an overcoming life.

4. Today I will play the role that God Himself has written for me, exactly as He envisioned it to be played. His will must be done in my natural earth-life as it is in heaven.

5. Today I will maintain loyalty to God on every level of my life so that He is able to see me clearly and show Himself mightily.

6. Today I will not hide my light under a bushel.

7. Today I will expect the grand finale of my present circumstance to have a happy ending to the glory of God. God is working all things together for my good, and the world is eager to see that goodness displayed. He never misses a performance - and neither will I. I am ready to take a bow today, and today I will live in the now!

Father, show Yourself strong in my behalf today. In Jesus' name, amen.

October 15
EXAMINE YOURSELF!

"Therefore whoever eats this bread or drinks this cup of the Lord in an unworthy manner will be guilty of the body and blood of the Lord. But let a man EXAMINE HIMSELF, and so let him eat of the bread and drink of the cup. For he who eats and drinks in an unworthy manner eats and drinks judgment to himself, not discerning the Lord's body. For this reason many are weak and sick among you, and many sleep [are dead]. For if we would judge ourselves, we would not be judged. But when we are judged, we are chastened by the Lord, that we may not be condemned with the world." (1 Corinthians 11:27-32)

1. Today I will live in the now! I will live in the now because I have the courage to tell myself the truth about my life — about the secret part of me that only God really knows. I will live the examined life today, judging myself properly and realistically, so that I will not be judged with the world.

2. Today I will examine my **motives** and will make sure that I am not wasting my time and energy on the performance of works of wood, hay and stubble that do not impress God and are of no real value to His Kingdom.

3. Today I will examine my **priorities** in an effort to line them up with God's priorities for my life. I will delight myself in the Lord so that he can instill *His desires* in my heart, making them *my desires* in the process.

4. Today I will examine my **belief system** and will discern the difference between what is real — what has been birthed by God in my spirit — and what is just religious tradition that has been passed down to me from people in my life, or from previous generations. Whatever is not of faith is sin, so I will search for the genuine faith in my heart that has come to me by correctly hearing the rhema word of God, and I will discard everything else.

5. Today I will examine my **world-view**, and will move into a place of mature authority that will enable me to see the world as God sees it, so that I can live my life in a way that will help His will to be done here on earth as it is in heaven.

6. Today I will examine my **self-perception**, so that I can be sure that I see myself correctly — as God sees me. I am who God says I am . . . I can do what God says I can do . . . I have what God says I have!

7. Today I will properly discern the body of Christ and will derive health from that discernment in my physical body, and will add years to my life because of my embracing it. By faith, I will drink the cup and eat the bread worthily today, and today I will live in the now!

Father, help me to examine my real life today. In Jesus' name, amen

October 16
SECRETS REVEALED!

"The secret things belong to the Lord our God,
but those things which are revealed belong to us and to our children forever,
that we may do all the words of this law." (Deuteronomy 29:29)

"The secret of the Lord is with those who fear Him,
and He will show them His covenant." (Psalm 25:14)

1. Today I will live in the now! I will live in the now because I dwell in the secret place of the Most High, and abide under the shadow of the Almighty, where God is revealing secret things – intimate things — to my spirit and to my renewed mind. There is an unveiling and uncovering of mysteries that I am walking in that is connecting all the broken pieces of my life. Revelation knowledge is logically explaining the illogical to my natural mind, creating vision, and explaining the deep things of God. And because deep calls unto deep, I have the spirit of wisdom and revelation in the knowledge of Him!

2. Today I will walk in understanding with those who usually confound me.

3. Today I will walk in the faith that takes the unmanifested things to a new level of tangibility. Today anything is possible — and the secret of the Lord is preparing me for a new thing that I cannot explain with my natural language — but I know that *it is real* and that *it is here!*

4. Today I will walk as a spiritual person who judges all things, and yet is judged by no man.

5. Today I will walk in godly insight, perception and discernment. The Mind of Christ is being revealed through process and earth-time to my eternal awareness of "now."

6. Today I will be released from anxiety and agitation because I understand what is really happening to me. I can see the big picture. I get it.

7. Today I will be a revealer of truth and light to those who sit in darkness, by my words and thoughts and actions. The access that I have to God-secrets will enable me to speak as one who has authority, and not as the Pharisees. I will not say anything that I do not hear the Father say today, and today I will live in the now!

Father, reveal Yourself to me today. In Jesus' name, amen.

October 17
GRACE REALITY!

"And last of all He appeared to me also, as to one prematurely and born dead [no better than an unperfected fetus among living men] . . . but by the grace (the unmerited favor and blessing) of God I am what I am, and His grace toward me was not [found to be] for nothing (fruitless and without effect). In fact, I worked harder than all of them [the apostles], though it was not really I, but the grace (the unmerited favor and blessing) of God which was with me." (1 Corinthians 15:8, 10 - AMP)

1   Today I will live in the now! I will live in the now because I accept the reality that I am what I am by the grace of God. I believe that the timing of the events in my life is by His grace, and that even though I may be "born out of season," I will arrive at the ultimate destination of my purpose right on time!

2   Today I will flow in faith with the fact that my anointing is what it is by the grace of God!

3   Today I will purposely make peace with the perspective that my calling is what it is by the grace of God!

4   Today I will actualize my abilities with the awareness that my individuality is what it is by the grace of God!

5.   Today I will take in the totality of the truth that my vision is what it is by the grace of God!

6.   Today I will base the business at hand on the belief that my purpose is what it is by the grace of God!

7.   Today I will be ready to run for the goal by the revelation that my destiny is what it is by the grace of God! Today I will realize that I have been "graced" to do great things as only I can do them, and today I will live in the now!

Father, give me the grace to be me today. In Jesus' name, amen.

October 18
I SAY!

"When Jesus came into the region of Caesarea Philippi, He asked His disciples, saying, 'Who do men SAY that I, the Son of Man, am?' So they said, 'Some SAY John the Baptist, some Elijah, and others Jeremiah or one of the prophets.' He said to them, 'But who do you SAY that I am?' Simon Peter answered and said, 'You are the Christ, the Son of the living God.' Jesus answered and said to him, 'Blessed are you, Simon Bar-Jonah, for flesh and blood has not revealed this to you, but My Father Who is in heaven. And I also SAY to you that you are Peter . . . .'" (Matthew 16:13-18)

1. Today I will live in the now! I will live in the now because I know that *Jesus is to me who I SAY that He is.* "Now Jesus stood before the governor. And the governor asked Him, saying, 'Are you the King of the Jews?' Jesus said to him, 'It is as you SAY'" - Matthew 27:11)! I also know that I am who He says that I am — and that it is imperative that I say that *I am who God SAYS that I am!*

2. Today I will say that Jesus is my Savior and my Lord! Flesh and blood has not revealed this to me.

3. Today I will say that Jesus is my Healer and my Baptizer! Flesh and blood has not revealed this to me.

4. Today I will say that Jesus is my Rewarder and my Provider! Flesh and blood has not revealed this to me.

5. Today I will say that Jesus is my Friend and my Brother! Flesh and blood has not revealed this to me.

6. Today I will say that Jesus is my Intercessor and my King — He is the Christ, the Son of the living God! Flesh and blood has not revealed this to me, because it cannot reveal it to me. With my mouth confession is made unto salvation. I am the redeemed of the Lord, and I SAY so!

7. Today I will say that I am the righteousness of God in Christ, a son of God, His workmanship, a new creation, the redeemed of the Lord, an heir of God and joint-heir with Christ, a partaker of the divine nature, an individual member of the Body of Christ, the temple of the Holy Spirit, an able minister of the New Testament, an overcomer, more than a conqueror, the healed of the Lord, sanctified, justified, set apart, bought with a price, blood-washed, forgiven, regenerated, transformed, translated from the kingdom of darkness into the Kingdom of the Son, blessed, successful, prosperous, the head and not the tail, above only and not beneath, called, anointed, appointed, and delivered! I have what I say today, and today I will live in the now!

Father, reveal to me today what flesh and blood cannot. In Jesus' name, amen.

October 19
HEAVENLY TREASURE!

"Don't hoard treasure down here where it gets eaten by moths and corroded by rust or – worse! – stolen by burglars. Stockpile treasure in heaven, where it's safe from moth and rust and burglars. It's obvious, isn't it? The place where your treasure is, is the place you will most want to be, and end up being. Your eyes are windows into your body. If you open your eyes wide in wonder and belief, your body fills up with light. If you live squinty-eyed in greed and distrust, your body is a dank cellar. If you pull the blinds on your windows, what a dark life you will have! You can't worship two gods at once. Loving one god, you'll end up hating the other. Adoration for one feeds contempt for the other. You can't worship God and Money both." (Matthew 6:19-24 - The Message)

1. Today I will live in the now! I will live in the now because my treasure is in heaven — my financial interests are Kingdom-related.

2. Today *I will have things* without letting *things have me*.

3. Today I will declare my independence from the world's economic system by returning the Lord's tithe to Him, giving my offerings, thinking about affluence from His perspective, and prophesying my prosperity and provision by my faith-filled words.

4. Today I will repent of greed, stinginess, or any other small-minded attitude or paradigm. My Father owns the cattle on a thousand hills and there is more than enough for me. The earth is the Lord's, and the meek are inheriting it!

5. Today I will seek first the Kingdom of God by not worrying about what I am going to eat or what I am going to wear.

6. Today I will serve one God with my whole heart.

7. Today I will rise above an earth-bound mentality concerning finances, which will, in turn, cause me to think out of the box and supersede the cosmos (world-system) in every other area of my life. My real life is hidden with Christ and God (Colossians 3:1-4), and I am putting on the new man, who is renewed in knowledge according to the image of Him Who created him! Today I am making significant, heavenly investments and deposits, and today I will live in the now!

Father, help me keep my heart where my treasure is today. In Jesus' name, amen.

October 20
REMIND ME!

"I, even I, am He who blots out and cancels your transgressions, for My own sake, and I will not remember your sins. Put Me in remembrance [REMIND ME of your merits]; let us plead and argue together. Set forth your case that you may be justified (proved right)." (Isaiah 43:25, 26 - AMP)

1. Today I will live in the now! I will live in the now because I know that God has blotted out my transgressions for His own sake, so I will not bring them up to Him anymore!

2. Today I will remind God of my merits and, in so doing, I will remind myself.

3. Today I will not speak of sins that have been long forgiven. There is therefore now no condemnation to me because I am in Christ, and He is faithful and just to forgive me and to cleanse me from all unrighteousness!

4. Today I will put God in remembrance of His Word concerning every area of my life.

5. Today I will forget those things which are behind, and bring myself into the now!

6. Today I will walk in righteousness-consciousness rather than sin-consciousness. I celebrate the fact that I am in Christ and that I am accepted in Him Who is the Beloved!

7. Today I will only say good and positive things about myself, because I belong to God and I refuse to insult the beauty of His new creation! I will walk with a healed and sanctified memory, making peace with my past — making peace with my life! I have peace with God today, and today I will live in the now!

Father, be reminded of my merits today. In Jesus' name, amen.

October 21
CHRIST'S EPISTLE!

"Do we begin again to commend ourselves? Or do we need, as some others, epistles of commendation to you or letters of commendation from you? You are our epistle written in our hearts, known and read by all men; clearly you are an epistle of Christ, ministered by us, written not with ink but by the Spirit of the living God, not on tablets of stone but on tablets of flesh, that is, of the heart." (2 Corinthians 3:1-3)

1. Today I will live in the now! I will live in the now because I realize that God's living word is being presently published through my life, to be read by the people around me so that they can have illustrated truth readily available to them. I have a story to tell and I am telling it in every day that I live. It is my own personal story, but it is really the story of Christ — it is a part of the living gospel!

2. Today I will overcome the accuser of the brethren by the word of my testimony, because I know that he has been defeated by the Blood of the Lamb in the atonement.

3. Today I will embrace all of my history. My life is what it is — God's providence working through the consequences of my choices — but, ultimately, He has caused all things to work together for my good. Therefore, I do not second-guess my decisions or regret my life-choices. I have chosen the right path, and I will make the most of what I have to work with today.

4. Today I will draw strength from my experiences, having learned from my mistakes and realizing the importance of putting away the childish things that prevent me from taking full responsibility for my life. God and I together are co-creating my destiny, and His perfection more than makes up for my inadequacies in this area.

5. Today I will celebrate and exalt my victories — not to bolster my ego — but to boast in the Lord! I will let MY light so shine before men that they may see MY good works, and glorify my Father in heaven.

6. Today I will not be in denial about my defeats or recklessly forgetful of my failures. I will admit them and accept them as a part of the whole experience of my life, and then move on to rise above them and become a better person.

7. Today I will make it my aim and personal goal to work out my own salvation – my "designer salvation," individually, tailor-made for my unique relationship with God. I will live my life by my own word from God today, and today I will live in the now!

Father, write me on the hearts of those who need to see You today. In Jesus' name, amen.

October 22
KING'S GLORY!

"It is the glory of God to conceal a matter,
but the glory of kings is to search out a matter." (Proverbs 25:2)

1. Today I will live in the now! I will live in the now because the King of Kings has made me a king and a priest, and the glory of kings is to search out the mysteries that God has concealed. As in the legend of King Arthur and the sword in the stone, I am proving my divine rights to royalty by pulling the sword of the Lord (Hebrews 4:12; Ephesians 6:17) out of the Rock, Who is Christ! The part of the sword (Word) that is exposed is the logos Word given to everyone. That Word shows the way to salvation and all of its benefits and is available to "whosoever will." But the part that is hidden deep in the stone (the Cornerstone that the builders rejected) is the rhema word for my life, destiny and individual purpose. It is the word that is written to me only. No one can extract that sword from the rock (Rock) but me, and I assume my responsibility in finding my own path – working out my own salvation – surviving my own Garden of Gethsemane – so that I can pray, alone, through my own drops of blood for God's perfect will to be done in my life!

2. Today I will search out the meaning of my past experiences.

3. Today I will search out the meaning of my personal prophecies.

4. Today I will search out the meaning of my gifts and callings.

5. Today I will search out the meaning of my relationships.

6. Today I will search out the meaning of my fiery trials.

7. Today I will search out the meaning of my whole life – past, present, future – who I am and who I am becoming. I will work at pulling the sword from the stone today, and today I will live in the now!

"Oh, the depth of the riches both of the wisdom and knowledge of God! How unsearchable are His judgments and His ways past finding out! 'For who has known the mind of the Lord? Or who has become His counselor? Or who has first given to Him and it shall be repaid to him?' For of Him and through Him and to Him are all things, to whom be glory forever. Amen." (Romans 11:33-36)

Father, teach me how to live like a king today. In Jesus' name, amen.

October 23
CHEERFUL GIVER!

"[Remember] this: he who sows sparingly and grudgingly will also reap sparingly and grudgingly, and he who sows generously [that blessings may come to someone] will also reap generously and with blessings." *(2 Corinthians 9:6 – AMP)*

1. Today I will live in the now! I will live in the now because I have a good attitude concerning giving, and that is why I am so blessed! I have defined my terms and written my own ticket with God. Simply put, He loves to give to me because I love to give to Him! ("Let each one [give] as he has made up his own mind and purposed in his heart, not reluctantly or sorrowfully or under compulsion, for God loves (He takes pleasure in, prizes above other things, and is unwilling to abandon or to do without) a cheerful (joyous, 'prompt-to-do-it') giver [whose heart is in his giving]." - 2 Corinthians 9:7 - AMP)

2. Today I call myself free from any religious spirit concerning giving. I am free from the law concerning giving. I am free from tradition concerning giving. I give because I am in covenant with God, and I am more than happy to do it!

3. Today I will be in the flow because of my obedience to God.

4. Today I open supernatural doors through which prosperity may enter my life. I will make contact with those who are supposed to give to me - good measure, pressed down, shaken together, running over. I will be at the right place at the right time, say the right thing to the right person, and receive the right response!

5. Today I will not worry for a minute about my needs being met. "And God is able to make all grace (every favor and earthly blessing) come to you in abundance, so that you may always and under all circumstances and whatever the need be self-sufficient [possessing enough to require no aid or support and furnished in abundance for every good work and charitable donation]" - 2 Corinthians 9:8 – AMP. I will be self-sufficient in Christ's sufficiency today!

6. Today I will scatter abroad and give to the poor. My deeds of justice and goodness and kindness and benevolence will go on forever! And God, Who provides seed for the sower and bread for eating, will also provide and multiply my resources for sowing and increase the fruits of my righteousness, which manifests itself in active goodness, kindness and charity. I will be enriched in all things, and in every way, so that I can be generous, and my generosity will bring forth thanksgiving to God!

7. Today my cheerful giving will help to make the world a better place in which to live, and today I will live in the now!

Father, help me to stay cheerful in my giving today. In Jesus' name, amen.

October 24
FULFILLED PURPOSE!

"God answer you in the day you crash,
The name of God-of-Jacob put you out of harm's reach,
Send reinforcements from Holy Hill,
Dispatch from Zion fresh supplies,
Exclaim over your offerings,
Celebrate your sacrifices,
Give you what your heart desires,
Accomplish your plans.

When you win, we plan to raise the roof
And lead the parade with our banners.
May all your wishes come true!

That clinches it – help's coming,
An answer's on the way,
Everything's going to work out."
(Psalm 20:1-6 – The Message)

"May He grant you according to your heart's desire, and fulfill all your PURPOSE."
(Psalm 20:4)

1. Today I will live in the now! I will live in the now because I know that the Lord saves His anointed!

2. Today I will plan my work and work my plan ("May He grant you according to your heart's desire, and fulfill all your plans" - Psalm 20:4 - AMP).

3. Today I will believe that God is fulfilling all of my secret petitions (Psalm 20:5).

4. Today I will find direction.

5. Today I will walk in the peace that passes understanding.

6. Today I will believe that everything is going to be all right, because the Lord perfects that which concerns me!

7. Today I will be fulfilled. I will make the decision to feel fulfilled and will flee from the fear of failure, remaining full of faith in the faithfulness that I find in God, and freeing myself by forgetting what is forever behind me! I will make my life count today, and today I will live in the now!

Father, fulfill Your purposes in me today. In Jesus' name, amen.

October 25
SHOW TIME!

"Then the Lord said to Moses, 'Rise early in the morning and stand before Pharaoh, and say to him, 'Thus says the Lord God of the Hebrews: "Let my people go, that they may serve Me, for at this time I will send all My plagues to your very heart, and on your servants and on your people, that you may know that there is none like Me in all the earth" . . . but indeed for this purpose I have raised you up, that I may show My power in you, and that My name may be declared in all the earth." (Exodus 9:13, 14, 16)

1. Today I will live in the now! I will live in the now because I know that God is using me, along with the current circumstances in my life, to show His mighty power. This is not a time for me to be down - discouraged, disappointed or depressed – it's Show Time! – time to display a definite miracle! – time for me to dynamically declare and demonstrate His divine power to deliver me from defeat, destruction, demons and death!

2. Today I will rejoice that God's show is the greatest show on earth and that He always saves the best for last! He will turn the ordinary water of my life into the finest wine!

3. Today I will be open to the working of unusual, creative, and unprecedented miracles . . . signs and wonders . . . Gifts of the Spirit . . . confirmations . . . the pulling down of strongholds . . . manifestations of supernatural success, favor and promotion . . . prophetic words and insights . . . supernatural occurrences of revelation knowledge . . . angelic visitations . . . dreams and visions . . . anything and everything that brings attention to God and makes His name more famous. I will not just think outside of the box through the possibility of these things today, I will destroy the box altogether!

4. Today I will live a life of genuine testimony that bears witness to the greatness of God!

5. Today I will uninhibitedly tell my story, and sing my song of triumph with abandon and spiritual vigor!

6. Today I will not be surprised when I see the wicked gnash with their teeth at the sight of my vindication. I will comfort the afflicted, and afflict the comfortable, with my provocative presentation of the precious redemption that I possess in Christ.

7. Today I will be godlike ("So the Lord said to Moses: 'See, I have made you as God to Pharaoh . . .'" - Exodus 7:1). I will confidently walk in the commitment to my calling, and today I will live in the now!

Father, show me off for Your pleasure today. In Jesus' name, amen.

October 26
SUPERNATURAL SIGNS!

"Now the Lord said to Moses, 'Go in to Pharaoh; for I have hardened his heart and the hearts of his servants, that I may show these SIGNS of Mine before him, and that you may tell in the hearing of your son and your son's son the mighty things I have done in Egypt, and My SIGNS which I have done among them, that you may know that I am the Lord.'" (Exodus 10:1, 2)

1. Today I will live in the now! I will live in the now because my life up to this point is a sign and a wonder, God miraculously working through me and for me – even in spite of me – to show Himself strong on my behalf!

2. Today I will see God turn a hopeless situation into a testimony of deliverance.

3. Today I will look beyond what seems to be accidents, flukes or coincidences, and see the hand of God ordering the events of my life to bring about His purposes.

4. Today I will recognize the people who have been supernaturally connected to me for Kingdom reasons.

5. Today I will hold on to my vision and will believe that the events of this day, no matter how mundane or ordinary, are an essential part of the fulfilling of my destiny.

6. Today I will notice and count every little miracle – every good and fortunate thing that happens to me – and I will thank God for every one of them.

7. Today I will see signs and wonders confirm the power of the gospel in my life. I will make myself comfortable with the unusual and unprecedented. I will be miracle-minded today, and today I will live in the now!

Father, perform Your signs and wonders through me today. In Jesus' name, amen.

October 27
STAND STILL!

"And Moses said to the people, 'Do not be afraid. Stand still, and see the salvation of the Lord, which He will accomplish for you today. For the Egyptians whom you see today, you shall see again no more forever.'" (Exodus 14:13)

1. Today I will live In the now! I will live in the now because I am seeing the saving deliverance of God in my life – God's great show that is "standing room only" – and I am seeing it up close and first hand! It is written: "Therefore put on God's complete armor, that you may be able to resist and STAND your ground on the evil day [of danger], and having done all [the crisis demands], to STAND [firmly in your place]. STAND therefore [hold your ground] . . . " (Ephesians 6:13, 14 - AMP). Today I will do all that the crisis demands, and then I will bravely stand in faith — patiently, but not passively — for my stand is an act of aggression against the powers of darkness.

2. Today I will be still and know that God is God.

3. Today I will stand up and be counted for what is right. I am on the good side. I am on the Lord's side!

4. Today I will get back up after a fall. Even if I am hedged in and pressed on every side — even if I am troubled and oppressed in every way. — I will refuse to be cramped or crushed! It doesn't matter if I suffer an embarrassment. I will not be moved if I feel perplexed and can't seem to find a way out — I will not be driven to despair!

5. Today I will not be afraid of persecution. Even if I am hard driven and pursued, I know that I will not be deserted, and I will not have to stand alone! I may be struck down to the ground, but I will never be struck out! I make the decision to keep standing today; therefore, I know that I will never be destroyed!

6. Today I will keep my head held high, looking for my miracle as I continue to stand in faith. I will stand still, and stand firm, confident and undismayed by the threats of my enemies. I will not feel overwhelmed today — the Greater One indwells me and He is STANDING UP FOR ME, ever living to make intercession.

7. Today I will stand up to everything the enemy throws my way. I will be prepared for whatever comes today, and when it's all over but the shouting, I'll still be on my feet! I am looking for the salvation of the Lord to be manifested like never before today, and today I will live in the now!

Father, help me to stand still and see what You're doing today. In Jesus' name, amen.

October 28
GOD'S STRATEGY!

"Surely the Lord does nothing, unless he reveals His secret to His servants the prophets."
(Amos 3:7)

1. Today I will live in the now! I will live in the now because I am on the Lord's side and He is revealing to me His secret strategies for my life, for the Kingdom, and for the world. Jesus said: "However, when He, the Spirit of Truth, has come, He will guide you into all truth; for He will not speak on His own authority, but whatever He hears He will speak; and He will tell you things to come" (John 16:13). "He" is here now and He is my resource and source of information. I am a watchman on the wall - sober and vigilant. I will not be blind-sided by trouble or calamity, because the Helper is in constant revelation mode in my life!

2. Today I will be wise as a serpent, yet harmless as a dove.

3. Today I will master the art of war in the heavenlies.

4. Today I will believe the words of my friend, Jesus, Who said, "No longer do I call you servants, for a servant does not know what his master is doing; but I have called you friends, for all things that I heard from My Father I have made known to you" (John 15:15). As a friend of Christ, I am a child of light, so I never need to fear a thief in the night!

5. Today I will develop a master plan for my prosperity and productivity by meditating on the Word and allowing God to reveal His secrets of success to me.

6. Today I will utilize and employ with perception every piece of the panoply of God.

7. Today I will listen closely to the still, small voice in my inner man, and today I will live in the now!

. *Father, let me be a sanctuary for Your secrets today. In Jesus' name, amen.*

October 29
DESERT ROSES!

"Wilderness and desert will sing joyously, the badlands will celebrate and flower – like the crocus in spring, bursting into blossom, a symphony of song and color. Mountain glories of Lebanon – a gift. Awesome Carmel, stunning Sharon – gifts. God's resplendent glory, fully on display. God awesome, God majestic." (Isaiah 35:1,2 – The Message)

1. Today I will live in the now! I will live in the now because I am claiming the promise of God that the desert will bloom like a rose! I am believing that I am receiving fulfilled prophecies - answered prayers - dreams coming true - the dry bones living again - my second wind - the refreshing of the Spirit - the watering of the Word. I prophesy to the wind that life is manifesting its triumph over death!

2. Today I will walk in resurrection power. I speak these words: "Energize the limp hands, strengthen the rubbery knees. Tell fearful souls, 'Courage! Take heart! God is here, right here, on His way to put things right and redress all wrongs. He's on His way! He'll save you! Blind eyes will be opened, deaf ears unstopped, lame men and women leap like deer, the voiceless break into song. Springs of water will burst out in the wilderness, streams flow in the desert" (Isaiah 35:3-6 – The Message). It is raining on my desert today! I am alive and awake! I am renewed and refreshed! I am fruitful and flourishing! I will be a life-giver today, for God is pouring out of His Spirit through my spirit. It is raining *through me* today!

3. Today I will rejoice that hope springs eternal!

4. Today the hot sands of persecution, heated by the fiery trials that I have been experiencing, will become a cool oasis of Holy Ghost life. The thirsty ground will become a splashing fountain of faith. The barren grasslands will flourish richly as miracles begin to spring up everywhere. I see it! I receive it!

5. Today I will draw water out of the wells of salvation with joy. It's time to be happy! It's time to laugh! It's time to sing and rejoice! It's time to thrive in the spirit of celebration. I celebrate God today! I celebrate the Kingdom! I celebrate the now! I celebrate the day. I rejoice and am glad – very glad – in every minute of it. *IT'S ALL GOOD!*

6. Today I will drink from the rivers of living water flowing from my inner man, building myself up on my most holy faith by praying in the Spirit!

7. Today I will see a real change for the better, and today I will live in the now!

   Father, let the desert bloom like a rose today. In Jesus' name, amen.

October 30
INVISIBLE IMAGE!

"He is the image of the invisible God, the firstborn over all creation. For by Him all things were created that are in heaven and that are on earth, visible and invisible, whether thrones or dominions or principalities or powers. All things were created through Him and for Him. And He is before all things, and in Him all things consist. And He is the head of the body, the church, Who is the beginning, the firstborn from the dead, that in all things He may have the preeminence. For it pleased the Father that in Him all the fullness should dwell." (Colossians 1:15-19)

1. Today I will live in the now! I will live in the now because I recognize the reality of the Christ in my world . . . in my life . . . in the now — the exalted firstborn Son of God reigning *over* and *through* me so that He can ultimately reign *with* me! I am being changed into His likeness today as I hear the sound of His voice speaking to my current situation. Jesus, the prophet, is speaking to my destiny. Jesus, the priest, is praying for me to fulfill my purpose. Jesus, the king, is revealing Himself to me as the undisputed ruler of the universe. I am beginning to look and talk like Him . . . to think like Him . . . to be like Him in this earth . . . to walk in the reality of the invisible God, making Him visible here in the material world.

2. Today I will confess that in Him all things consist! I boldly confess that Jesus Christ is Lord – absolutely and entirely - to the glory of God the Father!

3. Today I will declare that He is the Head of the Church! I will do my part to rid it of the antichrist religion that tries to rob it of its mission and vision. I will pray that the Church will give birth to the Kingdom in dynamic demonstration!

4. Today I will recognize that in all things He has the pre-eminence! Christ is all! Christ is the victor!

5. Today I will find my voice in the Kingdom. I will speak my part of the vision, and bring restoration to my part of the earth. I will be a visionary healer today who speaks a word of reconciliation and deliverance to a nation.

6. Today I will agree with the Father in that it will please me that, in Christ, all of the fullness should dwell. I am full today because Christ is full, complete, perfect, entire, and whole. I am whole in Him! I am complete!

7. Today I will prophesy to creation and announce that the earth is the Lord's. I will pull out of the invisible realm what needs to become visible to the natural eye. I will not be passive, but I will manifest the image of the invisible God as I walk in my authority and enforce my Kingdom influence. I will walk in real power today, and today I will live in the now!

Father, reveal the invisible things through me today. In Jesus' name, amen.

October 31
NO MONSTERS!

"You shall tread upon the lion and the cobra,
the young lion and the serpent you shall trample underfoot." (Psalm 91:13)

"Behold! I have given you authority and power to trample upon serpents and scorpions,
and (physical and mental strength and ability) over all the power that the enemy [possesses];
and nothing shall in any way harm you." (Luke 10:19 - AMP)

1. Today I will live in the now! I will live in the now because I am free from every curse — I do not fear demons or witchcraft or any work of darkness. My light cannot be overtaken and God has not given me a spirit of fear, but of power and of love and of a sound mind!

2. Today I will not be afraid of "the beast," or of Armageddon, or the sign of 666. I know that God has given me dominion on this planet, and I hold the keys of the Kingdom!

3. Today I will not fear the future. I declare the end from the beginning!

4. Today I will not fear any accusation from the brethren's accuser, because I am covered with the blood of Jesus and I am familiar with the word of my testimony.

5. Today I will not be afraid in my house – no plague will come near my dwelling! I am not afraid of the terror by night or of the arrow that flies by day, nor of the pestilence that walks in darkness, nor of the destruction that lays waste at noonday!

6. Today I will not be afraid of any accident or calamity, for the angel of the Lord sets up camp around me and bears me up in his own hand.

7. Today, even though I walk through the valley of the shadow of death, I will fear no evil, for God is with me! His rod and His staff comfort me today, and today I will live in the now!

Father, keep me safe today. In Jesus' name, amen.

November In The Now!

◆N◆O◆V◆E◆M◆B◆E◆R◆

A month to count your blessings . . .

Time for thanksgiving for the harvest . . .

Time to show an attitude of gratitude . . .

The seeds you have sown
are all finally full-grown!
It's time to say thanks
for all that you own.

You've reached for the prize,
and attained! For your eyes
have been brightened by blessed
Harvest Moons in the skies.

You've not ceased to believe,
Now it's time to receive,
and enjoy the fruits of
what you've longed to achieve.

Harvest time now is here,
There's no reason to fear,
You have more than enough –
It's your bumper crop year!

"So let's not allow ourselves to get fatigued doing good
At the right time we will harvest a good crop if we don't give up, or quit."
(Galatians 6:9 – The Message)

November 1
CREATIVE IMAGINATION!

" . . . and now nothing they have IMAGINED they can do will be impossible to them."
(Genesis 11:6 – AMP)

1. Today I will live in the now! I will live in the now because I am shaping my future by the God-given creativity resident in my divinely inspired imagination. I will work toward developing an understanding of REVELATION in relation to ENLIGHTENMENT. "[For I always pray to] the God of our Lord Jesus Christ . . . may grant you a spirit of wisdom and revelation [of insight into mysteries and secrets] in the [deep and intimate] knowledge of Him, by having the eyes of your heart flooded with light, so that you can know and understand . . . " (Ephesians 1:17, 18 - AMP). As revelation is being imparted to me by the rhema word of God, enlightenment is coming to me from within as I let that abide in me which I heard from the beginning. These components comprise my creative imagination.

2. Today I will seek to understand linear time in relation to cyclical time ("That which is NOW already has been, and that which is to be already has been; and God seeks that which has passed by [so that history repeats itself]" Ecclesiastes 3:15 - AMP). As Jesus was actually crucified 2,000 years ago, but was also crucified from the foundation of the world, so there is more to what is happening in my life right now than what I can see on this particular date in history. I will walk CIRCUMSPECTLY (seeing in a circle - Ephesians 5:15), so that I can comprehend how I am coming, full cycle, into the perfect will of God for my life. These two dimensions locate my creative imagination.

3. Today I will understand the relationship between my recreated spirit and my renewed mind, knowing that He has made everything beautiful in its time and has planted eternity in my heart, divinely implanting a sense of purpose in me that has been working through the ages. The eternal life in my spirit assures my heavenly destiny, but the renewing of my mind transforms me here in the material world.

4. Today I will understand the balance between the God-kind of faith and "the things we hope for," using my imagination to release things for which I believe.

5. Today I will understand the relationship of my Kingdom authority to the sovereignty of God (". . . the sword of the Lord, *AND* of Gideon!" – Judges 7:18).

6. Today I will be mature enough to discern the balance between creative *ability* and creative *responsibility*. I will use the power of my soul only for the good.

7. Today I will understand how the future relates to the *now* (the future IS now). I will own this understanding today, and today I will live in the now!

Father, bless my imagination today. In Jesus' name, amen.

November 2
KINGDOM AUTHORITY!

"Therefore I exhort first of all that supplications, prayers, intercessions, and giving of thanks be made for all men, for kings and ALL WHO ARE IN AUTHORITY, that we may lead a quiet and peaceable life in all godliness and reverence." (1 Timothy 2:1, 2)

1. Today I will live in the now! I will live in the now because I am living a quiet and peaceable life in all godliness and reverence as a direct result of my understanding and appreciation of authority figures - in the church, in the Kingdom, and in society. I am free from the bondage of a spirit of rebellion!

2. Today I will comprehend the meaning of Kingdom authority, which is:

    A - ccepting the system of government that God has ordained for His creation (Romans 13:1-7)
    U - nderstanding the flow of command in the Kingdom (Matthew 22:15-22)
    T - rusting in the power of submission (Matthew 8:9)
    H - onoring those in authority for the right reasons (1 Thessalonians 5:12, 13)
    O - beying with a cheerful heart (Hebrews 13:17)
    R - esting in the liberty that comes from proper submission to authority (1 Peter 2:13-17)
    I - nvesting in the restoration of all things (Acts 3:21)
    T - aking dominion over the present world-system, and its god (Revelation 11:5)
    Y - ielding ultimately and completely to the Lordship of Jesus (Ephesians 5:22-24)

3. Today I will win in life by understanding how the system works.

4. Today I will intercede for those in authority.

5. Today I will have order in my life.

6. Today I will have authority, being under authority myself. "For I am a man under authority, having soldiers under me. And I say to this man, 'Go' and he goes; and to another, 'Come' and he comes; and to my servant, 'Do this,' and he does it" (Matthew 8:9).

7. Today I will exercise spiritual authority, winning the war against principalities, powers, the rulers of the darkness of this world, and spiritual wickedness in high places. I will prevail over strongholds, and Jesus will marvel at my faith because of my insight into the authority that I have in Him, in three worlds (heaven, earth, hell). I will take charge of my life today, and today I will live in the now!

Father, let Your Kingdom come today. In Jesus' name, amen.

November 3
DECIDE NOW!

" . . . choose for yourselves THIS DAY . . . . " (Joshua 24:15)

1. Today I will live in the now! I will live in the now because I appreciate and discern the power of a decision in my life and the importance of timing to the discovery of my destiny. A decision CHANGES CIRCUMSTANCES (James 1:5-8; 4:8), and today I will begin the process of changing what needs to be different or better in my life by simply making the decision to do it! Today's decisions will become tomorrow's realities!

2. Today I will anticipate directional dialogue, realizing that a decision COMMANDS RESPONSE (Joshua 24:14, 15). I decide today that, as for me and my house, we will serve the Lord and I will be prepared to deal with every reaction to that decision, whether positive or negative.

3. Today I will prepare for something new in my world and sphere of influence, knowing that a decision CREATES EVENTS (Luke 15:18). My decision-making skills will make positive things happen for me and take me to the next level of success.

4. Today I will not worry about getting my needs met, because I know that a decision CALLS PROVISION (2 Corinthians 9:10). The money, finances or resources that I need will be pulled toward me by the force of my decision – they will be drawn in like steel to a magnet. My decision to prosper drives a stake in the mental and emotional ground of my life, and the surrounding circumstances will conform to the power of it!

5. Today I will cross paths with the right person for every situation that arises, because I am aware that a decision CONNECTS PEOPLE (Amos 3:3). I will find a place of agreement and harmony with someone who flows with my vision, because of our mutual decisions and because our steps are ordered.

6. Today I will break ties with any long-held affection for my comfort zones, because I know that a decision CHALLENGES MEDIOCRITY ("For whoever has, to him more will be given; but whoever does not have, even what he has will be taken away from him" - Mark 4:25).

7. Today my iron-like resolve will sharpen the iron in someone else, because a decision COMMUNICATES FAITH (Proverbs 27:17). I will realize that two will be better than one today, and today I will live in the now!

Father, help me to make good decisions today. In Jesus' name, amen.

November 4
REAL SUBSTANCE!

"Now faith is the SUBSTANCE of things hoped for . . . ." **(Hebrews 11:1)**

1. Today I will live in the now! I will live in the now because my faith gives substance* or matter** to the intangible and invisible things for which I hope. [*Substance: that which has mass, occupies space, and can be perceived by the senses.] [**Matter: a material of a particular kind or constitution; the most central and material part; essence; solid, substantial quality or character; physical density; body.] Faith makes it real. Faith says "I have it now!" Today I will rejoice to know that **FAITH IS AVAILABLE** (Romans 12:3)!

2. Today I will be aware that **FAITH IS MOBILE**. It can come from somewhere else (Romans 10:17) and it can walk me to somewhere else (2 Corinthians 5:7).

3. Today I will be grateful that **FAITH IS ACCESSIBLE**. It works by love (Galatians 5:6), and love is mine through the impartation of the Holy Spirit (Romans 5:5).

4. Today I will be confident in the fact that **FAITH IS VISIBLE** (". . . when Jesus SAW their faith . . ." – Mark 2:5), and I will demonstrate it to the sense-ruled world today!

5. Today I will remember that **FAITH IS VERBAL**. It is written: "And since we have the same spirit of faith, according to what is written, 'I believed and **THEREFORE I SPOKE**, we also believe, and therefore SPEAK" (2 Corinthians 4:13). I will speak to the mountain today, and I will believe that what I say is coming to pass!

6. Today I will enjoy the fact that **FAITH IS TANGIBLE!** I will believe that I receive WHEN I PRAY (Mark 11:24), and will not have to wait until I see a manifestation to thank God for the answer. In the world, seeing is believing . . . in Christ, *believing is seeing!*

7. Today I will not waver from the truth that **FAITH MAKES ALL THINGS POSSIBLE** ("Jesus said to him, 'If you can believe, all things are possible to him who believes!'" – Mark 9:23)

Father, thank You for the measure of faith given to every person.
Help me to increase mine by my belief in Your Word.
Show me how to give substance to the things that I hope for today. In Jesus' name, amen.

November 5
CHRIST'S EARTH!

"The earth is the Lord's, and all its fullness, the world and those who dwell therein."
(Psalm 24:1)

1. Today I will live in the now! I will live in the now because I know that God has given us dominion on the earth so that we can reclaim it for His glory and present it back to Him in wholeness. Jesus is held in the heavens until the restoration of all things (Acts 3:21), and I am resolved to do my part in restoring order, under His Lordship, to the chaotic environment in which I live. I will help to restore order to the earth by my **CONSISTENT INVOLVEMENT IN THE PRAISE AND WORSHIP OF GOD**. I will bless the Lord at all times; His praise shall continually be in my mouth!

2. Today I will help restore order to the earth by my **COMPLETE SUBMISSION TO SPIRITUAL AUTHORITY**. I will demonstrate my trust in God's method of government by my humility and service to others. In God's Kingdom, the way up is down!

3. Today I will help restore order to the earth by my **COMPREHENSION OF THE TITHE**. I will walk in the understanding that tithing is more than an action or a confession — it is an attitude resulting in a lifestyle that declares its own independence from the world's present, cosmetic financial system.

4. Today I will help restore order to the earth by my **CAPACITY FOR CHANGE** as I continually repent my way into the deep things of the Kingdom. In Him I live, and in Him I MOVE – change, grow, expand, and experience transition and transformation.

5. Today I will help restore order to the earth by my **COOPERATION WITH THE CHURCH – CHRIST'S BODY.** I will remember that unity is the instrumentation for the implementation of the Kingdom — we might not have it all together, *but together we have it all!*

6. Today I will help restore order to the earth by my **COMMITMENT TO COVENANT**, understanding the importance of the relationships in my life which provide the personal proving ground for my part in the Kingdom.

7. Today I will help restore order to the earth by my **COMPASSION FOR THE WHOLE WORLD**. My world-view will be inclusive and tolerant, because I know that there are those who know His name, but do not know Him – and there are those who know Him, but do not know His name! I will do what I can to reconcile them to God today, and today I will live in the now!

Father, help me to heal Your world today. In Jesus' name, amen.

November 6
RESURRECTION REALITIES!

"When they saw Him, they worshipped Him; but some doubted. And Jesus came and spoke to them, saying, 'All authority has been given to Me in heaven and on earth. Go therefore and make disciples of all the nations, baptizing them in the name of the Father and of the Son and of the Holy Spirit, teaching them to observe all things that I have commanded you; and lo, I am with you always, even to the end of the age!' Amen." (Matthew 28:17, 18) ". . . if you . . . believe in your heart that God raised Him from the dead, you will be saved. For with the heart one believes unto righteousness . . ." (Romans 10:9, 10)

1. Today I will live in the now! I will live in the now because I believe that God raised Jesus from the dead – not just with my head (intellectually, factually, through information), but with my heart (intuitively, spiritually, by revelation). I believe that God has brought me to this place in my life to reconcile my revelation of the resurrection to my comprehension of the role that I am to play in history. His resurrection has direct bearing on my personal destiny. Jesus was raised from the dead for a certain purpose; I was born when I was born, and have lived long enough to see the 21st century, for a certain purpose. It is my time to bring these two concepts into harmony with one another!

2. Today I will establish myself on the truth that ALL authority has been given to Jesus and, because I am His joint-heir, I am a partaker and shareholder of that authority. I don't *think* that I am, *I know that I am!*

3. Today I will obey the commandment to disciple nations, beginning with my realm of influence – my neighborhood, my place of employment, my community – because I have the confidence of knowing that He is with me until the end of the age (Gr. "Aion" meaning: until there isn't time anymore . . . until we operate in the now). Christ has revealed God as the "Ancient of Days" (Daniel 7:9, 10, 13, 14), which means "the One Who existed before there were days – One Who is older than the advent of days." Light was created before the sun, moon and stars — before the earth began to rotate on its axis (Genesis 1:1-5). I will do my part to disciple the earth until it returns to its eternal state where there is no time, and the Lamb is its light! Jesus is the Light of the World!

4. Today I will remember that God did not rest on the 7th day until He had given man dominion on the 6th day, passing the baton to His creation (Genesis 1:26)!

5. Today I free myself from doubt and unbelief.

6. Today I will free myself from intimidation and feelings of inferiority.

7. Today I will be fully alive in Christ, and today I will live in the now!

Father, help me make the resurrection a reality to my world today. In Jesus' name, amen.

SURVIVAL INSTINCTS!

"But we're not quitters who lose out. Oh, no! We'll stay with it and SURVIVE, trusting all the way." (Hebrews 10:39 – The Message)

1. Today I will live in the now! I will live in the now because I am developing the ability to **THINK BIG!** The bigger my vision, the larger my potential for success, so I will overcome any attack on my vision, even if it comes from people who are close to me! I will assume my responsibility to protect my vision, because I realize that a vision-assault in my life is simply an effort to diminish me and my effectiveness in the Kingdom!

2. Today I will **TALK MY WAY INTO SUCCESS!** I will win the battle with hell for the control over my tongue ("The tongue is a fire, a world of iniquity . . . and it is set on fire of hell." James 3:6), because that is where my creativity resides. My tongue will be inspired by heaven today as I speak God's words and release the miracle that is in my mouth!

3. Today I will **TRUST MY INSTINCTS**. I will walk in the Spirit, and pray without ceasing, until I am able to walk without second-guessing the Mind of Christ in me. I will have faith in my faith and will not mistrust my ability to hear from God.

4. Today I will **TAKE RISKS**, if necessary. I know that I will never discover new oceans until I am willing to lose sight of the shore, so I will break any unhealthy addictions that I have to my comfort zones. I will give no place to demonic powers that are resistant to change (Matthew 12:43, 44; Mark 5:9-12).

5. Today I will **TEAM UP WITH WINNERS**. I will not allow words, or works of the flesh, to separate me from those who could potentially speak into my life and help me get to the next level. I will attract, and be attracted to, great people.

6. Today I will **TRANSCEND MY PROBLEMS**, rising above and surpassing the temptation to look at the temporal, visible things. My faith will enable me to see the big picture, and realize that the current problem may actually be a blessing in disguise, so I will rethink it and see it as a great opportunity for a breakthrough in my life! I will focus on the solution. I will keep my eyes on Jesus, the Author and Finisher of my faith.

7. Today I will **TRY AGAIN**. I will not listen to any voice from the dark side that would attempt to persuade me to quit. I will run and not be weary today, and today I will live in the now!

Father, help me to keep going today. In Jesus' name, amen.

November 8
DREAM WEAVER!

"When the Lord brought back the captives [who returned] to Zion, we were like those who DREAM [it seemed so unreal]." (Psalm 126:1 – AMP)

1. Today I will live in the now! I will live in the now because I am daring to develop my dream, no matter how out of context it is with my current, real-life experience. I am weaving it on the loom of faith which calls those things that are not as though they are, with threads of imagination, vision and the prophetic word of God. My dream demands that I think in a whole new way, so today I will begin to **ERASE MY OLD TAPES**. I will update my mental files and prepare myself for the new thing that God is birthing in me through the power of dreams.

2. Today I will **ENTER MY FUTURE BY RELEASING MY PAST**. I will not weave the threads of old, irrelevant thought patterns into the fabric of my faith in the now!

3. Today I will **ENJOY THE GOODNESS OF GOD**, without feelings of unworthiness . . . without believing a lie that says I don't deserve the best. The realization that God is turning my captivity is not too good to be true. He does not think that it is, and neither do I!

4. Today I will **EXPERIENCE, FULLY, THE THRILL OF VICTORY**. My past failures or mistakes do not dictate my future. That was then – this is now! My real dream has a happy ending!

5. Today I will **EXAMINE THE LINE BETWEEN THE SEEN AND UNSEEN REALMS**, and will be aware when the membrane that separates the spiritual from the natural begins to become thin enough to indicate to me that birth and breakthrough are imminent!

6. Today I will **EXPECT NOTHING BUT GOD'S BEST**. The centripetal force of my expectation will draw God's very best blessings into the happenings of my life as I hold on to my dreams.

7. Today I will **EXPAND MY CAPACITY TO DREAM BIGGER DREAMS**, knowing that a mind once stretched by a new idea never regains its original shape or dimension! I will locate the dream of God for my destiny, and then I will use my inner strength and commitment to make that dream come true. I will do the impossible today, and today I will live in the now!

Father, help me to make it happen today. In Jesus' name, amen.

November 9
LOVE CAN!

"For [if we are] in Christ Jesus, neither circumcision nor uncircumcision counts for anything, but only faith activated and energized and expressed and working through LOVE."
(Galatians 5:6 – AMP)

"Love never fails . . ." (1 Corinthians 13:8)

1. Today I will live in the now! I will live in the now because I am allowing the power of love to be the dominant force in my life. I will be faithful in my relationships today, because **LOVE COMMITS** (Ruth 1:16, 17; 1 Samuel 18:1-4; 20:16, 17).

2. Today I will reach out to someone who has been disconnected and do what I can to restore them, because **LOVE CONFIRMS** (2 Corinthians 2:1-11).

3. Today I will shower the people I love with love, and show them the way that I feel, because **LOVE COMMUNICATES** (Proverbs 16:13).

4. Today I will not involve myself with gossip or passing on rumors, because **LOVE CONCEALS** (Proverbs 11:13).

5. Today I will protect the reputation of others, because **LOVE COVERS** (Proverbs 10:12, 17:9; James 5:19; 1 Peter 4:8).

6. Today I will have the courage to tell the truth to someone who needs to hear it, because **LOVE CORRECTS** (Proverbs 9:8; 27:5, 6).

7. Today I will win in the game of life, because **LOVE CONQUERS** (1 Corinthians 13:4-13). I will not fail today because of love, and today I will live in the now!

Father, love through me today. In Jesus' name, amen.

November 10
MISSION: POSSIBLE!

"I'm glad in God, far happier than you would ever guess . . . . Actually, I don't have a sense of needing anything personally. I've learned by now to be quite content whatever my circumstances. I'm just as happy with little as with much, with much as with little. I've found the recipe for being happy whether full or hungry, hands full or hands empty. Whatever I have, wherever I am, I CAN MAKE IT THROUGH ANYTHING in the One Who makes me who I am." (Philippians 4:13 – The Message)

1. Today I will live in the now! I will live in the now because I have learned how to walk in the kind of balance that comes from experience and maturity. This balance enables me to boldly say that I can do all things through Christ – I can deal with anything that arises - because the accomplishing of my mission is more important to me than external conditions, and my balanced life makes it possible for me to prevail over every problem! Today I will walk in the balance of having **REVELATION WITHOUT RELIGIOSITY.** Much of religion is built on what God **has said**, but revelation is the manifestation of what God **is saying**!

2. Today I will walk in **SPIRITUALITY WITHOUT SUPERIORITY** (" . . . Knowledge puffs up, but love edifies" - 1 Corinthians 8:1). I will cherish my spiritual life and relationship with God, without feeling that I am better than those who do not share my Christ-experience.

3. Today I will walk in **LIBERTY WITHOUT LAWLESSNESS.** I will not be reckless in my righteousness, flaunting my liberty before weaker believers. I will remember that all things are lawful, but not all things are helpful or profitable (1 Corinthians 6:12).

4. Today I will walk in **BELIEF WITHOUT BONDAGE.** I will not let myself become mechanical in my faith and will embrace and celebrate the *spirit* of the law, rather than the *letter* of it. I will go with the flow, even if the flow takes me into uncharted waters.

5. Today I will walk in the balance of **DISCIPLINE WITHOUT DEPRIVATION**. Jesus' burden is easy, and His yoke is light. In Him I am able to deny mysel, without engaging in self-abuse. I can humble myself without compromising my self-respect, and I can be a servant without being taken advantage of.

6. Today I will walk in **EXCELLENCE WITHOUT EXTRAVAGANCE**. I know how to be abased and I know how to abound, because my real wealth is internal.

7. Today I will walk in **COMPASSION WITHOUT COMPROMISE**. I will be merciful, yet maintain a high moral standard, and today I will live in the now!

Father, help me to live a balanced life today. In Jesus' name, amen.

November 11
WINNING WAY!

*"Yet amid all these things we are more than conquerors
and gain a surpassing victory through Him Who loved us." (Romans 8:37 – AMP)*

1. Today I will live in the now! I will live in the now because I am a winner in life. I am a winner who walks in the spirit of excellence because of my **ASSOCIATION WITH GOD**. His victorious and prevailing nature manifests itself in me and will become obvious in my everyday life and through my personality, today.

2. Today I win the battle for my eternal destiny because of my **ACCEPTANCE OF THE LORDSHIP OF JESUS.** I have unbroken peace and fellowship with God because Jesus has saved (and is saving) me to the uttermost!

3. Today I will win in the arena of the supernatural because of my **ACQUAINTANCE WITH THE HOLY SPIRIT**. I am not bound to the limitations of the finite, material world, nor am I held back by the demands of natural law!

4. Today I will win the battle for my mind because of my **ATTITUDE TOWARD THE WORD**. I am being radically transformed, emotionally and intellectually, by the renewing of my mind as I develop the courage to begin to think the thoughts of God Himself!

5. Today I will win in prayer and spiritual warfare because of my **AGREEMENT WITH BELIEVERS**. Two are better than one and they can put ten thousand to flight. There is strength in numbers and safety in the multitude of counselors!

6. Today I will win in the game of success because of my **ALTERATION OF WRONG THINKING.** This book of the law – meditated and spoken by me – will advance me into the arena of accelerated achievement.

7. Today I will develop and demonstrate a *winning* attitude because of my **APPRECIATION OF EVERY BLESSING**. I will rise to the top today, and today I will live in the now!

Father, help me to be a gracious winner today. In Jesus' name, amen.

November 12
SATISFIED HEART!

"A SATISFIED soul loathes the honeycomb,
but to a hungry soul every bitter thing is sweet." (Proverbs 27:7)

"O God, You are my God; earnestly will I seek You; my inner self thirsts for You,
my flesh longs and is faint for You, in a dry and weary land, where no water is.
My whole being shall be SATISFIED . . ." (Psalm 63:1, 5 – AMP)

1. Today I will live in the now! I will live in the now because the pursuit of God is my satisfaction. He has satisfied me by giving me all the **ATTENTION** that I need ("The eyes of the Lord are on the righteous, and His ears are open to their cry" – Psalm 34:15). The same Jesus Who felt the touch of the woman with the issue of blood, and noticed Zaccheus in the sycamore tree, will always hear my cry and will leave the other ninety nine sheep to go and find me, regardless of where I am!

2. Today I will be satisfied because He has given me all the **ACCEPTANCE** that I need. The righteousness of God in Christ has made me accepted in the Beloved (Ephesians 1:6)!

3. Today I will be satisfied because He has given me all the **APPRECIATION** that I need ("His Lord said to him, 'Well done, good and faithful servant . . . enter into the joy of the Lord'" - Matthew 25:21). God is faithful to notice me and reward me!

4. Today I will be satisfied because he has given me all the **AFFIRMATION** that I need ("If you instruct the brethren in these things, you will be a good minister of Jesus Christ, NOURISHED in the words of faith and of the good doctrine which you have carefully followed" - 1 Timothy 4:6). His words nourish me spiritually and emotionally, satisfying me deeply in the inner man!

5. Today I will be satisfied because He has given me all the **AFFECTION** that I need ("Be kindly AFFECTIONATE to one another with brotherly love . . ." - Romans 12:10). God has touched me and embraced me, directly (by His Spirit) and indirectly (through others who demonstrate their love to me).

6. Today I will be satisfied because He has given me all the **APPROVAL** that I need ("He has not dealt with us according to our sins . . . " - Psalm 103:10).

7. Today I will be satisfied because He has given me the **AFFINITY** that I need ("Then God said, 'Let Us make man in Our image . . ." - Genesis 1:26). I will walk in kinship and fellowship with my Creator today, and today I will live in the now!

Father, thank You for giving me everything that I need today. In Jesus' name, amen.

November 13
VISION ADJUSTMENT!

". . . 'Lift your eyes now and look from the place where you are . . .'" (Genesis 13:14)

1. Today I will live in the now! I will live in the now because I am getting my world-view in line with God's perspective, so that I can see correctly and produce good things for the Kingdom. Instead of looking at everything through my personal window, I will see more accurately by **ADJUSTING THE CENTER OF MY UNIVERSE** — making sure that Jesus is enthroned in my vision. I will do His will even when I don't feel like it. I will not allow the plan of God to be obscured by my selfishness – by making everything about *me* – but I will put God's desires first, and consider His opinion in every decision that I make.

2. Today I will make sure that I see things clearly by **ABANDONING MY RELIGIOUS PREJUDICES**. I will not allow my tradition to make the Word ineffective (Mark 7:13). The only filter that I need for my information is the power of the Holy Spirit, and He is more than willing and able to help me!

3. Today I will improve my eyesight by **ADOPTING A BIGGER PICTURE OF MY PURPOSE**. I can do all things through Christ, regardless of my limitations.

4. Today I will walk in a better self-perception by **ACCEPTING MY RIGHTEOUSNESS** according to the Word of God. Seeing myself through the lens of sin-consciousness is not only a waste of time, it is antichrist! I have better things to do with my time than to spend it being absorbed with feelings of guilt and condemnation! I can see with my spiritual eyes *who* I am in Christ!

5. Today I will see the glass half-full by **ACCENTUATING THE POSITIVES IN MY LIFE**. I will consistently talk up the good stuff, and give God all the glory!

6. Today I will be able to walk out my vision by **ACQUIRING A PERCEPTION OF THE IMPORTANCE OF TIMING**. I will be able to pace myself, because I will be able to see where I am going by His Word that is a lamp for my feet (my immediate activities) and a light for my path (my destiny).

7. Today I will see things from God's perspective by **ASPIRING TO BE AN ACTIVE PARTNER IN HIS PROGRAM**. I want to be player – a mover and a shaker in the Kingdom – right in the middle of where the action is! Today I will lift up my eyes and look from the place where I currently *am* in my life, so that I can better see where I *am going*. I will open my eyes wide today, and today I will live in the now!

Father, adjust my vision so that I can see clearly today. In Jesus' name, amen

MOVING DAY!

"And all of us, as with unveiled face . . . are CONSTANTLY BEING TRANSFIGURED into His very own image . . . from one degree of glory to another . . . ." (2 Corinthians 3:18 – AMP)

1. Today I will live in thc now! I will live in the now because I am comfortable with being in a state of flux . . . of going with the flow . . . of growing and stretching. Change is good. Transition is necessary. TRANSITION IS:

    T - aking risks   (Psalm 18:29)
    R - eaching forward   (Philippians 3:13, 14)
    A - ccepting change   (Ecclesiastes 3:1-8)
    N - eeding more   (Isaiah 54:2, 3)
    S - eeing opportunities   (Romans 8:28)
    I - ncreasing vision   (Proverbs 29:18)
    T - rying again   (Proverbs 24:16)
    I - magining possibilities   (Ephesians 3:20)
    O - utlasting difficulties   (Matthew 7:24-27)
    N - ever quitting   (Ephesians 6:10-13)

2. Today I will embrace transition without the fear of the unknown, believing that God will perfect that which concerns me! I know that I am in charge of my life, but, ultimately, I know that my future is in His hands.

3. Today I will let go of the things that I need to release, and will move on to the next wave – the new current in the river of my life.

4. Today I will dare to be different than I have been before. I can change, and I can change for the better! It is not too late for me to become everything that God has ordained for me to be!

5. Today I will be in the moment and will enjoy what I have while I have it. I will not ask for more than my daily bread.

6. Today I will meditate on what Jesus meant when He said that he who loses his life shall save it (Luke 17:33). I will humble myself before Him and offer my body as a living sacrifice, which is my reasonable service.

7. Today I will celebrate being a new creation and will not mourn the passage of the old things. I will be fully mobile in Christ today, and today I will live in the now!

Father, help me to deal with transition graciously and maturely today. In Jesus' name, amen.

November 15
GETTING THERE!

"By faith Abraham obeyed when he was called to go out to the place which he would receive as an inheritance. And he went out, not knowing where he was going." (Hebrews 11:8)

1. Today I will live in the now! I will live in the now because I am willing to go out of my current reality if God tells me to, even if I don't know where I am going, because I know that He has a destination in mind for me. By faith I will **GET THERE**, wherever "there" is!

2. Today I will get "there" because I will **GET OVER IT** (Philippians 3:13, 14) and **GET A LIFE** (Matthew 7:1-5)! In other words, I will not let people hold me back from going to where I need to go.

3. Today I will get "there" because I will **GET A GRIP** (Ephesians 6:10) and **GET A CLUE** (Hosea 4:6)! In other words, I will not be moved by external things, but will search inwardly for the truth about what is happening in the now!

4. Today I will get "there" because I will **GET A PLAN** (Luke 14:28) and **GET UP** (Proverbs 24:16; Micah 7:8)! I will not stay down, but will proactively rise above my current problem.

5. Today I will **GET SMART** (Proverbs 4:7, 8) and **GET AHEAD** (1 Corinthians 9:24)! I will stop regretting my mistakes and will learn from them, so that I can better run my race – so that I can win!

6. Today I will **GET HAPPY** (Proverbs 17:22)! Attitude is everything, and mine will only move me forward!

7. Today I will **GET OUT OF HERE!** I have to leave "here" so that I can get "there" — dying on one level so that I can be resurrected on the next. I will recognize that today is a great day for a road trip, and today I will live in the now!

Father, help me to walk by faith and not by sight today. In Jesus' name, amen.

November 16
REINVENT YOURSELF!

"The spirit of man [that factor in human personality which proceeds immediately from God] is the lamp of the Lord, searching all His innermost parts." (Proverbs 20:27 – AMP)

1. Today I will live in the now! I will live in the now because I believe that it is possible for me to become the person that I have always wanted to be, because that desire was placed there by God Himself! I will **LOVE MYSELF UNCONDITIONALLY NOW** because love never fails (1 Corinthians 13:8), and I am not my sin, mistakes or bad behavior (Romans 7:17).

2. Today I will **LET GO OF MY PAST FAILURES** . . . I will live in the now!

3. Today I will **LEARN FROM MY MISTAKES** . . . I will grow up and be wise!

4. Today I will **LOOK AT WHO AND WHERE I WANT TO BE** . . . I will develop a vision that will produce a hope-image for my faith to give substance to!

5. Today I will **LAY DOWN ALL OF MY "IMPOSSIBILITY THINKING"** . . . I will pull down the mental strongholds that exalt themselves against the knowledge of God!

6. Today I will **LINE UP MY LIFE WITH THE WORD OF GOD** . . . I will be a doer of it and not a hearer only!

7. Today I will **LIVE THE LIFE FOR WHICH GOD CREATED ME** . . . I will take responsibility . . . I will take action . . . I will take the right road . . . I will start making necessary changes immediately – today – and today I will live in the now!

Father, show me how to become the new me. In Jesus' name, amen.

November 17
BRAIN-WASHED!

"So here's what I want you to do, God helping you: Take your everyday, ordinary life – your sleeping, eating, going-to-work, and walking-around life – and place it before God as an offering. Embracing what God does for you is the best thing you can do for Him. Don't become so well-adjusted to your culture that you fit into it without even thinking. Instead, fix your attention on God. You'll be changed from the inside out. Readily recognize what He wants from you, and quickly respond to it. Unlike the culture around you, always dragging you down to its level of immaturity, God brings the best out of you, develops well-formed maturity in you." (Romans 12:1, 2 – The Message)

1. Today I will live in the now! I will live in the now because I am being transformed by the renewing of my mind as it is being washed by the water of the Word! I am abandoning conformity to this world system and age, refusing to be fashioned and adapted to its external and superficial customs. My entire mind is being renewed for transformation – new ideals – new attitude. I am being transformed from **VICTIM TO VICTOR** because God is living big in me - bigger than my genetics - bigger than my family history - bigger than my dysfunctional circumstances. If God is for me, who can be against me!

2. Today I will be transformed from **CAPTIVE TO CONQUEROR** by the renewing of my mind! The Lord is turning my captivity as I exercise my authority and dominion in Him!

3. Today I will experience a transformation from **TRAGEDY TO TRIUMPH** by the renewing of my mind! All things are working together for my good!

4. Today I will embrace a transformation from **MEDIOCRITY TO MAGNIFICENCE** by the renewing of my mind! God has called me to greatness, and I have accepted the call!

5. Today I will discipline myself (my words, my attitude) for transformation from being a **WHINER TO A WINNER!** Life is in the power of my tongue!

6. Today I will be renewed and reinvigorated to be transformed from a state of **EXHAUSTION TO EXHILARATION!** My youth is being renewed like the eagle's!

7. Today I will be transformed from a paradigm of **REPRESSION** TO a perspective of **RIGHTEOUSNESS!** His nature in me has set me free from the law of sin and death. I will walk in a new mindset today, and today I will live in the now!

Father, wash my mind with Your Word today. In Jesus' name, amen.

November 18
VALIDATED LIFE!

"Even when we were dead (slain) by [our own] shortcomings and trespasses, He made us alive together in fellowship and in union with Christ; [He gave us the very life of Christ Himself, the same new life with which He quickened Him, For] it is by grace (His favor and mercy which you did not deserve) that you are saved (delivered from judgment and made partakers of Christ's salvation)." (Ephesians 2:5 - AMP)

1. Today I will live in the now! I will live in the now because I know that my life is an important part of God's plan for mankind. I am on this planet at this time in history for a distinct and unique purpose. I was pre-destined to function in the Kingdom of God (Romans 8:29, 30).

2. Today I will walk in the confidence that comes from knowing that I was not born by accident (Psalm 139:13-16).

3. Today I will make peace with myself, knowing that my personality came from God. He gave it to me as an equipping to help me successfully function in my own spiritual gifts and callings (2 Corinthians 12:9, 10).

4. Today I will stay focused on the fact that I have a destiny to fulfill (Jeremiah 1:4, 5), a destiny that has been waiting from the eternal past for my arrival!

5. Today I will accept the assertion that my ego does not need to be destroyed in order for me to please God. It simply needs to be sanctified and submitted to His will, for the sake of seeking the substance of His nature in my soul (1 Corinthians 4:16; 11:1)!

6. Today I will prevail in spiritual warfare, knowing that any unseen attack is just a pathetic ploy to prevent me from pursuing my personal assignment – to disconnect me by distraction (1 Peter 5:8)!

7. Today I will walk in peace and fulfillment by becoming the unique and special person that I was created to be (2 Peter 1:3-11). My life of individuality will be an inspiration to my world today, and today I will live in the now!

   Father, show me how to live a valid life for You today. In Jesus' name, amen.

November 19
ALL THAT!

"So they all ate and were filled. And they took up twelve baskets full of fragments and of the fish. Now those who had eaten the loaves were about five thousand men." (Mark 6:42-44)

1. Today I will live in the now! I will live in the now because God, the "El Shaddai," the One Who is more than enough, is an extravagant giver who gives good measure, pressed down, shaken together and running over! He is *"all that AND a bag of chips!"* He doesn't just fill my cup, He makes my cup run over! He doesn't just give me life, He gives me life more abundantly! He doesn't just do what I think that He'll do, He does exceeding abundantly above all that I can ask or think! He does not deprive me or make me live with shortages or in lack – He gives me **MORE THAN ENOUGH PROSPERITY**, so that I can be a prodigious giver (2 Corinthians 9:6-11)!

2. Today I will rejoice that He gives me **MORE THAN ENOUGH FORGIVENESS**, so that I can easily and freely forgive others (1 John 1:9-2:2).

3. Today I will appreciate the fact that He gives me **MORE THAN ENOUGH ATTENTION** (Psalm 139), so that I am able to be unselfish and secure in my relationships – so that I don't have to be needy and co-dependent. Freely I have received love, freely I am able to give love!

4. Today I will walk in confidence because He gives me **MORE THAN ENOUGH RIGHTEOUSNESS**. He does it so that I am able to be a prominent proclaimer of His realized righteousness to a fatally fallen world (Psalm 51:13)!

5. Today I will rest in the Lord because He gives me **MORE THAN ENOUGH PEACE**. He gives me His peace so that I can be a peacemaker (John 14:27).

6. Today I will be happy about the fact that He gives me **MORE THAN ENOUGH JOY**, so that I can create joy, happiness, and pleasure for others (John 15:9-11).

7. Today I will be thankful that He gives me **MORE THAN ENOUGH LOVE**, so that I can lay down my life for others, and bear much fruit (John 15:12-17). I will not panic when God asks me to do something that I cannot do. I will not feel overwhelmed when He asks me to give more than I can give. I will not be afraid when He tells me to fight battles that I can't win. I will obey Him in all things because he has met all of my needs ("Indeed I have all and abound. I am full . . ." – Philippians 4:18). Today I will praise God for being **ALL THAT**, and today I will live in the now!

Father, thank You for being more than enough today. In Jesus' name, amen.

"And do this, knowing the time, that NOW it is high time to awake out of sleep; for NOW our salvation is nearer than when we first believed." (Romans 13:11)

1. Today I will live in the now! I will live in the now because the concept of NOW is becoming more than just a concept to me — it is becoming my life's theme and daily lifestyle! My God is in the now! He is the I AM (Exodus 3:14), and those who come to Him must believe that HE IS (Hebrews 11:6)! Conformity to His image is causing me to "BE" in the eternal now ("Love has been perfected among us in this: that we may have boldness in the day of judgment; because as HE IS, SO ARE WE in this world" – 1 John 4:17)! He *is*, and I *am*!

2. Today I will walk in NOW faith. NOW FAITH IS . . . IS . . . IS . . . (Hebrews 11:1)! Faith is not *was* or *will be* – it *IS* the evidence of things not seen . . . it IS the substance of things hoped for!

3. Today I will see myself in the NOW as God sees me. I am in Christ and I am a new creation — old things have passed away — ALL THINGS have become NEW (2 Corinthians 5:17)! ALL THINGS have become NOW!

4. Today I will forget those things which are behind (Philippians 3:13). I will stop wasting my NOW by spending my time regretting the past!

5. Today I will forget tomorrow. I will take no thought for it (Matthew 6:34). I will not waste my NOW by spending my time worrying about the future!

6. Today I will not just *send the message* of Christ in the NOW to my world; I will *act it out* in front of the world! (". . . TODAY, if you will hear His voice, do not harden your hearts." - Hebrews 4:7; ". . . Behold, NOW is the accepted time; behold, NOW is the day of salvation." - 2 Corinthians 6:2) My life will be my sermon today, and I will preach it with conviction!

7. Today I will be productive for the Kingdom because of my perception of NOW ("I must work the works of Him Who sent Me while it is day; the night is coming when no one can work" – John 9:4). "THIS is the day the Lord has made . . . ." - Psalm 118:24. "Behold, I will do a new thing, NOW it shall spring forth . . ." (Isaiah 43:19). I will embrace these things today, and today I will live in the now!

Father, bring my whole thought-life, personality, will and emotions into Your NOW today. In Jesus' name, amen.

November 21
BIG RIVER!

(Ezekiel 47:1-6)

"Then he brought me back to the door of the temple; and there was water, flowing from under the threshold of the temple . . . and he brought me through the waters; the waters came up to my ankles . . . again . . . he brought me through; the water came up to my waist . . . again . . . and it was a river that I could not cross; for the water was too deep, water in which one must swim, a river that could not be crossed." (Ezekiel 47:1, 3-5)

1. Today I will live in the now! I will live in the now because I am moving into the deep things of God – into greater revelation and greater responsibility – into a mature faith that is a big river in which I must swim. It is too deep for wading or splashing around in the edges. Today I will go with the flow of the river of God. I will not be passive, but I will not struggle in the flesh, either.

2. Today I will find my balance in the river of God, praying specifically, without limiting my options as His co-laborer. He will allow me to decree a thing so that it may be established, but He will also do more for me than I can ask or think!

3. Today I will locate the current of faith, discerning what I can actually believe for. I will not pray beyond my faith, but I will not be afraid to launch out into the deep – to get in over my head — as the Holy Spirit prompts me to do so.

4. Today I will know when to let go. I can't swim while holding on to excess emotional baggage, so I will discover the power of acceptance, choosing my battles so that I don't exhaust myself out in the water. I will stand on the Word concerning the things that I absolutely know are the will of God for my life (salvation, healing, deliverance . . .), but anything outside of what has been provided for me in the atonement will be treated with flexibility. I will wait for a rhema word and, if I do not find one, I will let go of the petition and swim out further into the deep to find the perfect will of God destined for my life.

5. Today I will keep moving! I must swim or tread water to stay afloat, so my faith will be kept alive by my works – the demonstrated gospel in my life will be my flotation device!

6. Today I will pace myself in proportion to the size of the river in which I am to flow. I will live in the moment, and learn to pray for my daily bread.

7. Today I will enjoy my swim. A big river can be perceived as intimidating or exciting, depending on how it is seen. I will see God's great move of the water of life as an inviting, adventurous experience today, and today I will live in the now!

Father, help me to navigate Your big river today. In Jesus' name, amen.

November 22
POSSIBILITIES NOW!

"Do not remember the former things, nor consider the things of old. Behold, I will do a new thing, now it shall spring forth; Shall you not know it? I will even make a road in the wilderness and river in the desert." (Isaiah 43:18, 19)

1. Today I will live in the now! I will live in the now because I am aware that all things are possible with God, and that possibilities are available to me today. I am *not* trapped. My situation is *not* hopeless. There *is* a way *out*. There *is* a way *through*. There *is* hope for me. I must make room for the new thing that God wants to do for me. In Him I have UNLIMITED POSSIBILITIES!

2. Today I will create an environment of possibility through:

    P - lans   (God is a planner and always has an available plan B in case plan A fail.)
    O - ptions   (If Moses fails, there's Joshua: First Adam/Last Adam - Israel/the Church.)
    S - trategies   (God is a Master-strategist! – 1 Corinthians 2:7, 8)
    S - ynergy   (God is a team-player, even though He's always the Team Captain!)
    I - deas   (God is my source – the source of all creative thinking outside the box.)
    B - elief   (God shows me how to see the end from the beginning by faith.)
    I - nspiration   (God is the giver of all life – where there is life, there is possibility!)
    L - imitlessness   (There are no limits in the realm and dimension where God exists.)
    I - magination   (God is a dreamer . . . dreams create new worlds of possibility.)
    T - enacity   (God never gives up!)
    Y - outh-renewal   (God speaks through a child-like heart that says it's never too late! *)

    * *"Even the youths shall faint and be weary, and the young men shall utterly fall, but those who wait on the Lord shall renew their strength; they shall mount up with wings like eagles, they shall run and not be weary, they shall walk and not faint" (Isaiah 40:30, 31).*

    "Who satisfies your mouth with good things, so that your youth is renewed like the eagle's" (Psalm 103:5). I will relocate the sense of wonder and imaginative belief that I had as a child — the belief that anything was possible and that amazing things could happen!

3. Today I will do something new . . . go home a different way . . . alter my routine.

4. Today I will prepare for change . . . open my mind . . . eat something I've never eaten.

5. Today I will wear something different . . . respond in a new way to an enemy.

6. Today I will be optimistic . . . think positively . . . introduce myself to someone new.

7. Today I will enjoy the adventure of life, and today I will live in the now!

   Father, help me to prepare for new possibilities today. In Jesus' name, amen.

November 23
PROSPERITY'S PURPOSE!

"Therefore keep the words of this covenant, and do them,
that you may PROSPER in all that you do." (Deuteronomy 29:9)

". . . whatever he does shall PROSPER." (Psalm 1:3)

1. Today I will live in the now! I will live in the now because I know that my prosperity has purpose. I fare well, flourish and financially thrive, enjoying success and security to the glory of God, so that I may be a blessing to mankind. **PROSPERITY IN MY LIFE IS SOMETHING THAT GIVES GOD PLEASURE** (". . . Let the Lord be magnified, Who has PLEASURE in the PROSPERITY of His servant" – Psalm 35:27). God will be pleased with me like that today!

2. Today I will remember that **PROSPERITY IS AN INTEGRAL PART OF MY SALVATION** ("I will praise You, for You have answered me, and have become my salvation. Save NOW, I pray, O Lord; O Lord, I pray, send NOW PROSPERITY" – Psalm 118:21, 25). I know that I am saved like that today!

3. Today I will remember that **PROSPERITY BRINGS ME INTO CO-PARTNERSHIP WITH GOD** ("Only be strong and very courageous . . . that you may PROSPER wherever you go . . . for then you will make your way PROSPEROUS, and then you will have good success" – Joshua 1:7, 8). I will do great things like that for/with God today!

4. Today I will remember that **PROSPERITY IS SOMETHING THAT GOD USES TO GIVE ME FAVOR WITH OTHER PEOPLE** ("The Lord was with Joseph, and he was a successful man . . . and his master [Potiphar] saw that the Lord was with him, and that the Lord made all he did to PROSPER in his hand . . . The keeper of the prison did not look into anything that was under Joseph's authority, because the Lord was with him; and whatever he did, the Lord made it PROSPER" – Genesis 39:2, 3, 23). I will walk in that kind of favor today!

4. Today I will remember that **PROSPERITY IS SOMETHING THAT GOD USES TO BRING STABILITY TO MY LIFE** ("Now in my PROSPERITY I said, 'I shall never be moved.'" – Psalm 30:6). I will be stable and fixed like that today!

5. Today I will remember that **PROSPERITY IS ALWAYS INCLUDED IN GOD'S PLANS FOR MY RESTORATION** (Jeremiah 33:7-9; Zechariah 1:16, 17). I know that I am restored like that today!

6. Today I will remember that **PROSPERITY IS AN INDICATION THAT I AM WALKING WITH GOD** (3 John 2-4), even though gain is not godliness. I will keep these things in perspective today, and today I will live in the now!

Father, help me to believe for prosperity for all the right reasons today. In Jesus' name, amen.

November 24
HE LIVES!

"looking unto Jesus, the author and finisher of our faith, who FOR THE JOY THAT WAS SET BEFORE HIM endured the cross, despising the shame, and has sat down at the right hand of the throne of God." (Hebrews 12:2)

1. Today I will live in the now! I will live in the now because I am alive in the living Christ! In the world, death is the period at the end of the sentence. In the Kingdom of God, it is the beginning of a new paragraph. Jesus' empty tomb enables me to experience a paradigm shift concerning death and its necessity. I can't live at point B until I have died at point A, so death becomes a part of the natural progression of my life – dying on one level to live on the next! Instead of mourning the death of the caterpillar, I celebrate the emergence of the butterfly! The resurrection in my life represents a **RESTORATION OF THE HOPE THAT THERE IS LIFE ON THE OTHER SIDE OF DEATH** ("If in this life only we have hope in Christ, we are of all men most pitiable" - 1 Corinthians 15:19).

2. Today I will remember that the resurrection represents a **RECLAMATION OF GOD'S PROMISES *TO* ME, *FOR* ME AND *IN* ME** (". . . hard pressed on every side . . . not crushed . . . perplexed . . . not in despair . . . persecuted . . . not forsaken . . . struck down . . . not destroyed . . . always carrying about in the body the dying of the Lord Jesus, that the life of Jesus also may be manifested in our body . . . we who live are always delivered to death for Jesus' sake, that the life also may be manifested in our mortal flesh . . . death is working in us, but life in you" - 2 Corinthians 4:8-12).

3. Today I will remember that the resurrection results in a **REFORMATION OF MY UNDERSTANDING OF BEGINNINGS AND ENDINGS** (John 12:24).

4. Today I will remember that the resurrection represents a **REPARATION OF EVERYTHING THAT WAS DAMAGED IN MAN WHEN DEATH ENTERED THE WORLD** (Romans 8:11; 2 Peter 1:4).

5. Today I will remember that the resurrection represents a **REHABILITATION OF MAN'S TENDENCY TOWARD VICTIMIZATION**. The law of the spirit of life in Christ Jesus makes me free from the law of sin and death!

6. Today I will remember that the resurrection represents a **RECONCILIATION OF MORTAL AND FINITE BEINGS WITH AN IMMORTAL AND INFINITE CREATOR**. I have been crucified with Christ, yet I *live!*

7. Today I will remember that the resurrection represents a **REITERATION OF GOD'S TRUTH AND HIS WILLINGNESS TO WATCH OVER IT TO PERFORM IT** (1 Peter 1:23-25). Today I will live it fully, and today I will live in the now!

    Father, make the resurrection a living reality to me. In Jesus' name, amen.

November 25
RESOLVING ISSUES!

"But as for you, you meant evil against me; but God meant it for good . . . ." (Genesis 50:20)

1. Today I will live in the now! I will live in the now because I am learning how to work out my differences with people by observing and obeying Kingdom principles, and by choosing to live in the now. I will resolve my issues with others who may have offended me, or with those whom I may have offended, by recognizing the voices of righteousness that speak from my regenerated heart. I will listen to the voice of **REPENTANCE**, which asks, "What role did I play in this matter, and how can I best take responsibility for my actions?" I will do what I can to make things right.

2. Today I will listen to the voice of **REVELATION** (the spirit of understanding - Isaiah 11:2) which asks, "What was the other person thinking and feeling?" I will try to empathize with the other person and see the situation through their window.

3. Today I will listen to the voice of **RELATING**, which asks, "How can I effectively communicate exactly what hurts?" ("Confess to one another therefore your faults (your slips, your false steps, your offenses, your sins) and pray [also] for one another, that you may be healed and restored [to a spiritual tone of mind and heart]" - James 5:16 - AMP). I will not expect others to read my mind, but I will have the courage to be communicative if possible, and confrontational if necessary.

4. Today I will listen to the voice of **RELEASE**, which says, "I must forgive those who have hurt me." I will embrace the 70 x 7 forgiveness plan for my own sense of well-being and peace of mind.

5. Today I will listen to the voice of **REPLACEMENT**, which says, "I must find those who can heal me." I will ask God to bring people into my life who can, and will, restore in me what others may have damaged.

6. Today I will listen to the voice of **REVERSAL**, which says, "I must overcome hurt with healing" ("Do not be overcome by evil, but overcome evil with good" - Romans 12:21). I will be proactive in my relationships, because I have a winning attitude!

7. Today I will believe the voice of **RESTORATION**, which says, "I will be healthier now than I was before I was hurt!" All things work together for my good. I will enjoy the good stuff today, and today I will live in the now!

Father, help me to resolve my issues and move on today. In Jesus' name, amen.

November 26
BEST LIGHT!

"For it is the God who commanded light to shine out of darkness, who has shone in our hearts to give the light of the knowledge of the glory of God in the face of Jesus Christ. But we have this treasure in earthen vessels, that the excellence of the power may be of God and not of us." (2 Corinthians 4:6, 7)

1. Today I will live in the now! I will live in the now because I know that God sees me in the best light possible and, therefore, He makes me look good before the world! God sees me through the blood and faith of Jesus, and His power is greater than any negative thing in my life. I will be eternally grateful that **THE POWER OF GOD IN MY LIFE IS GREATER THAN MY FAULTS** (". . . with patience, bearing with one another and making allowances because you love one another" - Ephesians 4:2 – AMP)!

2. Today I will celebrate the fact that **THE POWER OF GOD IN MY LIFE IS GREATER THAN MY FAILURES** ("For a righteous man may fall seven times and rise again . . ." - Proverbs 24:16).

3. Today I will be encouraged in the knowledge that **THE POWER OF GOD IN MY LIFE IS GREATER THAN MY MISTAKES** (Psalm 19:12-14)!

4. Today I will derive confidence from knowing that **THE POWER OF GOD IN MY LIFE IS GREATER THAN MY EMBARRASSMENTS** (Isaiah 54:4)!

5. Today I will enjoy the revelation that **THE POWER OF GOD IN MY LIFE IS GREATER THAN MY POOR LIFE-CHOICES** (Joel 2:25-27)!

6. Today I will be blessed by the truth that **THE POWER OF GOD IN MY LIFE IS GREATER THAN MY SINS** (Isaiah 43:22-26; Ezekiel 36:16-32)!

7. Today I will be able to move into the next phase of my life, knowing that **THE POWER OF GOD IN MY LIFE IS GREATER THAN MY PAST** (2 Corinthians 5:17)! I will totally connect with the power of God in every part of my life today, and today I will live in the now!

Father, make me look better than I deserve to look today. In Jesus' name, amen.

November 27
MAXIMIZED POTENTIAL!

"The sower sows the word." (Mark 4:14)

1. Today I will live in the now! I will live in the now because I have not only received the Word, but I am developing the soil in which it must be planted (my heart and mind), so that it can produce more than thirty or sixty fold in my life. The Word sown in the garden of my heart will produce the MAXIMUM harvest of a one hundredfold return because of my diligence in maintaining optimal growing conditions! I will develop my dirt by EFFECTIVE TIME MANAGEMENT (Ephesians 5:14-17), A WINNING ATTITUDE (1 Corinthians 9:24-27), and A PROGRESSIVE VISION (Proverbs 29:18)!

2. Today I will develop my dirt by AN ABILITY TO SEE THE "BIG PICTURE" (2 Corinthians 4:17, 18), REAL COMEBACK POWER (Micah 7:8, 9), and through POSITIVE NETWORKING (Psalm 1:1-3; Ecclesiastes 4:9, 10; Proverbs 27:17)!

3. Today I will develop my dirt by A DETERMINATION TO STAY ON TOP (Deuteronomy 28:13), AN ABILITY TO PRIORITIZE (Matthew 23:23, 24), and A LOVE FOR DISCIPLINE (2 Timothy 2:3-5)!

4. Today I will develop my dirt by A DESIRE TO BE A TEAM PLAYER (1 Corinthians 12:14-24), A SKILL FOR DAMAGE CONTROL (Ephesians 4:27), and GOOD COMMUNICATION SKILLS (Proverbs 18:21)!

5. Today I will develop my dirt by EMOTIONAL MASTERY (Hebrews 4:12), POSITIVE REINFORCEMENT (Ephesians 4:14-16, 29), and PERSONAL ORGANIZATION (1 Corinthians 14:33, 40)!

6. Today I will develop my dirt by AN APPRECIATION OF THE CHAIN OF COMMAND (Matthew 8:5-13), A WORKING KNOWLEDGE OF KINGDOM POLICY (Hosea 4:6; Matthew 16:19), and AN UNDERSTANDING OF MY KINGDOM JOB DESCRIPTION (Mark 16:14-20)!

7. Today I will develop my dirt by A DESIRE FOR ADVANCEMENT (Hebrews 11:6), A SENSE OF PURPOSE (Romans 12:1-3), and A BELIEF SYSTEM THAT WILL ALWAYS PUT ME OVER (Ephesians 2:10)! I will cultivate my inner garden with these things today, and today I will live in the now!

Father, help me to produce the maximum for my potential today. In Jesus' name, amen.

November 28
THANKS GIVING!

"Enter into His gates with thanksgiving and with a thank offering, and into His courts with praise! Be thankful and say so to him, bless and affectionately praise his name! (Psalm 100:4 – AMP)

1. Today I will live in the now! I will live in the now because I can comprehend the power of the prayer of thanksgiving. I will pray with a thankful heart today, because I know that the prayer of thanksgiving evokes the presence of God (Psalm 95:1, 2), and in His presence is fullness of joy!

2. Today I will maintain a healthy mind and body by praying with thanksgiving, because it is that prayer that causes me to be able to keep my healing and to continually be made whole. ("And one of them, when he saw that he was healed, returned, and with a loud voice glorified God, and fell down on his face at his feet, giving Him thanks . . . and He said to him, 'Arise, go your way. Your faith has made you well [whole]).'" - Luke 17:15, 16, 19)

3. Today I will pray the prayer of thanksgiving, because it causes my supplications and requests to be made known to God (". . . in everything by prayer and supplication, WITH THANKSGIVING, let your requests be made known to God" - Philippians 4:6). I will say, as Jesus did at the tomb of Lazarus, "Father I THANK YOU THAT YOU ALWAYS HEAR ME" - and that prayer will make the dead things live again!

4. Today I will pray with thanksgiving because I know that, in so doing, I will keep myself established in the faith ("Rooted and built up in Him and established in the faith, as you have been taught, abounding in it WITH THANKSGIVING" - Colossians 2: 7).

5. Today I will improve my spiritual vision by praying the prayer of thanksgiving ("Continue earnestly in prayer, being VIGILANT in it WITH THANKSGIVING" - Colossians 4:2). Being thankful in my petitions will improve my perception and will enable me to "watch and pray" effectively.

6. Today I will remember that the prayer of thanksgiving enables me to live peaceably with all men (1 Timothy 2:1-3).

7. Today I will remember that the prayer of thanksgiving causes my good to be sanctified (1 Timothy 4:1-5). I will be thankful for everything and in everything today, and today I will live in the now!

Father, THANK YOU! THANK YOU! THANK YOU! In Jesus' name, amen.

November 29
THE CHURCH!

". . . I will build my church, and the gates of hades shall not prevail against it."
(Matthew 16:18)

1. Today I will live in the now! I will live in the now because I am a part of the true "Church" – the Body/Bride of Christ! Not some archaic, irrelevant religious system, but that universal company of called-out ones who are coming into the consummation of the third day! This "Church" – this living, breathing, vital organism – this many-membered man – is becoming the most bridge-building, cutting-edge, dream-inspiring, faith-accelerating, goal-oriented, relationship-building, upwardly-mobile, sold-out, forward-thinking, non-judgmental, non-religious, open-minded, ground-breaking, hard-working, life-giving, life-changing, success-oriented, Spirit-filled, Spirit-led, Spirit-controlled, worry-free, state-of-the-art, mountain-moving, vision-casting, uncompromising, unconventional, unprejudiced, unselfish, undefeated, understanding and prophetically powerful network of people in the world! The "Church" is the hope for the world, and I am a part of it!

2. Today I will pray for the "Church" of Jesus Christ, that it will stay fresh, current and relevant in the world . . . that Jesus will be able to look at His "Church," see the travail of His soul, and be satisfied!

3. Today I will have faith for the "Church" of Jesus Christ. I will have faith that the "Church" will be real and genuine, without hypocrisy or pretense — that it will reach out to the fallen world and embrace it lovingly and unconditionally!

4. Today I will believe in the vision of the "Church" of Jesus Christ. I will believe that the "Church" will put away childish things and begin to walk in dominion, growing into full stature in Christ.

5. Today I will do what I can to promote unity in the "Church" of Jesus Christ and will not be afraid to confront religious strongholds, doctrinal divisions, prejudice and racism, or unresolved offenses among believers. I will confess that love will conquer!

6. Today I will honor and hallow the "Church" of Jesus Christ, giving thanks for it and agreeing with Christ's intercession for its ultimate victory – the restoration of all things – so that He may be released from being held in the heavens.

7. Today I will pray that the "Church" of Jesus Christ would have a revelation of who she is and how she relates to the world, the Kingdom, and the Christ in the earth. I will do my part as one person to stand in the gap and make up the hedge today, and today I will live in the now!

Father, bless Your Church today. In Jesus' name, amen.

November 30
RESTORED SOUL!

"He restores* my soul . . . ." *(Psalm 23:3)*

"The strong spirit of a man sustains him in bodily pain or trouble,
but a weak and broken spirit who can raise up or bear?" *(Proverbs 18:14 – AMP)*

[*Restore: To bring back to a former or original condition, appearance, etc. as a painting; to put back in a former place or position; reinstate; to bring back to health and vigor; to give something back that was lost or taken away.]

1. Today I will live in the now! I will live in the now because God has restored my soul. I will say, "The Lord is my shepherd," because He has restored me by assuming the role of leader in my life.

2. Today I will say, "He makes me lie down in green pastures," because He is restoring my soul by bringing me to a place in relationships where I can find spiritual and emotional nourishment – where my self-esteem can be built up by unconditional love.

3. Today I will say, "He leads me beside still waters," because He is restoring my soul by helping me to find rest from the exhaustion that comes from maintaining unhealthy relationships.

4. Today I will say, "He leads me in the paths of righteousness for His name's sake," because He is restoring my soul by removing sin-consciousness from my self-image.

5. Today I will say, "In the valley of the shadow of death I will fear no evil," because He is restoring my soul by showing me how to appreciate my life as it is.

6. Today I will say, "He prepares a table for me in the presence of my enemies," because He is restoring my soul by making me take the initiative in resolving my "people problems."

7. Today I will say, "He anoints my head with oil and my cup runs over," because He is restoring my soul by renewing my mind and giving me more than enough. Goodness and mercy will follow me today, and today I will live in the now!

Father, let me dwell in Your house forever. In Jesus' name, amen.

December In The Now!

◊D◊E◊C◊E◊M◊B◊E◊R◊

A month for revelation.

'Tis the season

for

Celebration of the Incarnation (The Word made flesh)

and

Inspiration for the Imagination (The womb of the spirit) . . .

The babe laid in a manger . . .

Emmanuel, the embodiment and earthly expression of the eternal God –

Is now revealed TO you as

Christ IN you, the Hope of Glory,

Being revealed THROUGH you as the King of Kings . . .

Joy to the world, the Lord is come, let earth receive her King!

Now the hopes and fears of all the years

Can be met in the miracles made possible by your meditation in the Word.

Why waste the season by just walking in a winter wonderland

when you could be giving birth to the impossible?

December: A study in the Revelation of Jesus Christ . . .

December 1
THE REVELATION!

"[This is] the revelation of Jesus Christ [His unveiling of the divine mysteries]. God gave it to Him to disclose and make known to His bond servants certain things which must shortly and speedily come to pass in their entirety. And He sent and communicated it through His angel (messenger) to His bond servant John, Who has testified and vouched for all that he saw [in his visions], the Word of God and the testimony of Jesus Christ. Blessed . . . is the man who reads aloud [in the assemblies] the words of this prophecy; and blessed . . . are those who hear [it read], and who keep themselves true to the things which are written in it [heeding them and laying them to heart] for the time [for them to be fulfilled] is near." (Revelation 1:1-3 - AMP)

1. Today I will live in the now! I will live in the now because I readily recognize and receive the revelation of the resurrected Jesus Christ, acknowledging that it is only through Him that anything can be given. I will believe that the blessings bestowed upon my everyday life are the result of my response and reaction to what has been revealed to my regenerated and reborn spirit! The revelation of Jesus Christ imparts the life of Jesus Christ into me – the dominion, authority and power that I walk in are in direct proportion to my prophetic paradigm.

2. Today I will understand that the Jesus Who unveiled divine mysteries to John, the Apostle, on Patmos Island – the Jesus Who is the same, yesterday, today and forever – is still revealing Himself to His bond servants in the now. He does not desire to hide Himself or shroud Himself in unsolvable enigmas. He wants to be seen and known. He wants me to want to see and know Him. And, if He isolates me for a season, as He did John, I will believe that it is for the purpose of gaining my undivided attention, so that He can show me things to come!

3. Today I will stay strong, steady and stable by standing on the Word of God, and will triumph over every test or trial by trusting in the testimony of Jesus!

4. Today I will be blessed by hearing and reading aloud the words of this prophecy, and by laying them to heart. I will be a doer of the Word, and not a hearer only!

5. Today I will have a sense of knowing what is going on. Wisdom and understanding will be a natural part of my make-up, and I will bring insight into every conversation that I have today, speaking as one who has authority.

6. Today I will walk as a seer and a visionary, comprehending spiritual and abstract ideas, as I perceive the poetic nature of prophecy (the spiritual man judges all things – I Corinthians 2:15).

7. Today I will see beyond the veil, and today I will live in the now!

Father, help me walk in revelation today. In Jesus' name, amen.

December 2
THE BRIDE!

"Then one of the seven angels . . . came to me and talked with me, saying, 'Come, I will show you the bride, the Lamb's wife.' And he carried me away in the Spirit to a great and high mountain, and showed me the great city, the holy Jerusalem, descending out of heaven from God, having the glory of God. Her light was like a most precious stone, like a jasper stone, clear as crystal." (Revelation 21:9-11)

1. Today I will live in the now! I will live in the now because I will walk in a greater revelation and clearer vision of the bride, the Lamb's wife – the holy, hallowed and heaven-sent city of Jerusalem that is consecrated for Kingdom fulfillment, consummated by Christ's incorruptible seed and clothed in God's glory! I am a part of the body/bride of Christ. "So husbands ought to love their own wives as their own bodies; he who loves his wife loves himself. For no one ever hated his own flesh, but nourishes and cherishes it, just as the Lord does the church. For we are members of His body, of His flesh and of His bones." (Ephesians 5:28-30)

2. Today I will comprehend the city of God (the bride) and how I relate to it. ("But you HAVE COME to Mount Zion and to the CITY OF THE LIVING GOD, the heavenly Jerusalem . . ." - Hebrews 12:22). I know that I have already come to the city, to an innumerable company of angels, to the general assembly and church of the firstborn who are registered in heaven, to God the Judge of all, to the spirits of just men made perfect, to Jesus the Mediator of the new covenant, and to the blood of sprinkling that speaks better things than that of Abel. Therefore, today, I will not refuse Him Who speaks – Who speaks to me! I will embrace what He *IS SAYING* (rhema word) more than what He *HAS SAID* (logos word)! I cannot live by bread alone, but by every word that PROCEEDS out of the mouth of God.

3. Today I will recognize and release the glory of God in me – Christ IN me, the hope of glory (Colossians 1:27)! I will illuminate *my* world with *His* glory!

4. Today I will recognize and respect the glory of God ON me – I will arise and shine for my light has come (Isaiah 60:1)! The glory is risen UPON my life!

5. Today I will be faithful to my marriage to Christ ("For your Maker is your husband, the Lord of Hosts is His name; And your Redeemer is the Holy One of Israel; He is called the God of the WHOLE EARTH" – Isaiah 54:5).

6. Today I will walk in the confidence that comes from knowing that I have become "one flesh" with Him, and that the marriage covenant produces creativity in me.

7. Today I will be blessed "in the city," and today I will live in the now!

Jesus, sanctify and cleanse Your bride today with the washing of water by the Word!

December 3
JESUS' TESTIMONY!

"Then I fell prostrate at his feet to worship (to pay divine honors) to him, but he [restrained me] and said, Refrain! [You must not do that!] I am [only] another servant with you and your brethren who have [accepted and hold] the testimony borne by Jesus. Worship God! For the substance (essence) of the truth revealed by Jesus is the spirit of all prophecy [the vital breath, the inspiration of all inspired preaching and interpretation of the divine will and purpose, including both mine and yours]" (Revelation 19:10 - AMP)

1. Today I will live in the now! I will live in the now because I bear the testimony of Jesus in my life — I am His joint-heir! I do not have to worship angels, because I am in the God class, and my angels are here to *serve me*, and serve *with me* ("Are they not all ministering spirits sent forth to minister for those who will inherit salvation?" – Hebrews 1:14)! The testimony of Jesus in me demands that I worship God alone, and I will do that today with all of my heart and soul and mind and strength!

2. Today I will walk as a son of God in the earth, exercising my rightful dominion and authority as an heir to the throne. The testimony of Jesus in my life declares and claims sonship with Christ and kinship with the Father, recognizing the responsibility resident in royalty ("And because you are sons, God has sent forth the Spirit of His Son into your hearts, crying out, Abba, Father!" – Galatians 4:6). The Spirit of Christ is speaking through me – praying through me – doing exploits through me today — as I allow Him to cry out "Abba! Father!" from the depths of my inner man, with no sense of intimidation, trepidation or perception of my unworthiness!

3. Today I will understand how the testimony of Jesus is the spirit of prophecy in my dreams and visions, and in the prophetic words of my mouth. That testimony — that spirit of prophecy in my conversation today — will present my spirit with a preview of possibilities and will propel me into my purpose, projecting a positive attitude that personally promotes Kingdom principles and produces a plan that points progressively to a prosperous future prevailing over a poorly-navigated past!

4. Today I will listen to what Jesus says, with prophetic ears.

5. Today I will say what Jesus says, with a prophetic voice.

6. Today I will do what Jesus tells me to do, with prophetic skill.

7. Today I will embrace His true testimony, and today I will live in the now!

   Father, let Jesus' testimony live big in me today. In His name, amen.

December 4
FAITHFUL WITNESS!

". . . Grace to you and peace from Him Who is and Who was and Who is to come, and from the seven Spirits who are before His throne, and from Jesus Christ, the FAITHFUL WITNESS, the firstborn from the dead, and the ruler over the kings of the earth. To Him Who loved us and washed us from our own sins in His own blood, and has made us kings and priests to His God and Father, to Him be glory and dominion forever and ever. Amen."
(Revelation 1:4-6)

1. Today I will live in the now! I will live in the now because I believe in the faithfulness of God to me through Jesus Christ, the firstborn from the dead, Who is undeniably proving His unconditional love and care for me with unending grace and mercy! I was predestined to be conformed to His image, that He might be the firstborn among many brethren (Romans 8:29), so today I will fulfill that destiny by exercising my rights and privileges as a bona fide member of God's family!

2. Today I will confidently carry myself with an authoritative air, knowing that my faithful Elder Brother is the ruler over the kings of the earth! He is the ultimate authority figure, and He is on my side! I can reign because He rules; I can win because He watches over His Word to perform it!

3. Today I will stand on the promises concerning God's faithfulness, in Christ, for every situation of my life. It is written: "GOD IS FAITHFUL, by Whom you were called into the fellowship of His Son, Jesus Christ our Lord" (1 Corinthians 1:9) — ". . . but GOD IS FAITHFUL, Who will not allow you to be tempted beyond what you are able, but with the temptation will also make a way of escape, that you may be able to bear it" (1 Corinthians 10:13) — "HE WHO CALLS YOU IS FAITHFUL, Who also will do it" (1 Thessalonians 5:24) — "BUT THE LORD IS FAITHFUL, Who will establish you and guard you from the evil one" (2 Thessalonians 3:3) — "If we are faithless, HE REMAINS FAITHFUL; He cannot deny Himself" (2 Timothy 2:13) — "If we confess our sins, HE IS FAITHFUL and just to forgive us our sins and to cleanse us from all unrighteousness." (1 John 1:9)

4. Today I will be faithful over my sphere of influence, following the example of Jesus Who was faithful over all His house (Hebrews 2:17, 3:2, 5).

5. Today I will be a witness to the faithfulness of God, sharing my testimony with someone who really needs to hear it (or hear it again).

6. Today I will accept the responsibility of the throne, as well as the priesthood!

7. Today I will dare to take dominion, and today I will live in the now!

Father, help me to be a faithful witness today. In Jesus' name, amen.

December 5
FIRST LOVE!

"But I have this [one charge to make against you]: that you have left (abandoned) the love that you had at first [you have deserted Me, your first love]." (Revelation 2:4 - AMP)

1. Today I will live in the now! I will live in the now by repenting to rediscover, refresh and revitalize the romance in my relationship with the real Jesus, remembering the reality that was responsible for restoring me to right-standing with Him and, in retrospect, realizing that He is all that I've ever really required! Patience and perseverance have their place in the pavement of my personal path of discipline, but my Prince of Peace prefers that my passion take premier priority so that He can procreate progeny with me, producing powerful offspring for the Kingdom! He appreciates my dutiful diligence, but demands my devotion and desire! I am married to Him, with a mature love that must never become mundane to me!

2. Today I will gladly do my first works again if it is necessary for me to do so.

3. Today I will allow for an emotional, even physical, response to His manifested affection for me ("O God, You are my God; early will I seek You; my SOUL THIRSTS FOR YOU; my FLESH LONGS FOR YOU in a dry and thirsty land where there is no water" - Psalms 63:1).

4. Today I will love the Lord my God with all of my heart, mind, soul, and strength. I will bless the Lord with ALL that is within me!

5. Today I will be transformed by the renewing of my mind concerning the consummation of my covenant with Christ.

6. Today I will praise the Lord spontaneously and with total abandon, enjoying His presence without restraint, as young lovers enjoy the uninhibited and undivided attention of one another.

7. Today I will not just seek His Kingdom and His righteousness — I will not just seek the benevolent blessings of His hand — today I will seek His face and His heart FIRST, and today I will live in the now!

Father, help me to return to my first love today. In Jesus' name, amen.

December 6
KINGDOM PROCLAIMED!

"The kingdom of the world is NOW the Kingdom of our God and His Messiah! He will rule forever and ever!' The twenty-four Elders seated before God on their thrones fell to their knees, worshipped, and sang, We thank you, Oh God, Sovereign-Strong, WHO IS AND WHO WAS. You took Your great power and took over – reigned! The angry nations now get a taste of your anger. The time has come to judge the dead, to reward your servants, all prophets and saints, reward small and great who fear Your Name, and destroy the destroyers of the earth." (Revelation 11:15-18 – The Message)

1. Today I will live in the now! I will live in the now because I prophetically proclaim that the kingdom(s) of this world are coming under the authority of the Christ and that He is ruling in heavenly places NOW – crowned with many crowns NOW — and so shall He ever reign as the undisputed champion, commander and conqueror of all Creation! Not just the twenty-four Elders (representing the twelve tribes of Israel [Old Covenant] + the twelve Apostles [New Covenant] = Christ In The Now), but the whole Creation lifts its voice to sing His anthem of triumph, becoming, finally, a true UNIVERSE (uni: "one" - verse: "song")! Jesus Christ is Lord over the universe and over all existing things — the earth and all humankind, together with all its creatures, the heavens, the galaxies — all of it as a whole. JESUS CHRIST IS LORD OF ALL!

2. Today I will proclaim the rule of Christ, through me, over every situation that I am currently facing! In all these things I am more than a conqueror!

3. Today I will pronounce a blessing on God in Christ by the true praise and worship that flows like a river from my heart to His throne! I will say, "Great is the Lord and greatly to be praised! How excellent is Your name in all the earth! The heavens declare Your Glory! Of the increase of Your government there shall be no end! Hallelujah, for the Lord our God, the Almighty, reigns!"

4. Today I will pray His own prayer — "Your Kingdom come, Your will be done on earth as it is in heaven" – believing that I receive when I pray, knowing that my effectual, fervent prayer avails much!

5. Today I will prepare the kingdoms of my heart and soul for His total conquest! I will present my body as a living sacrifice, holy and acceptable to God!

6. Today I will protect the earth, for it is the Lord's and He will destroy those who try to destroy it.

7. Today I will prevail by Christ's authority, and today I will live in the now!

Father, help me to find my voice in the Kingdom today. In Jesus' name, amen.

December 7
THE MARK!

"He causes all, both small and great, rich and poor, free and slave, to receive a MARK* on their RIGHT HAND or on their FOREHEADS, and that no one may buy or sell except one who has the MARK or the name of the beast**, or the number of his name. Here is wisdom. Let him who has understanding calculate the number of the beast, for it is the number of a man: His number is 666." (Revelation 13:16-18)

(*Mark: Greek - "charagma" [English – "character"] - a stamp or impress)
(**Beast: Greek - "therion" - a wild, untamed beast; like the old nature)

1. Today I will live in the now! I will live in the now because I have the MARK OF THE LAMB, not the mark of the beast ("therion" - the old nature) on my forehead (my understanding, wisdom, and thought processes) or in my right hand (my strength, power and authority). I have passed from death unto life! "Then I looked, and behold, a Lamb standing on Mount Zion, and with Him one hundred and forty-four thousand, having His Father's name written ON THEIR FOREHEADS" (Revelation 14:1). "And there shall be no more curse, but the throne of God and of the Lamb shall be in it, and His servants shall serve Him. They shall see His face, and His name shall be ON THEIR FOREHEADS" (Revelation 22:3, 4). The Mark (character) of the Lamb is on my forehead, so I am not limited to think like a natural man with a fallen nature (represented by the number 6 – natural spirit, soul, and body = 666), but I think like a redeemed man with a renewed mind (represented by the number 7). "And these words . . . shall be in your heart. You shall teach them diligently to your children . . . talk of them while you sit in your house, when you walk by the way, when you lie down, and when you rise up. You shall bind them as a SIGN ON YOUR HAND, and they shall be as FRONTLETS BETWEEN YOUR EYES" (Deuteronomy 6:6-8).

2. Today I will not allow the mark of secular humanism to be on my forehead or in my hand. I confess that Jesus Christ is Lord to the glory of God the Father!

3. Today I will not allow confidence in the flesh to rule my mind or control my authority. Jesus is the vine; I am the branch. Apart from Him I can do nothing.

4. Today I will not take on the mark (character) of rebellion, which is as witchcraft.

5. Today I will not take the mark of idolatry. I will seek the Kingdom FIRST!

6. Today I will not take the mark of intellectualism that produces atheism. I believe!

7. Today I will not buy or sell according to the world system, refusing to bear the number of a man. I will bear *God's* seal today, and today I will live in the now!

Father, give me wisdom and understanding today. In Jesus' name, amen.

December 8
MARRIAGE CELEBRATION!

"And I heard as it were, the voice of a great multitude, as the sound of many waters and as the sound of mighty thunderings, saying, 'Allelujah! For the Lord God Omnipotent reigns! Let us be glad and rejoice and give Him glory, for the marriage of the Lamb has come, and His wife has made herself ready.' And to her it was granted to be arrayed in fine linen, clean and bright, for the fine linen is the righteous acts of the saints. Then he said to me, 'Write: Blessed are those who are called to the marriage supper of the Lamb!' And he said to me, 'These are the true sayings of God.'" (Revelation 19:6-9)

1. Today I will live in the now! I will live in the now because I am doing my part to bring God's will into the earth, because His reign cannot be complete until His will is fulfilled here as it is in heaven. My voice joins the voice of the great multitude, the sound of many waters, crying, "The Lord God Omnipotent reigns!"

2. Today I will assume responsibility for my own life and actions, knowing that, as a part of the bride/wife and body of Christ, I must do what I can to make myself ready. I will prepare myself by doing all that I can to lose and strip away everything that is opposed to the Bridegroom.

3. Today I will help array the bride in fine linen by performing righteous acts, even though I know that I cannot be saved by works. I will feed the hungry, clothe the naked, and visit the prisoner, demonstrating the gospel by my actions. I will walk in love, but I will love in deed, and not in word only.

4. Today I will be sensitive to the dearest desire of Jesus, expressed right before His death: "I do not pray for these alone, but also for those who will believe in Me through their word; that they ALL MAY BE ONE, as You, Father, are in Me, and I in You; that they also MAY BE ONE IN US, that the world may believe that You sent Me" - John 17:20, 21. I will confront and challenge division when I see it, knowing that ALL must become ONE, so that Jesus can reign in every place.

5. Today I will celebrate all of the benefits of the communion table . . . the elements that remember Jesus . . . the elements that remind me that I am bone of His bone, and flesh of His flesh. I will partake of the bread from heaven – Jesus, the Living Manna. I will not just pray, "Give me this day my daily bread;" instead, I will say, "Give me this day my daily Jesus!" I will know Him in the now!

6. Today I will not be offended when I hear Him say, ". . . unless you eat the flesh of the Son of Man and drink His blood, you have no life in you" (John 6:53). I have life in me! He is in me and I am in Him! We are married! We are one forever!

7. Today I will taste and see that the Lord is good, and today I will live in the now!

Father, help me to make myself ready today. In Jesus' name, amen.

December 9
GOD'S SALVATION!

"After these things I looked, and behold, a great multitude which no one could number, of all nations, tribes, peoples, and tongues, standing before the throne and before the Lamb, clothed with white robes, with palm branches in their hands, and crying out with a loud voice, saying, 'Salvation belongs to our God Who sits upon the throne, and to the Lamb!' All the angels stood around the throne and the elders and the four living creatures, and fell on their faces before the throne and worshipped God, saying: 'Amen! Blessing and glory and wisdom, thanksgiving and honor and power and might, be to our God forever and ever. Amen.'" (Revelation 7:9-12)

1. Today I will live in the now! I will live in the now because I am standing still and seeing the salvation of God in my life. No matter what happens to me in the natural realm today, I will remember that God and Christ, the Lamb, sit on the throne in power. I willingly fall on my face and proclaim blessing and glory and wisdom to God, giving Him all of my thanksgiving, honoring His mighty power forever. My lifestyle is the "amen" to my worship.

2. Today I will embrace the nations of the earth and pray for their salvation. I will not forget that the earth is the Lord's and that His knowledge is filling all of it as the waters cover the sea.

3. Today I will seek to understand every tribe of the earth and do what I can to extend a hand of reconciliation to them — to be a harbinger of God's salvation to the "tribes" of education and higher learning - of politics and government - of the arts and entertainment world - of finance - of science and technology - of the media - even the different tribes of the world's religions.

4. Today I will make the effort to reach out to all peoples, looking beyond our differences, and seeing how to make inroads into their cultural/societal experience with the message of salvation as it relates to the unique aspects of their lives.

5. Today I will hear with my spirit the languages and tongues of earth's citizens crying out to God for the salvation for which the whole creation groans, and will be a bridge-builder who speaks to them with relevance. I will search for the right words to present the Kingdom until I hear the people say, ". . . how is it that we hear, each in our own language in which we were born . . . we hear them speaking in our own tongues the wonderful works of God" - Acts 2:8, 11. I will be all things to all men, that I might by all means save some (1 Corinthians 9:22).

6. Today I will genuinely and unselfishly empathize with the lost.

7. Today I will live out my salvation in reality, and today I will live in the now!

Father, show Your salvation in my life. In Jesus' name, amen.

December 10
KNOCK! KNOCK!

"Behold, I stand at the door and knock; if any one hears and listens to and heeds My voice and opens the door, I will come in to him and will eat with him, and he [will eat] with Me." (Revelation 3:20 – AMP)

1. Today I will live in the now! I will live in the now because I can hear the voice of Jesus, and I recognize the sound of His knocking at the door of my heart. I am aware of His attempts to get my attention and His knocking is not a distraction – it is the most important thing to my life! Wisdom is crying out in the streets, and I have ears to hear it.

2. Today I will obey the voice of the Lord, even in the smallest things. I will not question or second-guess His instructions, even allowing for the foolish things of the world to confound the wise in *my* world. He is Lord – Adonai – my Master, Leader, Sovereign, Boss, Teacher, Instructor. His Word is the final word on every situation.

3. Today I will open the door to Him. I have nothing to hide because He already knows it all ("And there is no creature hidden from His sight, but all things are naked and open to the eyes of Him to whom we must give account." – Hebrews 4:13), and I will invite Him into every decision that I have to make.

4. Today I will recognize that His rebuke is an indication of His love for me, and I will receive it in a mature fashion. The correction of the Lord will not alienate me from Him. On the contrary, it will cause me to be zealous and eager to repent.

5. Today I will fellowship with Him at His table – the table of life – and all of my hunger will be satisfied with what He serves me.

6. Today I will make sure that my ears are awake to hear what God is saying. I will listen to the still, small voice in my inner man. I will listen to nature. I will notice the confirmation in the mouth of two or three witnesses. It is written: "Are your ears awake? Listen. Listen to the Wind Words, the Spirit blowing through the churches." (Revelation 3:22 – The Message)

7. Today I will refuse to be lukewarm toward Him, and today I will live in the now!

Father, help me to open every door to Jesus today. In His name, amen.

December 11
IRON ROD!

"And he who overcomes (is victorious) and who obeys My commands to the [very] end [doing the works that please Me], I will give him authority and power over the nations; And he shall rule them with a scepter (rod) of iron, as when earthen pots are broken in pieces, and [his power over them shall be] like that which I Myself have received from My Father." (Revelation 2:26, 27 – AMP)

1. Today I will live in the now! I will live in the now because I have power, authority and Kingdom rights that entitle me to take dominion on this planet and to subdue the earth for the sake of righteousness. I have authority because I am under authority. I have overcome the dysfunction of pride and rebellion and am qualified to hold the scepter of authority only because I have bowed my knees to the Lordship of Jesus, and because I am willing to be servant to all.

2. Today I will obey the (logos) commandments of God – those requirements *written in the Word* for every believer to live by.

3. Today I will obey the (rhema) commandments of God – those requirements *written on my heart* for the improvement and maintenance of my specific and unique relationship with God.

4. Today I will not shy away from assuming my authority over nations through warfare and intercession. I will pray that the Lord of the Harvest will send forth laborers to do the reaping.

5. Today I will recognize my influence and authority in the "nations" immediately around me – the youth nation, the cultural nation, the religious nation, the heathen nation, my city, my community, my neighborhood, my household — and every place that the sole of my foot touches will be claimed for the Kingdom!

6. Today I will reign over my soul . . . I will reign over my mind . . . I will reign over my will . . . I will reign over my emotions.

7. Today I will work the works that please God. It is written: "Then they said to Him, 'What shall we do, that we may work the works of God?' Jesus answered and said to them, 'This is the work of God, that you believe in Him Whom He sent'" (John 6:28, 29). Because I believe, I will do even greater works by His authority. I will reign in life because I am not afraid to move in faith today, and today I will live in the now!

Father, show me how to rule today. In Jesus' name, amen.

December 12
NO TEARS!

"Then one of the elders answered, saying to me, 'Who are these arrayed in white robes, and where did they come from?' And I said to him, 'Sir, you know.' So he said to me, 'These are the ones who come out of the great tribulation, and washed their robes and made them white in the blood of the Lamb. Therefore they are before the throne of God, and serve Him day and night in His temple. And He who sits on the throne will dwell among them. They shall neither hunger anymore nor thirst anymore; the sun shall not strike them, nor any heat; for the Lamb Who is in the midst of the throne will shepherd them and lead them to living fountains of waters. And God will wipe away every tear from their eyes.'" (Revelation 7:13-17)

1. Today I will live in the now! I will live in the now because, regardless of any tribulation that I must endure, I am of good cheer! Jesus said, "These things I have spoken to you, that in Me you may have peace. IN THE WORLD YOU WILL HAVE TRIBULATION; but be of good cheer, I have overcome the world" (John 16:33). My robes have been washed in the blood of the Lamb, and I have come through the fire of tribulation without the smell of smoke on them!

2. Today I will appreciate my position before the throne of God here on the earth. I will serve Him DAY AND NIGHT in His temple, before I go to heaven where there will be no day or night. He is dwelling with me, and in me, HERE and NOW!

3. Today I will stand on the promise of Jesus that they who hunger and thirst after righteousness will be filled! I cannot live by bread alone, but by every word that proceeds from the mouth of God, and I am nourished spiritually by the manna from heaven in the person of Jesus Christ.

4. Today I will not be overcome by the heat of the day – the stress, pressure and anxiety that comes from too much responsibility. Jesus' burden is easy and His yoke is light. He makes me lie down in green pastures and leads me beside the still waters. He restores my soul!

5. Today I will drink from the fountain of living waters – the artesian well of joy that flows in my life, even in the midst of hardship and persecution. With joy I will draw water from the wells of salvation, and I will be happy, even when I shouldn't be (according to the natural world). My joy comes from a supernatural source and provides me with supernatural strength.

6. Today I will sow in tears so that I can reap in joy! Weeping may endure for the night, but joy comes in the morning. God is wiping the tears from my eyes today!

7. Today I will choose to be happy, and today I will live in the now!

Father, fill my mouth with laughter today. In Jesus' name, amen.

December 13
EARTH'S HARVEST!

"Then I looked, and behold, a white cloud, and on the cloud sat One like the Son of Man, having on His head a golden crown, and in His hand a sharp sickle. And another angel came out of the temple, crying with a loud voice to Him who sat on the cloud, 'Thrust in your sickle and reap, for the time has come for You to reap, for the harvest of the earth is ripe.' So He who sat on the cloud thrust in His sickle on the earth, and the earth was reaped." (Revelation 14:14-16)

1. Today I will live in the now! I will live in the now because I know that God has not given up on His planet and that Jesus Himself will reap its harvest — He will not quit (and as His co-laborer, I will not quit), until all of it has been gathered in.

2. Today I will not be weary in well-doing, so that I can reap God's harvest in my own life. It is written: "And let us not lose heart and grow weary and faint in acting nobly and doing right, for in due time and at the appointed season we shall reap, if we do not loosen and relax our courage and faint." (Galatians 6:9 - AMP)

3. Today I will not worry about the tares that have been sown in God's field. He will take care of them in His own time and fashion.

4. Today I will be encouraged with the progress of the harvest, no matter how limited or incremental – first the blade, then the ear, then the full grain in the ear. The promise of harvest is inherited through faith AND patience!

5. Today I will pray for the lost — that all will find their own path to Christ.

6. Today I will preach the gospel – with my words, and by my lifestyle.

7. Today I will seek to have a sense of timing. I will not settle for an immature harvest, but I will not wait too long to reap, either. I have faith for the complete harvest today, and today I will live in the now!

Father, let me know when to thrust in the sickle and reap my own, personal harvest; and help me to be a good worker in Your big field today. In Jesus' name, amen.

December 14
WHITE GARMENTS!

"He who overcomes shall be clothed in white garments,
and I will not blot out his name from the Book of Life;
but I will confess his name before My Father and before His angels." (Revelation 3:5)

1. Today I will live in the now! I will live in the now because I have a witness of the Spirit that I am a child of God and, if a child, then an heir, and a joint-heir with Christ. He Who knew no sin became sin for me, that I might become the righteousness of God in Him, and He is now my Advocate and faithful High Priest.

2. Today I will remember that He has not dealt with me after my sin, nor rewarded me according to my iniquity. As high as the heaven is above the earth, so great is His mercy toward me, and as far as the east is from the west, so far has He removed my transgressions from me. He has thrown my sin into the depths of the sea and cast them behind His back!

3. Today I will enjoy peace with God, because there is therefore NOW no condemnation to me because I do not walk according to the flesh, but according to the Spirit. If He marked iniquities, how could I stand? But He was wounded for my transgressions, bruised for my iniquities; the chastisement of my peace was upon Him, and with His stripes I am healed!

4. Today I will believe that He is faithful and just to forgive my sins and to cleanse me from all unrighteousness. Where my sin abounds, His grace will much more abound in my life!

5. Today I will have confidence in the atonement – the completed work of Christ's blood sacrifice for me. He will not be ashamed of me in heaven, because I am not ashamed of Him on the earth. God did not send His Son to condemn me, but that I, through Him, might be saved!

6. Today I will not doubt that my name is indelibly written in God's book.

7. Today I will have abundant help from the angels because my name has been confessed before them – they know me well and respect me as a child of the Father. I will overcome today, and today I will live in the now!

Father, help me to see my white garments today. In Jesus' name, amen.

December 15
ALPHA, OMEGA!

"I am the Alpha and the Omega, the Beginning and the End, says the Lord God, He Who is and Who was and Who is to come, the Almighty (the Ruler of all) . . . I am the Alpha and Omega, the First and Last . . . then I turned to see [who was] the voice that was speaking to me, and on turning I saw seven golden lamp-stands, and in the midst of the lamp-stands [One] like a Son of Man, clothed with a robe which reached to His feet and with a girdle of gold about His breast. His head and His hair were white like white wool, [as white] as snow, and His eyes [flashed] like a flame of fire. His feet glowed like burnished (bright) bronze as it is refined in a furnace, and His voice was like the sound of many waters. In His right hand He held seven stars, and from His mouth there came forth a sharp two-edged sword, and His face was like the sun shining in full power at midday. When I saw Him I fell at His feet as if dead. But He laid His right hand on me and said, Do not be afraid! I am the First and the Last, and the Ever-living One [I am living in the eternity of the eternities]. I died, but see, I am alive for evermore; I possess the keys of death and hades, the realm of the dead." (Revelation 1:8, 11-18 - AMP)

1. Today I will live in the now! I will live in the now because I am experiencing life as a whole – a completion in Christ, the Alpha and Omega, Who is the firstborn of a nation of kings and priests coming full-circle in Him. All things are consummated in Him: the spirit realm and the natural realm – Son of God/Son of Man ruling sons of men becoming sons of God; Old Covenant/New covenant — the Word made one; my past, present and future — my life in the now; my spirit, soul and body — my complete self. *Christ is my all in all!*

2. Today I will draw strength from the eternal life already resident in me. I am alive forever, because He is alive forever; therefore, I know that I can certainly outlast the temporal problems that I am currently facing. The eternity in me wins!

3. Today I will develop an understanding of Jesus' requirements of me through His instructions to the seven angels of the seven churches represented by the seven stars held in His hand. Through these words to the church-at-large, I understand what He desires of me as a person, and in all these things I am an overcomer!

4. Today I will use, as Christ's joint-heir, the keys controlling the door of death, to gain dominance over the spirit of it. I close and lock that door in Jesus' name!

5. Today I will use, as Christ's joint-heir, the keys controlling the gates of hell, to gain dominance over its forces. I close and lock those gates today in Jesus' name!

6. Today I will see Jesus as He really is – as He is NOW – with eyes of spirit-vision.

7. Today I will hear the sound of many waters, and today I will live in the now!

Father, show me the A and the Z today. In Jesus' name, amen.

December 16
SIT DOWN!

"To him who overcomes I will grant to sit with Me on My throne,
as I also overcame and sat down with My Father on His throne." (Revelation 3:21)

"Conquerors will sit alongside me at the head table,
just as I, having conquered, took the place of honor at the side of My Father.
That's my gift to the conquerors!" (Revelation 3:21 – The Message)

1. Today I will live in the now! I will live in the now because I am seated on Christ's throne with Him by His own invitation! I am seated with Him in heavenly places! He generates energy from His throne as the manifestation of the 'I Am' – the energy of eternity – the life-force of NOW – and that energy is flowing mightily through me today!

2. Today I will rule over my circumstances and situations from the throne of God!

3. Today I will rule over my emotions and moods from the throne of God!

4. Today I will rule over the symptoms in my physical body from the throne of God!

5. Today I will rule over the flesh from the throne of God!

6. Today I will rule over the influence of the kingdoms of this world from the throne of God!

7. Today I will rule over religion – the antichrist spirit in the earth – and God, through Christ in me, will prevail. Today I will sit with Him and see the world from His perspective, and today I will live in the now!

"The Lord has established His throne in heaven,
and His Kingdom rules over all." (Psalms 103:19)

Father, rule and reign through me today. In Jesus' name, amen.

December 17
WHOEVER DESIRES!

"And the Spirit and the bride say, 'Come!' And let him who hears say, 'Come!' and let him who thirsts come. WHOEVER DESIRES, let him take of the water of life freely."
(Revelation 22:17)

"The [Holy] Spirit and the bride (the church, the true Christians) say, Come! And let him who is listening say, Come! And let every one come who is thirsty [who is painfully conscious of his need of those things by which the soul is refreshed, supported and strengthened]; and whoever [earnestly] desires to do it, let him come, take, appropriate, and drink the Water of Life without cost." (Revelation 22:17 – AMP)

1. Today I will live in the now! I will live in the now because I am in agreement with the Holy Spirit Who testifies of Jesus – we speak the same language ("For it seemed good to the Holy Spirit, and to us . . . " – Acts 15:28). He and I say to all who are thirsty, that Jesus has given them access to the fountain of life.

2. Today I will display the goodness of the Lord everywhere I go, so that it will be effective to lead people to repentance.

3. Today I will speak the *word* of reconciliation, by the *ministry* of reconciliation, as a repairer of the breach.

4. Today I will be a bearer of grace by my speech and conversation ("Let no corrupt word proceed out of your mouth, but what is good for NECESSARY EDIFICATION, that it may impart GRACE to the hearers" – Ephesians 4:29).

5. Today I will look beyond the exterior – the outward appearance – and I will allow God to show me how to look on the hearts of human beings and to know them after the spirit.

6. Today I will salt my area of the earth, light my part of the world, and carry the water to the desert.

7. Today I will let the Holy Spirit have His way in my life and persona, and today I will live in the now!

Father, help me to bring many sons - whoever desires - to glory today. In Jesus' name, amen.

December 18
HIDDEN MANNA!

"He who has an ear, let him hear what the Spirit says to the churches. To him who overcomes I will give some of the hidden manna to eat. And I will give him a white stone, and on the stone a new name written which no one knows except him who receives it." (Revelation 2:17)

1. Today I will live in the now! I will live in the now because I have a heart to seek out the mysteries of God – to search for the treasure buried in a field – to violently take the Kingdom by the force of my desire for revelation. It is written: "It is the glory of God to conceal a matter, but the glory of kings is to search out a matter" (Proverbs 25:2). As a king, I have the need to search out the hidden manna . . . to look for the truth hidden in parables . . . to dig deep for the pearl of great price!

2. Today I will remember that there is a white stone with my new name written on it. It is the standard by which the whole of my life is judged. It represents the ideal version of me that I am becoming as I am continually conformed to His image by going from glory to glory!

3. Today I will accept revelation of that new name (". . . a new name written which no one knows except him who receives it" – Revelation 2:17), developing a new self-perception in Christ. I am Who He says that I am, and I am becoming Who He says that I am becoming, whether anyone else can see it or not!

4. Today I will overcome in my attitude by being "up" in a down world. I will be a conqueror in my internal world. I will find hidden manna in the personality that God is helping to develop in me from the inside, out!

5. Today I will overcome in my reactions to negative forces released through the negative words of those around me. The shield of faith will flow in its function today!

6. Today I will overcome in my ability to believe for the impossible – to "hope against hope" – by the faith resident in me that overcomes the world!

7. Today I will overcome weakness through the knowledge that I have a white (pure, washed) stone (strength, revelation) with my new name written on it – I have godly strength, personalized for my life! I am empowered by the hidden manna today, and today I will live in the now!

Father, help me see into Your mysteries today. In Jesus' name, amen.

December 19
BABYLON'S FALLEN!

"After these things I saw another angel coming down from heaven, having great authority, and the earth was illuminated with his glory. And he cried mightily with a loud voice, saying, 'Babylon the great is fallen, is fallen, and has become a dwelling place for demons, a prison for every foul spirit, and a cage for every unclean and hated bird! For all the nations have drunk of the wine of the wrath of her fornication, the kings of the earth have committed fornication with her, and the merchants of the earth have become rich through the abundance of her luxury.' And I heard another voice from heaven saying, 'Come out of her, my people, lest you share in her sins, and lest you receive of her plagues.'" (Revelation 18:1-4)

1. Today I will live in the now! I will live in the now because I am redeemed – I am not of this world (system) – the cosmos . . . the cosmetic, superficial, temporary government, currently occupying certain places of authority on the Lord's earth. I declare the end from the beginning and I say that Christ rules this planet, ultimately, and that He rules my heart, actually (in the now)!

2. Today I will celebrate the fall of "Babylon" in my own life, declaring my independence from the influence of false religions, especially that strange mutation called "Christian religion." I know that Jesus did not appear on this planet to start a religion, but to save the world! I know that God's Kingdom should never have evolved into what we now call "Christianity," so I will call myself a Christian as a reference point, but will remember that the big picture is Christ's total, pure rule, beginning in my heart, worked out through my lifestyle.

3. Today I will enjoy guiltless, godly gain from the goodness of Jehovah Jireh, but I will not be entrapped by the fowler's snare of greed, covetousness, and the kind of money that can be a root to all evil. I will not be in the ministry for "filthy lucre." I will not allow the seed of the Word to be choked out by the deceitfulness of riches. I will worship God, and not mammon!

4. Today I will not be a partaker of the antichrist spirit in the earth. I will not be a rebel to spiritual authority. I will be a servant to all.

5. Today I will be patriotic, without losing perspective — my true citizenship is in the City of God! I will render unto Caesar what is Caesar's (pay taxes – Matthew 22:21), pray for those in authority, be a good citizen, and will fulfill the requirements of Romans 13 by obeying and honoring civil authorities – but I will remember that Babylon is Babylon, and that everything that *can* be shaken *will* be shaken!

6. Today I will say that sin shall not have dominion over me (Romans 6:14).

7. Today I will decree that Jesus Christ is Lord, and today I will live in the now!

Father, keep me free from the world-system today. In Jesus' name, amen.

December 20
HE'S WORTHY!

"The twenty-four elders fall down before Him Who sits on the throne and worship Him Who lives forever and ever, and cast their crowns before the throne, saying: 'YOU ARE WORTHY, O Lord, to receive glory and honor and power; for You created all things, and by Your will they exist and were created.'" (Revelation 4:10, 11)

1. Today I will live in the now! I will live in the now because I am casting my crown – my authority and right to dominion – gladly and absolutely at the feet of Jesus! He has given me a powerful, free will, and I am using that will to submit myself totally to His Lordship. I willfully worship the wonderful worthy Lamb Who reigns as King of Kings and Lord of Lords!

2. Today I will declare that the Lord is worthy to receive glory!

3. Today I will declare that the Lord is worthy to receive honor!

4. Today I will declare that the Lord is worthy to receive power!

5. Today I will seek to discern the purpose of creation by living my life in a way that pleases my Creator ("Thou art worthy, O Lord, to receive glory and honour and power: for Thou hast created all things, and FOR THY PLEASURE they are and were created" –Revelation 4:11 - KJV).

6. Today I will give God a sacrifice of praise and thanksgiving. It is written: "Therefore by Him let us continually offer the sacrifice of praise to God, that is, the fruit of our lips giving thanks to His name." (Hebrews 13:15)

7. Today I will take my worship to a whole new level. It will no longer just be something that I say or sing. It will not be limited to the lifting of my hands, the bowing of my knees, or the prostration of my body, but it will be my lifestyle . . . my manner of speech . . . the way that I move and act . . . how I relate to others . . . my attitude and demeanor . . . how I do business . . . how I show love and affection . . . my self-perception. It will all work together to become a worship-persona, a worship-existence, a worship-life! I was not created to please *myself*; I was created to please *God*. Today I will flow with my purpose for being here, and today I will live in the now!

Father, be pleased with me today. In Jesus' name, amen.

December 21
THE BOOK!

"For I testify to everyone who hears the words of the prophecy of this book: If anyone adds to these things, God will add to him the plagues that are written in this book; and if anyone takes away from the words of the book of this prophecy, God shall take away his part from the Book of Life, from the holy city, and from the things which are written in this book."
(Revelation 22:18, 19)

1. Today I will live in the now! I will live in the now because I accept the words of this prophecy with my whole heart. I will embrace it as the "apocalypses" – the unveiling of Christ and His purpose.

2. Today I will hear the words of this prophecy without religious prejudice.

3. Today I will hear the words of this prophecy without the influence of the traditions of men.

4. Today I will hear the words of this prophecy through the anointing of the Holy Spirit.

5. Today I will hear the words of this prophecy as a rhema word, relevant to my life.

6. Today I will hear the words of this prophecy in the now.

7. Today I will rejoice over His Word as one who has found great treasure, for the entrance of it brings light to my spirit and my mind. His Word is forever settled in heaven, and is a lamp for my feet and a light for my path because it does not return void to Him, but accomplishes what He sends it to do! It is like a hammer that breaks the rock in pieces, but it is sweeter than honey in the honeycomb! I will study it to show myself approved unto God, but I have no need for any man to teach it to me, because the anointing teaches me all things (I know it innately), and the Word is written on my heart! I will be a doer of the Word today without deceiving myself, and today I will live in the now!

Father, help me to rightly divide the Word today. In Jesus' name, amen.

December 22
NO NIGHT!

"Never again will there be any night. No one will need lamplight or sunlight. The shining of God, the Master, is all the light anyone needs. And they will rule with Him age after age after age." (Revelation 22:5 - The Message)

1. Today I will live in the now! I will live in the now because I dwell in the day of the Lord! His light — shining in and through me — the very glory of God – is developing daily, into a brilliant blaze of splendor — His revelation shining brightly at noonday! No matter how dark the night around me, the Lord is my light and my salvation, and He is bringing me into such an illumination of that fact that night is becoming irrelevant to me – a mere matter of perception! It is written: "And the Light shines on in darkness, for the darkness has never overpowered it [put it out or absorbed it or appropriated it, and is unreceptive to it]" (John 1:5 – AMP). I am not afraid of the "terror by night," because this is the DAY that the Lord has made. It is HIS day, forever!

2. Today I will welcome the eternal dawn of insight as the radiant Lamb of Glory establishes His permanent throne forever in my life (". . . and there was a rainbow around the throne, in appearance like an emerald . . . and from the throne proceeded lightnings, thunderings, and voices. Seven lamps of fire were burning before the throne, which are the seven Spirits of God" Revelation 4:3, 5). I decree that I walk in the light of the Spirit of the Lord . . . the light of the Spirit of wisdom . . . the light of the Spirit of understanding . . . the light of the Spirit of counsel . . . the light of the Spirit of might . . . the light of the Spirit of knowledge . . . the light of the Spirit of the fear of the Lord (Isaiah 11:2)!

   (* ". . . I saw, as it were, the appearance of fire with brightness all around. Like the appearance of a rainbow in a cloud on a rainy day, so was the appearance of the brightness all around it. This was the appearance of the likeness of the glory of the Lord." – Ezekiel 1:27, 28)

3. Today I will welcome the dawn of joy. Weeping may endure for the night, but joy comes in the morning!

4. Today I will welcome the dawn of mercy. His mercies are new every morning!

5. Today I will let my light shine before men, with no false pretense of bogus religious "humility." The Lamb is my light, and I am His reflection!

6. Today I will overcome the darkness of the traditions of godless men.

7. Today I will rule – in THIS age — and today I will live in the now!

   Father, shine Your light in me today. In Jesus' name, amen.

December 23
MORNING STAR!

"And he who overcomes, and keeps My works until the end, to him I will give power over the nations . . . and I will give him the MORNING STAR." (Revelation 2:26, 28)

1. Today I will live in the now! I will live in the now because, as the shepherds followed the star to find the Christ-child, I am following the true light – the light that is unconventional and set apart from the predictable – to find the real Jesus Christ, the Word made flesh ("Through the tender mercy of our God, with which the Dayspring from on high has visited us; to give light to those who sit in darkness and the shadow of death, to guide our feet into the way of peace" – Luke 1:78, 79)!

2. Today I will overcome by walking in real revelation and inspired insight into the manifold mysteries of God's goodness, so that I may receive the MORNING STAR!

3. Today I will overcome by walking in a growing grace that enables and empowers me, and the triumphant truth that fosters freedom, so that I may receive the MORNING STAR!

4. Today I will overcome by walking in the absolute authority of Christ, and in the accessible anointing of my Helper, the Holy Spirit, so that I may receive the MORNING STAR!

5. Today I will overcome by walking in a love for light, and a desire for discernment that produces a paradigm of total transformation, so that I may receive the MORNING STAR!

6. Today I will overcome by walking in a worldly wisdom that is Biblically balanced by a supernatural supply of Kingdom knowledge, so that I may receive the MORNING STAR!

7. Today I will overcome in Christ, and today I will live in the now!

"And we have the prophetic word [made] firmer still. You will do well to pay close attention to it as to a lamp shining in a dismal (squalid and dark) place, until the day breaks through [the gloom] and the MORNING STAR rises (comes into being) in your hearts. [Yet] first [you] must understand this, that no prophecy of Scripture is [a matter] of any personal or private or special interpretation . . . For no prophecy ever originated because some man willed it [to do so – it never came by human impulse], but as men spoke from God who were borne along (moved and impelled) by the Holy Spirit." (2 Peter 1:19-21 - AMP)

Father, help me to keep Your works until the end. In Jesus' name, amen.

December 24
SILENT NIGHT!

"The Life-Light was the real thing: Every person entering Life He brings into Light. He was in the world, the world was there through Him, and yet the world didn't even notice. He came to His own people, but they didn't want Him. But whoever did want Him, who believed He was Who He claimed, and would do what He said, He made to be their true selves, their child-of-God selves. These are the God-begotten, not blood-begotten, not flesh-begotten, not sex-begotten. The Word became flesh and blood, and moved into the neighborhood. We saw the glory with our own eyes, the one-of-a-kind glory, like Father, like Son, generous inside out, true from start to finish." (John 1:9-14 – The Message)

1. Today I will live in the now! I will live in the now because I believe in the possibility of the Word becoming flesh and dwelling with me.

2. Today I will receive Jesus in a deeper and greater dimension than ever before, with my whole heart. He has given me the authority to become a son, and I have the desire to become a full-grown son, with all of the responsibility of adulthood. I will always be His child, but I am ready to be His heir. Therefore, I will put away childish things and grow up into Him Who is the head of the church. (But tonight I will become as a little child again, experiencing deeply the wonder of the night before Christmas!)

3. Today I will not let the magnitude of the miracle of the Word becoming flesh get lost in the familiarity of holiday tradition. I will enjoy the traditions, without letting them make the Word ineffective in my heart. By the Spirit, Christmas will become new to me again . . . Christmas reborn . . . Christmas in the now!

4. Tonight I will recognize that all is calm, all is bright 'round the Christ-child – the holy infant so tender and mild – and I will make room for supernatural intervention because of His incarnation ("While You stretch out Your hand to cure and to perform signs and wonders through the authority and by the name of Your holy Child and Servant Jesus" - Acts 4:30 - AMP).

5. Tonight I will love pure light – the radiant beams from His holy face that bring the dawn of redeeming grace! ("But if we walk in the light as He is in the light, we have fellowship with one another, and the blood of Jesus Christ His Son cleanses us from all sin." – 1 John 1:7) His light brings healing tonight!

6. Tonight I will once again be shaken at the sight of glories streaming from heaven afar, and I will hear the heavenly hosts sing "Hallelujah!" It is the night of the dear Savior's birth! I am ready to rejoice!

7. Tonight I will sleep in heavenly peace, and tonight I will live in the now!

WELCOME, JESUS!

December 25
UNTO US!

"For unto us a Child is born, unto us a Son is given; And the government will be upon His shoulder. And His name will be called Wonderful, Counselor, Mighty God, Everlasting Father, Prince of Peace. Of the increase of His government and peace there will be no end, upon the throne of David and over His Kingdom, to order it and establish it with judgment and justice from that time forward, even forever. The zeal of the Lord of hosts will perform this." (Isaiah 9:6,7)

1. Today I will live in the now! I will live in the now because I joyously receive the revelation of the Incarnation in a personal way! Unto us – unto me! – a Child is born! A Son is given and He is well-received in my heart! **I WORSHIPFULLY WELCOME TO MY WORLD THE ONE CALLED "WONDERFUL"!** I welcome Him into my life . . . into my future . . . into my destiny! O come let us adore Him – *Christ the Lord!*

2. Today I will **CHOOSE TO CELEBRATE THE COMING OF THE ONE CALLED "COUNSELOR"!** Peace on earth and mercy, mild – God and sinners reconciled!

3. Today I will **MARVEL AT THE MAJESTY AND MIRACLE-BIRTH OF THE "MIGHTY GOD"!** The King of Kings lay in a lowly manger . . . in all our trials, born to be our friend!

4. Today I will **ECSTATICALLY EMBRACE THE ENTRANCE OF THE "EVERLASTING FATHER"!** I will welcome His entrance into the flesh existence, where He is touched with the feeling of my infirmities. He knows our need — our weakness is no stranger!

5. Today I will **PROUDLY PROCLAIM THE PREMIERE OF THE "PRINCE OF PEACE"!** Joy to the world, the Lord is come — let earth receive her King! Let every heart prepare Him room, and heaven and nature sing!

6. Today I will rest and be reassured in remembering that the government is on His shoulder, and that it will have no end! I will "let nothing me dismay," and remember Christ our Savior was born on Christmas day to save us all from satan's power when we were gone astray. I celebrate these tidings of comfort and joy!

7. Today I will trust that His Kingdom will be established in the whole earth. Joyful, all ye nations rise – join the triumph of the skies – with angelic hosts proclaim, "Christ is born in Bethlehem!" Today I will proclaim it – I will go tell it on the mountain today, and today I will live in the now!

HAPPY BIRTHDAY, JESUS!

December 26
THE KING!

"NOW I saw heaven opened, and behold, a white horse. And He Who sat on him was called Faithful and True, and in righteousness He judges and makes war. His eyes were like a flame of fire, and on His head were many crowns. He had a name written that no one knew except Himself. He was clothed with a robe dipped in blood, and His name is called The Word of God. And the armies in heaven, clothed in fine linen, white and clean, followed Him on white horses. NOW out of His mouth goes a sharp sword, that with it He should strike the nations. And He Himself will rule them with a rod of iron. He Himself treads the winepress of the fierceness and wrath of Almighty God. And He has on His robe and on His thigh a name written: "'KING OF KINGS AND LORD OF LORDS.'" (Revelation 19:11-16)

1. Today I will live in the now! I will live in the now because I confess that Jesus Christ is both Lord and King! His many names describe and define His perfectly multi-faceted nature and character, shown to me in every day of my life. I worship the One Who is called Faithful, and celebrate His great faithfulness to me today ("Through the Lord's mercies we are not consumed, because His compassions fail not. They are new every morning; Great is your faithfulness" – Lamentations 3:22, 23). I will worship the One Who is called True ("For the Lord is good; His mercy is everlasting, and His truth endures to all generations" – Psalms 100:5).

2. Today I will worship the One Who has a name written that no one knows but Himself. I will not be religiously smug or pompous enough to claim that I know everything about Him, or that I (or my system of fellowship) own the sole rights of access to Him. There is certainly more to the great King than what I know about — or than anyone else knows about! His revelation will be on-going and eternally progressive, and it is bigger and grander than the knowledge of men who know in part, and prophesy in part.

3. Today I will worship and pay homage to the One Who is called the Word of God ("In the beginning [before all time], was the Word (Christ), and the Word was with God, and the Word was God Himself" – John 1:1 – AMP).

4. Today I will worship, as a king myself, the One Who is called the King of Kings.

5. Today I will worship, as a lord myself, the One Who is called the Lord of Lords.

6. Today I will worship, without fear or dread, the One Who rules with a rod of iron.

7. Today I will follow Him into battle on the white horse of my own personal experience with Him. I will see the King today, and today I will live in the now!

Reign on, King Jesus! Long live the King! Amen.

December 27
EVERY NATION!

"And they sang a new song, saying: 'You are worthy to take the scroll, and to open its seals; for You were slain, and have redeemed us to God by Your blood out of EVERY TRIBE AND TONGUE AND PEOPLE AND NATION, and have made us kings and priests to our God; and we shall reign on the earth." (Revelation 5:9-10)

1. Today I will live in the now! I will live in the now because I embrace Christ's global vision – the one-world government birthed by His church, implemented by His Kingdom, and totally submitted to His authority. He must reign until His enemies be made His footstool!

2. Today I will celebrate diversity — challenge and expose racism, prejudice, and bigotry of any kind — and honor the importance of every nation to the grand scheme of things. Jesus is Lord over the kings of the earth, and the heart of every king is in the hand of the Lord. Jesus is Lord over the nations of the earth; it is His in all of its fullness. Jesus is Lord over the peoples of the earth – He is every color, and His truth prevails in every language!

3. Today I will meditate on what it means to be a king, and will watch the words of my mouth ("For the word of a king is authority and power, and who can say to him, 'What are you doing?'" – Ecclesiastes 8:4). I will expect my words to bear much weight, so I will use them wisely because I speak as one who has authority!

4. Today I will meditate on what it means to be a priest ("So I sought for a man among them who would make a wall, and stand in the gap before Me on behalf of the land, that I should not destroy it; but I found no one" - Ezekiel 22:30). I will assume the responsibility of intercession and will walk in the confidence that, if I ask anything according to His will, He will hear me and grant me my petitions!

5. Today I will reign – wherever I am – in whatever circumstance I find myself. It is written: "For if . . . death reigned through one, much more surely will those who receive [God's] . . . grace . . . REIGN AS KINGS in life through the One Man, Jesus Christ . . ." (Romans 5:17 – AMP). If Christ, the King of Kings, has made ME a king, then out of respect for Him, I will treat myself and think of myself today as royalty. I am a *servant*, and I am a *king!*

6. Today I will worship as a priest who offers up spiritual sacrifices to God (1 Peter 2:5) and, because I am a true priest, I will recognize the anointing of the priesthood on others.

7. Today I will pray for the nations of the earth, and today I will live in the now!

Father, bless every nation today. In Jesus' name, amen.

December 28
TEMPLE PILLAR!

"I'll make each conqueror a PILLAR in the sanctuary of My God, a permanent position of honor. Then I'll write names on you, the PILLARS: the Name of My God, the Name of God's City – the new Jerusalem coming down out of Heaven – and My new Name." (Revelation 3:12 – The Message)

1. Today I will live in the now! I will live in the now because I am not just a conqueror – I am *more* than a conqueror! Because I have responded correctly to the work of God's plan for my life, I am unmovable and unshakable – a pillar in the true temple of God, not made with hands. I am a rock. I am fixed. I am single-minded and, therefore, I am stable in all of my ways! No one can pluck me from God's hand because I have a permanent position of honor!

2. Today I will realize that God's name is written on me. I will not be moved by the words, opinions, rumors, lies or agendas of others. I will not accept their labels for me because my identification is settled — it's not up for discussion. I am who God says I am – period.

3. Today I will embrace the power of the name of Jesus, believing without reservation that every name that is named must ultimately bow to His name, recognizing Him as the final authority in every situation!

4. Today I will, as Abraham did, look for evidence of the City whose builder and maker is God – the City that is set on a hill that cannot be hidden – the Kingdom triumphant. And when I find entrance to the City I will go in and feel at home there, for its name is written on me, as well.

5. Today I will be unmoved by what I see in the natural realm.

6. Today I will be unmoved by what I hear from the natural realm.

7   Today I will be unmoved by what I feel as a result of my awareness of the natural realm. The Kingdom is what is real. The City of God is real. The living temple and sanctuary of Christ is real, and I am a support to that sanctuary – a pillar in the temple – my life is important to the economy of God. Today I will rise above chaos and turmoil. Today I will rise above the strife of tongues. I will not be moved or shaken today, and today I will live in the now!

Father, help me to live in a way that is worthy of one who bears Your name.
In Jesus' name, amen.

December 29
HEAVEN'S WAR!

"And war broke out in heaven: Michael and his angels fought with the dragon; and the dragon and his angels fought, but they did not prevail, nor was a place found for them in heaven any longer. So the great dragon was cast out, that serpent of old, called the devil and satan, who deceives the whole world; he was cast to the earth, and his angels were cast out with him. Then I heard a loud voice saying in heaven, 'NOW salvation, and strength, and the Kingdom of our God, and the power of His Christ have come, for the accuser of our brethren, who accused them before our God day and night, has been cast down. And they overcame him by the blood of the Lamb and by the word of their testimony, and they did not love their lives to the death.'" (Revelation 12:7-11)

1. Today I will live in the now! I will live in the now because Christ has conquered, and my overcoming life is part of the spoils of war. Jesus is Lord and Jesus is the victor. Greater is He Who is in me than he who is in the world!

2. Today I will demonstrate the truth of the Kingdom in the now: "NOW is the judgment of this world; NOW the ruler of this world will be cast out. And I, if I am lifted up from the earth, will draw all people to Myself" (John 12:31, 32). I will lift up Jesus in my life today to prove that satan has been cast down from his place of authority. By giving him no place in my life, I show forth Christ's triumph and validate His words.

3. Today I will not be vulnerable to accusation. I know what Jesus has done for me and I know who I am in Him. It is written: "Behold, I have created the smith who blows on the fire of coals and who produces a weapon for its purpose; and I have created the devastator to destroy. But no weapon that is formed against you shall prosper, and every tongue that shall rise against you in judgment YOU SHALL SHOW TO BE IN THE WRONG. This . . . triumph . . . is the heritage of the servants of the Lord . . . [in whom the ideal Servant of the Lord is reproduced] . . . the righteousness or the vindication which they obtain from Me . . . [which I impart to them as their justification] says the Lord." (Isaiah 54:16,17 – AMP)

4. Today I will celebrate the work of the Lamb's blood in my life — no record of rebellion, trace of transgression, instance of iniquity, or sign of sin anywhere in my history. It's all under His blood, and I win the war because I am washed!

5. Today I will trust in the power of my testimony to help me overcome. I have what I say, and I say that I am the righteousness of God in Christ! I win the war because I prophesy my victory!

6. Today I will not love my life to the death. My true life is the Christ-life!

7. Today I will win my personal battle, and today I will live in the now!

Father, help me be a good soldier today. In Jesus' name, amen.

December 30
GOD'S LAMB!

"Then I looked, and I heard the voices of many angels around the throne, the living creatures, and the elders; and the number of them was ten thousand times ten thousand, and thousands of thousands, saying with a loud voice: 'Worthy is the Lamb Who was slain to receive power and riches and wisdom, and strength and honor and glory and blessing!' And every creature which is in heaven and on earth and under the earth and such as are in the sea, and all that are in them, I heard saying: 'Blessing and honor and glory and power be to Him Who sits on the throne, and to the Lamb, forever and ever.'" (Revelation 5:11-14)

1. Today I will live in the now! I will live in the now because I am ascribing my **POWER** to the worthy Lamb Who was slain. He has empowered me to live my life as I choose, and I choose to live my life for Him! All of the power resident in my spirit, soul and body I willfully present back to Him, becoming an asset to the Kingdom – a viable, working part of the earth's solution and salvation.

2. Today I will give my **RICHES** to the worthy Lamb Who was slain. Where my treasure is, my heart is also, and as my riches represent my life – my pay is the exchange for my time – I give my whole life to Christ through the liberality of my soul.

3. Today I will give what **WISDOM** I have acquired to the purposes of the worthy Lamb Who was slain. I will use what I know (my testimony) to preach an intelligent message of the repentance-inducing goodness of God to those who are foolish enough to say that He doesn't exist.

4. Today I will give all of my **STRENGTH** to the Kingdom of the worthy Lamb Who was slain, and will use my authority to influence others to apply their strength to the advancement of His Kingdom.

5. Today I will give the **HONOR** that has been bestowed on me to the worthy Lamb Who was slain. I will give Him the glory for all of my accomplishments. I will let my light so shine before men that they may *see my* good works, and *glorify my Father* in heaven. I will honor Christ Jesus by acknowledging that it is in Him that I live, and move, and have my being.

6. Today I will give my **GLORY** – my light – to the worthy Lamb Who was slain. I will glorify Him in my praise and worship. I will glorify Him in my exploits of faith. I will glorify Him by overcoming.

7. Today I will ascribe any **POWER** that I have to the worthy Lamb Who was slain. If it is in the power of my hand to do great things, I will do them for His Kingdom. I give my all to Him today, and today I will live in the now!

Father, help me lay down my life today. In Jesus' name, amen.

December 31
IT'S DONE!

"Then He Who sat on the throne said, 'Behold, I make all things new.'
And He said to me, 'Write, for these words are true and faithful.'
And he said to me, 'IT IS DONE!
I am the Alpha and the Omega, the Beginning and the End.
I will give of the fountain of the water of life freely to him who thirsts.'"
(Revelation 21:5, 6)

1. Today I will live in the now! I will live in the now because I am whole and complete in Christ, in Whom everything begins and ends, having come full circle in my destiny as it relates to His Kingdom purposes in Creation. These words are not only faithful and true, they are indelibly written upon the tablets of my heart. Everything that has happened in my life – every experience, whether positive or negative – has been working together to bring me into Him in His fullness. He is not just **THE** Alpha (The "A") – He is **MY** Alpha! **My** "A!" He is **my** beginning, **my** starting point, **my** personal Genesis, **my** eternal source and history. He is not just **THE** Omega (The "Z") – He is **MY** Omega! **My** "Z!" The Author of my faith is the Finisher of my faith. The One Who began a good work in me will complete it until the day of the Lord. He will finish what He started in me! He is my destiny, my eternity, the consummation of my life experiences, my latter that is greater than my former, my happy ending . . . the One Who has been there all along, declaring the end from the beginning. The One Who has ever lived to make intercession for me in order to save me to the uttermost! I am utterly saved – utterly fulfilled – utterly complete – utterly vindicated – utterly in Christ!

2. Today I will look at every unanswered petition, every unmet need, every unfulfilled wish, every incomplete dream in my life, and boldly declare by the God-kind of faith, "It is done . . . finished . . . consummated . . . executed . . . complete!"

3. Today I will drink freely of the water of life and be totally satisfied and filled. Out of my own belly will flow rivers of living water. I am filled with the Spirit!

4. Today I will walk in the full revelation and demonstration of my sonship in Christ. Even though I am a son, I will learn obedience through my suffering and I will come through every fiery trial – no matter how hot – absolutely smoke-free!

5. Today I will overcome instead of looking for an escape. *Deliverance* is no longer my desire – my ultimate goal is to *inherit all things*! The Kingdom has come *in me*! Christ's work is finished in my behalf, and the travail of His soul is satisfied!

6. Today I will love His appearing – His revelation – in all aspects of my earth-life!

7. Today I will see all things made new, and today I will live in the now!

I decree that it is done! In Jesus' name, amen!

ABOUT THE AUTHOR

Bishop Jim Earl Swilley is a fourth-generation, full gospel minister who acknowledged his call into the ministry at the age of thirteen, on February 14, 1972. Since that time, he has proclaimed the gospel in song, ministry and prayer on street corners, in jungles, homeless shelters, churches, cathedrals, and coliseums throughout the United States and many foreign countries.

He graduated in 1980 from Southeastern College of the Assemblies of God, and then served as Assistant Pastor at Faith Memorial Assembly of God in Atlanta, Georgia, where he also served as President of New Life Bible School for a period of three years.

On Pentecost Sunday, May 26, 1985, he founded what is now known as Church In The Now. Through his leadership, this cutting-edge, multi-cultural, interdenominational church is impacting its community (and beyond — via television, streaming audio and covenant ministries) in a powerful way, with a life-changing message of restoration, and a progressive vision for the future.

Jim Swilley has served the ministry as a psalmist, evangelist, teacher, prophet, apostle, preacher and pastor, and was consecrated as a Bishop in the International Communion of Charismatic Churches (ICCC) in October of 1998. In this capacity, he gives oversight and covering to over 170 churches and ministries.

He is known for his unique ability to deliver deep revelation knowledge, with spontaneous humor and contemporary relevance. He is a seeker of the Truth who helps bridge the gap between God and man, while liberating the soul in bondage as he helps others to become REAL PEOPLE experiencing the REAL GOD in the REAL WORLD.

Bishop Swilley is devoted husband to Debye, and proud father of Jared, Christina, Judah and Jonah.

Appendix A
Featured Products by Bishop Jim Earl Swilley

Washed by the Word

This unique, anointed project will speak directly to your potential and your destiny as Bishop Jim Earl Swilley speaks the Word over live music . . . Don't miss out on this!

CD (NMD0100) $15
Cassette Tape (NMC0100) $10

Washed by the Word for Kids

A special project created live just for children. As they listen, they will understand how special they are and begin to memorize the Word of God . . . Your children will love this!

CD (NMD0103) $15
Cassette Tape (NMC0103) $10

Washed by the Word AM & PM
(2-CD set)

Washed by the Word – AM
"From the rising of the sun . . ."

Say "Good Morning!" to life and health and blessing and prosperity! Pour yourself a fresh, piping hot cup of the anointed Word of God, stir in some positive music to pump up your heart rate, and you're prepared to put your best foot forward, with the faith to face a day of favor and promotion!

Washed by the Word – PM
" . . . to the going down of the same, the Lord's name is to be praised!"

Say "Good Night!" in perfect peace and in the presence of God. Wash your face and brush your teeth before going to bed, but don't forget the most important part – the washing of your spirit, soul and body by the water of the Word! Get some quality rest in the Lord as you cast your care on Him!

CD (NMD0105) $20
Cassette Tape (NMC0105) $12

Activating the Power of Life and Death

By Bishop Jim Earl Swilley

In this easy-to-read edition, Bishop Swilley speaks to the issues of dominion by the power of choice and the authority of the spoken word to alter destiny. Written in a relevant, conversational style, he uses humor, personal anecdotes, and a wealth of scriptural insight to empower the reader with a vision for Kingdom lifestyle in everyday situations.

The book challenges the believer to demonstrate a high standard of living in faith, favor, health, and blessing, but does so with compassion and in a non-threatening, non-abrasive manner. You will be encouraged, enlightened, and even entertained, as you learn to choose life, and live it in the now!

Book #BK01 $8

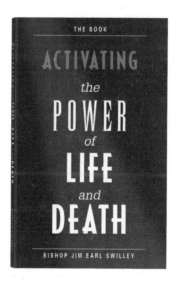

To receive a full listing of Bishop Swilley's products, write or call:

Jim Earl Swilley Ministries
P.O. Box 80876
Conyers, GA 30013

Phone: 678-607-3113
Email: orders@churchinthenow.org
Internet: www.ChurchInTheNow.org